From Arab Nationalism to OPEC

Indiana Series in Middle East Studies
Mark Tessler, General Editor

From Arab Nationalism to OPEC

Eisenhower, King Saʿūd, and the Making of U.S.-Saudi Relations

Nathan J. Citino

INDIANA
INDIANA
University Press
Bloomington & Indianapolis

This book is a publication of

Indiana University Press
601 North Morton Street
Bloomington, IN 47404-3797 USA

http://iupress.indiana.edu

Telephone orders 800-842-6796
Fax orders 812-855-7931
Orders by e-mail iuporder@indiana.edu

The paper used in this publication meets the minimum requirements of American National Standard for Information Sciences—Permanence of Paper for Printed Library Materials, ANSI Z39.48-1984.

MANUFACTURED IN THE UNITED STATES OF AMERICA

Library of Congress Cataloging-in-Publication Data

Citino, Nathan J.

From Arab nationalism to OPEC : Eisenhower, King Saʿūd, and the making of U.S.-Saudi relations / Nathan J. Citino.

p. cm. — (Indiana series in Middle East studies)

Includes bibliographical references and index.

ISBN 0-253-34095-0 (cloth : alk. paper)

1. United States—Foreign relations—Saudi Arabia. 2. Saudi Arabia—Foreign relations—United States. 3. United States—Foreign relations—1953–1961. 4. Eisenhower, Dwight D. (Dwight David), 1890–1969. 5. Saud, King of Saudi Arabia, 1902–1969. 6. Petroleum industry and trade—Political aspects—Arab countries—History. I. Title: From Arab nationalism to Organization of Petroleum Exporting Countries. II. Title. III. Series.

E183.8.S25 C58 2002
327.730538—dc21

2002020514

1 2 3 4 5 07 06 05 04 03 02

For my parents
David and Mary

Contents

Acknowledgments

I HAVE ACCUMULATED many debts while completing this book, and these brief sentences can serve only to recognize and not repay them. I received generous financial support from the Ohio State University Department of History and Center for International Studies, as well as an Abilene Travel Grant from the Eisenhower World Affairs Institute. Two Foreign Language and Area Studies (FLAS) Fellowships enabled me to study Arabic at the Ohio State University and the University of Chicago. The College of Liberal Arts at Colorado State University also provided helpful research support as I finished the final stages of the manuscript.

Several archivists graciously shared their knowledge of primary source material and made this book a richer study than it would otherwise have been. For their assistance, I wish to thank Herbert Pankratz, Bonita B. Mulanax, Kathleen A. Struss, and the staff of the Eisenhower Library; Milton Gustafson at the National Archives and Records Administration; and the staff of the Special Collections Division at Lauinger Library, Georgetown University.

My dissertation advisors, Michael J. Hogan, Peter L. Hahn, and Jane Hathaway, each made an indispensable contribution to this study. I am grateful to them for their encouragement and constructive criticism, and especially for the high standards they set as scholars themselves. Where I have failed to measure up, the responsibility is entirely mine. Professor Mahdi Alosh and Raghad Dwaik of the Ohio State University and Professor Farouk Mustafa and Anne Broadbridge of the University of Chicago deserve special thanks for helping me learn to read modern standard Arabic. I am also grateful to my fellow graduate students in the diplomatic history program at Ohio State for their friendship and helpful suggestions when I was just beginning the long process of writing and revising. Encouragement from the gang at the Wittenberg University Department of History was greatly appreciated. My new friends and colleagues in the History Department at Colorado State University have offered thoughtful evaluations of my work, both informally and in our department faculty seminar.

At Indiana University Press, Peter-John Leone supported my efforts to polish and publish this study, and Linda Oblack patiently answered my endless questions as I finished the manuscript. Jane Lyle and Drew Bryan spared no effort in editing the manuscript, and I appreciate their hard work. I also wish to thank those readers who offered their insightful comments and criticisms anonymously. Carol Marander at the Office of Instructional Services, Colorado State University, cheerfully prepared the maps despite numerous other commitments. Material first published in my article "Defending the 'Postwar Petroleum Order': The US, Britain, and the 1954 Saudi-Onassis Tanker Deal," *Diplomacy & Statecraft* 11 (July 2000): 137–60, appears with the permission of Frank Cass Publishers. Some of the many others to whom I owe a debt appear below, and I apologize for any omissions: Jennifer Bosworth, Jeff Giauque, Susan Jones, Burton Kaufman, Todd Kenreich and Amy Wei, Bruce Khula, Douglas Little, David Painter, Andrew Rotter, Robert Vitalis, Salim Yaqub, and Thomas Zeiler.

Finally, for their love and encouragement, I wish to thank my parents, David and Mary, and my siblings, Dominic and Maria. My extended family has always been supportive of my studies, and I am especially grateful to my grandparents, John, Mildred, Mary, and Robert, and to my uncle, Professor Robert M. Citino of Eastern Michigan University, who showed me how cool history could be. Most of all, my wife Sharon deserves my thanks for following me cross-country as I completed this book. But her willingness to move from Ohio to Colorado has been only the smallest part of her love and support. "Well, it ain't Ozzie and Harriet."

NJC
Fort Collins, Colorado
July 2001

Note on Transliteration

I HAVE GENERALLY rendered Arabic-language titles and the names of people in the manner recommended by the *International Journal of Middle East Studies*. Familiar place names, such as Dhahran and Riyadh, appear in the form most recognizable to speakers of English.

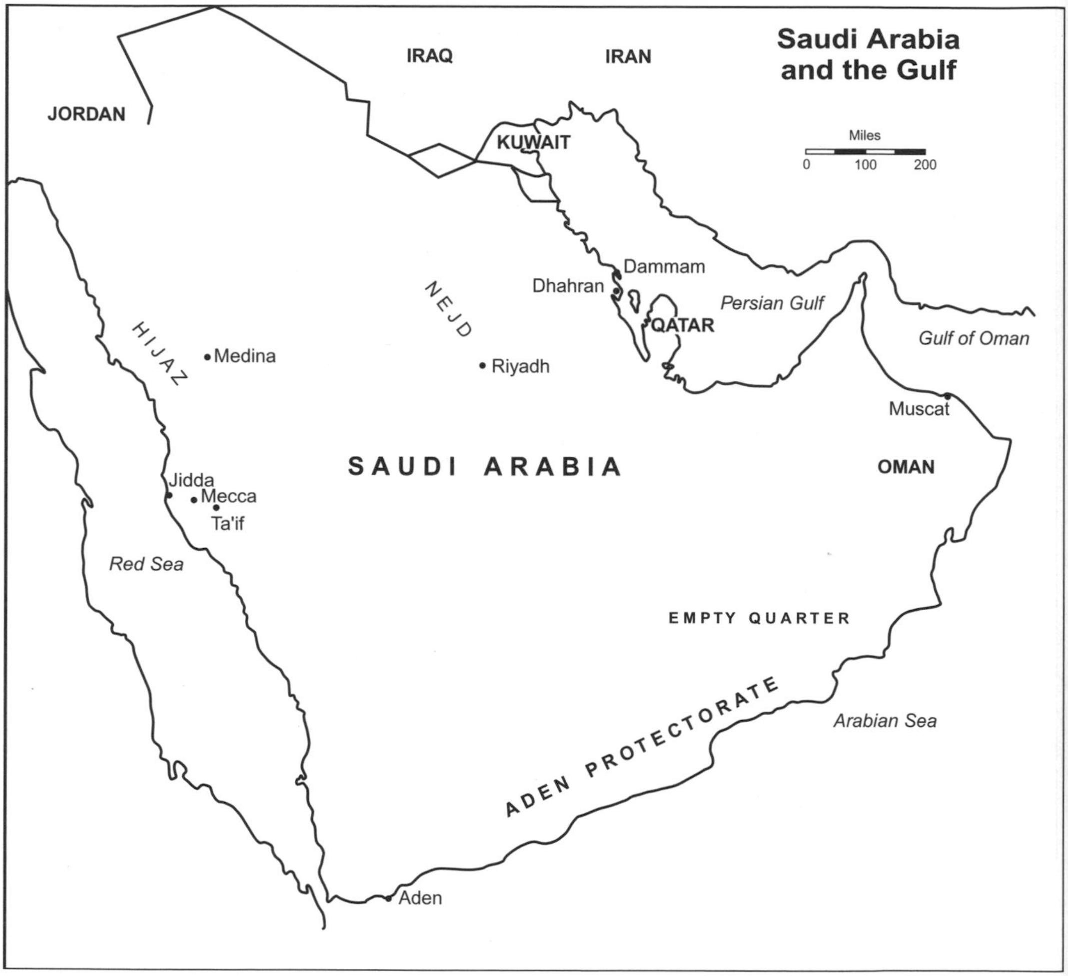
Saudi Arabia
and the Gulf
Miles
0
100
200
JORDAN
IRAQ
IRAN
KUWAIT
Dammam
Dhahran
Persian Gulf
QATAR
Gulf of Oman
HIJAZ
NEJD
Medina
Riyadh
Muscat
SAUDI ARABIA
OMAN
Jidda
Mecca
Ta'if
Red Sea
EMPTY QUARTER
ADEN PROTECTORATE
Arabian Sea
Aden

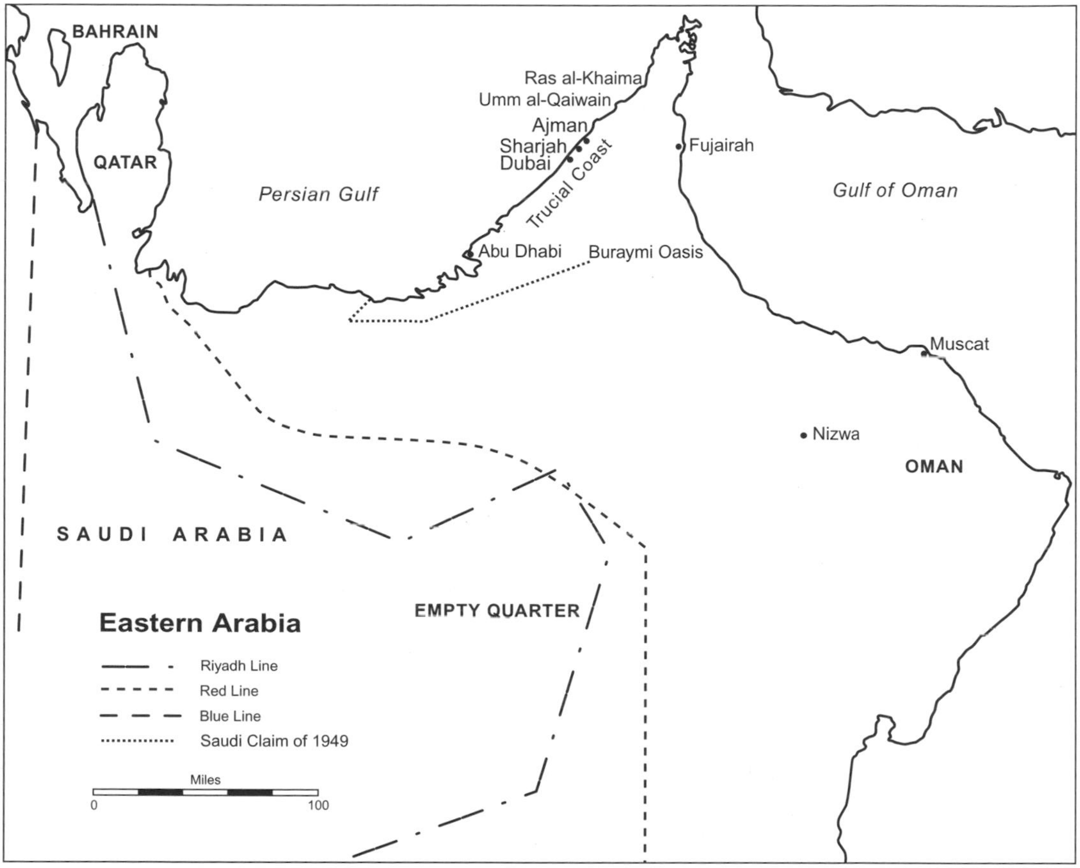

Based on maps found in J. B. Kelly, *Eastern Arabian Frontiers* (London: Faber and Faber, 1964); and Eden Visit (Jan. 30–Feb. 1, 1956) (2). Box 22, International Series, ACW, DDEL.

From Arab Nationalism to OPEC

Introduction: Saudi Arabia and the Anglo-American "Postwar Petroleum Order"

Prior to World War Two, recalled a U.S. diplomat, Saudi Arabia "had hardly been in the orbit of our cognizance." If Americans thought at all of the Arabian peninsula before the war, he said, it was as an endless desert and "a great emptiness." As the 82nd Airborne Division streaked toward Saudi Arabia in August 1990 to defend it from Ṣaddām Ḥusayn's armies, President George Bush declared the kingdom "of vital interest to the United States" and cited the "longstanding friendship and security relationship between the United States and Saudi Arabia."[1] What accounts for the dramatic change in Saudi Arabia's importance to the United States during the twentieth century, from a blank space on the map to the reason for the largest deployment of U.S. troops since the Vietnam War? Though the answer has a lot to do with oil, a full explanation requires studying the nature of American power in the postwar world.

Only after American petroleum companies discovered vast oil deposits in the kingdom's Eastern Province did policy makers in Washington come to regard Saudi Arabia as more than *terra incognita.* The history of American corporations' entry into the kingdom and early U.S.-Saudi relations has acquired almost legendary status. During the Great Depression, Standard Oil of California signed an exclusive agreement with King ʿAbd al-ʿAzīz ibn Saʿūd to develop his kingdom's oil resources and a few years later ceded a share of its concession to the Texas Oil Company. Their investment paid off in 1938, when Dammam Well No. 7 began gushing petroleum in commercial quantities. The outbreak of war piqued American fears of an oil shortage and fostered the growth of official ties between the U.S. and Saudi Arabia. At the behest of the oil companies, President Franklin D. Roosevelt, concerned about wartime petroleum supplies, declared the kingdom eligible for Lend-Lease aid. Roosevelt further acknowledged the importance of Saudi Arabia to the American war effort by meeting King ʿAbd al-ʿAzīz in 1945 aboard an American warship in the Suez Canal. Following the president's death, the two countries agreed to build an airfield at Dhahran, a concrete sign of the burgeoning American presence in the kingdom.[2]

These events became renowned largely through the public relations activities of the Arabian-American Oil Company (Aramco), the consortium formed by the major American petroleum corporations in Saudi Arabia. Another indication of Aramco's success at shaping historical interpretations of its role in the kingdom is the way in which some historians have celebrated the Aramco venture and echoed the company's own corporate promotion.[3] Indeed, Aramco was the basis of American foreign policy toward Saudi Arabia. But the story of U.S.-Saudi relations is neither a fable of Yankee entrepreneurship in the desert, nor the sort of bare statistical record of growing oil production and profits found in the company's annual reports. It is instead part of a more important historical epic about how the United States inherited custodianship of the global economy from Great Britain.

America's leading role in reforming the European economy through the Marshall Plan and permanent military presence in Western Europe after 1945 saddled Washington with formidable new responsibilities in the Middle East. Even before Roosevelt's shipboard meeting with ʿAbd al-ʿAzīz, American officials recognized that implementing their goal of multilateral free trade among developed economies would require secure access to the oil of Saudi Arabia and other Middle Eastern countries. The strategic value of these resources only increased as the Cold War with the Soviet Union intensified. In postwar Europe, economic reform was based on an Anglo-American compromise that introduced freer trade while salvaging the battered pound sterling as an international reserve currency and with it Britain's status as a global power. Meanwhile, a corresponding partnership developed in the Middle East, where the U.S. counted on the stabilizing influence of the British Empire. The two allies shared an interest in preventing any disruption in the free flow of Mideast oil, whether by Soviet expansion or nationalist revolution, that would upset their European arrangement.

The Anglo-American transfer of authority over the global economy encompassed a related, yet more gradual, changing of the guard in the oil-rich Persian Gulf.[4] There, the United States pursued a specific strategy for appeasing Arab nationalism: reliance upon private, corporate interests. This approach, intended to accommodate expanding U.S. power to the anti-colonial currents of postwar global politics, differed from the much older British presence in the region and its Victorian legacy of protectorates, political residents, and local military forces commanded by British officers. Saudi Arabia was the oil-producing Arab country in which the Americans pursued their approach to the fullest extent. But this strategy provided no guarantee that Middle Eastern oil would remain available to fuel European reconstruction. It did not provide an answer to the growing radicalism among the non-oil-producing Arab states or to the Arab-Israeli conflict, and close relations with the U.S. threatened to isolate Saudi Arabia from the rest of the Arab world. Saudi conflicts with neighboring Gulf states and with their British colonial patron also hindered Anglo-American cooperation. As anti-colonialism and nationalism swept the Arab Middle East, American policy makers faced a choice between their desire to assuage these political forces and their collaboration with Great Britain to extract the region's oil.

The distinct *modus operandi* practiced by each of the Anglo-American allies grew out of their different historical experiences in the Gulf. Parker T. Hart, U.S. consul and later ambassador in Saudi Arabia, noticed this disparity when he met King ʿAbd al-ʿAzīz for the first time in 1946. Hart attended a royal audience with his British counterpart in the Saudi kingdom, Sir Laurence B. Grafftey-Smith, who was, unlike Hart, fluent in Arabic. Grafftey-Smith wore an elaborate Arab costume, including a royal gold *ʿiqāl* on his headdress and the king's traditional colors, a custom signifying his adoption as ʿAbd al-ʿAzīz's "son." Hart, dressed in the standard Arab clothes issued to Western visitors by the king, observed the British minister bow in the royal presence and kiss the king's hand. "I decided as an American not governed by traditions of royalty," Hart wrote, "to simply do an emphatic handshake and give a respectful verbal salutation."[5]

This quintessentially American gesture—the businesslike handshake—symbolizes the approach the U.S. employed toward Saudi Arabia. Dispensing with the formal trappings of empire, Washington sought to rely mainly on the U.S. oil corporations that had operated in the kingdom since the 1930s to cultivate good relations with the producing government and secure the oil resources so vital to American strategic goals. U.S. officials promoted amicable company-government relations and comparatively generous royalty payments to Riyadh as insurance against the disruption of oil supplies to Europe. But the U.S. also needed Britain in the region, both as the dominant military power in the Gulf and because Britain's continued access to Gulf oil was necessary if it was to be part of the European economy Washington envisioned.

For Saudi Arabia, the emergence of American power in the Gulf held special implications. ʿAbd al-ʿAzīz had once been a client of Great Britain, as other Gulf rulers were still in the 1950s, but his decision to grant an oil concession to U.S. companies made his kingdom part of an informal American empire knitted together by private enterprise and corporate investment. The private basis of this informal American imperium had consequences for the evolution of the Saudi state. Aramco not only extracted the kingdom's petroleum, but by managing development, infrastructure, and welfare projects out of enlightened self-interest, it functioned in place of a genuine Saudi state bureaucracy. Royalty advances paid by Aramco to the Saudi government, intended by corporate leaders and American officials to smooth U.S.-Saudi relations, also delayed the establishment of a state budget in Saudi Arabia and a political process to determine how revenues would be spent. But after ʿAbd al-ʿAzīz's death, his heirs confronted fierce challenges from radical Arab nationalism at home and abroad. In domestic policy, Saudi leaders reformed relations between the king and ruling family and decided to distribute oil revenues in a limited way as the price of retaining their monopoly on political power. At about the same time, the Saudi government rejected Arab nationalist demands that Gulf oil wealth be shared with the poorer and more populous non-oil-producing Arab states. Together with Arab and non-Arab producers, Saudi Arabia formed the Organization of Petroleum Exporting Countries (OPEC) to secure the best price available from the major oil corporations.

Understanding the history of U.S.-Saudi relations therefore involves exploring the historic transfer of power from London to Washington and the new kind of empire built by the U.S. after 1945. It was during Dwight D. Eisenhower's administration that the foundations of the postwar U.S.-Saudi relationship and the American role in the Gulf took shape. The 1950s witnessed the beginning, though not the completion, of the Anglo-American changing of the guard in the Gulf. Eisenhower first grappled with the contradictions posed by the transition from British imperial hegemony to an American capitalist order, and the decisions he made ensured that the passing of the baton would be mostly a cooperative process. By 1960, too, the Arab nationalist threat to Western oil supplies had been contained. Saudi Arabia and other Arab oil producers organized OPEC with non-Arab oil states to present a united front in pricing negotiations, forsaking the Arab nationalist agenda of seizing Western oil assets and using them as a common resource for the development of the Arab world. Finally, ʿAbd al-ʿAzīz's heirs established the fundamentals of the modern Saudi state during these years, thereby reconciling the patrimonial nature of the kingdom he had created before American oilmen waded ashore in the Eastern Province with the challenges of Arab nationalism and integration into the global economy.

The introductory essay that follows provides necessary background on these issues and sets the stage for the Eisenhower era in several ways. First, it surveys the historiography of American oil diplomacy, which historians have described as part of a process continuous with the economic development of the U.S. and in terms of the public-private cooperation characteristic of the American political economy. Second, it scrutinizes the notion of an Anglo-American "special relationship" in oil diplomacy and contends that the two allies based their policies in the Middle East primarily on common economic concerns in postwar Europe. Third, it traces the emergence of revolutionary Arab nationalism, the most serious challenge faced by Eisenhower and other leaders who during the 1950s sought to preserve access to Mideast oil on the West's terms. Finally, it departs from earlier, oil-company-inspired accounts by addressing the consequences of integration into the global economy for Saudi Arabia itself and by exploring the theme of state building in both the American and Saudi contexts.

A substantial body of literature on U.S.-Saudi relations and American foreign oil policy during the 1940s argues that American officials responded to the wartime emergency by resorting to oil policies based on state intervention in the petroleum industry. When U.S. interest in Saudi oil as a wartime resource was at its height, American policy makers envisioned a direct role for the U.S. government in developing Arabian petroleum. In 1943, interior secretary and head of the Petroleum Reserves Corporation Harold Ickes proposed that the U.S. government purchase controlling shares in the development of Saudi oil, and in the following year he launched an ambitious plan to build a pipeline from the Gulf oil fields to the Mediterranean. By the end of World War Two, however, these wartime expedients had given way to approaches that emphasized private investment in developing Middle Eastern petroleum. Following the war, Standard Oil of New York and Jersey Standard joined Aramco, and the corporate partners organized a company to build the trans-Arabian pipeline initially conceived by Ickes as a government project. By offering its diplomatic support to these enterprises, the U.S. government entrusted corporations with developing foreign petroleum in exchange for profit.[6]

As corporatist historians have argued, American foreign oil policy replicated the state-industry relationships characteristic of the domestic political economy. Public-private cooperation emerged from a historical process originating in the Progressive era, through which government and industry leaders attempted to bring order to an increasingly complex, integrated national economy. This process had yielded a partnership between the most highly organized industries and a limited government to maximize economic abundance as a way of defusing political arguments about the distribution of resources. The techniques of industry-government collaboration they pioneered to rationalize the domestic economy found expression in American diplomacy during the 1920s, when the U.S. became a global economic power and a major creditor to Europe. Refined by the innovations of the New Deal, this approach also shaped American policy toward European reconstruction after World War Two, the reform of the global economy, and economic strategies for containing communism. Public-private cooperation in oil was therefore part of the general thrust of U.S. foreign economic policy. This approach was based on a belief that the capitalism Americans had perfected at home offered a blueprint for an international prosperity free of both the autarky that had characterized the Great Depression and the overweening centralized control of state-driven economies.[7]

Through the private investment of the Aramco partners, Saudi Arabia became part of what Daniel Yergin has called the "postwar petroleum order."[8] Broadly construed, this phrase can be used to refer to a set of arrangements that sustained both recovery and remilitarization in Western Europe and reconciled growing U.S. domestic consumption with the escalating demands of American Cold War foreign policy. For the U.S., a net importer of oil from 1948, Gulf petroleum provided a means for fueling foreign policy in Europe without siphoning off the western hemisphere reserves crucial to domestic prosperity. The "postwar petroleum order" consisted of a tangible infrastructure for delivering Mideast oil to Europe, including two pipelines and the Suez Canal, but more importantly it involved a series of relationships among producing states, transit countries, major petroleum firms, and the Western powers. In the volatile Middle East, the terms of these relations were not fixed but continuously contested and subject to challenge. The postwar petroleum order and its set of relationships therefore evolved as part of a historical process shaped by Arab nationalism, efforts by producing states to increase their revenue, and the Anglo-American determination to preserve Western access to Mideast oil.

In the case of Saudi Arabia, the U.S. government fulfilled its part of the corporatist bargain by offering diplomatic support for Aramco's venture. The fifty-fifty profit-sharing deal concluded between Aramco and the Saudi government at the end of 1950 illustrates how public-private cooperation underpinned the postwar petroleum order. Aramco headed off more far-reaching challenges to its concession by offering the Saudi government half of the net revenue it earned from the sale of Saudi crude to its parent companies. Harry S. Truman's administration then permitted Aramco to deduct the Saudi share of profits from corporate taxes the company paid in the United States as part of a strategy to safeguard Aramco's investment, enhance the income—and therefore stability—of the Saudi government, and help guarantee the continued flow of oil to Western Europe.[9]

Anglo-American cooperation sustained the postwar petroleum order. As Irvine Anderson, Michael J. Hogan, and William Stivers have shown, cooperation between the allies in oil dated to the 1920s and 1930s, when American companies gained their first footholds in the British Empire.[10] The two countries played leading roles in the 1928 Red Line agreement, which was designed to curb overproduction, contain nationalism, and stabilize the oil industry, and they were also signatories to a petroleum agreement in 1944 intended to formalize joint control over Middle East oil.[11] After the agreement foundered in the U.S. Senate, the Americans and the British continued to pursue their joint interests, but through contrasting approaches toward the producing states of the Middle East. This tactical divergence, rather than direct economic competition, accounts for Anglo-American differences in the Gulf and on the Arabian peninsula during the early Cold War.

Historians of oil diplomacy during the war decade have discerned real instances of Anglo-American antagonism. American oilmen endorsed the offer of Lend-Lease aid to ʿAbd al-ʿAzīz out of concern that financial necessity would force the king to grant British firms a share of Saudi oil. At the same time, the British resented the growing U.S. presence in Saudi Arabia, where the United Kingdom had once commanded unchallenged influence. The abrogation of the Red Line Agreement in 1947 permitted the American partners in the Iraq Petroleum Company to join Aramco, which represented a reversal in the Anglo-American power relationship in Mideast oil. British diplomats in the region and policy makers in London consequently grew suspicious of Aramco, the very instrument chosen by Washington to develop Saudi oil.[12]

Although these scholars have ably catalogued Anglo-American tensions during and after World War Two, their regional or single-country focus slights the dramatic ways in which the postwar Middle East became incorporated into the Western European economy. For the U.S. and its European allies, the years 1947–1954 witnessed a series of events that made Middle Eastern oil resources central to economic policy and strategy. Not by chance, the Marshall Plan coincided with the consolidation of the large, oil-producing consortiums, and the Korean conflict and Cold War rearmament coincided with the opening of the major Middle Eastern pipelines. As this economic interdependence progressed, the U.S. relied on British hegemony in the Gulf to secure one of the greatest resources controlled by the

Western allies and the key to a strong and prosperous Europe. Lately, scholars studying U.S. Cold War diplomacy and the British Empire in the Middle East have identified these broad common interests between the two allies without sweeping genuine tensions under the rug. While offering greater sophistication than the myth of Winston Churchill's "special relationship," current interpretations also challenge earlier claims that the U.S. actively maneuvered after 1945 to replace Britain as the leading Mideast power. This reinterpretation, central to recent scholarship on Egypt and Iran, has yet to influence the comparatively sparse analysis of the Anglo-American relationship on the Arab side of the Gulf. The argument developed here not only extends recent historiographical trends to that oil-rich region, but also seeks to provide the sort of historical framework still needed in the literature for understanding Anglo-American collaboration and conflict throughout the Middle East.[13]

The postwar petroleum order contained at its heart an Anglo-American understanding in oil diplomacy that both regulated the allies' relationship in the Middle East and facilitated cooperation in Europe. The bargain combined U.S. plans for multilateral free trade with attempts to address Britain's large balance-of-payments deficit. U.S. policy makers recognized that progress toward their free-trading vision for Europe, enshrined in the Bretton Woods system, the Marshall Plan, and the GATT agreements, required preserving the British imperial presence in the Gulf. Washington promoted European integration, as Hogan has argued, qualified by support for the United Kingdom's special role as banker to the sterling area, or those countries in Britain's imperial orbit maintaining currency balances in pounds on the London market. This policy had direct implications in the Middle East, whose oil exports were a major factor in Britain's balance-of-payments position. By neglecting such considerations and the European context in which American and British officials shaped Middle Eastern policy during the early Cold War, some scholars have misinterpreted allied oil diplomacy and have exaggerated Anglo-American "competition" for Mideast petroleum after 1945.[14]

Indeed, Britain's efforts to manage its postwar "dollar drain" were closely tied to oil, and the import of dollar petroleum was one reason in particular that the United Kingdom was chronically short of the foreign exchange it needed to finance reconstruction. Attempting to slow the depletion of its hard currency reserves, Britain cut off imports of dollar oil to the sterling area in 1949, a step incompatible with the U.S. campaign against imperial preferences and for more open and integrated economies in Western Europe. In response, the Economic Cooperation Administration threatened to withhold Marshall Plan aid from Britain, and an Anglo-American confrontation was averted only through the kind of public-private diplomacy that characterized the postwar petroleum order. The major American oil companies entered into specific dollar-saving agreements with the British government, pledging to reinvest dollar profits in the sterling area. Nevertheless, the crisis had a lasting effect on British policy in the Middle East, where maintaining control of petroleum that could be purchased with sterling became a top priority. It also demonstrated to the Americans the necessity of preserving London's authority over its Gulf clients and access to the sterling oil they produced in order to permit British participation in the postwar multilateral economy.[15]

Far more threatening to the postwar petroleum order than Anglo-American competition was nationalism in the oil-producing and oil-transit countries. In the Arab states, growing anti-colonial sentiment during and after World War Two corresponded to a broadening of the social foundations of Arab politics. Scholars have explained these changes in the context of the Ottoman past. Albert Hourani and his students have shown that the earliest constituency for Arab nationalism came from a notable elite that coalesced in the Ottoman Arab provinces during the nineteenth century. European economic penetration and *Tanzimat* reforms synthesized a social leadership consisting of families who enjoyed both local prestige and the patronage of imperial authorities. Such powerful urban households controlled the agricultural surplus of the countryside and maintained extensive clientage networks. These social patterns survived the collapse of the Ottoman Empire and continued to define politics in the Arab successor states during the early decades of their independence.[16]

By the time of World War Two, however, the explosive Palestine issue and the travails of war had roused a new generation of educated Arab teachers, lawyers, and journalists, who challenged the social leadership of the urban notables. The Syrian Baʿth party, founded in 1942 by teacher Michel ʿAflaq, exemplified Arab technocrats' increasingly radical opposition to both Western imperialism and the economic privilege of notable families. Following the humiliation of the Palestine War in 1948, Arab military officers became imbued with the new Arab nationalism and grew hostile toward Israel, Western colonialism, and the Ottoman-era elite that continued to dominate the successor states. This revolutionary Arab nationalism emerged in Egypt and the countries of the Fertile Crescent, encompassing Palestine, Lebanon, Jordan, Syria, and Iraq, states that not only shared the Ottoman legacy but that also cradled the major oil-transit facilities.[17]

The founding of Israel in 1948 dramatically politicized the postwar petroleum order. According to historian David S. Painter, the Americans hoped that the distinction between corporate enterprise and official diplomacy would deflect Arab resentment over U.S. government recognition of Israel and prevent attacks on Western oil supplies. One American oil executive, for example, even declared the trans-Arabian pipeline a "little Marshall plan" for the Middle East that could promote development and curb Arab radicalism. But Arab League members subjected Saudi Arabia to intense pressure to withhold petroleum from Western countries that recognized Israel. Confronted with demands for an embargo, yet utterly dependent upon oil revenues, ʿAbd al-ʿAzīz faced a choice between risking isolation within the Arab world and abnegation of his income. The king opted against an embargo, while using rhetoric to stake out a recalcitrant position opposing the establishment of the Jewish state. His policy, however, failed to mitigate the contradiction between Arab nationalism and Saudi integration into the postwar petroleum order. Throughout the 1950s, Arab nationalism would continue to pose a dilemma for Saudi foreign policy and would even threaten the Saudi kingdom from within.[18]

Saudi Arabia experienced Arab nationalism differently from Egypt and the Fertile Crescent countries. Scholars have noted that with the exception of the Hijaz—the western province that is home to Mecca and Medina, the holy cities of Islam—the Saudi kingdom did not exhibit the politics of urban notables characteristic of the Ottoman successor states.[19] For nomadic inhabitants of the Arabian peninsula (still an estimated 40 percent of the Saudi population during the 1950s), social life revolved less around patronage networks consisting of urban households than tribally based lineage and kinship relations.[20]

In describing the kingdom's development, historians have invoked the *Muqaddimah* of Ibn Khaldūn, a fourteenth-century scholar who discerned a pattern of state building and decay among dynasties in North Africa based upon the central dialectic between nomadic and settled peoples.[21] According to Ibn Khaldūn, during a period of political consolidation, a tribal leader rallied the allegiance of disparate nomadic groups, often on the basis of a religious revival movement, and established a royal dynasty. As the dynasty expanded, it absorbed the culture and material comforts of urban societies, and the nature of the dynasty shifted from nomadic to sedentary. Over time, the basis of the dynasty's cohesion, as well as the fighting prowess of once-fierce bedouin, waned as royal charisma and revivalist zeal gave way to urban bureaucracy and religious legalism. The dynasty was therefore susceptible to decay and vulnerable to raids by nomadic bedouin, who perpetuated the cycle.

Founded by ʿAbd al-ʿAzīz ibn Saʿūd, modern Saudi Arabia is the twentieth-century echo of two previous Saudi states that in the late eighteenth and nineteenth centuries challenged Ottoman authority in Arabia and the Fertile Crescent. ʿAbd al-ʿAzīz's ancestor Muḥammad ibn Saʿūd built an alliance with the Islamic revivalist Muḥammad ibn ʿAbd al-Wahhāb, who preached an austere form of Sunni Islam dedicated to eradicating what he regarded as polytheistic accretions to the "pure" Islam, such as veneration of saints' tombs. From the central Arabian settlements of Nejd, Muḥammad ibn Saʿūd and his successors spread Wahhābī Islam and Saudi authority throughout much of the Arabian peninsula, including the Hijaz. When the Saudis imposed their severe version of Islam on the holy cities and advanced toward Baghdad and Damascus, the Ottoman sultan commissioned Muḥammad ʿAlī Pasha, governor of Egypt, to defeat the Wahhābī. Though Muḥammad ʿAlī's forces destroyed the Wahhābī empire in 1818, a second Saudi state rose from the ashes of the first by the mid-1820s and provoked renewed Egyptian intervention. By exploiting strife among rival Saudi heirs, the Sublime Porte next attempted in 1871 to impose its authority over eastern Arabia through an unsuccessful military expedition led by the governor of Baghdad. The second Saudi state finally collapsed in the late 1880s, when the Saudis' rivals, the Rashīdī, captured Riyadh and in 1891 drove the young ʿAbd al-ʿAzīz and his family into exile.[22]

With his recapture of Riyadh in 1902, ʿAbd al-ʿAzīz began a bid to recreate his predecessors' achievements. In Ibn Khaldūnian fashion, ʿAbd al-ʿAzīz employed Wahhābī Islam as the basis for unifying the tribal peoples of the Arabian peninsula under his rule and forged a zealous military force, the Ikhwān, to wage his campaigns of conquest. ʿAbd al-ʿAzīz also combined Wahhābī proselytism with the settlement of nomadic peoples; he intermarried with and co-opted leading tribal families such as the Jiluwī, Shaykh, and Sudayrī, and carefully cultivated British patronage during World War One. After seizing control of the Hijaz from the Hashemite sherifs in 1925, ʿAbd al-ʿAzīz refrained from imposing Wahhābī strictures upon pilgrims to the holy cities, a practice that had been the undoing of the first Saudi state. The final consolidation of ʿAbd al-ʿAzīz's power involved a ruthless suppression of rebellious Ikhwān, whose religious fervor, an asset when directed against an enemy, was incompatible with supreme Saudi authority. In 1932, three decades after reconquering Riyadh, ʿAbd al-ʿAzīz declared himself king of Saudi Arabia.[23]

Unlike his predecessors, ʿAbd al-ʿAzīz defied the logic of the *Muqaddimah* by accepting Western support for the consolidation of his kingdom, and he signed treaties with the British that established internationally recognized boundaries along Saudi Arabia's borders with Iraq and Kuwait.[24] But petroleum, most of all, set ʿAbd al-ʿAzīz's creation apart from the previous two Saudi states. Just as British patronage had helped to transform ʿAbd al-ʿAzīz's confederation of tribes into a kingdom, sharing in the American oil profits contributed to the establishment of a modern Saudi state. Ironically, however, Saudi Arabia's absorption into the world petroleum economy after 1945 had destabilizing consequences for the state that ʿAbd al-ʿAzīz had so assiduously fashioned. Oil revenues financed the overseas education of an elite group of Saudis, and these educated few, many of them urban Hijazis, composed a growing constituency for Arab nationalism in the kingdom. In the Eastern Province, Aramco employed thousands of Saudi and non-Saudi Arab workers, and labor unrest fueled by Arab nationalism erupted within this work force, most seriously in 1953. With the emergence of nationalist opposition, the new Arab politics threatened to act as a solvent on the bonds that ʿAbd al-ʿAzīz had forged in the making of his kingdom. His successors inherited a foreign policy ambivalent toward Arab nationalism, but ʿAbd al-ʿAzīz also bequeathed to his heirs the larger challenge of preserving the kingdom itself against radical new political forces.[25]

During the 1950s, President Eisenhower and other American officials conducted policy toward Saudi Arabia in the context of an Arab nationalist challenge to the postwar petroleum order and its carefully ordered set of relationships among private companies, Middle Eastern states, and Western consumers. The decade corresponded to an era of high expectations in Arab politics following the July 1952 revolution in Egypt, and for American policy makers, nationalism posed the principal obstacle to securing Mideast petroleum resources. From "Mossadeq through Nasser and Khomeini, to Saddam," Simon Bromley notes, the major threat to Western oil supplies in the Middle East "has come not from the USSR but from indigenous social and national movements." Although Cold War concerns dominated Eisenhower's oil diplomacy, as they did virtually every issue of foreign relations during his presidency, his policy in the Gulf focused less on confronting Soviet expansion directly than on tending the postwar petroleum order. This objective involved coping with Arab nationalism while managing the shift from British to U.S. dominion in the region. The postwar history of the Mideast oil economy, Bromley explains, "coincided with and was deeply formed by the transition from an era of European colonial empires and British hegemony to a postwar epoch of Cold War, independent nation-states, and U.S. hegemony." Before 1955, when Moscow offered to sell arms to Riyadh, Arabia and the Gulf went largely ignored in Soviet Cold War diplomacy. In 1950, only the Americans and the British maintained embassies in the Saudi kingdom. Though Moscow had been the first government to recognize Saudi Arabia in 1926, its mission to the kingdom shut down in 1938, and full diplomatic ties were not restored until 1990. Officials in Washington worried about potential Soviet initiatives in the oil-rich Gulf, and the Saudi leadership, in pursuit of U.S. military aid, sought to manipulate American fears. Superpower antagonism is an essential element of the story that emerges in the following pages, but it provides the background for a discussion of how the U.S. sought to perpetuate the existing arrangements for extracting Gulf oil. Cheap petroleum was indispensable to maintaining high levels of both civilian consumption and military spending within what contemporary policy makers called the "free world." Indeed, since the collapse of the Soviet Union, the U.S. has assumed a dramatically more prominent role in defending the region's oil, a responsibility Washington inherited by degrees following the British withdrawal from the Gulf three decades ago. Born in the early years of the U.S.-Soviet conflict, the postwar petroleum order has outlived the Cold War.[26]

Eisenhower, like his predecessor, hoped that by working through enlightened corporate interests he could prevent Arab nationalism from threatening the petroleum so vital to the economic system nurtured by the U.S. As Eisenhower revisionists have shown, Ike was a more active decision maker than previously supposed and did not simply follow the lead of his vocally anti-communist secretary of state, John Foster Dulles. In relations with the Saudis, Eisenhower personally promoted efforts to build up the regional prestige of King Saʿūd, and the president even waded into the diplomatic morass of the eastern Arabian frontiers problem. But scholarship on Eisenhower has moved beyond revisionism, as "post-revisionists" have questioned the wisdom of the policies Eisenhower actively helped to create.[27] This study, unlike work by both Eisenhower revisionists and post-revisionists, does not make the president himself the focus of the analysis. While recognizing the importance of Eisenhower's role in managing the Anglo-American changing of the guard, it asserts that the president operated in circumstances largely shaped by the economic structures of the postwar petroleum order. Political economy, more than personality, was the major influence on American foreign oil policy during the 1950s. This emphasis is intended to devote as much attention to the consequences of U.S. diplomacy as to how American foreign policy is made and by whom.

Specifically, this study contends that the private structure of U.S. oil diplomacy had an important influence on the Saudi state. This argument both adopts corporatist historians' insights into the political economy of U.S. diplomacy and raises questions that they have neglected. Although corporatism has provided a new way of understanding the ideology and practice of state-industry collaboration in U.S. foreign policy, it has not emphasized the social and political impact of American economic expansion. Influenced by such historians of the U.S. economy as Robert Wiebe, Ellis Hawley, and Alfred Chandler, corporatism has enabled scholars to explain the public-private framework of American diplomacy, as well as the ideological rationale behind it.[28] But like the associational scholarship on which it is based, the corporatist literature on American foreign relations has been less evaluative than descriptive of public-private cooperation. It has sought to transcend the acrimony of earlier debates between New Left scholars and their detractors through an interpretation of policy focused more on organizational structure and ideology than on the consequences of U.S. global power.[29] Corporatism introduced a sophisticated account of political economy and multilateral economic relations into the discussion of American foreign relations, but it simultaneously shifted attention from outcomes to processes and abandoned direct criticism of America's twentieth-century empire. Scholarship on U.S. oil diplomacy typifies this sort of analysis by examining the role of corporate enterprise in official policy while ignoring how American investment affected the politics of Middle Eastern countries.[30]

Meanwhile, literature on Saudi Arabia has approached the 1950s as a crucial era during which the social effects of economic growth challenged Saudi authority. But scholars have yet to consider how the private structure of U.S. diplomacy constrained Saudi responses to Arab nationalism at home and abroad. Most recently, Sarah Yizraeli has defined these years in terms of a personal struggle between the late ʿAbd al-ʿAzīz's sons, Saʿūd and Fayṣal, who pursued clashing visions for the future of the Saudi kingdom following the death of their father. Other analysts have portrayed the Saudi government's dilemma in terms of balancing the competing interests of "new" social groups associated with oil development, such as workers and the middle class, against the demands of "traditional" constituencies, such as tribal and religious leaders. Yet these political and social tensions emerged as the result of private investment by American corporations and of Saudi Arabia's integration into the postwar petroleum order.[31]

Britain's role in Iraq and other oil-producing Gulf states provides a valuable contrast to the American experience in Saudi Arabia. Building on their historic colonial presence, the British had by the early 1950s established and staffed official development boards in Iraq and Kuwait dedicated to channeling oil revenues into development projects, rationalizing governmental administration, and co-opting political dissenters among the populations and within the ruling families. Conversely, these efforts came later in Saudi Arabia, where the U.S. government offered assistance only on such technical questions as currency stabilization and military development, and ceded responsibility for oil-funded projects to Aramco. In 1950, the U.S. did grant the kingdom an Export-Import loan for development, but this $15 million credit was earmarked for projects already planned by Aramco's construction contractor, Bechtel International.[32] Only in 1958, when Prince Fayṣal headed a reform government born of financial necessity, did the regime pursue fiscal accountability and seek to institutionalize the ruling family's role in the bureaucracy.

This argument should not be confused with Aramco's claims that its paternalism brought Saudi Arabia into the twentieth century, nor should it be equated with nostalgia for British imperialism. The purpose instead is to distinguish the American and British approaches toward the oil-producing countries of the Gulf. British efforts to foster development and London's political dominance in an area crucial to Britain's economy met with less-than-complete success. Paul Kingston has shown how British development plans for Iraq failed to live up to their stated goal of improving the quality of life for "peasants, not pashas." A more dramatic failure for British policy occurred in 1958, when the Iraqi revolution destroyed British influence and the social authority of Britain's elite collaborators. Jill Crystal has noted that although the 1950s began with the expectation that oil-funded development would enhance British influence in Kuwait, London was forced to concede Kuwaiti independence in 1961.[33] Britain's policies of colonial administration were therefore incompatible with postwar Arab nationalism. For their part, U.S. officials formulated their oil diplomacy in conscious contrast to the British approach and believed that corporate investment could coexist with, and even tame, the radical new political forces that were remaking the Middle East. They promoted private initiative as an enlightened way of doing business, as a means to differentiate the American presence abroad from that of the Europeans and the Soviets, and as a way to advance economic growth and pacify Arab nationalism.

State building emerges as a key theme in this study because it offers a way to merge a discussion of U.S. foreign economic relations during the early Cold War with an account of how oil revenues and Arab nationalism transformed ʿAbd al-ʿAzīz's dynasty. As corporatist historians have explained, U.S. oil diplomacy was a product of economic development in North America. Government and corporate elites subdued the Hobbesian chaos of Gilded Age capitalism through bureaucratic management within industry, backed by limited official administration. They identified economic growth as a panacea for social conflict. This is precisely the approach that oilmen and policy makers used to cope with nationalist challenges to the postwar petroleum order. The nature of U.S. Cold War diplomacy as it emerged from the domestic political economy helps to explain why and how Washington supported the Saudi regime, why the United States government assumed certain responsibilities in the Saudi kingdom, and why it ceded others to private interests. If the Saudi kingdom was part of an informal American empire, then the characteristics of that empire are traceable directly to the historical experience of *American* state building in the first half of the twentieth century.[34]

At the same time, the modern history of Saudi Arabia must be appreciated within a broad context of comparative Islamic state building. The particular circumstances of 1950s oil diplomacy, Arab nationalism, and rapid social change should not obscure the fact that the Saudi leadership confronted difficulties faced by previous Middle Eastern dynasties that each sought to negotiate the transition from an expanding, Islamic movement composed of diverse elements into a bureaucratic government.[35] Twentieth-century pressures complicated efforts by ʿAbd al-ʿAzīz's fractious heirs to fulfill the process of state formation he had begun decades earlier. But far from being passive in this situation, Saʿūd, Fayṣal, and other Saudis courted or spurned the U.S. as part of their strategies for addressing the challenges faced by the kingdom and as they maneuvered for advantage in their rivalries with one another.

The six chapters of this study situate the shifts in U.S.-Saudi relations during the 1950s within the contexts of Arab nationalism, the Anglo-American relationship, and Saudi state building. With the United States caught uneasily in the middle, the British and Saudis wrangled for years over a remote group of settlements in eastern Arabia. In discussing the Buraymī dispute, the first chapter shows how fundamentally different kinds of British and American empires in Arabia and the Gulf interfered with Anglo-American cooperation in the Middle East. Chapter 2 introduces Eisenhower's foreign policy by explaining his concerns that Arab nationalism endangered Europe's oil supplies, by illustrating how his administration was torn between improved relations with the Arab states and Anglo-American cooperation, and by showing that labor unrest in the Saudi kingdom raised serious questions about the ability of private interests to manage revolutionary nationalism.

Chapter 3 discusses strains in U.S.-Saudi relations following the accession of King Saʿūd. When Washington's northern-tier defense policy exacerbated the Saudi rivalry with Hashemite Iraq, Saudi Arabia joined Egyptian president Gamāl ʿAbd al-Nāṣir in opposing it. As chapter 4 explains, however, the Suez crisis and growth of a domestic Nāṣirist opposition led King Saʿūd to cautiously seek closer cooperation with the United

States. This important shift in Saudi foreign policy coincided with an ill-considered campaign by the administration to invest Saʿūd with the leadership of the Arab world, a policy derived from persistent Orientalist assumptions about Islam. The Eisenhower Doctrine is the subject of chapter 5, which describes the administration's inability following the Suez crisis to establish Saʿūd as a pro-Western alternative to Nāṣir and Washington's missed opportunity to restructure its policy in the Middle East.

After the collapse of Saʿūd's leadership, the Saudi government retreated from Arab politics and became preoccupied with struggles between Fayṣal and Saʿūd over internal reform and political power. Chapter 6 portrays Fayṣal's policies as an attempt to place the Saudi regime's authority on a more rational basis and explains how the fundamental nature of the U.S.-Saudi relationship foreclosed possibilities for further political reform. At the same time, burgeoning supplies undermined the price of crude oil and weakened the political leverage of producing states. Expanded production, as well as rising tensions within the Arab world, reduced the possibility that Arab nationalism could deprive Western Europe of petroleum. In response to falling prices, the Saudi government joined other producing states in establishing OPEC. Previous analysts have portrayed the birth of OPEC as evidence of producing countries' growing strength and as a realignment of power in the global oil economy that ultimately worked to the detriment of consumers. But the 1970s oil embargo overshadowed the fact that OPEC represented an abandonment of Arab nationalist goals by oil-producing Arab states. Through their alliance with non-Arab oil exporters in founding OPEC, this study concludes, Saudi Arabia and other Arab oil states signaled a willingness to bargain within the existing terms of the postwar petroleum order.

Despite American fears, the postwar petroleum order survived as the consequence of growing oil production, antagonism among the Arab states, and the dependence of Saudi Arabia and other producers on the Western corporations. This account of U.S.-Saudi relations during the Eisenhower era is largely the story of how both Americans and Saudis sought to defend their stake in the postwar petroleum order, and how an informal American empire gradually replaced a more formal British one. Only in the fullness of time will historians be able to assess the implications of these developments for the Middle East and the political and social costs of what U.S. policy makers counted as one of their greatest achievements in economic diplomacy.

1
A Dutch Uncle: The U.S. and Buraymī, 1952

On August 31, 1952, the Saudi Amīr Turkī ibn ʿAbdullah ibn ʿUṭayshān accompanied Rashīd ibn Ḥamad from Saudi Arabia to the settlement of Ḥamāsā, located in the Buraymī oasis on the eastern fringe of the Arabian peninsula. Turkī arrived at the oasis with forty armed men, and his escort of Rashīd ibn Ḥamad, chief of one of the clans settled in Ḥamāsā, represented a forceful assertion of Saudi Arabian sovereignty over Ḥamāsā and the eight other settlements of the Buraymī oasis. This Saudi claim directly challenged the authority of the kingdom's smaller Gulf neighbors, Abu Dhabi and the Sultanate of Muscat and Oman, over Buraymī. The ruler of Abu Dhabi claimed six of the settlements at the oasis, the Sultan of Muscat the remaining three, including Ḥamāsā.[1]

Conflict over the hinterland separating Gulf sultanates and Saudi empire builders of the Arabian interior had a history of more than a century. Clearly demarcated geographic borders did not exist in eastern Arabia, where political authority was defined instead by garnering the allegiance of the region's semi-nomadic inhabitants. The tenuous nature of such political authority and its cycles of consolidation and decay were observed by Ibn Khaldūn in the *Muqaddimah,* which modern scholars have interpreted more broadly as a basic state-building pattern characteristic of Middle Eastern societies.[2] Historians have pointed out that the Buraymī oasis, as the "northern gateway to the Sultanate of Muscat and Oman," occupied a position of strategic importance in the eastern Arabian desert, situated about an equal distance between Abu Dhabi on the Persian Gulf to the west and the Gulf of Oman to the east and watered by runoff from nearby mountains. Several fortifications in the oasis, the largest built by the Wahhābī in the mid-nineteenth century, testify to its strategic value. But control of Buraymī was also key to asserting political authority over eastern Arabia, because semi-nomadic tribes needed the oasis for agriculture, for watering their livestock, and as a center for trade. Only by controlling access to Buraymī could a sedentary dynasty hope to impose its authority over the region's inhabitants.[3]

Although the conflict had its origins in an earlier period of Saudi expansion, the twentieth-century Buraymī dispute hinged on a new factor, the discovery of vast deposits of crude oil in the area, and postwar European demand for this petroleum opened a new chapter in the struggle for eastern Arabia. What had been a local dispute involving the extent of Saudi authority in the east and the Gulf rulers' hegemony over their hinterlands intensified as Western oil companies scrambled to define petroleum concessions in geographic terms. The region's rapid integration into the global economy after 1945 gave Buraymī international significance beyond the mere question of who controlled a remote oasis in southeastern Arabia.[4]

The detailed account of the Buraymī dispute in this chapter serves a dual purpose. First, it outlines the historical background of a complicated diplomatic problem that American, British, and Saudi diplomats tried unsuccessfully to solve throughout the 1950s. This conflict emerged from the ways in which oil development and state building affected societies in the Arabian peninsula during the twentieth century. Second, Buraymī helps to illustrate the different strategies in oil diplomacy—indeed, the contrasting imperial styles—that Britain and the U.S. employed in the Middle East after World War Two. Though the allies understood that the success of their policies in Europe depended on joint development of Mideast petroleum, they utilized different means in pursuit of their mutual goals. While the British sought to preserve their formal colonial presence in the Gulf, the U.S. worked through private oil companies to forge a relationship American officials believed could accommodate Arab nationalism. This discussion of Buraymī is therefore meant not only as background for the U.S.-Saudi relationship during the 1950s, but also as a first step toward reinterpreting Anglo-American relations in the Middle East during the same period. Anglo-American friction in the region was not, as some have assumed, the result of a competition for oil resources. It arose instead from basic differences in the two nations' oil diplomacies and from their distinct historical experiences in the Middle East.

Turkī's expedition to Ḥamāsā showed how private American oil investment helped to define the territory of the modern Saudi state, and it posed an uncomfortable foreign policy dilemma for the United States government. Since Aramco's consolidation after World War Two, Washington had backed the private efforts of the company to develop Saudi oil. Not surprisingly, Aramco took a direct interest in the eastern Arabian frontiers dispute, and researchers in its Arabian Affairs Division even helped to develop the kingdom's legal claim to Buraymī with the help of Saudi government tax collectors who had worked among the tribes of southeastern Arabia. Turkī himself had once served as governor of Ras Tanura in the Eastern Province of Saudi Arabia where Aramco maintained a huge refinery, and the amīr and his armed guards reportedly arrived at Ḥamāsā in Aramco-owned vehicles. Efforts by the company to map the limits of its concession reinforced the Saudis' historic ambition to dominate their Gulf neighbors.[5]

But Great Britain, bound by treaty to defend Abu Dhabi and arbiter of the Sultan of Muscat's foreign policy since the nineteenth century, directly opposed this Saudi-Aramco expansion in the east. In order to secure shipping lanes to its Indian empire, London had negotiated a treaty system that by 1853 gave Britain authority over Abu Dhabi and six other Gulf shaykhdoms. During the second half of the nineteenth century, London entered into subsequent agreements with what became known as the Trucial Shaykhdoms and concluded treaties with states of the upper Gulf including Bahrain, Kuwait, and, during World War One, Qatar. By the time Standard Oil of California (Socal) negotiated the earliest concession agreement in Saudi Arabia, Britain's treaty system had grown into a formal imperial presence that consisted of political residents and British-officered defense forces. Indian independence in 1947 eliminated the historical basis for the British presence in the Gulf, but a new set of concerns replaced the earlier rationale. The Gulf became a vital source of petroleum for Great Britain, and this resource was doubly valuable because Gulf oil could be purchased with sterling, rather than with precious American dollars, and its sale provided a crucial source of hard currency. Kuwaiti oil alone accounted for roughly half of Britain's foreign exchange. Under London's authority, British companies had also negotiated a series of oil concession agreements with the lower Gulf states, but when Petroleum Concessions Limited, a subsidiary of the Iraq Petroleum Company, organized explorations in the disputed territory of eastern Arabia in 1949, the Saudi government responded by claiming Buraymī.[6]

The conflict over the frontiers of eastern Arabia therefore caught the United States between two allies. Washington consistently offered diplomatic support for Aramco's operations in Saudi Arabia and had promised Riyadh military aid as a quid pro quo for renewal of the Dhahran base lease in June 1951; yet, at the same time, Great Britain was the principal U.S. ally in the Cold War and the key to Western defense strategy in the Middle East. After the Saudis advanced their unprecedented claims, the

U.S. sought unsuccessfully to coax the parties into a negotiated settlement. Pressured by both the Saudis and the British to choose sides, American officials found themselves having to allay the suspicions of each country that Washington secretly backed the cause of the other.[7]

Despite British suspicions of U.S. connivance with the Saudis, Anglo-American differences in Arabia and the Gulf were actually much narrower than naked economic competition, and instead involved a controversy over how best to preserve the postwar petroleum order. The Americans sought to assuage nationalist sentiment in producing countries through modest, judicious concessions administered privately by the oil corporations. Aramco's fifty-fifty deal with Saudi Arabia exemplified this approach, but the Aramco-Saudi agreement had prompted Iranian premier Muḥammad Musaddiq to nationalize the Anglo-Iranian Oil Company. Compromise with Musaddiq, the British believed, would encourage other challenges to Britain's Mideast interests. Instead, London wished to close ranks with the U.S. to prevent destabilizing concessions similar to the Aramco deal and to present nationalist challengers with a united Anglo-American front. As recently as March 1952, the British embassy had proposed a joint petroleum policy to the U.S. State Department, where officials worried that such overt cooperation would fan the very nationalism it was intended to address and threaten Western interests in the Middle East.[8]

While the Americans hesitated to endorse a common petroleum policy, the British looked to the United Kingdom's historic relationships with the Gulf rulers as an anchor of stability in a turbulent region. The nationalization of the Anglo-Iranian Oil Company gave added importance to ties with Kuwait and the Trucial states. In a paper titled "Middle East Oil Policy" circulated at a conference of British Middle East diplomats in June 1952, the Foreign Office set out the broad outlines of its plans for a partnership with the Gulf rulers and the United States. London would foster cooperation with the Gulf regimes, promoting the wise use of their oil revenues and guaranteeing their security against internal and external threats. Anglo-American cooperation remained the highest British priority, but U.S. officials appeared

> apprehensive of anything which smacks of cartels or "ganging up" against the Middle East oil States. Indeed the State Department appear to be more pre-occupied by allegations of restrictive practices on the part of the companies than by the necessity for them to stand together to resist exorbitant demands from the oil countries.

In order to address these problems and secure Anglo-American cooperation, the paper recommended a regional "oil forum," a revival of the 1944 agreement, through which the U.S. and the U.K. could regulate Middle Eastern petroleum.[9]

But the Foreign Office's plans for a partnership with *both* the U.S. *and* the Gulf rulers involved a contradiction. Ritchie Ovendale has noted that American officials found Britain's relationships with its Gulf clients "anachronistic." The British ambassador in Jidda, George Pelham, was aghast at suggestions by his American counterpart, Raymond Hare, for overhauling the British treaty system in the Gulf. When Hare proposed a federation encompassing all the Gulf states including Saudi Arabia, the Foreign Office sought assurances from Washington that seeking such a federation was not official U.S. policy. For London to continue its traditional imperial role in the Gulf, it also had to take a hard line against the Saudis in eastern Arabia, which frustrated American efforts to defuse the Buraymī conflict.[10]

For the U.S., Buraymī posed a particularly serious dilemma that can be understood only from a global perspective encompassing Western Europe as well as the Middle East. Intent on improving relations with the Arab states and preventing expansion of Soviet influence in the Middle East, the Americans were wary of appearing to be accomplices to British imperialism. At the same time, the sterling oil of the Gulf was essential to economic policy in Europe and to British participation in the free-trading, multilateral economy so cherished by American policy makers. Those historians who portray Buraymī as a transparent attempt by the United States to encroach on British oil ignore the importance that Gulf petroleum held for U.S. interests and Anglo-American cooperation in Europe. They also slight the major role played by the Saudis in shaping the conflict and Riyadh's repeated frustration in attempting to enlist Washington's support.[11]

As for the two parties to the dispute, neither the Saudis nor the British regarded the eastern Arabian controversy in isolation but in the context of regional politics. King ʿAbd al-ʿAzīz had grown to distrust his former patron, Great Britain. After World War Two, Labor foreign secretary Ernest Bevin sought to recast Britain's relations with its mandates Transjordan and Iraq, controlled by Hashemite monarchs, through the negotiation of new treaties. ʿAbd al-ʿAzīz interpreted Bevin's foreign policy as a British endorsement of the Hashemite Fertile Crescent scheme to unify the Arab world, and perhaps even of Hashemite revanchist designs on the Hijaz. Nadav Safran explains that by 1949, the historic Anglo-Saudi understanding—British restraint of Hashemite ambition in exchange for a Saudi *détente* with British Gulf clients—had broken down.[12]

In reaction to Bevin's policy, the Saudi king not only cultivated ties with the government of Egypt and with the anti-Hashemite Syrian politician

Shukrī al-Quwwatlī, but he also looked to the United States to provide security against the Hashemite threat. According to George McGhee, assistant secretary of state for near eastern affairs, U.S. officials hoped that the Tripartite Declaration issued by the United States, Britain, and France in May 1950 would quiet Saudi concerns about Hashemite aggression. In October 1950, President Truman also sent a personal message to King ʿAbd al-ʿAzīz declaring that "the United States is interested in the preservation of the independence and territorial integrity of Saudi Arabia," and that "[n]o threat to your Kingdom could occur which would not be a matter of immediate concern to the United States." Such assurances failed to eliminate Saudi concerns about the Hashemites, however, and close relations with the U.S. raised additional dangers for Riyadh. Cooperation with the principal supporter of Israel threatened to isolate the Saudi kingdom in the Arab world, undermining King ʿAbd al-ʿAzīz's efforts to win Arab allies against the Hashemites. The dispute with Britain over Buraymī, in other words, heightened the chronic Saudi sense of regional insecurity, which stemmed from both the Arab-Israeli conflict and from political antagonism among the Arab states themselves.[13]

For Britain, eastern Arabia was one issue in a constellation of questions related to its postwar position in the Middle East. Bevin's foreign policy had run up against fundamental social changes in the Arab world. His plan to revise treaty relations with the Arab states involved alliances with an earlier generation of Arab nationalists, such as the Hashemites and Iraqi prime minister Nūrī al-Saʿīd, who had been part of the Ottoman elite. Balanced precariously on these narrow social foundations, Bevin's policy encountered difficulties at every turn. Although Britain successfully negotiated a treaty with Jordan in 1948, anti-British riots followed the conclusion of the Portsmouth treaty with Iraq that same year. Great Britain had also been compelled to relinquish its Palestine mandate in 1948, and U.S. support for Israel threatened to upset British plans for Middle Eastern stability and friendly relations with the Arab states.[14] Even more frustrating were attempts to negotiate a new treaty with the Egyptian government over the vast Suez military base. British negotiators had sought to couch a new agreement within a proposed Anglo-American defense organization, the Middle East Command. But in October 1951, the Egyptian prime minister, Muṣṭafā al-Naḥḥās, amid escalating violence in the canal zone, rejected the Middle East Command and abrogated the existing Anglo-Egyptian treaty.

That very month, the British electorate returned the Tories to power and Winston Churchill to 10 Downing Street. Churchill's approach toward the Middle East sought to revive the wartime cooperation of the English-speaking allies by encouraging the United States to accept greater responsibility for regional defense through the Middle East Command while Britain pared its own commitments and military presence. But Churchill was determined to hold the line in the Gulf, the chief source of Britain's petroleum, and to maintain intimate relations with the Gulf rulers. This became especially apparent in 1953, when for several months the prime minister assumed direct conduct of foreign affairs and struggled, without success, to reconcile Anglo-American cooperation in the Middle East with a tough stand on Buraymī.[15]

The evolution of the eastern Arabian frontiers question itself reflected not merely the souring of the Anglo-Saudi relationship but also major changes in the Arabian peninsula over half a century. In July 1913, an Anglo-Ottoman convention had fixed the boundary between the Gulf shaykhdoms and the Ottoman *sanjaq* of Nejd at a "Blue Line" running south from the Gulf coast west of the Qatar peninsula to the great desert of the Rubʿ al-Khālī, or Empty Quarter. Following his defeat of the Rashīdī, ʿAbd al-ʿAzīz had been recognized as *vali,* or governor, of Nejd by the Ottoman Porte, which exercised nominal authority in central Arabia. In theory, at least, Saudi dominions therefore extended to the Blue Line, but the outbreak of war in 1914 complicated the politics of Arabia and the Gulf and aligned Britain and the Ottoman Empire against one another. In December 1915, the British signed a treaty with ʿAbd al-ʿAzīz, who revolted against his Ottoman superiors, and following the defeat of the Central Powers and partition of the Ottoman Empire, Britain received a mandate over Iraq that confirmed its status as the dominant power in the Gulf.[16]

Several factors led ʿAbd al-ʿAzīz to seek revision of the Blue Line in his favor. First, the Saudi defeat of the Hashemites and capture of the Hijaz represented a major aggrandizement of Saudi status. King of Nejd, Hijaz, and their dependencies by 1925, ʿAbd al-ʿAzīz aspired to control the entire peninsula. Second, the Ottoman collapse meant that Saudi ambitions were no longer constrained by Anglo-Ottoman diplomacy. ʿAbd al-ʿAzīz had come to power by playing the British and Ottomans against one another, and he became adept at employing great-power patronage in the service of internal consolidation. To ratify his early victories in Nejd over the Rashīdī, he had first sought the sanction of the Porte, and then a treaty with the British, who finally obliged with the advent of the war. A new Saudi treaty with Britain, signed at Jidda in 1927, was followed by his suppression of the Ikhwān. King of Saudi Arabia by 1933, ʿAbd al-ʿAzīz awarded a petroleum concession to Standard Oil of California (Socal) to generate revenue for his empty treasury. In subsequent years, American oil companies would become another kind of great-power patron for Saudi Arabia, as well as, the king hoped, a new foil for British power in the Gulf.[17]

The advent of oil politics in the kingdom was the third decisive factor that contributed to Anglo-Saudi conflict in eastern Arabia. Dispute over the extent of Saudi authority in the east followed closely on the award of the Socal concession. The British informed the U.S. government that it still considered the Blue Line the Saudi boundary with the Gulf shaykhdoms, while a series of Anglo-Saudi negotiations during the years 1935–1937 failed to settle the matter. The "red" line proposed by Saudi representatives in 1935 elicited a British counter-proposal for a "green" line. This rainbow of proposed revisions for the political boundaries of eastern Arabia was based on the rulers' putative authority over indigenous, nomadic tribes. The British proposed the so-called "Riyadh" line the following year as a compromise, but that proposal fell a full hundred miles short of the extensive Saudi claims made in 1949. By this time, Aramco represented a powerful new American presence in the Arabian peninsula, and ʿAbd al-ʿAzīz's attitude toward Buraymī had also merged with his concern over Bevin's Hashemite diplomacy. Seeing potential enemies in neighboring Jordan and Iraq, as well as along the Gulf, the king began to complain to Washington of "Anglo-Hashemite encirclement."[18]

Seeking a diplomatic solution to the dispute, the two sides agreed in 1950 to suspend oil prospecting activities and the movement of military forces in eastern Arabia pending new talks, yet substantive Anglo-Saudi negotiations in London during August 1951 focused on maritime boundaries and did not address the Buraymī dispute directly. Negotiators also organized a joint fact-finding commission to investigate eastern Arabian claims, but they failed to reconcile Saudi ambitions in eastern Arabia with British interests in the Gulf. Following the collapse of a new round of Anglo-Saudi talks at Dammam, Saudi Arabia, in early 1952, Riyadh appealed for American intervention to settle the dispute. The Saudi foreign minister, Prince Fayṣal, demanded that the U.S. sponsor Saudi claims in the way the British defended the interests of their Gulf clients.[19] The Saudis also sought to invoke President Truman's October 1950 assurances of the kingdom's territorial integrity in the eastern Arabian border conflict, but Truman had offered this commitment in order to dispel King ʿAbd al-ʿAzīz's Hashemite concerns and not to provide a blank check for a Saudi drive to the east. His guarantee occasioned a serious misunderstanding with the Saudis, who believed that because American companies were developing the kingdom's oil, Riyadh was entitled to the support of the U.S. government in the Buraymī dispute.[20]

For the British too, Buraymī fostered a misunderstanding with the Americans based on confusion about the nature of public-private cooperation in U.S. oil diplomacy. Because the Saudi claims on Buraymī amounted to trespassing in British eyes, the Foreign Office resented the unwillingness of the U.S. government to actively oppose Saudi and Aramco territorial ambitions. "We expect something more from the State Department than mediation and impartial advice to both sides," wrote Archibald Ross, head of the Eastern Department. Anglo-American relations over Saudi Arabia were already irritated by the growing American presence in the kingdom. Saudi-American military cooperation, for example, grew as the eastern Arabian question drove a wedge between Riyadh and London, while plans to coordinate the American military training mission with a British mission still operating in the kingdom were never implemented. The British viewed Aramco as the cause of the decline of British influence with the Saudis and as a partner in ʿAbd al-ʿAzīz's eastern Arabian adventures. "Ibn Saud has moved from being a grateful pensioner of ours," Ross wrote Bernard Burrows, counselor at the Washington embassy, "to being the recipient of a shower of American produced wealth." Ross warned that Aramco's role in driving Saudi expansionism should not be underestimated.[21]

The State Department opposed siding with the Saudis and stressed to the American ambassador in London, Walter Gifford, the drawbacks to U.S. involvement. Resumption of direct Anglo-Saudi talks was crucial to keeping the eastern Arabian question out of the United Nations, where the Soviets would exploit tension between two Western-aligned states. Though the U.S. had "wanted to remain aloof" from the Buraymī dispute since 1949, eventual American involvement might become unavoidable if a protracted crisis in eastern Arabia threatened the British position in the Middle East "to which we attach great importance." U.S. policy on Buraymī sought Anglo-Saudi compromise, but a strong British presence in the region remained the overriding American priority.[22]

Meanwhile, Saudi frustrations over the Dammam talks led ʿAbd al-ʿAzīz to increase pressure on the ground in Buraymī. On March 29, the Saudi government protested the visit of the British political resident in Oman to the Buraymī oasis as a violation of Saudi sovereignty, and in July, a Saudi party harassed a mission sent by the Petroleum Concessions Limited Company into territory that Britain claimed belonged to Abu Dhabi. These Saudi moves, which culminated in Turkī's occupation of Ḥamāsā on August 31, threatened to incite violent conflict. In response to Turkī's arrival, the Sultan of Muscat mobilized tribes under his authority, and by October, 8,000 men had been assembled on the Gulf coast. The

British political resident in the Gulf ordered forces of the Oman Trucial Levies to forts in the Abu Dhabi–claimed settlements in Buraymī and organized Royal Air Force overflights of the oasis.[23]

For the United States, a difficult situation had become dangerous. The British Foreign Office protested Turkī's occupation of Ḥamāsā to the Saudi government, and the British consul in Jidda warned that his government would "protect its position."[24] The U.S. government had to entice the parties back to the negotiating table before violence erupted, and in doing so faced the nearly impossible challenge of convincing both sides that it was an honest broker.

While the U.S. politely rebuffed Saudi entreaties to enforce the kingdom's territorial integrity, the State Department simultaneously sought to dissuade the British from additional military action that would escalate the crisis. King ʿAbd al-ʿAzīz sent a message to the State Department on September 17 requesting U.S. assistance on the basis of the Truman letter, and the Saudi ambassador Asad al-Faqīh asked the U.S. to be prepared to assist Saudi Arabia in the event Britain followed through on its threats to impose a military solution. The department informed the embassy in Jidda, however, that al-Faqīh had left his meeting with American officials without "aid or comfort."[25] At the same time, Robert Sturgill of the Bureau of Near Eastern Affairs assured a British embassy official that the U.S. had no prior knowledge of Saudi plans to occupy Ḥamāsā and expressed concern about RAF overflights at Buraymī. Sturgill urged restraint on the part of Britain and its Gulf clients, but the British were not inclined to accept the Saudi challenge passively. "What would you have us do," retorted British minister Ronald Bailey, "take the whole thing lying down?"[26]

As talks in Jidda deadlocked, the Saudis sought mediation by Washington, but the U.S. was reluctant to abandon the neutrality officials had sought to maintain since 1949. American diplomatic representatives in Saudi Arabia and Britain offered the State Department contradictory advice on the mediation question. From Jidda, Ambassador Hare warned that a refusal to mediate could damage U.S.-Saudi relations and argued that Saudi Arabia had a "quite tenable position" in claiming sovereignty over the oasis. In London, however, U.S. Ambassador Gifford advocated continued restraint, noting that U.S. meddling in eastern Arabia could jeopardize the Anglo-American partnership in regional defense. Neither of the ambassadors' recommendations was without risk. Mediating the Buraymī crisis could involve alienating one or both of the disputants, yet State Department officials also realized that inaction could lead to a rancorous clash between two U.S. allies at the United Nations and a propaganda victory for the Soviet Union.[27]

Meanwhile, British forces had blockaded Buraymī to prevent resupply of the Saudi party. Ambassador al-Faqīh protested the blockade in a meeting with officials of the State Department's Bureau of Near Eastern Affairs on September 29 and also renewed threats to bring the Buraymī dispute before the United Nations Security Council, a move near eastern affairs assistant secretary Henry Byroade hoped would not be necessary. Instead, the American officials expressed optimism over a new message from King ʿAbd al-ʿAzīz to British foreign secretary Anthony Eden that protested the British blockade but also expressed willingness to negotiate.[28]

A controversy over whether Turkī should be permitted to remain at Ḥamāsā during negotiations prevented the resumption of the Anglo-Saudi talks that had collapsed the previous winter. On September 30, British embassy counselor Bernard Burrows told near eastern affairs director Parker T. Hart that London would not permit Turkī to stay because that would constitute a clear indication that the Saudis "have won their point." Burrows rejected Hart's suggestion of mutual withdrawal pending a diplomatic settlement, because the Saudi claim lacked "any legitimate basis" and because mutual withdrawal would be an unacceptable blow to British prestige.[29] Opting to stay out of the dispute while the king awaited a reply from Eden, the State Department instructed Ambassador Hare on October 2 to "hold at bay" Saudi demands for American involvement. In the meantime, the U.S. would continue to advocate Anglo-Saudi negotiation, the success of which was crucial to avoiding "exploitation" of Buraymī by enemies of the "free world."[30]

With no reply from Eden, the Saudi king summoned Hare to Riyadh for an audience on October 6. The king was despondent over the Buraymī situation and declared himself "ill" from thinking about it. He protested British overflights and the blockade of Buraymī and complained that he had received no help from the United States. Apparently, the king still believed that the U.S. had given him a blank check of support in the form of the Truman letter, which he planned to put "to the test." He requested American mediation of the dispute but responded favorably when Hare suggested a lifting of the British blockade and RAF overflights, a maintenance of the status quo in Buraymī, and new Anglo-Saudi negotiations.[31]

In a memo to his superiors, John Jernegan expressed the preference of the Near Eastern Affairs Bureau for mutual withdrawal, but emphasized the importance of getting the parties to negotiate lest this "very minor incident" lead to "trouble out of all proportion to its importance." If the Buraymī situation escalated, it would "result in even greater difficulties than those in which we now find ourselves in the Middle East." Given the Truman letter and U.S. interests in the kingdom, the U.S. could not ignore

ʿAbd al-ʿAzīz's pleas for American involvement, and the U.S. also had to take seriously the king's threat to appeal to the Security Council. Jernegan identified Britain's "rather unyielding" stance that Turkī withdraw before talks resume as a major obstacle to a resolution. Without judging the merits of the case, Jernegan argued that the British were capable of greater "ease and flexibility" than the Saudis. State Department officials, he recommended, should propose to the British the same three suggestions that Hare had put to the Saudi king.[32] Later that day, undersecretary David Bruce placed these proposals before British ambassador Sir Oliver Franks. "Regardless of the merits of the case," Bruce explained that only a compromise could keep ʿAbd al-ʿAzīz from taking Buraymī to the U.N. or requesting formal U.S. mediation. In response, Franks agreed to forward the proposals to the Foreign Office and insisted that London had already sent a favorable reply to ʿAbd al-ʿAzīz's request for new talks.[33]

Although American officials had some reason to be optimistic about a resumption of negotiations on Buraymī, the standoff over the oasis remained tense. The State Department cabled Hare on October 8 with reports of a Saudi force of 700 troops massing in the region of al-Kharj, southeast of Riyadh. The British agreed to cease RAF overflights of the oasis, but the Sultan of Muscat had mobilized a large force, possibly intending to dislodge Turkī from Ḥamāsā, and it seemed likely that new incidents on the ground could torpedo efforts to work out a diplomatic resolution despite British promises to restrain the sultan.[34]

Eden agreed to the resumption of talks following a simultaneous withdrawal of British and Saudi forces from Buraymī, but the king told Hare that he "categorically refused" mutual withdrawal, because he could not be expected to evacuate his own territory. ʿAbd al-ʿAzīz insisted that only U.S. mediation could end British attempts to cut Turkī's supply lines and prevent a drastic Saudi reaction. That same day, the department informed the Foreign Office that "for all practical purposes" Washington had received a formal Saudi request to mediate the dispute. The U.S. wished to avoid assuming such a role and also wanted to avoid the referral of Buraymī to the U.N. Security Council. Therefore Washington suggested that the two countries submit Buraymī to impartial arbitration. The following day, Eden accepted a standstill agreement provided it did not prejudice the claims of either party at Buraymī. The Foreign Office was prepared to return to direct negotiations and resort to arbitration if bilateral talks failed.[35]

While the State Department hoped to avoid a public arbitration that would provide grist for the Soviet propaganda mill, the British were eager to push ahead to arbitration, where they believed that their stronger legal claims to Buraymī on behalf of the Gulf rulers would prevail. Meanwhile, the Saudis floated a new idea when they invited the U.S. to participate in a tripartite commission that would visit the oasis and ascertain the allegiances of the indigenous tribes. This scheme was a clever attempt by the Saudis to play their strongest card at Buraymī, where, since his arrival in August, Turkī had been paying subsidies to local tribes in a bid to win their fealty for ʿAbd al-ʿAzīz. A commission charged with administering some kind of plebiscite could give the king his best chance of asserting his sovereignty over Buraymī, especially, the Saudis believed, if the U.S. could tip the balance of the commission in favor of Riyadh.[36] American officials demurred on the commission idea, however, and stressed to al-Faqīh the need for prompt resumption of bilateral negotiations. On the same day, October 18, the State Department urged the Foreign Office to approach the king in order to arrange for new talks. To convey the importance it attached to the new negotiations, the department shared with the British embassy the contents of Truman's October 1950 letter in which the president promised to defend Saudi territorial integrity.[37]

After a week in Riyadh, Ambassador Pelham hammered out a standstill agreement with Saudi deputy foreign minister Yūsuf Yāsīn and other officials. Initialed on October 26, the agreement permitted both parties at Buraymī to remain in place and receive supplies, but prohibited reinforcements. Military actions were to cease, and no attempt would be made to interfere with the inhabitants of the oasis. The standstill agreement did not resolve the basic dispute, however, and King ʿAbd al-ʿAzīz still insisted that the status of the Buraymī oasis could be determined only through his tripartite commission scheme. Pelham, returning to Jidda from Riyadh, told Hare that he was pessimistic about new bilateral talks. He predicted the two sides would soon have to resort to arbitration, and he condemned the Saudi seizure of Ḥamāsā as "imperialism."[38]

While the Buraymī issue was far from settled, the U.S. had, at least temporarily, defused a potentially explosive situation. American officials had brought the two sides back to the negotiating table without committing the U.S. to the responsibility of formal mediation. Although the U.S. professed impartiality, its insistence on restoring direct Anglo-Saudi negotiations benefited the weaker party in the dispute. ʿAbd al-ʿAzīz had seriously miscalculated by trying to invoke the Truman letter, but American pressure on Britain to concede to a standstill agreement permitted Turkī to remain at Buraymī, where the Saudi claim was dubious at best.

The crisis over Buraymī erupted during a sensitive period in U.S.-Saudi relations. American policy makers had been debating whether the kingdom would receive military aid, which negotiators had held out as an inducement for the Saudis to renew the Dhahran air base agreement. American and Saudi representatives initialed the renewal on June 18, 1951, and the Saudis looked to the Americans to fulfill their promises. Their demands went unanswered, however, because the American bureaucracy was divided over the question of aid for the kingdom and the Truman administration remained preoccupied by larger questions in Middle East diplomacy.

In April 1952, the Near Eastern Affairs Bureau complained that the Joint Chiefs had reneged on commitments given during the Dhahran negotiations to support limited aid for Saudi Arabia. Secretary of State Dean Acheson subsequently reminded Defense Secretary Robert Lovett of these promises and explained that honoring U.S. assurances to the Saudis was essential to continued good relations. In addition, the Defense Department had requested expanded base rights at Dhahran, and Acheson warned that it would be "very difficult" to secure these rights without a favorable decision on aid.[39] In June, the Defense Department therefore assented to "token grant military aid" if such aid were politically necessary in negotiations over base rights, but the Joint Chiefs' recommendation for such assistance was so lukewarm that State Department proposals for aid to the kingdom stood little chance of approval by the White House.[40] Meanwhile, Hare attempted to use the promise of aid as a carrot in new negotiations with the Saudis over expanding U.S. base rights at Dhahran and the establishment of a Military Assistance Advisory Group (MAAG). He conducted two rounds of negotiations with the Saudis on the MAAG agreement, the first concluding on July 26, a month prior to Turkī's occupation of Ḥamāsā, and the second in October, as the Saudis and British were working out a standstill agreement.[41]

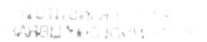

For the Saudis, base negotiations with the Americans involved the delicate issue of sovereignty and the politics of Arab nationalism. King ʿAbd al-ʿAzīz was squeezed between his dependence on the U.S. for his defense requirements and the danger of appearing to cooperate too intimately with a Western power, especially the patron of Israel. He wished to spare Saudi Arabia the violent demonstrations that had shaken Iraq following the military base agreement between Baghdad and London, and, after the Suez base became a rallying point for Arab nationalists, the Saudi government grew reluctant to knuckle under to the United States on Dhahran. For these reasons, the twenty-five-year lease on the air base the Americans initially requested was whittled down to five years, and the Saudi king sought U.S. aid to avoid the appearance of submitting to U.S. demands without any compensation. Indeed, Ambassador Hare recognized that in offering the U.S. a lease renewal at Dhahran, the king was "swimming very much against the current" of Arab anti-imperialism.[42] Significantly, the Saudis remained recalcitrant in their insistence that American Jews not be permitted at the Dhahran air base. The U.S.-Saudi base agreement gave the Saudis the right to exclude from the American contingent at Dhahran "objectionable persons," a euphemism for Jews, whose presence would have seriously embarrassed the king in the Arab world.[43]

These considerations help to explain why ʿAbd al-ʿAzīz, and later his successor, Saʿūd, found it nearly impossible to retreat on the Buraymī issue. Interest in the potential oil resources of eastern Arabia, fear of Anglo-Hashemite encirclement, and a desire to redeem the claims of the previous century all contributed to the Saudi preoccupation with Buraymī. But in addition to these factors, an intransigent attitude toward the British at Buraymī provided the king with some nationalist cover against charges that his country was dominated by Western oil companies and the U.S. military. Just as Aramco took pains to publicize the anti-colonial character of its relations with Saudi Arabia, ʿAbd al-ʿAzīz felt compelled by Arab nationalist pressures to show his opposition to Western imperialism. Ill-prepared for an actual armed confrontation with the British, the king nevertheless kept the Buraymī issue alive for its political value, relying on the U.S. government to prevent any serious consequences.

Following their standstill agreement on October 26, both the Saudis and the British continued to seek American support for their respective positions on Buraymī. King ʿAbd al-ʿAzīz pressed his plebiscite scheme, while the British prevailed upon U.S. officials to force the Saudis into arbitration. The State Department maintained its preference for direct talks and cabled Hare in Jidda that the Saudi scheme sought to manipulate the U.S. "in ways not compatible" with friendly Anglo-American relations. The department wanted to avoid participating in a fact-finding commission and, indeed, "any substantive involve[ment]" in settling the dispute.[44] Again offering conflicting advice, Ambassador Gifford commended the Foreign Office's proposal for arbitration as the "most promising method" for resolving the conflict, while Hare expressed suspicion of both British and Saudi motives.[45] Assistant Secretary Byroade explained to the Saudi ambassador on November 8 that the U.S. "cannot be umpire between disputants" who are both friends, because "each will expect special appreciation" for its position. He expressed regret that the Saudis had attached the commission scheme as a condition to the resumption of talks and urged the Saudi government to "give direct talks a trial." On November 23, the Foreign Office finally proposed to the Saudis that Buraymī go to arbitration. The British decided to appeal to Prince Fayṣal, who was then at the United Nations in New York and who they hoped would be more receptive to arbitration than the aged king.[46]

Fayṣal, however, proved no more amenable to arbitration than his father was. Undeterred by the American rejection of a plebiscite commission, the prince approached Secretary Acheson at the Seventh General Assembly of the U.N. on December 2 and dismissed any arbitration of claims to such an "integral part of Saudi Arabia" as Buraymī. He renewed the Saudi request for U.S. participation in a plebiscite commission, but the meeting concluded after nearly an hour with no promises of U.S. support. In a conversation with a member of the U.S. delegation two days later, the prince vented his frustrations and alluded ominously to negative consequences in the Middle East if the U.S. failed to improve relations with the Arab states. "Don't place too much faith in what Arab leaders may tell you that Communism is incompatible with Islam," he warned. "A drowning man will grasp at a snake—even a poisonous one—if it is the only chance he has to prevent his going under for the last time!"[47]

The Saudis rejected arbitration in a note to the British Foreign Office on December 6, and British officials complained that U.S. inaction had allowed ʿAbd al-ʿAzīz to keep alive his hopes for a plebiscite commission. The British embassy in Washington communicated Eden's desire that the U.S. "make unmistakable" its support for arbitration, and the department cabled Hare that it was "strongly inclined" to support such a step. In Jidda, Ambassador Pelham expressed regret to the U.S. ambassador that Turkī had not been "ejected" from Buraymī early on, and he blamed U.S. "passivity" for Saudi intransigence. Meanwhile, frustrated by the Saudis' refusal to submit Buraymī to arbitration, the British were readying plans to retake the oasis by force if necessary.[48]

Concerned about the ongoing stalemate with the Egyptians on the Suez base treaty and the Anglo-Iranian crisis, the British Conservative government was unwilling to suffer another black eye in the Middle East at Buraymī. Eden's secretary, Evelyn Shuckburgh, recorded on December 2 feeling "very depressed about the world in general. . . . [A]fter Persia and Egypt, the sheikdoms on the Persian Gulf are now being absorbed by Saudi Arabia." On December 11, Shuckburgh described his boss as "very tired and very impatient." Eden "thinks we are giving way too much to Neguib over the Sudan; [he] also thinks the Office [is] being casual and inactive over the Persian Gulf sheikdoms in which our position is being undermined by Saudi Arabia." In the wake of the "stunning blow" to British prestige in Iran, Eden wrote the cabinet, another setback in the Middle East could prompt the Gulf rulers to "reassess" their traditional relations with Britain, whose economy was utterly dependent on the region's oil. The foreign secretary advocated taking a "firm line" with the Saudis, defending the Gulf clients, and above all protecting sterling oil. In accord with this stance, Eden announced that a local buildup of forces was underway on the Gulf coast, and the Chiefs of Staff were preparing to send the H.M.S. *Ceylon* and two frigates into the Gulf. Eden stopped short of accusing the United States of sponsoring the Saudi campaign for Buraymī, but he noted that the U.S. maintained its position in the kingdom by "yielding constantly to Saudi pressure." Voicing his persistent suspicion of Aramco influence in Saudi Arabia, Pelham wrote Eden that the U.S. was "now unmistakably the bigger firm and spare no pains to show it," and that the Americans "seem to find us embarrassing partners."[49]

British suspicions would have appeared ironic to Saudi officials, whose repeated demands for U.S. participation in the plebiscite scheme fell on deaf ears. Prince Fayṣal apparently still hoped for a favorable reply to his formal request for U.S. involvement, but the Saudi prince shifted his strategy as the Truman administration entered its final weeks. On December 30 in New York, the prince approached John Foster Dulles, Secretary of State–designate in the incoming Eisenhower administration. Dulles recorded that Fayṣal "poured out his grievances" and talked about his "hopes" for the new American leadership. The prince was uneasy that the British would shape the ideas of the new administration on Buraymī and other matters before the Saudi case could be heard, and Fayṣal's concern increased when it became known that Winston Churchill was planning a trip in early 1953 to consult with Eisenhower and renew Anglo-American friendship. Fayṣal therefore canceled a meeting with Acheson on January 5 to focus his attention on the new administration. The next day, Eisenhower urged Dulles to "bring the Prince in for a talk" so that "he could not kick about me talking to W[inston] C[hurchill]."[50]

In Jidda, Hare decided that the U.S. should support arbitration, but the ambassador wanted to avoid the impression of "having teamed up" with Britain. As in the Anglo-Egyptian talks, it was imperative that the U.S. maintain its distance from London and speak like a "Dutch uncle" to both sides if it hoped to develop good relations with the Arab states. In spite of Fayṣal's decision to snub Acheson, the State Department on January 8 summoned al-Faqīh for a meeting with Bruce, who again explained that because the U.S. was an "intimate friend" to both parties in the dispute, it could not participate in any tripartite commission. Bruce strongly recommended that Buraymī be submitted to arbitration, but the Saudi government remained adamantly opposed. Truman administration officials had failed to solve the eastern Arabian frontiers question, and Eisenhower's invitation to Fayṣal was only the beginning of his administration's equally frustrating efforts.[51]

Clearly, Eisenhower would inherit formidable challenges in the Middle East. Buraymī was only one of a collection of issues that posed a dilemma between siding with Britain and pacifying anti-colonial nationalism. Adding to these difficulties was the legacy of Truman's decision to recognize Israel. This factor posed a major obstacle to formulating a regional defense policy and improving U.S.-Saudi relations. Hare reported the Saudis' "dissatisfaction and disillusionment" with the level of American military aid, which he attributed to U.S. failure to follow through on the assurances given in June 1951. The ambassador knew that U.S. aid to the Saudis was linked to the pending decision about assistance for the Free Officers' regime of Muḥammad Negīb in Cairo. Washington was considering offering military aid as a way of enticing Egypt into an agreement with Britain and a proposed Middle East Defense Organization (MEDO). Hare worried that the Saudis would become indignant if aid were awarded first to "some other Middle Eastern country." Washington told Hare on January 16, however, that assistance for the Saudis would not be forthcoming. Though the State Department had pressed for aid to Egypt, Truman approved only token assistance for Cairo. According to an official in the Near Eastern Affairs Bureau, the president opposed close ties with Arab countries because "Israel and Jewish groups in the United States protested strongly." Truman's support for Israel had seriously compromised U.S.-Arab relations, and it was unlikely that U.S. oil corporations, no matter how generous their policies toward Arab oil-producing and oil-transit countries, could overcome Arab mistrust of Washington. At the close of his administration, the lame-duck president passed the buck on all of these Middle Eastern questions to Eisenhower and Dulles.[52]

At Buraymī, U.S. policy makers had to choose between their partnership with Great Britain and assuaging Arab nationalism. Open cooperation with Britain to safeguard the postwar petroleum order was sure to incite anti-colonialism in the region, alienate the producing states, and hand the Soviets a golden opportunity to increase their influence in the Middle East. At the same time, Buraymī demonstrated to officials in Washington how unqualified support for Aramco and Saudi Arabia could strain the Anglo-American relationship and threaten British authority in the Gulf. This authority was crucial to broader U.S. foreign policy goals in the region and in Europe that depended upon British strength and prosperity.

While American policy makers firmly believed that support for private enterprise offered the best hope for preserving the postwar petroleum order, they also remained committed to an alliance with Britain, which pursued a quite different strategy based upon its long history as an imperial power in the Middle East. Buraymī was far from an Anglo-American proxy war for oil resources, as some have portrayed it. In fact, the U.S. repeatedly refused to endorse Saudi claims in eastern Arabia, and Washington regarded its reliance on private companies as a way to avoid official involvement in Middle Eastern political disputes. Instead, the conflict reflected the contrasting approaches employed by the U.S. and Britain to secure oil resources in the age of radical Arab nationalism. The U.S. government, having encouraged Aramco to accede to reasonable Saudi demands as the basis of its oil diplomacy, found it impossible to restrain the company-government campaign to expand into eastern Arabia. The British, economically dependent on sterling oil, could hardly retreat in the face of a Saudi drive to absorb potential oil-producing territory claimed by British imperial clients. Throughout the Eisenhower administration, these different historical approaches in the Middle East would complicate Anglo-American cooperation toward the common objective of defending the postwar petroleum order.

2
Old Soldiers: Eisenhower and ʿAbd al-ʿAzīz ibn Saʿūd, January–November 1953

DWIGHT D. EISENHOWER, no less than Truman, confronted a dilemma between preserving the Anglo-American postwar petroleum order and accommodating new political realities in the Arab world. American Cold War priorities in Europe depended upon access to inexpensive Mideast crude, yet overt collaboration with Great Britain, the dominant imperialist power in the oil-rich Gulf, threatened to inflame Arab nationalism. In its relations with the Saudi kingdom, the administration pressed for an Anglo-Saudi compromise on Buraymī as bitter, protracted negotiations dragged on over the status of the parties at the oasis. As part of the basic American strategy to assuage Arab nationalism through private diplomacy, the administration also supported Aramco's efforts to appease the Saudis by sweetening the terms of the fifty-fifty agreement for Riyadh. The British, intent on defending sterling oil and the security of their Gulf clients, felt threatened on both fronts. In the spring of 1953, Winston Churchill presented the Saudis with an ultimatum intended to bring them to arbitration. Meanwhile, British officials continued to lobby their American counterparts for a coordinated Anglo-American petroleum policy calculated to pre-empt challenges from the producing countries. Early in the new administration, the discrepancy between American and British foreign oil policies became apparent, and the Saudi kingdom lay at the center of this divergence.

As King ʿAbd al-ʿAzīz's health deteriorated, the dynasty's ability to sustain itself against foreign and domestic threats grew increasingly uncertain. ʿAbd al-ʿAzīz's heir, Saʿūd, and the kingdom's foreign minister, Prince Fayṣal, faced the challenges of shaping domestic reforms and navigating the kingdom through the turbulent waters of Arab politics. During 1953, labor unrest in the Aramco work force signaled that the kingdom was not immune to revolutionary Arab nationalism and called into question Eisenhower's faith in enlightened corporate policies as the key to preserving access to Arab oil. The Americans also decided on a regional defense policy based on the "northern tier" countries of the Middle East, a strategy that would come to include the Saudis' Arab nemesis, Hashemite Iraq, and precipitate an anti-Western turn in Saudi foreign policy.

Though Eisenhower revisionists have done important work by recasting the president as an active policy maker, the most significant early decisions Eisenhower made about the Middle East involved leaving the structure of American oil diplomacy unchanged. Reliance on private industry to tap the strategic oil resources of the Gulf had consequences for U.S. relations with both Great Britain and Saudi Arabia. Britain, protector of Abu Dhabi and Oman, mistrusted Aramco over the company's role in the Buraymī dispute, and the British generally felt that Aramco's policy of acceding to Saudi demands threatened Britain's Middle Eastern oil interests. But for the Saudis, the private nature of U.S. oil diplomacy held even greater importance. Ironically, Eisenhower's support for corporate statesmanship, a policy intended to distance the U.S. from Britain's formal colonial presence in the region, left a deep imprint on Saudi Arabia during the transition from ʿAbd al-ʿAzīz to his successors and as the kingdom developed into a modern state.

Eisenhower's attempt to cope with Arab nationalism has developed as the central theme in the literature on U.S. Middle East diplomacy during the 1950s.[1] Historians associate Arab nationalism with Gamāl ʿAbd al-Nāṣir, who emerged from Muḥammad Negīb's shadow following the July Revolution to become the leading political figure in Egypt and the Arab world, and scholarship has therefore focused on U.S. relations with Egypt and the American role in the Suez crisis.[2] Arab nationalism transcended Nāṣir's undeniable charisma and importance, however, and reflected the broadened social base of Arab politics since the war. The Truman administration, seeking cooperation in regional defense, attempted to cultivate ties with the Free Officers in Cairo, but this policy, which the Eisenhower administration continued, proved insufficient to address the challenges that social revolution posed to U.S. interests in the Arab world.[3]

Arab nationalism presented the U.S. and its allies with a triple threat. First, Nāṣir and others called for pan-Arab unity and the expulsion of Western influence, which would preclude the maintenance of military bases in the region. Second, administration officials feared an alliance between the pan-Arab movement and the Soviet Union, and just such a partnership appeared to be forming when the Soviets severed relations with

Israel in February 1953 expressly to garner favor with the Arab states. Finally, Arab nationalism threatened vital Gulf oil resources. Arab League member states discussed the formation of a petroleum committee that would exercise political control over Arab oil, a campaign that gained momentum following the nationalization of a Western oil company by non-Arab Iran. Nāṣir himself identified petroleum as the "vital nerve of civilization," and the key to unlocking the Arabs' economic potential and wielding true power on the world stage.[4] At the beginning of the Eisenhower administration, U.S. officials were therefore haunted by the specter of a unified Arab world in control of the region's oil resources and allied with the Soviet Union.

Eisenhower articulated his concerns in this regard following the January 6 reunion with his old acquaintance Winston Churchill, a meeting that had worried Prince Fayṣal. Churchill suggested that a renewed alliance could help solve problems in Egypt and Iran. But Eisenhower rejected Churchill's "almost childlike faith" in Anglo-American partnership in light of drastic changes in world politics since 1945. "Nationalism is on the march," Eisenhower wrote, "and world communism is taking advantage of that spirit of nationalism to cause dissension in the free world." To prevent Moscow from exploiting this crisis, "the two strongest Western powers must not appear before the world as a combination of forces to compel adherence to the status quo." Excessive reliance on Britain in the Middle East would wreck American attempts to grapple with Arab nationalism.[5]

The other stumbling block in U.S.-Arab relations was Israel, though as Eisenhower prepared to take office, expectations of a change in U.S. policy toward Israel increased. The incoming Republican president had few of the ties to the Jewish leaders and organizations that had influenced Truman, and he also owed no political debt to Jewish Americans, three-quarters of whom had voted for Democratic candidate Adlai Stevenson. Indeed, Israeli officials and Zionist organizations in the U.S. became alarmed that the new administration would abandon Truman's commitments to the Jewish state. They had a "general fear," as Israeli ambassador Abba Eban later wrote, "that Truman's successive interventions had been a one-time act of grace that could not be relied upon when his successor would come to office." At the same time, Arabs hoped that the Eisenhower White House would be sympathetic to their concerns. Following Eisenhower's election, *Al-Bilād al-Saʿūdiyya* conjectured that the Republican might be less cordial toward Israel than the Democratic president who preceded him. But as Eisenhower's policy in the Middle East evolved, these hopes (and fears) proved largely unjustified. Eban was relieved to find that the new administration "did not drastically change anything in American-

Israeli relations," though "in an effort to win Arab smiles, [it] avoided the traditional rhetoric of friendship with Israel." The administration did commit itself to seeking a solution to the Arab-Israeli conflict, however, which Dulles regarded as among the "thorniest problems" facing the new administration.[6]

As Eisenhower revisionists have shown, the president directed and supervised Dulles's forays into the thorny problems of the Middle East. Dulles, a corporate lawyer with a family pedigree in diplomacy, took a personal interest in the complexities of the Arab-Israeli conflict and regional defense strategy. Most importantly, however, as architect of the D-Day invasion and former commander of Allied forces in Europe, the president appreciated better than anyone the strategic importance of petroleum and understood that the military effectiveness of NATO depended upon defense of the postwar petroleum order. Eisenhower's persistent anxiety about Western European prosperity and security formed the basic consideration in his Middle East foreign policy. He warned in his inaugural address: "No free people can for long cling to any privilege or enjoy any safety in economic solitude. . . . This basic law of interdependence, so manifest in the commerce of peace, applies with thousand-fold intensity in the event of war."[7]

Concerns about Mideast oil also touched directly on Eisenhower's core beliefs regarding the international and domestic economies. Without the petroleum of the Gulf, American efforts to promote prosperous, more open economies in Western Europe were doomed. On the domestic front, as Robert Griffith has argued, Eisenhower envisioned a flourishing economy based on corporate growth and tended by modest government power.[8] Threats to Mideast oil supplies therefore jeopardized not only U.S. defense and economic policies in Europe, but also Eisenhower's vision of the economy at home, because diverting western hemisphere oil to Europe would require unacceptable governmental controls on domestic consumption. On a personal level, Eisenhower relied on advisors recruited from the American petroleum industry who shared his beliefs, such as Herbert Hoover Jr., to conduct the administration's oil diplomacy.

In accord with his faith in private initiative fortified by limited state power, Eisenhower supported those American companies in the business of extracting Middle East petroleum. As part of this policy, his administration approved recommendations developed by the State Department under Truman to quash criminal proceedings against major oil companies for antitrust violations. Given the importance of petroleum for the security of the U.S. and its allies, as well as to the ongoing war in Korea, the administration resolved to go ahead with a civil proceeding only. Secretary

Dulles even opposed Attorney General Herbert Brownell's plans for bringing a civil case, citing a "dangerous effect on our national security." But the president authorized a civil suit, adding that antitrust laws should be changed "as soon as possible" to prevent the necessity of further legal proceedings. These early decisions indicated Eisenhower's willingness to subordinate antitrust concerns to preservation of the postwar petroleum order and its underlying pattern of government-industry collaboration.[9]

Middle Eastern oil continued to be indispensable to economic recovery and defense in Western Europe. National Security Council Paper 138/1, drafted on the eve of Eisenhower's inauguration, deemed inexpensive Mideast oil "crucial to the strength and balance-of-payments position of this area which is vital to our security." At the same time, the U.S. preferred that private corporate interests address the nationalist challenge by offering producing states favorable terms, rather than coordinating oil policy with London. NSC 138/1 explained that U.S. petroleum policy must "avoid giving strength to the claim that the American system is one of privilege, monopoly, private oppression, and imperialism." Indeed, the administration withdrew its criminal case against the oil companies precisely because charges of collusion and price-fixing fostered this impression. The preservation of order in the oil-rich Gulf, however, remained a British responsibility. Opposed to greater U.S. military responsibilities in the Middle East, the National Security Council kept a planned Defense Department study examining the Gulf "in a deferred status." State Department officials, while criticizing the nineteenth-century character of Britain's relations with its Gulf clients, nevertheless acknowledged British primacy in this vital area. Byroade wrote Hare on February 20 that the British treaty system was "anachronistic," and he recommended prevailing upon the British "to adapt their thinking to changing times." But the assistant secretary simultaneously opposed any "radical changes." Eisenhower therefore backed what he considered to be enlightened, corporate development of oil resources, while at the same time his administration relied on Britain's imperial presence in the Gulf.[10]

As it had under Truman, the Arabian-American Oil Company spearheaded U.S. foreign oil policy in the Middle East. Since the opening of the Trans-Arabian Pipeline (Tapline) in 1950, Saudi Arabia had come to rival Kuwait in production and exports. Aramco exported about 32.1 million metric tons of Saudi oil in 1952, almost half of which passed through Tapline to its terminus at Sidon on the Lebanese coast. The remaining crude was loaded into tankers on the Gulf for shipment through the Suez Canal or processed in the Aramco refinery at Ras Tanura. As Eisenhower took office, Saudi production was increasing, in part to supply markets ordinarily serviced by Iranian oil, now under international embargo in response to Musaddiq's nationalization of the Anglo-Iranian Oil Company.[11]

While continuity defined the new administration's oil policy, events permitted Eisenhower to accede to Saudi demands for military assistance in ways his predecessor could not. Soon after Eisenhower's inauguration, Hare summarized the arguments in favor of aid to the Saudis. The ambassador stressed the "implied *quid pro quo*" used by the U.S. during the June 1951 negotiations over the Dhahran base and predicted a negative reaction by the Saudis if "any other Arab country or Israel" received aid first. Meanwhile, Britain and Egypt had made some progress toward resolving their dispute over the status of the Sudan. In early February, the two countries agreed that Egypt's demand for union with Khartoum, a major obstacle to a Suez base agreement, should be decided through free Sudanese elections. As a result of this development, the Eisenhower administration felt able to offer limited aid to Negīb's government in the form of military training. With the logjam broken, Hare's recommendations concerning the Saudis proceeded up the chain of authority in the new administration. On February 26, the Near Eastern Affairs Bureau sent a memo to the new secretary of state outlining the importance of military aid to U.S.-Saudi relations. Undersecretary Walter Bedell Smith commended the department's recommendations to Mutual Security Director Harold Stassen, who presented them to Eisenhower. On March 14, the president declared both Egypt and Saudi Arabia eligible for a limited grant of aid.[12]

Buraymī, however, still posed for American officials a contradiction between their goals in oil diplomacy and their desire to assuage Arab nationalism. The Saudis evinced a sense of betrayal at American refusals to back Riyadh in the eastern Arabian controversy. Hare cabled from Jidda that Prince Saʿūd persisted in asking why British aggression did not trigger President Truman's assurances to defend Saudi security. The prince also wanted to know why the Americans had rejected the Saudi plebiscite proposal, while heartily endorsing British calls for arbitration. To the Saudis, wrote the ambassador, "we now appear to be joining forces with [the] British." American professions of neutrality yielded only a "heavy drain on our reserve of goodwill with little by way of return."[13]

Dulles, meanwhile, followed through on promises to arrange a meeting between Prince Fayṣal and Eisenhower. In their conversations with Fayṣal, Dulles and the president sought to demonstrate their desire to improve U.S.-Arab relations. The secretary told the prince on March 2 that his meeting with the president was evidence of the Americans' wish "that the spirit of cordiality between ourselves and the Arab nations be restored." Fayṣal had been present at the United Nations in November 1947, when the U.S. voted in favor of partitioning Palestine. To him, American support for partition and recognition of Israel the following May represented a betrayal of Franklin Roosevelt's promises to King ʿAbd al-ʿAzīz to consult the Arabs on Palestine. This episode had been the prince's formative experience in relations with the U.S., and afterward, Fayṣal told Eisenhower "he had determined never to revisit the United States." Only following the 1952 election, the prince explained, did he agree to resume his role as head of the Saudi delegation to the U.N. While Fayṣal was hopeful "that the advent of the new administration meant a change for the better in United States-Arab relations," the president recognized the need for "a restoration of the spirit of confidence and trust which had characterized our relations with the Arab nations until the last few years." Eisenhower made it clear that in exchange for listening to Arab concerns, he expected cooperation in fostering regional stability and bringing about the "intellectual defeat of communism" in the Middle East.[14]

Although Fayṣal's conversation with Eisenhower remained on the level of generalities, the prince raised three specific issues with Dulles and State Department officials. First, his government desired formal renewal by the new administration of the Truman security guarantee. Second, Fayṣal expressed Saudi impatience at U.S. foot-dragging over military and economic aid, which remained stalled in the American bureaucracy. Finally, the Saudi foreign minister demanded U.S. support for Saudi claims in eastern Arabia. The prince rejected Dulles's suggestion that Buraymī be submitted to arbitration, insisting instead that the oasis was "indisputably Saudi territory."[15]

By the time of his departure from the U.S., Fayṣal had received favorable responses on the first two issues, but U.S.-Saudi relations remained troubled. Bedell Smith informed Ambassador al-Faqīh that the current administration "emphatically" reiterated the assurances given to Saudi Arabia by its predecessor and announced the president's willingness to aid the Saudis. Still, Buraymī threatened to stymie the U.S.-Saudi cooperation touted by Eisenhower and Dulles during the prince's visit. Despite the continued American preference for arbitration, Smith agreed to raise alleged British violations of the standstill agreement with Eden, who was also in Washington. At an embassy dinner, however, Smith intimated to Eden that the U.S. was "acutely embarrassed" by Saudi stubbornness and that the Anglo-Iranian Oil Company crisis, Egypt, and Buraymī were "in danger of wrecking Anglo-American understanding throughout the area." Despite Eisenhower's hopes for improved relations with the Arab states, his administration's reliance on Anglo-American cooperation in the Middle East kept it mired in the Buraymī quagmire.[16]

Soon after Eden's return from Washington, the Churchill government opted to confront ʿAbd al-ʿAzīz with an ultimatum backed by force that would compel him to accept arbitration or would result in Turkī's eviction from Buraymī. Either outcome, the British believed, would bolster their sagging prestige in the Gulf and help to secure sterling oil. On March 12, the Saudi king dispatched officials to Buraymī with orders to collect *zakāt*—or alms tax—from the indigenous tribes, a symbolic as well as administrative act signifying sovereignty in Islamic societies. Eden sent a memo to the cabinet four days later noting Saudi violations of the October agreement and expressing concern about the U.K.'s declining prestige with its Gulf clients. Britain, he recommended, should declare itself no longer bound by the standstill agreement and send forces to occupy a set of locations in Abu Dhabi territory, cutting off Turkī from his supplies. At the same time, Eden said, London should renew offers of arbitration. In this manner, Britain could force ʿAbd al-ʿAzīz to abandon the plebiscite idea, which was a "transparent fraud" because of Turkī's subversive activities at Buraymī. As for the American reaction, Eden calculated that Washington would acquiesce in British military moves so long as London remained willing to arbitrate the dispute.[17]

The British implemented their plan on April 2 by dispatching additional Oman Trucial Levies to blockade Buraymī, and Ambassador Pelham informed the Saudi government that the British no longer considered themselves bound by the agreements of the previous October. To soften the blow, Churchill sent a friendly note to ʿAbd al-ʿAzīz dated March 30, explaining that the U.K. simply could not forsake its duty to its Gulf clients. The prime minister renewed his appeal for arbitration: "If neither of us can convince the other, is it beyond the power of statesmanship to find means of reconciling our views with justice and honour?" A Saudi Foreign Ministry official told Hare that Churchill's letter created a favorable atmosphere, but that British military moves sent mixed signals about London's desire for a peaceful settlement. Nonetheless, new Saudi-British negotiations opened on April 8. The king agreed to a "middle Course" between his plebiscite scheme and the arbitration proposed by London, and though the king also insisted on a return to the status quo in eastern Arabia prior to the British moves of April 2, Pelham wrote Churchill that ʿAbd al-ʿAzīz had agreed in principle to arbitration. The British, the ambassador recommended, should offer some concession—"display our largesse of mind and spirit"—to save ʿAbd al-ʿAzīz's face and win the king away from his more hawkish advisors, led by Deputy Foreign Minister Yūsuf Yāsīn.[18]

But Churchill disregarded the advice of Pelham and officials at the Foreign Office who urged a conciliatory policy toward the Saudis. From

April 1, Churchill assumed direct conduct of British foreign affairs from an ailing Eden. The prime minister opposed the appearance of retreat in the Gulf not only out of concern for British prestige, but also because members of his own party would bristle at any new Middle East setback that compounded the crises in Iran and Egypt. Minister of State Selwyn Lloyd proposed to Churchill concessions Britain might offer the Saudis to ease the path to arbitration, including neutral supervision in eastern Arabia and withdrawal of some of the troops introduced on April 2. The prime minister rejected Lloyd's compromises, replying, "I would not have sent my personal telegram to Ibn Saud if I had thought that the policy of concessions was to follow from it."[19]

The British gambit appeared to pay off both because it elicited Saudi agreement in principle to arbitration and because the U.S., as predicted, raised no objection to the military action. In late March, the State Department wound up an independent investigation into territorial rights in eastern Arabia and concluded that the Saudi claim to Buraymī was weak. On April 2, the department cabled its conclusion to Hare that no Saudi ruler had occupied Buraymī since 1869 and that Saudi Arabia could not invoke Truman's letter because the Saudis had no definitive claim on Buraymī. Britain's military action and the State Department's findings compelled the Saudis to drop the issue of the Truman letter and abandon the plebiscite scheme. Near Eastern Affairs officials expressed growing department skepticism toward Saudi claims in a meeting with Aramco vice president James Terry Duce and Saudi legal counsel on April 3. Richard Young, an American lawyer retained by Aramco for the Saudi government, attempted to justify ʿAbd al-ʿAzīz's "emotional attachment" to Buraymī. When the officer in charge of Arabian peninsular affairs, Andrew D. Fritzlan, questioned the king's sudden affection for a remote locale his family had not possessed since 1869, Young retorted that Fritzlan must have been "reading British propaganda." Although support for Aramco anchored U.S. foreign policy toward Saudi Arabia, the administration's cautious position on Buraymī revealed that such support was balanced against concern for Anglo-American relations.[20]

Meanwhile, the Eisenhower administration was in the process of rethinking its Cold War strategy in the Middle East. The administration sought to settle the question of regional defense, whose resolution remained blocked by ongoing Anglo-Egyptian disagreement over the Suez base. As part of the re-evaluation of Middle East policy, Secretary Dulles, accompanied by Mutual Security Director Harold Stassen and other officials, undertook a tour of the region in May. During a stop in Riyadh on May 18–19, the secretary hoped to continue the dialogue begun with

Fayṣal in the U.S., but the British moves a month earlier had poisoned the atmosphere. Saudi officials, the aged King ʿAbd al-ʿAzīz foremost among them, were bitter over what they perceived as American duplicity regarding Buraymī.[21]

The visit showcased the personalities who shaped Saudi foreign policy. Dulles met first with the seventy-eight-year-old founder of Saudi Arabia, ʿAbd al-ʿAzīz, who was crippled by arthritis and in frail health generally. Since his celebrated expedition to Riyadh in 1902, the Middle East had been changed almost beyond recognition by the Ottoman collapse, oil politics, and the Arab-Israeli conflict. Most recently, the clarion call of nationalism had mobilized Arabs against Western imperialism, and the monarchy in Egypt had been a casualty of the new Arab politics. How the kingdom built by ʿAbd al-ʿAzīz would survive in the postwar Middle East would be a question for the dying king's heirs.

Politics within the Saudi royal family during the 1950s is the story of two half-brothers. In Riyadh, Dulles met with both the hand-picked successor of ʿAbd al-ʿAzīz, Crown Prince Saʿūd, and Foreign Minister Fayṣal. Of the two, the more seasoned in international affairs was Fayṣal, who in 1919 had represented his father on a state visit to London. Following the Saudi recapture of the holy cities, Fayṣal, a direct descendant of Muḥammad ibn ʿAbd al-Wahhāb on his mother's side, had served as viceroy in the Hijaz, the Islamic heartland. This important post required him to manage the annual pilgrimage, which was crucial to good relations with other Arab and Muslim countries. Later, Fayṣal served abroad in various capacities, including representative to the United Nations, which placed him in New York during the fateful vote on Palestine in November 1947. Embittered then by the Americans' "betrayal," Fayṣal had expressed sympathy for nationalist demands that the kingdom embargo oil to the West.

After an influenza epidemic claimed ʿAbd al-ʿAzīz's eldest son, the king named Saʿūd his successor. The crown prince served as his father's viceroy in Nejd, the Saudis' traditional, central Arabian home, which was much less cosmopolitan than the Hijaz. Though Saʿūd had traveled to the United States, he lacked the diplomatic experience and sensitivity to regional and international politics possessed by his half-brother. It was assumed that Fayṣal would continue to have a prominent role in the Saudi government, but the responsibility for managing the transition after the death of the kingdom's founder and for negotiating the hazards of Arab nationalism belonged to the ill-prepared Saʿūd.[22]

Another leading influence on Saudi diplomacy was the deputy foreign minister, Yūsuf Yāsīn. A protégé of ʿAbd al-ʿAzīz's Syrian ally Shukrī al-Quwwatlī, Yāsīn remained deeply suspicious of Anglo-Hashemite influence in the Middle East. The Americans were familiar with Yāsīn's tenacious bargaining during negotiations over the Dhahran air base and Saudi compensation from Aramco, and the deputy foreign minister used his influence in equal measure to oppose any compromise with the British over eastern Arabia.[23]

Both princes, along with Yāsīn, attended the elderly king when he greeted the American delegation on May 18 in Riyadh. Referring to the Buraymī dispute, ʿAbd al-ʿAzīz desired to know whether "his friends had deserted him." He explained that his decision two decades earlier to award an oil concession to an American company had offended London, which was the reason that the British were now attempting "to chase Saudi subjects from their own country." The king was not satisfied with Dulles's explanation that the Americans had consistently counseled the British against drastic military action. ʿAbd al-ʿAzīz insisted that the U.S. "execute its promises" under the security guarantee issued by Truman and renewed by the current administration. He also made the extravagant claim that his family had owned Buraymī for five hundred years. Dulles then abruptly requested an end to the royal audience.

The Americans met subsequently with Saʿūd, Fayṣal, and Yāsīn, who were increasingly responsible for making foreign policy as the king's faculties declined. Dulles told Saʿūd bluntly that Buraymī was not covered by Truman's security guarantee, reaffirmed by Eisenhower, while Saʿūd reiterated his father's accusations that the British caused starvation through their blockade and committed "terrorism" against innocent people. The morning after enduring these tongue-lashings from the king and crown prince, Dulles held more businesslike discussions with just Yāsīn and Fayṣal, who treated the Americans to an extensive, if partisan, history of the Buraymī dispute. While the Saudis had responded favorably to Churchill's call for arbitration, Fayṣal insisted that the British continued to violate the standstill agreement. That very day, Fayṣal revealed, he had received a telegram from Turkī at Ḥamāsā reporting that British forces had interdicted supply caravans to Buraymī. Fayṣal conceded that Churchill had agreed to let Turkī draw supplies from the local store at Buraymī during arbitration, but he pointed out that in the meantime the British blockade remained in place. The prince called for the restoration of the status quo before April 2 and demanded British adherence to the standstill agreement. Dulles praised the Saudis' willingness to submit Buraymī to arbitration and acknowledged that the U.S. "could do more" to help resolve the dispute.[24]

Prior to departing Saudi Arabia, Dulles cabled the U.S. embassy in London and instructed the new U.S. ambassador Winthrop Aldrich to seek

British accommodation with the Saudis. But, annoyed at Dulles's interference over Egypt and Buraymī, Churchill told Aldrich "it was slightly irritating that Dulles, in his globe-trotting progress, should be taking pains at every point to sympathise with those who were trying to kick out or do down the British." Churchill opposed any retreat and wanted to concede only to a "gentleman's agreement" with ʿAbd al-ʿAzīz that the 300 British troops surrounding Buraymī would not take additional action while arbitration proceeded. He explained to Lloyd on May 24 that he did not want to reinforce the view, which "grew up from the Abadan scuttle," that "you only have to kick the British or push them and they will clear out." He instructed: "Let us sit resolute and phlegmatic on this high ground and see what happens."[25]

After being cajoled by Foreign Office officials, however, the prime minister finally relented and agreed to mutual withdrawal of the two parties from Buraymī. Lloyd replied on May 29, urging Churchill to reconsider his opposition to face-saving concessions and appealing to Churchill's sense of priorities in the Middle East. The minister of state reasoned that mutual withdrawal would get Turkī out of Buraymī and force the Saudis to make a humiliating 300-mile retreat. It would also pave the way for arbitration, which had the support of the U.S. Mutual withdrawal would therefore safeguard U.K. prestige in the Gulf and remove an impediment to Anglo-American cooperation. Faced with these arguments, Churchill sent a new message to ʿAbd al-ʿAzīz on June 2, explaining that "[t]rue equality will best be established if we both recall our forces."[26]

Dulles reported to the National Security Council on June 1 that relations with the Saudi kingdom "were at the moment poor." The "old and crotchety" ʿAbd al-ʿAzīz, angry over a lack of American support in eastern Arabia, might be inclined to cancel the Aramco oil concession and evict the Americans from Dhahran. Although the Buraymī question seemed "a minor affair," failure to bring the British and Saudis to arbitration "could have very bad consequences for the United States." In general, Dulles concluded from his trip that Western prestige in the region was "very low," and the U.S. "suffered from being linked with British and French imperialism." Eisenhower asked the secretary why the British "insisted on hanging on" at Buraymī, and Dulles replied that oil was London's main consideration. The president suggested that responsibility for compromise lay with London, and Eisenhower predicted that should the parties fail to reach agreement, "we should have more Irans on our hands."[27]

At the behest of Dulles, who wished to make amends for his unpleasant audience with the Saudi king, the president sent ʿAbd al-ʿAzīz a conciliatory message on June 15. Eisenhower expressed his dismay at accusations that the U.S. had abandoned its commitments to Saudi Arabia. Pleased that the king had agreed in principle to arbitration, Eisenhower contended that Washington's evenhanded policy on this issue had demonstrated American friendship for Saudi Arabia. "You and I are both old soldiers," Eisenhower concluded in a personal appeal to the king, "and I believe that we shall understand each other fully."[28]

But following Dulles's trip, new clouds formed on the horizon of U.S.-Saudi relations. Historians have identified the secretary's tour as pivotal to shifting U.S. regional defense strategy away from Egypt to the countries of the "northern tier." Substantial controversy surrounds the origins of the northern-tier idea, largely owing, as Nigel John Ashton has observed, to Anglo-American disagreements once the northern-tier concept evolved into the Baghdad Pact and to the polarizing effects the Pact had on the Arab world. Early American discussions concerning a northern-tier defense strategy focused on the non-Arab countries of Turkey and Pakistan, but it is clear from Dulles's statements and from discussions of military aid to Middle Eastern countries in 1953 that officials also envisioned an Iraqi role in the northern-tier concept. This change in American defense strategy could hardly have been more troubling to the Saudis. Rather than focusing on the Saudi kingdom's most important Arab ally, Egypt, U.S. plans for regional defense would involve its principal Arab antagonist. Washington's shift to the northern tier disappointed the long-standing Saudi hope for U.S. protection against Britain's Hashemite and Gulf clients and subordinated Saudi requests for aid to those of the northern-tier countries. Department officials recognized that this change in priorities would strain relations with the Saudi kingdom, but the magnitude of these tensions would become apparent only after the Saudi patriarch departed the scene.[29]

For the moment, the boundary dispute with Britain's Gulf clients continued to preoccupy the Saudis. Despite Churchill's willingness to offer mutual withdrawal of both parties from Buraymī, the Saudis rejected any compromise that would force them to recall Turkī and relinquish their hard-won foothold in the disputed territory. Anglo-Saudi progress toward arbitration effectively stalled during the summer of 1953 over the two parties' status at the oasis. As for the Americans, renewed violence sent State Department officials in search of British concessions out of fear that the specter of Western imperialism would enhance Soviet influence in the Middle East. In late June, elements of the Banī Kaʿab tribe, regarded by ʿAbd al-ʿAzīz as Saudi subjects, battled British forces at Buraymī. The Saudi king protested to Eisenhower that the British sent armored cars and RAF planes to attack civilians on June 27. According to the British, Banī

Kaʿab gunmen had attempted to stop traffic between Buraymī and Britain's Gulf protectorate of Sharjah four days earlier, and a Banī Kaʿab faction loyal to the Sultan of Muscat had requested British protection. Reports indicated that three Banī Kaʿab loyal to ʿAbd al-ʿAzīz had been killed and four wounded.[30] The Near Eastern Affairs Bureau argued on June 30 that because the Saudis had already expressed their opposition to mutual withdrawal, London's continued insistence on that point was futile. In light of the urgent need to conclude an arbitration agreement and Britain's superior military position at Buraymī, "the British can well afford to go out of their way to reach a satisfactory solution." The Saudi proposal for equality of forces had "considerable merit," and the paper recommended lifting the blockade, ending RAF overflights, and curtailing subversive activities by both sides among the Buraymī population. A neutral observer could be appointed through mutual agreement to monitor both parties.[31]

Churchill's concessions had not extracted an arbitration agreement from the Saudis, and the British now feared that their appeals for compromise would be interpreted as a sign of weakness. "If Turki does not go voluntarily," the Foreign Office cabled its ambassador to the U.S., Roger Makins, "we do not see how we can reasonably be expected to refrain much longer from pushing him out." British officials, encouraged by the Saudi ambassador in London, hoped that ʿAbd al-ʿAzīz would agree to mutual withdrawal if Eisenhower proposed it. But Dulles told Acting Foreign Secretary Lord Salisbury, in Washington for talks with the Americans and French, that the U.S. was "under great pressure from the King, who often referred to the Truman letter, to help him." Byroade added that a retreat would "cause a serious loss of face to Turki" and that ʿAbd al-ʿAzīz would never consent to mutual withdrawal.[32]

The Americans were willing to recommend only the terms specified by the Near Eastern Affairs Bureau on June 30, and Eisenhower sent another message to the king suggesting a new standstill agreement with neutral supervision. Impressed with Dulles's firmness, Salisbury cabled the Foreign Office that "we should not persuade the Americans to make any better proposal than the present one in the President's reply to Ibn Saud," but the cabinet rejected the American terms on July 16.[33] Belatedly, Salisbury concurred with the cabinet decision, explaining that the U.S. desired solely to "placate" ʿAbd al-ʿAzīz, and American officials seemed "ready to deprecate our actions as symptomatic of what they regarded as a reactionary attitude towards the problems of the Middle East as a whole." Critics within the Conservative party also forced the Churchill government into an obdurate stance. Evelyn Shuckburgh wrote that an Anglo-Egyptian agreement over the canal zone would "gravely upset the Tory backbenchers." He recommended to Salisbury that following any deal with Egypt, "we should at once occupy Buraimi to show that we can be tough as well." The acting foreign secretary therefore wrote Dulles on July 27 rejecting a stay-in-place arrangement as incompatible with Britain's obligations to its clients, while reminding Dulles that British prestige in the Gulf was a major Western asset in peacetime as well as in the event of war.[34]

As the players in the Buraymī crisis seemed to repeat the same lines, the protracted drama on the eastern side of the Gulf reached its climax with the American-backed overthrow of the Musaddiq government on August 18. Scholarship on the Iran coup has emphasized anti-communism as the primary motive on the part of the Americans, who feared that Musaddiq's growing ties with Iran's communist Tudeh party would leave the premier beholden to the Soviet Union. But Musaddiq's ouster, first planned by the British as "Operation Boot," was also a calculated defense of Western oil assets against nationalist expropriation. Following the coup, Eisenhower charged Herbert Hoover Jr. with negotiating a new Iranian oil consortium of both British and American firms to reintegrate Iran into the postwar petroleum order. Foreign Office advisors convinced Eden of the necessity of U.S. involvement in resurrecting the Iranian oil industry, an approach consistent with the British desire for greater Anglo-American coordination in petroleum policy.[35]

Recent literature has undermined the notion that American companies leapt eagerly at an opportunity to break the British monopoly in Iran. Reluctant American majors were wary of overproduction and feared antitrust prosecution, but the administration secured their cooperation on the grounds that the stability of the industry depended on it and by offering them broad antitrust immunity. Nevertheless, the Eisenhower administration's handling of the Iran episode fed Anglo-American misunderstanding because the British interpreted U.S. actions regarding Iran as evidence of greater willingness by Washington to coordinate foreign oil policies generally. American policy makers, however, remained mindful that the appearance of collaboration with British imperialism created dangers in the Middle East. They invoked U.S. antitrust laws to justify holding the British at arm's length, which frustrated British officials, particularly after the Iran case demonstrated the administration's willingness to dispense with antitrust concerns when national security required it.[36]

British desire for a common Anglo-American front increased during the fall of 1953 because Aramco and Saudi Arabia were renegotiating the terms of the fifty-fifty deal. The Saudi government demanded a higher, fixed price per barrel at which its share of Aramco's profits would be computed, and it wanted retroactive payments to make up the difference in the kingdom's income since 1951. Simultaneous negotiations were underway regarding a formula for compensating the Tapline transit countries.[37] Scarred by their Iranian ordeal, the British were alarmed when Aramco concessions to the Saudis prompted additional demands by Baghdad on the Iraq Petroleum Company. Saudi and Iraqi officials coordinated their oil policies, and in July Arab oil experts exchanged information at a Cairo meeting. Following the Cairo oil summit, the Foreign Office cabled the British embassy in Washington that the "dangers of this are obvious and are particularly acute in view of the recent 'ganging up' between the Saudis and the Iraqis and the new demands now being made on I.P.C." The Foreign Office found it "most undesirable that one American company should jeopardize our joint oil interests not only in this but in other areas."[38]

Bedell Smith accepted a British request on August 17 for informal discussions on oil policy, but stressed the American preference that the petroleum companies "accept the realities of the situation and make the best bargains they could to retain their foothold in the Near East."[39] Smith's comments again reflected the faith U.S. policy makers placed in corporate, rather than official, statesmanship to secure Mideast oil. Near Eastern Affairs oil economist Richard Funkhouser spelled out the American approach in a long memo drafted in July and revised during Anglo-American oil talks in September. Western interests, he contended, "cannot be protected by guns or governments but only by enlightened thought, understanding and compromise." Flexibility and competition were essential to adapting to nationalist politics, and, Funkhouser believed, "the *industry* not government must lead in this." He derided what he termed the "hold the line," "big stick," "British" school of oil diplomacy. In contrast to the Anglo-Iranian Oil Company, Aramco's independence of government interference accounted for "its present highly successful operations." Companies lacking similar vision and flexibility, he warned, may go the way of the "unversatile dinosaur family that sank in the mud when the weather changed." Official skepticism regarding governmental coordination of policy was shared by the oil companies themselves. Aramco vice president Duce told Byroade and Parker Hart at the end of August that if the British and Americans concerted their oil policies, the Western powers would be the ones charged with "ganging up" by the Saudis and other producers.[40]

Anglo-American petroleum talks opened in Washington on August 27 with the British side agitated over the Aramco negotiations, yet hopeful of greater Anglo-American cooperation in the wake of the Iran coup. At the opening session, Harold Beeley of the British embassy explained the strategic importance of Mideast petroleum to Western Europe and the dependence of the U.K. on sterling oil. Beeley also mentioned rising nationalist pressures on Western oil interests and remarked that nationalism "enjoyed a measure of success due primarily to a lack of coordination between the American and British Governments and companies." During the third session, Beeley suggested that the two governments arrange consultations between British and American companies over the Aramco pricing and Tapline issues. While State Department representatives agreed to pass the proposal along to the American majors, Hart and other officials who had previously met with Duce knew that Aramco opposed Anglo-American "ganging up." At the next session in late September, they invoked U.S. antitrust laws to explain the unwillingness of American companies to consult with their British counterparts. Although American oilmen such as Duce and Charles Darlington of Socony-Vacuum had expressed concerns to the State Department about prosecution, antitrust also offered a convenient pretext for avoiding the sort of Anglo-American collaboration the administration opposed for political reasons.[41]

While the two allies had decidedly different ideas about how to handle nationalist demands by producing countries, they diverged most noticeably when it came to supervising the producers' use of oil revenues for development and state-building projects. The development board in Kuwait, which British officials had helped to establish and staff by 1952, reflected London's concerns about the politically explosive potential of large oil revenues concentrated in the hands of the ruling family. Charged with overseeing expenditures of oil revenues for public welfare projects and with planning the future development of Kuwait City, the board's work became bogged down in family disputes between the Kuwaiti ruler, ʿAbdullah Salīm al-Ṣabāḥ, and his brother Fahd. Despite British frustrations, the board's work had certain political implications beyond the investments it supervised in hospitals, education, and construction. It forced ʿAbdullah to come to terms with Fahd, whom he appointed head of the board, after a clash between the ruler's British advisors and Fahd brought ʿAbdullah to the point of abdication. Battles over the development board compelled ʿAbdullah to devise a strategy for assuaging opposition within his own house.[42]

By contrast, U.S. officials played a considerably more modest role in the Saudi kingdom and only offered technical advice regarding military development and currency stabilization. In late 1949, a U.S. military mission under Brigadier General Richard J. O'Keefe had issued recommendations for the development of the Saudi armed forces. Though never fully implemented, O'Keefe's recommendations formed the basis for subsequent Saudi requests for U.S. military aid. In the civilian sector, the U.S. had established a Point Four mission in the kingdom shortly after the 1951 renewal of the Dhahran lease agreement. A Point Four advisor, Arthur Young, helped to establish a Saudi Arabian Monetary Agency (SAMA) dedicated to stabilizing the Saudi riyal, and SAMA issued a pilgrims' receipt scrip, which served as the kingdom's first paper currency. Unlike Britain, the U.S. did not become directly involved in quarrels within the ruling family over reforms and the expenditure of oil revenues.[43]

In talks with the British, American officials held up Aramco as the exemplar of Western adaptation to nationalism in the producing states. Aramco had pioneered the fifty-fifty principle in the Middle East, and the company took pride in its relations with the Saudi government as well as with its Arab labor force. So dependent was ʿAbd al-ʿAzīz's government on oil revenue that Aramco is often described as a state within a state, providing many of the services ordinarily associated with governments, such as building schools, transportation infrastructure, and hospitals. Its government services division helped staff the royal household, and it maintained an agricultural research program at al-Kharj. Bechtel International, the company's construction contractor, had built not only Tapline, but also the Aramco-financed Dammam-to-Riyadh railroad and the Dammam and Jidda harbors, among other projects. Although Aramco's willingness to advance the Saudi government funds against future oil revenues helped secure Aramco's petroleum concession, it also subsidized profligate spending on luxuries by the royal family and postponed budgetary and political reform. "While this practice may have the merit of keeping Company-Government friction to a minimum," observed one U.S. official, "it renders impossible the institution of modern budgetary procedures so desperately needed by this country."[44]

It was in labor relations that Aramco attempted most earnestly to embody the principle of "enlightened self-interest." Michael Sheldon Cheney, a clerk for Bechtel before working in public and government relations for Aramco, contrasted the American approach in the Middle East with both European empires and Soviet expansionism. He explained that Aramco oilmen were motivated by "Salvation Army" values, and, indeed, the array of benefits provided by Aramco to its employees exceeded the nineteenth-century company town and came closer to the modern welfare state. Saudi employees lived in company-owned, dormitory-style dwellings, were transported to work and to their home villages on the weekends in company busses, and could take advantage of a company loan plan to finance construction of their own homes. Aramco offered vocational and literacy training to its employees and sent a handful to the American University of Beirut or to the United States for a college education. Saudi employees dined in company commissaries, and their dependents could receive treatment in company-run hospitals. As a confidential Aramco report from the mid-1950s explained, such measures corresponded to the welfare capitalism practiced by American corporations at home:

> Many corporations in the United States, on the basis of enlightened self-interest, give corporate assistance to public services and encourage employee participation in public affairs. Aramco, on a similar basis supports or participates in projects and public services conducive to the progress of Saudi Arabia and its people in their efforts to build a stable self-reliant society for the benefit of all segments of the population in the area of operations. By so doing Aramco may develop such attitudes in Saudi society that the resources and industrial experience of Aramco and the enterprise of the Saudis can complement one another to their mutual advantage.

Such paternalism exemplified the approach State Department officials commended to the British. Aramco represented the humane face of American capitalism, distinct from European imperialism and Soviet communism, which the United States desired to exhibit in the Middle East.[45]

In spite of Aramco's "enlightened self-interest" in industrial relations, during October the company suffered serious labor unrest and a strike, which assumed political overtones beyond the immediate demands of workers. For all of Aramco's well-publicized welfare capitalism, worker discontent was evident throughout much of 1953, and Cheney criticized Aramco management for not anticipating trouble. Although a token number of Saudis had received vocational and advanced training, more than two-thirds of Saudi workers remained in the lowest unskilled positions. Most lived in crude dormitories, a marked contrast to the luxurious suburban-style homes of the Aramco senior staff in Dhahran. Cheney's first glimpse of the senior staff community evokes an idyll of 1950s American suburbia transplanted to the Arabian peninsula:

> We were literally entering another world. Ahead, a broad, paved avenue curved away past neat blocks of houses set in lush gardens. Homes built of stone, mellow orange brick and white plaster, with broad windows and long verandas, rested in the shade of palm, acacia and feathery tamarisk. Smooth lawns lay between jasmine hedges and clumps of oleander heavy with bright pink blossoms. Arcs of spray from whirling sprinklers flashed in the sunlight.

Reinforcing these disparities in the status of Aramco's Saudi and American employees, management enforced racial segregation of public facilities in the company's compounds. Said K. Aburīsh, a harsh critic of the Saudi royal family and Aramco's role in the kingdom, writes that American oilmen were "rednecks" from Oklahoma and Texas who "treated the Saudis the way they treated the blacks in America." Company policies, Helen Lackner observes, made Saudi employees feel "like third class citizens in their own country."[46]

While these issues provided the proximate cause for worker unrest, the events of October 1953 can be understood only in the context of Arab nationalism. A large proportion of the Aramco labor force belonged to Saudi Arabia's persecuted Shīʿa minority, who, according to Mordechai Abir, "were attracted by radical anti-western Arab nationalism which held out the promise of social and political equality." At the same time, a handful of Saudis educated abroad by Aramco returned to the Eastern Province unwilling to tolerate the company's discriminatory policies, and they formed the natural leadership of the workers' movement. Finally, non-Saudi Arabs directly influenced by the nationalism of the Arab heartland, including more than a thousand Palestinians, also made up part of the Aramco labor force. These factors set the stage for the 1953 strike, in which worker grievances merged with Arab nationalism.[47]

Labor unrest began in May, when worker representatives from Dhahran, Ras Tanura, and the oil fields at Abqaiq presented the company with a petition demanding better "working conditions and privileges."[48] The document also protested the company policy of granting living allowances only to non-Saudi employees. Aramco management met with seven worker spokesmen on June 30, but balked when they demanded the right to bargain on behalf not only of the 155 intermediate-level employees who had signed the petition, but also in the name of Aramco's entire Saudi labor force. After the company rejected the principle of collective bargaining, Saudi labor leaders organized support among Aramco workers and published criticism of the company in the Bahrain newspapers. One leader protested in a letter to Aramco management that, among other grievances, he had been barred by company policy from entering a segregated theater to view the Charlie Chaplin film *Limelight*.

Literature critical of the company, the Saudi government, and the U.S., as well as rumors of a strike, circulated among the Aramco work force. Early in September, 6,000 to 7,000 Saudi employees of Aramco signed a new petition addressed to Crown Prince Saʿūd, urging him to recognize their leaders as representatives of all Saudi workers. Though labor unions were strictly forbidden in the kingdom, the crown prince agreed to appoint a royal commission to investigate Aramco's industrial relations. But when the commission arrived in Dhahran at the beginning of October, it quickly rejected the leaders' calls for collective bargaining. Accused by worker spokesmen of being "sons of Aramco," government officials ordered the arrest of labor leaders on October 14 and 15.

The arrests triggered demonstrations and violence on the part of Aramco workers. On Friday, the Muslim holy day and a non-workday, more than 500 employees gathered at Dhahran to listen to speeches. When a U.S. Air Force bus carrying American military personnel from the Dhahran base passed along a nearby road, demonstrators pelted it with rocks, smashing the windows. The crowd also attacked a vehicle belonging to Trans-World Airlines, and there were reports of local officials being roughed up by demonstrators. Ninety percent of Aramco's Saudi employees failed to report to work on Monday, October 19, and 85 percent of the Saudis who worked at the Dhahran airfield were absent. In response to worker unrest, the Saudi government moved about 2,000 troops into the Eastern Province and, according to the U.S. consul, arrested 1,000 people by the evening of October 20. A government statement threatened that any employee not back at work by October 21 would be fired. Though Aramco management had criticized the Saudi government for a slow response when trouble began, the company objected when Saudi troops entered the three Aramco camps at Dhahran, Abqaiq, and Ras Tanura and began "screening" employees to identify agitators. The U.S. consul euphemistically reported that labor leaders were "closely interrogated" before being sent into internal exile, and shortly thereafter, five non-Saudi workers, including three Palestinians, were deported. Saudi suppression of the unrest broke the strike in little over a week, and more than 60 percent of Aramco's Saudi employees, many of whom had awaited the outcome of the work stoppage in their home villages, had returned to their jobs by November 1.

While the episode troubled U.S. officials, it did not lead them to reexamine their assumption that private interests could successfully assuage Arab nationalism. The American consul in Dhahran, Windsor Hackler, concluded that the unrest was stirred up by outside agitators who "may have been Communist." Most Saudi workers were not sympathetic to communism, Hackler explained, but literature found in the leaders' possession and their use of terms such as "capitalist" and "American imperialist" suggested that the strike was communist-inspired. Director of Central Intelligence Allen W. Dulles told the National Security Council on October 29 that the unrest was "really a strike against the government" of Saudi Arabia, though he conceded that it "might prove serious for the company and for U.S. interests in the area." Comparing events in the Eastern Province with the Anglo-Iranian crisis, a British official cabled the Foreign Office that "the spectre of Abadan has been haunting top Aramco executives" and speculated that the strike would impair Aramco-Saudi relations. But any such comparison was lost on American policy makers, who emerged from the Saudi strike of 1953 with their faith in enlightened corporate statesmanship intact.[49]

As order was being restored in the Eastern Province, the British and Saudis achieved a breakthrough in the Buraymī dispute. Ḥāfiẓ Wahba, the Saudi ambassador to Britain who had worked for Anglo-Saudi compromise during the summer, traveled to Jidda in September for consultations. When Ḥāfiẓ returned to London, he announced that the Saudis were willing to withdraw Turkī if the British conceded to form a joint police force for the oasis. The British and Saudis would each appoint a dozen persons to keep order at Buraymī while the dispute went to international arbitration.[50]

Eden, who had meanwhile returned to the Foreign Office on October 5, placed less of a premium on humoring the Americans than the aging Churchill did, and the foreign secretary expressed annoyance that Turkī had not been evicted. During Eden's convalescence, however, a debate had unfolded at the Foreign Office pitting Ambassador Pelham, who advocated compromise with the Saudis, against Bernard Burrows, London's resident at Bahrain and a staunch defender of British prestige in the Gulf. Pelham explained that Arab nationalism was bound to affect the Gulf states in the near future. "The better Arab/British relations as a whole then are," he wrote, "the greater our chance of maintaining our dominant position in the Gulf despite this growing Arab solidarity." The ambassador's call for accommodating the Saudis won the day in part, as Evelyn Shuckburgh noted in his diary, because the British needed American support in Iran and Egypt. On October 14, Eden put aside his own preference for strong action and recommended that Churchill accept Ḥāfiẓ's offer. At the end of October, Pelham traveled to Jidda to negotiate specific terms, and Eisenhower sent the Saudi king a message on October 27 expressing his gratification at the progress made toward resolving the Buraymī dispute. But news from the royal palace at Ṭā'if in the Hijaz brought negotiations to a halt on November 9: ʿAbd al-ʿAzīz was dead.[51]

Contrary to the fears of some in the U.S. and Britain, the kingdom did not unravel with the death of its founder. Saʿūd succeeded to the throne unchallenged, the clear heir to his father, who in October had designated him head of the recently formed Council of Ministers. But as ʿAbd al-

ʿAzīz, following Wahhābī custom, was buried in an unmarked grave near Riyadh, serious questions of foreign and domestic policy confronted the new king. It was becoming increasingly difficult for Saudi Arabia to straddle the widening fissure between the West and its Arab allies Syria and Egypt. While Buraymī and British ties to the Hashemites had undermined the historic Anglo-Saudi relationship, the United States had proven to be an unreliable ally in the eastern Arabian controversy and was now contemplating aid to Iraq. At home, Saʿūd faced the daunting challenge of balancing the leading families of the kingdom, the ʿulamāʾ, and members of his own house, a feat his father had accomplished through the sheer strength of his personality. Even if Saʿūd were equal to this task, it was unclear whether his father's personal style of leadership could address the challenge Arab nationalism posed to the stability of the kingdom.[52]

The Saudi king's death had not taken the Americans by surprise. As early as March 1952, the Truman administration had composed a letter to be given to ʿAbd al-ʿAzīz's successor as soon as the elderly king succumbed. Eisenhower, who replaced Truman's name on the letter with his own soon after his inauguration, now sent his representative to Riyadh to pledge U.S. support for Saʿūd. The president wrote the new king that the Saudi people "are indeed fortunate to have their destiny served by a ruler so progressive and devoted to their welfare as yourself." Allen Dulles, less effusive than Eisenhower but more accurate, told the National Security Council that the "situation in Saudi Arabia was quiet at the moment," though Saʿūd "was not yet in complete control of the country."[53]

The scripted American response to ʿAbd al-ʿAzīz's death reveals the importance of Saudi Arabia to U.S. foreign policy. Washington was committed to supporting Aramco and the Saudi royal family as pillars of the postwar petroleum order. As symbolized by the letter to Saʿūd, Eisenhower continued his predecessor's policies, investing private corporations with responsibility for developing Middle Eastern oil. At the same time, the U.S. remained bound in equal measure to a partnership with Britain to sustain economic reconstruction and security in postwar Europe. But Eisenhower's reliance on private diplomacy in the Gulf exasperated policy makers in London, who grew frustrated by Washington's unwillingness to coordinate oil diplomacy through official agreements and to force the Saudis into abandoning their claim in eastern Arabia.

American collaboration with Britain and continued U.S. support for Israel undermined Eisenhower's efforts to improve relations with the Arab world. In October, the administration antagonized the Arab states by offering Israel a $26 million aid package after Israeli leaders agreed to shelve their controversial hydroelectric project at B'not Yaakov.[54] The Aramco strike showed that private diplomacy alone could not guarantee the security of Saudi oil resources from Arab nationalist agitation within Saudi Arabia. As King Saʿūd's diplomacy would also demonstrate, Aramco policies and the administration's token gestures of military aid could not prevent Saudi Arabia from challenging the terms of the postwar petroleum order.

3

Reaching a Crossroads: The U.S. and King Saʿūd, December 1953–November 1955

King ʿAbd al-ʿAzīz's passing marked a transition in U.S.-Saudi relations. His successor, Saʿūd, not only lacked his father's prestige and abilities, but also operated in regional and domestic circumstances transformed by Arab nationalism. During 1954, Gamāl ʿAbd al-Nāṣir prevailed in his power struggle with Muḥammad Negīb in Egypt, Saudi Arabia's principal Arab ally. After securing British withdrawal from the Suez base, Nāṣir sought to lead the Arab campaign against Israel and block Western efforts to build a new regional defense system. As Cairo's influence over Saudi foreign policy grew stronger, internal opposition also threatened the stability of the kingdom. In both his diplomacy and domestic policies, the new king struggled to reconcile the contradiction he had inherited from his father between Arab nationalism and the Saudi role in the postwar petroleum order.

Three issues seriously strained U.S.-Saudi relations early in Saʿūd's reign. First, Saʿūd's government signed an agreement with Greek shipping magnate Aristotle Onassis to organize a Saudi-owned oil tanker company. The Onassis deal, opposed by both Aramco and the Eisenhower administration, represented a bold Saudi attempt to revise the relationships that constituted the postwar petroleum order. Second, U.S. aid to Hashemite Iraq and the American northern-tier defense policy angered the Saudis, who joined the Egyptian camp after the formation of the Baghdad Pact divided the Arab world. Finally, the Saudis renewed their charges of American betrayal over Buraymī when the long U.S. campaign to settle the dispute through arbitration collapsed, and the British presented the Saudis with a military *fait accompli.*

The Buraymī arbitration treaty finally concluded between the British and Saudis in July 1954 coincided with the Anglo-Egyptian base agreement and development of an oil consortium in Iran. These measures represented the culmination of Winston Churchill's foreign policy in the Middle East, but Anthony Eden, who became prime minister in April 1955, soon faced a heightened Arab nationalist challenge to British interests. His decision to resort to force in eastern Arabia reflected not only his concern for sterling oil and a willingness to act independently of Washington, but also the degree to which the British identified their interests in the Middle East with the security of their Gulf clients. American officials regarded the timing of Eden's action as poor and, more significantly, continued to prefer private investment as the basis of the Western presence in the region over what they regarded as outmoded colonial relationships. Yet, to the Saudis' dismay, Washington responded in a restrained manner to Eden's reoccupation of Buraymī out of concern for the allies' partnership in the Cold War and the continued economic viability of Western Europe.

By the time of Saʿūd's accession, Arab nationalism had begun to exert powerful strains on every part of the postwar petroleum order. U.S.-Saudi and Saudi-Aramco relations grew contentious because Saʿūd's government sought greater control over the country's Western-dominated oil industry. Arab nationalism also complicated Anglo-American cooperation, as leaders in each country redoubled their commitment to the policy they believed would protect Western oil interests. While Washington backed Aramco's position in the kingdom, London intervened militarily on behalf of its historic clients in the Gulf. For King Saʿūd's part, Arab nationalism forced him to follow a foreign policy similar to Nāṣir's. The Saudi king felt besieged by the forces of nationalism emanating not only from outside his country but also from an increasingly vocal opposition within it. As the U.S., Britain, and Saudi Arabia each defended its interest in the postwar petroleum order, their different responses to Arab nationalism threatened to unravel the system of relationships they had so carefully cultivated.

ʿAbd al-ʿAzīz had left behind an ambiguous legacy in terms of Saudi Arabia's foreign and domestic policy, and his sons Saʿūd and Fayṣal disagreed bitterly over the kingdom's future. By the time of his death, ʿAbd al-ʿAzīz had created the façade of a modern government by organizing the Council of Ministers, yet his selection of the conservative Saʿūd as the next king suggests that the founder of Saudi Arabia did not desire the rapid development of his kingdom into a modern state with a ministerial government. Indeed, by making a grand tour of the kingdom upon his succession, King Saʿūd immediately indicated his desire to rule in the patriarchal style of his father. Saʿūd met with leading tribal families and dispensed largesse to bedouin in exchange for their loyalty, while his personal funds remained indistinguishable from government revenues. As crown prince, Saʿūd had built himself a gaudy palace at Naṣriyya outside Riyadh, but after becoming king, he ordered its demolition and the construction on the site of a vastly larger edifice of pink stone with triumphal arches, swimming pools, and broad thoroughfares for the royal Cadillacs. This Shangri-La symbolized Saʿūd's intention to perpetuate a type of government in which the king held unfettered authority.[1]

As the new crown prince, Fayṣal hoped to reform the Saudi government by subordinating the king's power to the wishes of the royal family. Opposed to the genuine democratization of Saudi Arabia, Fayṣal instead sought greater power sharing within the ruling elite and the establishment of an efficient administration. Soon after Saʿūd became king, Fayṣal successfully maneuvered to become prime minister, and he blocked Saʿūd's attempt to combine the power of that office with his regal authority. Fayṣal refused to relinquish his role as viceroy in the Hijaz unless he was appointed prime minister, a threat that raised the possibility of the kingdom's disintegration. Pressured by the royal family, Saʿūd acquiesced and agreed to share power with his half-brother, but this uneasy compromise did not resolve the fraternal struggle, which would help shape both the domestic and foreign policies of Saudi Arabia during the 1950s. In an attempt to create a base of power apart from the royal family, Saʿūd brought outsiders into the government, including the Yemeni entrepreneur Shaykh Muḥammad Bin Lādin. The king's tactic did not necessarily succeed, however, because Saʿūd lacked the political skills of his father and could not always control his commoner appointees.[2]

As the Onassis affair demonstrated, Saʿūd's weakness held consequences for U.S.-Saudi relations. The Saudi collaboration with Onassis originated with Muḥammad ʿAlī Riḍā, whom Saʿūd appointed commerce minister in March 1954. A son of the Jidda governor, ʿAlī Riḍā was thought to be sympathetic to Fayṣal, whose power base remained in the Hijaz, and Saʿūd may have appointed him as part of the power sharing compromise forced upon the king. The commerce minister first met Onassis in August 1953 while vacationing in Cannes, France, in an encounter arranged by Spyrion Catapodis, an Onassis colleague. Catapodis later sought to wreck the agreement after a falling out with Onassis, who denied that he had ever promised Catapodis a share of its proceeds in exchange for introducing him to ʿAlī Riḍā.[3]

An Izmir-born Greek, Aristotle Onassis had fled Anatolia amid the violence surrounding the Ottoman collapse and the birth of modern Turkey. Settling briefly with his family in Athens, Onassis immigrated in 1923 to

Argentina, where he prospered importing tobacco, but he accumulated his fortune by anticipating the central role petroleum would play in the world economy. In the late 1930s, he invested heavily in huge oil tankers. During the war, the U.S. Maritime Commission paid a handsome price for vessels leased from Onassis, who reaped even larger profits when peace returned and major oil companies, including Mobil and Texaco, concluded long-term tanker contracts with him. Boasting a fleet worth a reported $300 million in 1953, Onassis had grown fabulously wealthy servicing the postwar petroleum order.[4]

Not satisfied with his profitable relationships with the oil companies, Onassis proposed the creation of a Saudi Arabian Maritime Tanker Company. He offered to provide the Saudi government with a national tanker fleet in exchange for a guaranteed share in the transportation of Saudi oil. ʿAbdullah Sulaymān, the experienced Saudi finance minister, negotiated a draft agreement with Onassis's hired consultant and Hitler's former advisor Dr. Hjalmar Schacht. By December 1953, the agreement was complete, and Onassis traveled to Jidda to meet with Saʿūd. ʿAlī Riḍā's demands for bribes totaling hundreds of thousands of pounds and a cut of the profits delayed implementation of the deal, at least according to Catapodis, and it was not until January 1954 that Onassis and Saʿūd finally signed a contract sealing the agreement.[5]

Aramco immediately opposed the scheme as prejudicial to its rights under the company's oil concession. Particularly troubling was Article 4 of the Saudi-Onassis contract, which required that Saudi crude be transported either in tankers in use before 1954 or in ships of the Saudi Arabian Maritime Tanker Company. This clause meant that as the oil companies retired aging vessels, Onassis tankers would replace them until the Greek mogul acquired a monopoly on the transportation of Saudi petroleum. The Aramco executive committee protested to the Saudi government, arguing that an Onassis monopoly would result in a "serious loss of markets" for Saudi oil, while Aramco's parent companies appealed for help to Secretary Dulles and Undersecretary for Near Eastern Affairs Henry Byroade.[6]

Just prior to ʿAbd al-ʿAzīz's death, the experienced Middle East diplomat George Wadsworth had replaced Raymond Hare as U.S. ambassador in Jidda. Like many of the State Department's Arab experts, Wadsworth had attended the American University of Beirut. He had been a leading critic within the department of Truman's support for a Jewish state in Palestine, but his appeal to Truman in 1945 on behalf of the administration's ambassadors to the Arab states had been ignored. Now sixty years old, he had served as ambassador to Iraq, Turkey, and Czechoslovakia before taking up the difficult assignment of managing U.S.-Saudi relations following Saʿūd's succession. The Onassis affair was the first in a series of crises that would test his skills.[7]

The Eisenhower administration also looked unfavorably on the tanker deal as an infringement on Aramco's concession and as a threat to the cheap petroleum that fueled European reconstruction and Western defense. On February 3, Wadsworth raised concerns about Onassis with King Saʿūd. Undersecretary Walter Bedell Smith told Wadsworth that the department planned to support Aramco, but that the U.S. would intervene with the Saudis only if the company's appeals failed. Defense Secretary Charles Wilson subsequently alerted Dulles that the Saudi-Onassis agreement threatened an existing oil contract between the U.S. Navy and Saudi Arabia. In response, Navy Secretary Robert Anderson and the Joint Chiefs demanded explicit assurances that no "foreign shipping enterprise" would obstruct U.S. military access to Saudi oil.[8]

The list of opponents to the agreement continued to grow. A lawyer representing Onassis's brother-in-law and bitter rival in the shipping business, Stavros Niarchos, met with Deputy Assistant Secretary of State John Jernegan on March 16. Niarchos stood to lose business if Onassis garnered a monopoly on transporting Aramco oil, and to prevent fulfillment of the deal, Niarchos's representative suggested that the State Department prevail on Onassis's creditors, National City Bank and Metropolitan Life, to withhold the necessary capital. Jernegan rejected this proposal, however, explaining that although the U.S. was concerned about the agreement, the State Department wanted Aramco to take the lead in opposing it.[9]

Department officials remained optimistic that the dispute could be resolved through negotiations among the Saudi government, Aramco, and Onassis. Saʿūd told Wadsworth on April 30 that the Onassis deal did not affect the Saudi contract with the U.S. Navy and did not impair Aramco's concession. While he intended to exercise his country's "sovereign rights," the king remained flexible. Byroade and Parker Hart, director of the Near Eastern Affairs Bureau, discussed a possible compromise with Onassis himself, who insisted that he was forced to cooperate with the Saudis, lest their plans for an independent tanker company deprive him of revenue in an already depressed shipping market. He disputed the ironclad interpretation of Article 4 as prohibiting the replacement of obsolete ships and offered to renegotiate the agreement to appease the oil companies. Onassis reportedly "gave the impression of . . . a man who is in a tight spot" and "wishes to make an accommodation to save himself further ill-will." The next day, Byroade urged Aramco vice president Duce to "consider coming to some arrangement" with Onassis.[10]

The State Department's handling of the Onassis affair reflected not only its consistent preference for private oil diplomacy but also its distaste for an official Anglo-American common front that might compromise U.S. relations with Arab oil-producing and oil-transit states. In a discussion with representatives of the British embassy on May 12, Hart insisted that the two countries could not collaborate on a response because the full text of the Saudi-Onassis agreement was not available. Nevertheless, London pushed for a joint policy against Onassis's venture. Officials in the U.K. worried that the deal might prove injurious to British shipping, which was a source of considerable "invisible" income, and, more importantly, the Saudi tanker company threatened Britain's interests in Kuwait, a major supplier of its oil. Riyadh had announced plans to require the use of Onassis vessels by J. Paul Getty's Pacific Western Oil Company, which held the Saudi concession to petroleum produced in the neutral zone that Kuwait shared with Saudi Arabia. By controlling the transportation of Pacific Western's oil, the Foreign Office feared, Onassis could expand his tanker operations into Kuwait. Officials also observed that state tanker companies provided an additional basis for the sort of collaboration among producing states that threatened British interests.[11]

Reluctance by the Americans to coordinate a response raised suspicions in London. One British official surmised that this "underhand affair" gave Onassis the exclusive right to transport only the Saudi oil not shipped in Aramco tankers, which would harm U.K. shipping interests and leave the Americans unscathed. When British petroleum attaché John Brook handed Byroade a copy of the Saudi-Onassis agreement obtained from Kuwait on May 24, Byroade remarked that the U.S. had been in possession of the contract "for some time." Brook expressed shock at Byroade's statement, which directly contradicted recent American claims that the agreement was not yet available.

Rebuffed by the U.S., Churchill's government considered unilateral action against Onassis, and the relentless Niarchos suggested a new way to obstruct the deal by crippling Onassis financially. In June, lawyers for Onassis's antagonist urged the British government to deny Onassis the right to transfer to the U.S. dollars earned from his tanker contract with Shell. This step would deprive him of the dollar credits he needed to repay the American lending institutions that were financing the Saudi deal. A debate over Niarchos's proposal emerged among the Foreign Office, the Treasury, and the Ministry of Trade and Civil Aviation. While the Foreign Office backed strong action, the Treasury vetoed Niarchos's plan as dangerous to public confidence in sterling and unlikely to achieve the desired goal. In lieu of stronger measures, Eden had to settle for a stern protest to the Saudis, which the foreign secretary himself delivered to the Saudi ambassador in early July.[12]

By this time, momentum was building in the U.S. for more forceful action by the Eisenhower administration, in part because Getty's Pacific Western Oil Company was on the verge of signing a tanker agreement with Onassis. The first tanker procured by Onassis for the Saudis, the 46,000-ton *King Saʿūd I,* had been launched in Hamburg, and Getty had made an oral agreement with Onassis to charter the new vessel. Department officials, concerned this agreement would legitimize the Saudi tanker company, asked Getty to back out of the deal.[13] Executives from Aramco's parents told Deputy Undersecretary Robert Murphy that Aramco would refuse to load any Onassis tanker attempting to take on oil at Ras Tanura, and Benjamin Jennings, president of Standard Oil of New York, explained that Aramco was intent on defending its rights even at the risk of "shutdown" and "nationalization." He asked that the department make "immediate diplomatic representations" in support of Aramco, and the National Security Council, with Eisenhower presiding, responded by resolving to take a more active role in opposing the Onassis deal. The administration's new basic document on Middle East policy, NSC 5428, called for "all appropriate measures to bring about the cancellation of the agreement between the Saudi Arabian Government and Onassis for the transport of Saudi-Arabian produced oil." Guided by this policy, Ambassador Wadsworth submitted an aide-mémoire to the Saudi government on August 3 protesting its joint venture with Onassis.[14]

Despite the blunt language of the new policy paper, State Department officials were reluctant to chastise Riyadh over the Onassis affair because the U.S.-Saudi relationship was already deteriorating on other fronts. NSC 5428 enshrined the Eisenhower administration's northern-tier strategy, under which military aid requests from Iraq received priority over Saudi appeals. Dissatisfied with the $5 million earmarked for Saudi Arabia and eager to enhance his nationalist credentials, Saʿūd refused to sign the advisory agreement required under the Mutual Security Act. Such a commitment, Yāsīn told Wadsworth, would not only "reflect badly on Saudi Arabian standing in all Arab States," but would also weaken the regime at home. If Prince Fayṣal signed an agreement to accept U.S. military advisors, "his blood would be shed in the Nejd."[15]

The anti-American drift in Saudi foreign policy also illustrated a growing Egyptian influence on King Saʿūd. ʿAbd al-Nāṣir traveled to Saudi Arabia in 1954 to perform the ḥajj and found Saʿūd a natural ally against the northern-tier defense scheme. U.S. ambassador to Egypt Jefferson Caffery believed that Nāṣir sought to manipulate Saʿūd by "inflating the

Sa'udi King's view of his own abilities and role as a Near Eastern political leader." Saudi newspapers reprinted critical comments from the Egyptian press concerning Turco-Pakistani negotiations on a mutual defense treaty, talks supported by Washington as the initial step in the northern-tier policy. A March editorial in *Al-Bilād al-Saʿūdiyya* amplified official Egyptian condemnations of Iraqi plans to sign an arms agreement with the United States. After the U.S.-Iraqi exchange of notes sealing the arms deal in April, *Al-Bilād* published an editorial suggesting that Iraqi ties with the West were incompatible with membership in the Arab League. To underscore his displeasure with the U.S., Saʿūd expelled American Point Four personnel and shut down the economic advisory program, which had operated in the kingdom since 1951.[16]

The expulsion of the Point Four advisors punctuated the decline in U.S.-Saudi relations and prompted speculation by National Security Council staffers that the U.S. might have to abandon the Dhahran base. Nadav Safran writes that Saʿūd's decision was in part retaliation for U.S. aid to Iraq, but Prince Fayṣal told a U.S. embassy official on June 3 that the Council of Ministers approved closing the Point Four mission to protest the lack of U.S. support over Buraymī. Saʿūd appeared determined to prosecute the Saudi claim in eastern Arabia first advanced by his father. Indeed, political circumstances made Buraymī even more valuable to Saʿūd than it had been to ʿAbd al-ʿAzīz, as the king sought to shore up relations with Egypt and to portray himself as an Arab nationalist struggling against British imperialism. This approach was not only calculated to overcome Saudi isolation in the Arab world just as the Western powers courted Hashemite Iraq, but Saʿūd and his advisors might also have hoped to pressure the U.S. into modifying its Middle Eastern policies on aid, Israel, and Buraymī itself. In U.S.-Saudi relations, Fayṣal remarked, "there has been one tragedy, Palestine," and "we do not want Buraimi to be another."[17]

New problems hobbled Anglo-Saudi progress toward a Buraymī arbitration agreement, which on the eve of ʿAbd al-ʿAzīz's death had briefly seemed imminent. In early December 1953, Petroleum Concessions Limited struck oil in disputed territory, and this discovery threatened to complicate already difficult negotiations. Attempting to detach the issue of oil concessions from the national boundary question, Eden suggested that American and British companies together build a consortium to produce oil in eastern Arabia as they had in Iran. The foreign secretary told the cabinet on January 7 that it "would be to the general advantage if . . . both British and American companies were interested in the exploitation of oil in each of the oil-producing countries of the Middle East."[18] Not all parties on the

British side, however, accepted Eden's idea. From Bahrain, political resident Bernard Burrows criticized any compromise with Aramco as "inequitable" and "immoral," while Iraq Petroleum Company president Horace Gibson believed that a consortium "would be detrimental to I.P.C. interests all over the Gulf." Concerned about jeopardizing Anglo-American cooperation in Iran, Minister of State Selwyn Lloyd observed "that it is better not to seem to hold a pistol at Aramco's head." Pending consultations with Aramco, the consortium idea was therefore left off the list of Britain's new arbitration terms presented to the Saudis on February 12.[19]

The Foreign Office notified the U.S. embassy of its revised terms on February 15. As it had the previous October, Britain expressed a willingness to evacuate posts in Abu Dhabi–claimed territory, provided that Riyadh agreed to a joint police force for the Buraymī oasis and that the Saudi intruders, led by Turkī, quit Ḥamāsā. An arbitration tribunal would then decide the boundary question. In return for these compromises, the Foreign Office insisted that British oil exploration continue and suggested that if the parties involved agreed, Anglo-Iranian and IPC seek "concessionary rights in any disputed area which might pass to Saudi sovereignty." The State Department endorsed these terms as "going far to meet Saudi demands," but Aramco objected strenuously to continued exploration by the British companies and rejected proposals for a joint Anglo-American consortium.[20] Aramco lawyer George Ray complained that London's new terms reflected an "aggressive" British campaign to usurp Aramco's legitimate rights. Parker Hart noted "that Aramco itself had not been entirely innocent of aggressive tactics," and Byroade told Aramco chairman Fred Davies that the department was "interested primarily in getting this troublesome boundary dispute settled." Nevertheless, the department promised to "do everything it properly can to protect Aramco's interests," and Byroade suggested to Bedell Smith on April 1 that the U.S. request revision of the British terms to address Aramco's concerns.[21]

Meanwhile, Saudi officials, who had long accused Washington of duplicity in the Buraymī dispute, were themselves double-dealing. A surprised Ambassador Pelham reported on April 15 that Saʿūd expressed his willingness to offer a concession to British companies, and Yūsuf Yāsīn requested British help in convincing the Americans to accept the joint-concession scheme. "As Aramco would make difficulty over this," Pelham quoted Yāsīn in the ambassador's report to the Foreign Office, "we would no doubt be prepared to help the Saudis to settle the matter with the Americans." While keeping Aramco in the dark about his British contacts, Yāsīn was even so bold as to request that the company's Arabian Affairs

Division prepare maps for his use prior to departing for Bahrain to meet with British officials. Secret Anglo-Saudi talks proceeded at the very time that Fayṣal was castigating Aramco officials over U.S. failure to uphold Saudi rights, and while Yāsīn accused Aramco of colluding with the British in drafting London's new, "inflexible" arbitration terms. Separately, Wadsworth and British embassy officials in Washington concluded that the Saudis were playing their two countries against one another. Once Aramco's attitude became apparent, the Foreign Office dropped the joint-concession idea, and Pelham reported that in subsequent audiences with Saʿūd, who had himself proposed the British consortium, the king appeared unaware of the negotiations later conducted by his representatives at Bahrain.[22]

With arbitration talks stalled again, this time over the right of the British companies to continue oil exploration, a new crisis loomed. In late May, Saʿūd demanded that Aramco organize its own expedition into disputed territory to prospect for oil. State Department officials urged the company to refuse the request and proposed that both sides suspend exploration during the hot months. But Aramco felt compelled to honor Saʿūd's demand, and Selwyn Lloyd feared that a new incident would "be disastrous for Anglo-American relations." Despite such concerns, the British government was more worried about defending its prestige in the Gulf. London refused to suspend British oil prospecting and pledged to intercept any Aramco expedition into Abu Dhabi–claimed territory. "Unless we repel this incursion," Lloyd wrote the cabinet, "the confidence of the rulers whom we protect will be further shaken."[23]

Although the Aramco expedition during early June produced some tense moments in London and Washington, Tore Tingvold Petersen has exaggerated the potential danger of "British-led soldiers killing American civilians at the height of the cold war." In fact, the excursion was carefully stage managed by British and American officials to minimize the risk of violence. Aldrich told Lloyd that Aramco would only make an appearance in eastern Arabia to placate Saʿūd, do no drilling, and promptly retreat. Four days later, Aramco informed Pelham in Jidda about the precise makeup of its expedition: twelve Americans with six to ten Saudi escorts in a half-dozen vehicles. Churchill, worried about an Anglo-American incident but determined to defend the Gulf clients, approved the instructions for confronting the Aramco expedition. While Eden wanted British forces to shoot out the tires of Aramco vehicles as a last resort, Churchill, fearing injury to Americans, ordered "no firing except in self-defence."[24] Assistant undersecretary at the Foreign Office Evelyn Shuckburgh lobbied for tougher measures, claiming that failure to confront the Saudis again would be "heart-breaking," but Churchill was delighted when direct confrontation proved unnecessary. On June 5, Royal Air Force planes dropped leaflets over the position of the Aramco expedition protesting that it was "committing trespass" against Abu Dhabi. By June 10, the party had withdrawn, and Churchill could portray the episode as "another case of Peace through Strength."[25]

For their part, American officials hoped new British concessions could facilitate an arbitration agreement. In a National Security Council meeting on the eve of the Aramco expedition, John Foster Dulles insisted that British refusals to suspend explorations had produced the present crisis. Herbert Hoover Jr., who had raised Buraymī with the British while negotiating the Iran consortium, explained that the U.K. had staked its prestige in eastern Arabia. Eisenhower again argued that the "British seemed to be behaving in a very high-handed fashion" and instructed Dulles to "press the British pretty hard on this issue."[26]

To the satisfaction of administration officials, Britain and Saudi Arabia made rapid progress toward an agreement following the withdrawal of the Aramco party. In addition to the joint police force, the British government agreed to a neutral zone, or "no-oilman's-land," which would prevent conflict over oil rights without prejudicing the verdict of arbitration. During a trip to Washington, Churchill, accompanied by Eden, continued discussions of Buraymī with Eisenhower and Dulles. Though the prime minister groused that "it was oilism and not colonialism which was evil in the world today," Eden assured the Americans that Buraymī "was under control and moving toward a solution." At long last, the parties signed the arbitration agreement in Jidda on July 30, just three days after the Anglo-Egyptian agreement on the Suez base and as negotiators were completing the details surrounding the Iranian oil consortium. This series of initiatives reflected Churchill's desire for Anglo-American partnership and the fulfillment of his foreign policy design for the Middle East.[27]

Churchill's vision alone did not determine the timing of the arbitration treaty. Rather, the evidence suggests that the Saudis delayed signing until after conclusion of the Anglo-Egyptian agreement. Saʿūd wanted to avoid breaking ranks with Egypt and taking the first risky step of signing a treaty with the leading Western imperial power. If the king hoped that achieving British withdrawal from Buraymī would pay some political dividend, however, he was likely disappointed. As agreed, Turkī departed Ḥamāsā with eighty men on the morning of August 13, but he refused a British escort back into Saudi Arabia and promptly lost his way in the desert. A British detachment rescued him several days later "in a state of collapse from heat exhaustion, with his convoy nearly disintegrated." This ignominious end to Turkī's two-year expedition foreboded new Buraymī troubles for the Saudis. Now, the conflict shifted from eastern Arabia to a legal forum in which the British were convinced they would prevail.[28]

With Buraymī headed safely for arbitration, American officials could concentrate on nullifying the Saudi-Onassis deal, though they had to move cautiously to avoid hastening the deterioration in U.S.-Saudi relations. In early August, Prince Fayṣal rehashed to a State Department official the list of Saudi grievances against the U.S. According to Fayṣal, Buraymī demonstrated that "there is no difference between a useless friend and a harmless enemy." The U.S. had also reneged on promises to offer substantial military and economic aid and was now meddling in Saudi-Aramco relations over the Onassis affair. At the same time, executives from Aramco's parent companies complained that the State Department's objections to the tanker deal were "not strong enough." Beset by these conflicting pressures, the State Department attempted to break the impasse through private channels. After consultations with Undersecretary Walter Bedell Smith and other officials, the Greek-American president of Twentieth-Century Fox, Spyros Skouras, met with Onassis in Paris. As a compromise, Skouras hoped to broker the sale of Onassis tankers intended for the Saudis to the oil companies instead. But Onassis was unwilling to sell his vessels at a loss as the companies demanded, and he was confident that he would prevail if the matter went to the courts. Onassis, noted Bedell Smith, was not "in a chastened mood."[29]

As these efforts stalled, the impetus for more vigorous action shifted to Onassis's Greek enemies, Spyrion Catapodis and Stavros Niarchos. In September, Catapodis, bitter over what he perceived to be Onassis's betrayal, gave a lengthy deposition and documents to the British consul in Nice, France, implicating his former partner in bribing ʿAlī Riḍā and other Saudi officials. Niarchos, who immediately purchased copies of these documents, saw an opportunity to discredit Onassis. He promptly sent the Catapodis dossier to Shell Oil Company executive Frank Hopwood, who deposited copies of the documents with the British Foreign Office and proposed threatening their publication unless the Saudis reversed course on the Onassis deal. But the British government had already decided to cede the initiative in the Onassis affair to Washington. One official wrote that the Saudis might perceive leaking the Catapodis documents as a British "plot." A more important consideration was that American and British companies were completing negotiations surrounding the Iranian oil consortium, and British meddling in Aramco's affairs might jeopardize that cooperation.[30]

On the same day as Hopwood's meeting in London, a private investigator hired by Niarchos delivered the Catapodis file to the State Department and told John Jernegan that "these papers should be gotten into the hands of King Saud," who could use them to blame the Onassis affair on his advisors and as a pretense for abrogating the contract. Niarchos had already passed the documents to the Central Intelligence Agency for delivery to King Saʿūd and had recruited oil geologist Karl Twitchell to carry the documents to Saudi Arabia. Twitchell, who had conducted some of the earliest oil exploration in the Saudi kingdom and had helped broker the original American concession, planned to present the bribery charges to Saʿūd during a September 29 royal audience.[31]

Onassis's biographers and more than one historian of Saudi Arabia have argued that Niarchos's covert campaign prompted Saʿūd to abandon Onassis in favor of a compromise with Aramco. But King Saʿūd fired Finance Minister ʿAbdullah Sulaymān, architect of the Onassis deal, on August 30, weeks prior to the Twitchell mission. Self-interest, rather than Niarchos's cloak-and-dagger activities, lay behind the king's change of heart. Whatever his difficulties with the U.S., Saʿūd carefully avoided burning his bridges with Washington and jeopardizing his lucrative relationship with Aramco. Reaching a draft accord regarding the pricing issue on October 3, Aramco offered the kingdom $70 million in retroactive royalty payments. As a result, the British embassy reported that Aramco found Saʿūd "reasonably disposed to talk sense" concerning the Onassis affair.[32]

At the end of October, King Saʿūd summoned Onassis to Jidda, where the Greek shipping magnate found the Saudi government and Aramco aligned against him. Saʿūd undercut Onassis's position by telling Aramco that Saudi Arabia would "support any understanding they could reach with Onassis," including modification of Article 4. Confronted by Aramco's unwillingness to budge "even an inch of the way," wrote a British official, Onassis left Jidda "a dejected man." Commerce Minister Muḥammad ʿAlī Riḍā, who negotiated the initial Saudi contract with Onassis, now resigned, and the matter finally went to arbitration in January 1955. Wadsworth reported that Saʿūd was relieved to find a face-saving avenue out of his tanker deal and finally to "finish with Onassis."[33]

With the risk of offending the Saudi government diminished, the administration felt able to support Aramco more aggressively. Dulles followed through on the administration's campaign to destroy the Onassis deal by prevailing on Attorney General Brownell to file suit against Onassis in an unrelated case. Onassis had been indicted in October 1953 for concealing the foreign ownership of a company seeking to purchase vessels from the U.S. government, a violation of the 1946 Merchant Ship Sales Act. As the

Saudi tanker issue went to arbitration, the Justice Department kept the pressure on Onassis by rejecting his $5.7 million settlement offer in the Ship Sales case. Some in the Justice Department resented "holding the bag on account of State's intervention," but in this instance, as in the oil cartel case, the Justice Department's priorities took a backseat to a foreign policy based on supporting corporate enterprise.[34]

Arbitration of the Onassis affair represented a positive turn for American diplomacy. As with Buraymī, it offered an expedient for preserving the postwar petroleum order that did not compromise Saʿūd's carefully cultivated image as an Arab nationalist. In subsequent months, however, developments in the Middle East would make it increasingly difficult for the king to maintain both an Arab nationalist profile and his close relationship with the U.S.

In late 1954, the American and British governments organized a new Mideast initiative designed to resolve the Arab-Israeli conflict. As the considerable scholarship on the Alpha plan has shown, policy makers hoped to replace the beleaguered 1949 armistice with an enduring peace by enticing Egypt and Israel into a set of compromises on borders, refugees, and security. Such an approach, its framers believed, would also deprive the Soviet Union of leverage in relations with the Arab states. But Alpha was in significant respects incompatible with the existing northern-tier defense strategy. While seeking ʿAbd al-Nāṣir's cooperation on Alpha, the allies simultaneously alienated the Egyptian leader by supporting northern-tier defense and courting Nāṣir's Arab rival, Iraqi prime minister Nūrī al-Saʿīd.[35]

London and Washington diverged over how to address this dilemma. At a Cairo meeting in February 1955, Eden learned firsthand that Nāṣir could never be reconciled to the new Western defense scheme. In subsequent weeks, the British government reversed its early reservations about northern-tier defense and opted formally to join its client Iraq, the key to defending the vital sterling oil of the Gulf, in what became known as the Baghdad Pact. The Eisenhower administration, which had first sponsored the northern-tier concept, refrained from adhering out of concerns about wrecking Alpha, angering pro-Israeli interests in the U.S., and causing a crisis with the Saudis by embracing their Hashemite enemies. Faced with opposition to the northern-tier strategy, American officials sought to safeguard the postwar petroleum order and to prevent Moscow from deriving any advantage from Arab polarization.[36]

Saudi-Egyptian cooperation accelerated following the conclusion of the Baghdad Pact treaty between Nūrī al-Saʿīd and Turkish President Adnan

Menderes on February 24 and Israel's military strike on the Gaza strip four days later. As Nadav Safran writes, the Saudis regarded the Baghdad Pact as "a resurgence in a most virulent form of the old Hashemite threat," while at the same time, any intensification of Arab-Israeli hostilities sharpened the basic contradiction faced by Saudi diplomacy. The Baghdad Pact made it imperative for the Saudis to join with Nāṣir in opposing long-standing Hashemite ambitions to dominate the Fertile Crescent. Prince Fayṣal proclaimed that Saudi Arabia and Egypt shared "one policy" opposing Nūrī's alliance with Turkey and a common spirit that united the two countries. Meanwhile, Saudi newspapers repeatedly condemned Iraqi deals with "foreigners" and attempted to counter Iraqi broadcasts ridiculing Riyadh's meager contribution to the struggle against Israel. These trends culminated in early March, when Saudi Arabia, Egypt, and Syria signed an agreement pledging support for a federal Arab union.[37] With the establishment of the Baghdad Pact, ʿAbd al-Nāṣir also became a leader in the non-aligned movement, launched at the Bandung conference in late April, and the Saudi government vocally supported neutralism. Prince Fayṣal led a delegation to Bandung amid great official fanfare, and accounts of the conference dominated the Saudi press. One article in *Al-Bilād* asked, "Is Bandung the beginning of the end of imperialism?" The Saudi press provided supportive coverage of Bandung while criticizing the Baghdad Pact as imperialism by other means, based on Britain's alliance with the "henchman of imperialism," Nūrī al-Saʿīd.[38]

The direction of Saudi foreign policy disturbed State Department officials such as Herbert Hoover Jr., who observed that U.S.-Saudi relations were "reaching a cross-roads." Yet Hoover dismissed the possibility that the administration could change its policies on Israel and the northern tier. King Saʿūd, Hoover predicted, was likely to demand unprecedented levels of aid in exchange for renewing the Dhahran lease in 1956, but Saʿūd must understand that the U.S. would not be "blackmailed." George V. Allen, assistant secretary for near eastern affairs, had difficulty convincing Saudi ambassador al-Faqīh of the Baghdad Pact's "indigenous character." Disputing this contention, al-Faqīh pointed to the conviction widely held among Arabs that Britain and the U.S. were the prime movers behind the Pact, a suspicion that seemed validated by formal British adherence on April 5. London's membership in the Baghdad Pact cemented the alliance between Saudi Arabia and Egypt against Anglo-Hashemite influence in the Middle East and brought the two countries' foreign policies into alignment on issues ranging from regional defense to Buraymī.[39]

Despite concerns in Washington, the Saudis' support for neutralism and an Arab union with Egypt and Syria was less than absolute. Ghassan Salamé has argued that Saudi Arabia never wholeheartedly embraced the spirit of Bandung. Profit derived from supplying oil to the West constituted the basis of its foreign policy, and, indeed, the Saudi leadership appeared unwilling to forsake the benefits it enjoyed from the postwar petroleum order. Similarly, the Saudis offered only qualified support for union with Egypt and Syria. A government statement issued in early March hailed the pact among the three countries as "a wide-ranging step on the way to their union." The ambiguity of this declaration revolves around the Arabic word *ittiḥād,* whose meanings range from literal political "union" to mere "unity" or "agreement." Historians have noted that while important as an Arab nationalist gesture, the tripartite agreement achieved little practical significance.[40]

The ambivalent Saudi foreign policy also reflected a fear that Arab nationalism was undermining royal authority at home. By the time of Saʿūd's accession, Arab nationalism and the domestic impact of integration into the world petroleum economy posed mutually reinforcing challenges to the Saudi state. The government had forcibly suppressed the 1953 strike, and Aramco subsequently offered concessions to placate workers, including 10 to 20 percent wage increases and higher subsidies for food and housing. Despite these measures, Lackner writes that "discontent simmered just below the surface," and Abir identifies the 1953 strike as pivotal "in the re-emergence of militant opposition" to Saudi rule for the first time since the 1920s. In addition to workers, educated urban Hijazis, who had access to the Egyptian media, formed a constituency for Arab nationalism inside the kingdom. Following the strike, labor leaders and Hijazi opponents of the Saudi regime organized the National Reform Front (NRF), which sought social justice and political freedoms. A Free Officers' movement emerged in the Saudi military by 1955 as well, the unintended consequence of an Egyptian military training program. Such activity went on underground because the regime had criminalized political organizations. Political parties remained illegal, and opposition leaders fled the country to avoid arrest. In mid-1955, Saʿūd's government rounded up and deported more than one hundred Palestinians suspected of subversion, prompting complaints by Aramco about official harassment of its workers, and the king also prohibited any Saudi citizen from studying abroad unless he had permission to pursue a university degree. The Saudi response to Arab nationalism therefore combined a cautious partnership with Nāṣir in foreign policy and severe repression at home.[41]

Saʿūd's organization of the Council of Ministers was an empty gesture in terms of governmental reform that did not substantially alter the structure of the state bequeathed to him by ʿAbd al-ʿAzīz. Politics continued to be the exclusive domain of the royal family in Saudi Arabia, which lacked a middle class, possessed a military establishment divided between modern forces and the tribally based "White Army," and a leftist opposition suppressed by the government. For his part, Saʿūd still desired to rule, as his father had, by courting leading tribal clans, though Fayṣal and members of the ruling family had forced him to share power. As Arab nationalist pressures intensified outside and within Saudi Arabia, the antagonism between Saʿūd and Fayṣal escalated, while the two half-brothers battled for influence over the younger generation of princes. At the same time, no formal plan existed for applying oil revenues to development, despite Saʿūd's effort to expand education in the country and his establishment of a health ministry. While oil income for 1954 topped $230 million, Saʿūd failed to balance the budget, which existed only on paper, and spending on luxuries, a short-term ploy for defusing quarrels within the royal family, consumed revenue faster than it could be earned.[42]

Just as continuity characterized the Saudi state following Saʿūd's accession, the official American role in the kingdom remained confined within the narrow limits that had existed under ʿAbd al-ʿAzīz. That presence revolved around the Dhahran airfield, and American concerns about the renewal of the base's lease agreement gave the Saudis added leverage when demanding military aid. By further arming the Saudi regime and militarizing the postwar petroleum order, however, the U.S. reinforced Arab nationalist discontent in the kingdom. The NRF and other opponents of Saʿūd's government made scant distinction among the king's repression, the royal family's excesses, the presence of Aramco, and the foreign military base at Dhahran. A manifesto listing the NRF's demands included:

> 1. The full liberation of the country from imperialist domination and from the economic yoke of Aramco and the other oil companies.
>
> 2. The introduction of a constitution with guarantees of an elected parliament, the freedom of the press, the right to hold assemblies and set up parties and trade unions, and the right to engage in demonstrations and strikes. . . .
>
> 5. The revision and amendment of agreements with the oil companies in order to use the country's resources for its social, economic and cultural progress.

Joining the growing chorus of revolutionary nationalists throughout the Arab world, opponents of the Saudi regime combined anti-imperialism with calls for social justice and an end to repressive, Western-aligned governments. Saudi leaders began to seek American military aid as reinforcement not against the forces of international communism but against an increasingly frightening array of Arab nationalist opponents inside and outside the kingdom.[43]

The Saudis succeeded in exploiting Washington's Cold War preoccupations to secure military aid. In May 1955, the Eisenhower administration agreed to sell Saudi Arabia B-26 aircraft and to consider a Saudi request for M-47 and M-41 tanks. Wadsworth and American military experts endorsed the sale of eighteen M-41s, which, the ambassador explained, King Saʿūd desired as part of an expansion of his armed forces. Failure to honor Saudi requests for tanks would have an "unfortunate effect" on U.S.-Saudi relations, he warned, and might even prompt Saʿūd to "purchase them elsewhere."[44]

Not surprisingly, the British objected to expanded U.S. military aid to Saudi Arabia, and discussions about the potential impact of this aid in eastern Arabia were part of a wider Anglo-American dialogue on Mideast defense during the summer of 1955. During meetings between U.S. officials and a British delegation at the end of June, the Americans sought support for Alpha and tried to blunt British expectations of U.S. aid to the Baghdad Pact. For their part, the British desired U.S. adherence to the Pact as well as substantial aid to Nūrī, whose foreign policy had left him isolated in the Arab world. To the disappointment of the British, Hoover declared on June 23 that he was "unable to express any view" on possible U.S. membership, but by the time of the Geneva conference, the U.S. was offering limited support for Britain and the Baghdad Pact.[45] Eisenhower agreed to finance part of the cost of British-made Centurion tanks for Iraq, though the president was "emphatic" that the U.S. should prevail on the British "to dig further into their own resources." Eisenhower personally explained to Eden on July 20 at Geneva that the U.S. would assume only partial and not "full financial responsibility" for arming the Iraqis. Though the U.S. would accept a greater share of the financial burden for the northern-tier strategy, defense of the Middle East remained to a great extent Britain's responsibility.[46]

In August, news that Egypt had concluded an arms agreement with the Eastern Bloc came as a blow to the northern-tier strategy. The Baghdad Pact had not only failed to contain Soviet influence, but its polarizing effects on the Arab world had encouraged a Soviet initiative in the Middle East and crippled administration efforts to "woo Nasser" with offers of military aid. Meanwhile, Alpha elicited less-than-enthusiastic responses from Arabs and Israelis after Dulles unveiled it in a speech on August 26. When presented with a copy of Dulles's remarks, Prince Fayṣal snapped, "Why should I read it. . . . We can never live with Israel. Will Americans ever understand this fact[?]; nothing they can do can change it."[47]

After achieving their breakthrough with Egypt, the Soviets took the opportunity to make overtures to Saudi Arabia. In late July, Yāsīn told Wadsworth that the Soviets had offered to provide arms in exchange for full diplomatic relations and had secured an invitation for Fayṣal to visit Beijing. The State Department immediately recognized Yāsīn's announcement as a Saudi maneuver for more substantial U.S. aid. During a visit by King Saʿūd to Tehran in early August, the Soviet embassy renewed offers of arms, and Saʿūd dutifully reported these contacts to U.S. officials. As a "staunch friend" of the U.S., the king was saddened by Washington's "unfulfilled, if not actually broken, promises," and he regretted that he had to consider the Soviet offers seriously. With less subtlety, Defense Minister Prince Mishʿal threatened that the Saudis would, if necessary, buy tanks "even from the devil."[48]

Offers to sell arms to Riyadh represented the first major Soviet initiative in the Gulf, a threat the State Department believed held "particularly dangerous potential." Washington warned Saʿūd that communism was inimical toward Islam and that Soviet ties were incompatible with his responsibilities as guardian of the Muslim holy places. But Saʿūd, despite rumors of a Saudi delegation to Prague in December, regarded Moscow's overtures simply as a means to pressure the U.S. for more aid. Though Saudi leaders mouthed the slogans of neutralism, their fundamental economic relationship with the U.S. prevented them from following ʿAbd al-Nāṣir's lead.[49]

The intensification of the Cold War in the Middle East also strained Anglo-American cooperation. Despite British protests, the U.S. approved Saudi requests for tanks, and Eden concluded after Geneva that he could count on only limited American support for the Baghdad Pact. He therefore determined that Britain must act independently to support Iraq and safeguard Gulf oil. Eden told the cabinet:

> We should not therefore allow ourselves to be restricted overmuch by reluctance to act without full American concurrence and support. . . . Our policy should be based on the need to help our acknowledged friends and allies, such as Iraq, and the Trucial States on whom our oil depend[s].[50]

Eden's first opportunity to demonstrate his more independent approach came in eastern Arabia. The Buraymī arbitration process, vested in a tribunal seated at Geneva, had been in serious trouble since a fire devastated the village of Ḥamāsā in late July. Saudi officials complained that Britain had violated the arbitration agreement by introducing aid workers into Buraymī, while the British countered with accusations that Saudi agents deliberately set the suspicious fire. In September, just prior to the opening of formal hearings on Buraymī, arbitration collapsed following the resignation of the British delegate to the tribunal, Oxford professor Reader Bullard. Citing Saudi malfeasance, the British withdrew from arbitration.[51]

British accusations against the Saudis fell into several categories. First, the British argued that the Saudis continued to bribe local leaders and to smuggle guns into the oasis. Second, London charged Riyadh with attempting to influence the Pakistani member of the tribunal, Dr. Mahmoud Hasan, during Hasan's pilgrimage to Mecca. Third, Bullard cited improper conduct by the Saudi delegate to the tribunal, Minister of State Yūsuf Yāsīn, as the immediate reason for his resignation. Bullard contended that Yāsīn's contacts with the Saudi political agent at Buraymī, whom the tribunal had subpoenaed as a witness, "hopelessly compromised" the proceedings. Finally, the British government accused the Saudis of plotting a "coup d'etat" in Abu Dhabi by attempting to bribe Shaykh Zayid ibn Sulṭān, brother of the ruler, into supporting Saudi territorial claims.[52]

Of all these accusations, the most extensive evidence exists to substantiate the first. At Buraymī, the British uncovered a voluminous correspondence between the head of the Saudi police contingent and Saʿūd ibn Jiluwī, the Saudi governor of the Eastern Province, detailing smuggling activities in the oasis. As for the charges regarding Dr. Hasan, the British government abandoned efforts to prove Saudi bribery out of fear of provoking Pakistan, which joined the Baghdad Pact in September, though evidence indicates that Yāsīn somehow obtained notes taken by Hasan during the initial meetings of the arbitration tribunal and passed those documents to Aramco officials. The Saudis did not deny Bullard's accusations against Yāsīn himself, but argued that his contacts with the Saudi witness were part of Yāsīn's official responsibilities. Saudi propaganda charged Bullard with contriving this pretext for his resignation when he realized that arbitration might not yield as decisive a British victory as London had hoped.[53]

Events surrounding the overture to Shaykh Zayid remain complicated by historians' claims that Saudi designs on Abu Dhabi were part of a CIA scheme financed by Aramco, charges neither refuted nor proven by available documentation. In discussing this issue, W. Scott Lucas and Ritchie Ovendale rely primarily on the unsubstantiated claim of British journalist Leonard Mosley. Even if Mosley's account is accurate, however, maneuvering in eastern Arabia was reflective less of a U.S.-Saudi plot to undermine the British than of consistent efforts by the ruling families of the Gulf to play stronger powers against one another. Believers in an anti-British conspiracy ignore the Saudis' secret offer to London of an oil concession in the spring of 1954. As King Saʿūd had then, Zayid allegedly courted both American and British interests, first by entertaining Saudi offers and then by hastening to inform the British authorities about the bribes. Previous accounts of this matter therefore seem flawed by nearly exclusive focus on the supposed rivalry between the Western powers and an unwillingness to ascribe agency to the dynasties of the Gulf themselves.[54]

Given British awareness of local subversion since Turkī's expedition in 1952, Saudi corruption alone cannot account for the timing of the British decision to seize Buraymī. Aware of Saudi activities, Eden nonetheless consented to arbitration in October 1952, urged Churchill to accept arbitration a year later, and approved the treaty with the Saudis in July 1954. Only the subsequent intensification of Arab nationalism led Eden's government to forsake arbitration and secure its interests through more drastic measures. Once overshadowed by imperial crises in Egypt and Iran, Buraymī became a symbol for Britain of its commitment to the Baghdad Pact, its prestige in the Gulf, and its stake in sterling oil. In addition, British officials concluded that they could not trust arbitration to yield an acceptable outcome. As early as March 1955, Burrows worried that a compromise on Buraymī "will of course lean far more towards the Saudi side than towards ours." A member of the British team at Geneva complained that Reader Bullard "has no grasp at all of . . . the issues in the Arbitration, though we have done our best to coach and help him." The decision to withdraw from arbitration came, according to Shuckburgh, when the tribunal indicated its intention "to declare our bribery charges not proved." Shuckburgh resolved "that we must do everything possible to prevent such a decision by the Tribunal," and on September 16, Bullard announced his resignation.[55]

Concerns about the possible American response delayed the British resort to force. Ian Samuel of the Foreign Office's Eastern Department wrote that if the British seized Buraymī, Saudi Arabia would likely appeal to the U.N. Security Council, where the U.S. position would be "decisive." During consultations on Alpha, Shuckburgh told a State Department official that it might be best to "let the Arbitration Agreement die," draw the Saudi–Abu Dhabi boundary unilaterally, and "stand by this line." Though he made no mention of a military solution, Shuckburgh wrote that in his talks with the Americans he had "prepared the ground" for one. The Foreign Office concluded in the meantime that by sharing evidence of Saudi bribery, Britain could secure "benevolent neutrality" from Washington.[56]

These decisions cleared the way for military action by the British and implementation of Eden's independent policy in the Middle East. In a memo to the cabinet on October 15, Foreign Secretary Harold Macmillan explained that if the Saudis took over the oasis,

> we should be regarded as having betrayed the Rulers for whom we are acting and the value of British protection would slump heavily all the way from Kuwait to Aden. The consequences of this on our position in the Persian Gulf and throughout the Middle East would be very grave. . . . If we were to allow the Saudis to impose a major defeat upon us—and the loss of Buraimi would be that—the whole of our position might easily slip away.

Early on October 26, British-led forces seized Buraymī, overcoming the small Saudi police force, while the Foreign Office simultaneously declared a new Saudi–Abu Dhabi boundary based on the 1935 Riyadh Line. Eden told the House of Commons that he undertook the action "to protect the legitimate interests" of Britain's Gulf clients, though the prime minister left the door open to "minor rectifications" of their boundaries with the Saudis as circumstances required.[57]

Aramco reacted to the British raid with outrage, and Vice President Duce quickly impressed Aramco's interpretation of these events on the director of central intelligence. Allen Dulles conveyed to his brother Duce's view that the British had "sabotaged arbitration" when an unfavorable decision became likely. The British move further undermined Alpha by legitimizing violent means for resolving Mideast conflicts, while Moscow's offer of arms would also now seem "even more attractive" to the Arab states. Another Aramco official predicted that if Washington failed to side with the Saudis, Americans would be tossed out of the kingdom: "[W]e will not be able to stay. I am sure of it." For the moment, Saudi protests seemed oddly pro forma, and King Saʿūd appeared paralyzed by the British attack. He awaited the return of Fayṣal, who was in Egypt signing a new agreement with Nāṣir, before deciding on a response.[58]

As the British had hoped, however, official U.S. reaction was mild. Eisenhower, who had insisted on the need for British compromise, was recovering from a heart attack. Dulles told Macmillan in Paris that Washington was "annoyed about the suddenness of the British action," yet "Dulles took this all very calmly," Macmillan wrote, "and, having ticked off this item, did not press it." Acting Secretary Hoover conceded to the National Security Council that the military action was necessary if Britain was to avoid being "pushed out of all the sheikdoms in the area." The U.S. and Britain, Hoover gently chided British ambassador Roger Makins, would have to "play it together from now on." Moderate reactions by U.S. officials reflected the premium placed by the administration on Anglo-American cooperation in the Middle East. After meeting Soviet foreign minister Molotov in Geneva, Dulles made a report to the NSC, assembled at Camp David where Eisenhower continued his recuperation. Dulles explained that "the Soviets had deliberately opened a new cold war front." Soviet expansion amounted to "a very grave situation," because the "loss of the oil of the Middle East would be almost catastrophic for the West." Therefore, Dulles concluded, "no significant cleavage between the U.S. and the UK on Near Eastern policy could be permitted."[59]

Britain's reoccupation of Buraymī confronted the Eisenhower administration with a difficult choice between supporting Saudi Arabia and Aramco on the one hand and maintaining British prestige in the Gulf on the other. Both were essential elements of the postwar petroleum order. But Britain's access to sterling oil, without which American policy in Western Europe would be impossible, trumped the administration's other priorities in the Middle East. American officials consequently muted their complaints about the seizure of Buraymī while they awkwardly tried to reassure the fuming Saudi leadership that the U.S. had no prior knowledge of Britain's plans.[60]

The different British and American responses to Arab nationalist crises early in King Saʿūd's reign exemplified their distinct approaches in the Middle East. While the U.S. resolved the Onassis dispute by relying on Aramco to increase its payments to Saudi Arabia, Eden used military force at Buraymī to secure the territory and sterling oil of Britain's Gulf clients. Yet the two allies found common ground in the defense of the postwar petroleum order, and the friction generated by Britain's military action was therefore minimal. But the early years of King Saʿūd's reign witnessed a more serious deterioration in the U.S. relationship with Saudi Arabia. Aramco and the Eisenhower administration regarded the Onassis deal as a threat to the postwar petroleum order, and U.S. aid to Iraq aligned Washington with the Saudis' historic enemies. Saudi officials continued to accuse the Americans of siding with the British over Buraymī, while heightened Arab nationalism in the region forced Saʿūd's government into closer relations with Egypt and flirtations with neutralism. As a result, Saʿūd cancelled the American Point Four mission to his kingdom and threatened to evict the Americans from Dhahran.

During the same period, however, the Saudis demonstrated their unwillingness to sever ties with Washington altogether. Saʿūd capitulated on the Onassis deal and rejected Soviet offers of military aid. The king recognized his stake in the postwar petroleum order and understood that Arab nationalism strengthened domestic opponents of his regime, whose stability was already undermined by serious divisions within the ruling family and a power struggle between Saʿūd and Fayṣal. As Arab nationalism intensified, Eisenhower concluded from the king's behavior that he could cast Saʿūd to play the leading role in the administration's defense of the postwar petroleum order, which would soon face its most serious crisis since the foundation of Israel.

4

A Tangled Skein: Suez, December 1955–December 1956

BRITAIN'S REOCCUPATION of the Buraymī oasis placed serious strains on each side of the triangle connecting the United Kingdom, the United States, and Saudi Arabia. Unless London withdrew its forces from Buraymī and returned to arbitration, King Saʿūd threatened to submit the issue to the United Nations Security Council. At the same time, the Saudis attacked the Americans for failing to condemn British actions and hinted that Washington's refusal to support the Saudi claim over Buraymī could prevent renewal of the lease at the Dhahran airfield. Finally, Buraymī became part of a larger Anglo-American controversy at the end of 1955 over how best to preserve the postwar petroleum order in the Middle East.

In accord with the policy that had led to military action at Buraymī, Prime Minister Eden sought to strengthen relations with rulers of the oil-producing Gulf states and to fortify the Baghdad Pact. When Britain attempted to bring Jordan into the alliance, Saudi Arabia lobbied vigorously against what it regarded as an Anglo-Hashemite bid to dominate the Arab world. Eden's government, in turn, angry over Saudi patronage of Egyptian president Gamāl ʿAbd al-Nāṣir's anti-Pact campaign among the Arab states, criticized the U.S. for failing to invest Saudi oil revenue constructively, as the British had in Kuwait and Iraq. Britain considered Saudi Arabia the major financier of Arab nationalist attacks on its interests, while the Americans still promoted the kingdom as a showplace for their policy of assuaging Arab nationalism through private largesse.

In January–February 1956, the allies seemingly overcame their disagreements following meetings between Eden and President Eisenhower. Britain agreed to re-open direct talks with the Saudis on Buraymī, and by March, Eisenhower had abandoned plans for an Arab-Israeli settlement and had opted instead to isolate Nāṣir's Egypt. The president tapped Saʿūd to lead a pro-Western coalition in the Arab world and hoped that the king, as keeper of the holy places of Islam, could transmit Western influence to other Arab and Muslim countries. Though this policy ignored Saʿūd's personal deficiencies, this chapter argues that it also borrowed misconceptions about Islam from European Orientalism.

But just as Eisenhower embarked on his new departure and as the British and Saudis resumed their negotiations over Buraymī, President Nāṣir nationalized the Suez Canal. In his attempts to prevent war, Eisenhower enlisted the help of King Saʿūd, whose authority at home was increasingly threatened by renewed labor violence and growing support for Nāṣir. After the invasion of Egyptian territory by Israel, Britain, and France, the administration worked with the oil industry to restore the postwar petroleum order while demanding the aggressors' withdrawal. When the crisis subsided, however, the U.S. had failed to resolve the essential contradiction in its policy between collaboration with Britain and a desire for improved relations with the Arab states. Through his burgeoning relationship with Saʿūd, Eisenhower hoped to hold on to the prestige earned by the U.S. as a result of its anti-colonial stand during the crisis, even as the president brokered a post-Suez Anglo-American reconciliation.

Although Suez has been portrayed elsewhere as a breach in the "special relationship," as evidence of Anglo-American competition for oil, or as the death throes of British power in the Middle East, the crisis is depicted here as a grave shock to the postwar petroleum order. That set of relationships among oil producers and transit states, major petroleum corporations, and the Western powers had been the foundation of the "free world" economy since the early days of the Cold War. By threatening to shut off the flow of Mideast oil, the crisis jeopardized U.S. officials' free-trading vision for Western Europe and the entire postwar American project of simultaneously building a prosperous consumer society at home while assuming major responsibilities abroad. Suez also illustrated in the starkest way imaginable contrasting U.S. and British ideas regarding how the West should maintain its access to Mideast oil. Though the transition from British colonial to American capitalist hegemony in the Middle East produced Anglo-American tensions during the 1950s, it was during the second half of 1956 that the allies' different policies came closest to destroying the postwar petroleum order.

Initially restrained, the Saudi reaction to Britain's seizure of Buraymī grew bellicose by early November 1955. In a speech delivered in Dammam to a crowd reportedly numbering twenty thousand, King Saʿūd called for a jihād against the British and vowed, "I shall be the first soldier to go . . . we shall defend our country with our lives." From November through the early months of 1956, *Al-Bilād al-Saʿūdiyya* published scores of telegrams from Saudis offering to sacrifice themselves in a war against Britain. U.S. Ambassador Wadsworth told his British counterpart that Saʿūd was determined "to do something spectacular to vindicate his honour in the eyes of tribal leaders and others who were now urging him to start a holy war." Despite this posturing, the Saudis were powerless to return to Buraymī by military force, and genuine support in the kingdom for confrontation with Britain appeared weak. The Saudi government worked instead to garner U.S. support for pressuring Britain to resume arbitration and threatened an appeal to the U.N. if London refused. Saudi Arabia's "direction is towards [the] United Nations Security Council," Fayṣal warned Wadsworth, and Aramco lawyers were already preparing to present the Saudi case. At the same time, Riyadh sought U.S. support for King Saʿūd's five-year military development plan and took the opportunity to ratchet up the level of military aid it demanded in exchange for renewing the Americans' lease at Dhahran.[1]

Concerned by the possibility of Saudi action in the Security Council, where the Soviet Union was soon scheduled to assume the chair, the Eisenhower administration promised to consider Saudi demands for arms and sought British compromise over Buraymī. Though Dulles was "not prepared to pay an unreasonable price" for the Dhahran renewal, State Department officials agreed to study a new Saudi request for 467 military items. Undersecretary Hoover urged the British Foreign Office to return the Buraymī issue to arbitration or to re-open negotiations, and he prevailed on ʿAzzām Pasha, former Arab League secretary and now Saudi delegate to the U.N., to delay any appeal to the Security Council pending the British reply.[2]

For their part, the British were unwilling to depart from Eden's policy of stronger support for Britain's Gulf allies and the Baghdad Pact. The Foreign Office continued to believe that threats to publish the incriminating documents seized at Buraymī would dissuade the Saudis from U.N. action and convince the U.S. of Saudi malfeasance. ʿAbd al-Nāṣir also told Britain's ambassador in Cairo that he opposed Security Council involvement and would advise Saʿūd against introducing Buraymī. Brandishing captured documents, Minister of State Anthony Nutting rebuffed the Saudi ambassador's request for new talks on November 10. The Foreign Office refrained, however, from publicizing the documents, and with the Saudis decisively evicted from Buraymī, some officials argued for compromise to avoid alienating both the United States and friendly Arab countries. Assistant Undersecretary Evelyn Shuckburgh proposed a "more or less ingenuous offer to talk" with Riyadh in order to "keep the Saudis in play" while British officials tried to change American views about Saudi foreign policy.[3]

British and American attitudes toward the kingdom diverged sharply at the end of 1955, as London became alarmed by Saudi financial support for opponents of both the Baghdad Pact and Britain's authority in the Gulf. The Foreign Office accused the Saudi government of bankrolling anti–Baghdad Pact political candidates and newspapers in Syria, Jordan, and other Arab states, while the Saudis were also supporting an insurgency against one of Britain's Gulf clients.

Saudi connections to Syrian opponents of Hashemite influence, such as Shukrī al-Quwwatlī, dated to the reign of ʿAbd al-ʿAzīz. The question of whether Syria should join a united Fertile Crescent dominated by Hashemite Iraq had been a key fault line in Syrian politics since the French mandate, when Ottoman-era notables still controlled the major parties. The British campaign to expand the Baghdad Pact radicalized Syrian politics, however, and helped to strengthen a new generation of Baʿth and Communist Party politicians, who staunchly opposed the Pact as a new vehicle for Hashemite ambition and Western imperialism. The Saudi government's support for these interests and especially its association with Khālid Baqdash, a Kurdish lawyer who was the first Communist Party member elected to the Syrian National Assembly, prompted British accusations that Saudi activities benefited communism.[4] "[I]t is no exaggeration," Harold Macmillan wrote Eden, "to say that American (Aramco) money is being spent on a vast scale (about £100 million a year) to promote communism in the Middle East." In December, when Eden sent Sir Gerald Templer to Amman to negotiate Jordan's entry into the Baghdad Pact, a step the U.S. opposed, rioting followed and the Jordanian government collapsed. Some in the Foreign Office blamed Saudi subversion among West Bank Palestinians for the failure of the Templer mission. "If Saudi/Egyptian/Communist intrigue can prevent Jordan [from] joining the Pact," Shuckburgh wrote, " . . . how far the rot has spread!"[5]

At the same time, the Saudis supported a revolt against the Sultan of Muscat and Oman, Saʿīd ibn Taymūr. A British client, the sultan made his capital at Muscat, which faced the Gulf, though he also claimed authority over a broad hinterland populated by tribes whose allegiance he commanded only nominally. In the Omani interior, Ibāḍī khārijism, an austere separatist sect with early Islamic origins, exerted a powerful influence tied to the leadership of an elected imām, whose authority overlapped the sultan's. Oil exploration in Oman, as elsewhere in eastern Arabia, introduced new tensions into societies consisting of nomadic populations ruled by settled dynasties. The sultan granted a concession to a subsidiary of the

Iraq Petroleum Company, which claimed rights over all the sultan's lands. Ghālib ibn ʿAlī al-Hināʾī, the Ibāḍī imām elected in 1954, challenged this claim and sought, with his ambitious brother Ṭālib, to establish an independent state among tribes in the Omani interior. Both Saudi Arabia and Egypt backed the imāmate's petition for independent representation in the Arab League, and Britain's cache of captured documents from Buraymī revealed that the Saudis had sent the imām 100,000 Indian rupees in August 1955. Intent on completing its campaign begun at Buraymī, Britain launched a military operation in December aimed at destroying the imāmate. The sultan's forces captured the imām's stronghold of Nizwā, and Ṭālib, who led a weak resistance, fled into Saudi territory.[6]

Britain's growing conviction that Saudi Arabia, well-financed by Aramco, had a hand in subversive activity across the Arab world became the mirror image of Saudi complaints about Anglo-Hashemite encirclement. British officials tried to convince the U.S. that Saudi Arabia was an anti-Western force in the Middle East. Moreover, Britain proposed curtailing Saudi political activities through a temporary moratorium on Aramco royalty payments, a measure first suggested by Iraqi premier Nūrī al-Saʿīd. In an attempt to reconcile the U.S. to British policy and to reshape American views, the Foreign Office gave the State Department some advance warning of military action at Nizwā, unlike at Buraymī, and soon afterward decided to share evidence of Saudi bribery. But on December 13, Dulles asked that Britain "make every effort to restrain [the] Sultan." Concerned that action in Oman would force the Saudis' hand in the Security Council, where the Soviets had already expressed support for a Saudi petition, Dulles also requested a restoration of the Buraymī arbitration process. Shuckburgh wrote that British officials were "thrown into a rage" by Dulles's requests, and Permanent Undersecretary Ivone Kirkpatrick made what he called a "fairly savage attack" on U.S. minister Walworth Barbour.[7]

Both allies, however, recognized the need for cooperation against Soviet initiatives in the Middle East, a joint effort that involved negotiations with Nāṣir for Western financing of the Egyptian Aswan Dam. In Paris for a NATO ministers' meeting, Dulles set aside his preference for an immediate solution to Buraymī and agreed that Eden and Eisenhower could address the Saudi question during talks scheduled for January. Evelyn Shuckburgh would precede Eden to the U.S, and ʿAzzām Pasha, advised by Aramco to delay, promised to refrain from Security Council action in the meantime.[8]

Anglo-American differences over Saudi Arabia transcended both Washington's unwillingness to restrain the Saudis and a lack of appreciation for the value of British treaty relationships in the Gulf. Rather, such tensions involved the fundamentally different approaches the two allies employed toward the oil-producing states. Reliance upon private economic diplomacy made it impossible for Washington to accede to British requests that it force Aramco to reduce the oil revenues paid to the Saudi government. This sort of interference with corporate enterprise would not only undermine the strategy U.S. officials thought most likely to preserve the postwar petroleum order, but would also violate norms governing public-private relations whose historical roots ran deep in the domestic political economy. Eisenhower remained unwilling to overstep precedent by assuming a larger official role directing economic development in the Saudi kingdom as Britain had in Iraq and Kuwait. For their part, the British felt that just such a step on Washington's part was needed to break the alliance between Saudi money and Arab nationalism.

The basic nature of this divergence became clear during Shuckburgh's January 1956 mission. In talks with officials in the Bureau of Near Eastern Affairs, Shuckburgh argued that recent unrest in Jordan "proved that the Palestinian refugees have been infused with Communism and Saudi-Egyptian anti-Western propaganda." He blamed well-financed Saudi intrigue for growing Arab nationalism and stressed the need to control the Saudis' use of oil revenues. In contrast to Iraq, where he claimed that 60 percent of royalties helped to support development, and Kuwait, whose profits were invested in bonds on the sterling market, Shuckburgh contended that "in Saudi Arabia the oil revenues have not been harnessed to constructive development." A Saudi development board was therefore necessary to divert oil revenues from more sinister purposes. Assistant Secretary George V. Allen deemed such paternalism impossible in the current political atmosphere and hoped instead that private oil investment would foster a "responsible middle class in Saudi Arabia" that was immune to revolutionary politics. If the British compromised on Buraymī, Herbert Hoover Jr. added, "Saudi Arabia might be persuaded to reorient its current anti-Western policies and activities," whereas attempts to curtail Saudi revenues would have the opposite effect. Citing Saudi threats to go to the Security Council, Hoover suggested a return to arbitration, a proposal Shuckburgh dismissed as "very unsatisfactory."[9]

Indeed, as Eisenhower and Eden prepared for their summit, Anglo-American differences over Saudi Arabia seemed irreconcilable. On January 16, Eden warned the president about the Saudis' collusion with "the Russians, the Egyptians and the Syrians to undermine western influence in the Middle East." The prime minister, U.S. Ambassador Aldrich reported, "lost his temper" during his trans-Atlantic voyage when Aldrich raised the possibility of compromise over Buraymī. Dulles intimated to Eugene

Holman of Jersey Standard his apprehension that the British would place "a strong urge upon us to align ourselves with them in a way which the Saudis would undoubtedly consider as unfriendly." The Saudi question threatened to drive a wedge between the two allies just as British and American officials were jointly trying to prevent further Soviet gains in the Middle East.[10]

During the summit, however, Eisenhower's personal intervention on two key points preserved Anglo-American cooperation while avoiding a clash with Riyadh. First, Eisenhower relented on the U.S. demand that Britain return to arbitration of Buraymī. Suggesting a resumption of direct talks instead, the president proposed that London grant the Saudis access to the Gulf east of the Qatar peninsula, a territorial compromise that had been on the table when the Dammam talks collapsed in 1952. Second, to address Eden's concerns about the subversive use of oil funds, Eisenhower proposed "selling arms to the Saudis to absorb money." With some quid pro quo involving U.S. military aid imminent during negotiations on Dhahran, Eisenhower could portray arms sales as a solution to the Saudi problem in the Middle East. Most importantly, the president's suggestion did not require expanding the U.S. role in the kingdom to encompass development planning as the British demanded.[11]

By every appearance, Eisenhower's two-pronged compromise on Saudi Arabia seemed successful in the weeks following the summit. The British cabinet approved re-establishing direct talks with the Saudis and the "mopping up" of Saudi funds through the sale by Washington of what Eden called "obsolete arms." Near Eastern Affairs officials informed Saudi ambassador ʿAbdullah al-Khayyāl of the proposal for new talks, and the Saudi government approached Britain about resuming negotiations. Through private channels, the U.S. also sought to persuade King Saʿūd to curb his support for radical Arab causes and forgo plans to transfer Saudi accounts from U.S. to Swiss banks. At Aramco's request, President John J. McCloy of Chase Manhattan, Saudi Arabia's principal creditor, traveled to Riyadh for this purpose. Meanwhile, Eden agreed for the moment to continue Eisenhower's policy of trying to work with Nāṣir. Negotiations proceeded on financing Egypt's Aswan Dam, and in January Eisenhower's special envoy, Robert Anderson, held separate discussions with Nāṣir and Israeli prime minister David Ben-Gurion on an Arab-Israeli settlement.[12]

Within a short time, however, election-year politics threatened to upset Eisenhower's compromise. After Egypt announced its purchase of Czech arms, U.S. officials had worked to expedite the sale of light tanks to Saudi Arabia. Meanwhile, the Israeli government lobbied Washington intensely for military aid and a security guarantee. Though Eisenhower supported third-party arms sales to Israel, he believed that any hope for an Arab-

Israeli settlement would disappear if the U.S. armed Israel directly. Not surprisingly, the Israelis publicly protested the sale of U.S. tanks to Riyadh, and domestic supporters of Israel pressured the Eisenhower administration to suspend the transaction. The political storm broke on February 17, as eighteen M-41 tanks sat on lighters at a Brooklyn pier awaiting shipment to Saudi Arabia. Eisenhower was at his home in Georgia, while Secretary Dulles vacationed in the Caribbean, leaving Herbert Hoover Jr. in charge at the State Department. When news radio broadcasts publicized the tank shipment, presidential press secretary James Hagerty woke a sleeping Eisenhower, who ordered a temporary suspension of export licenses for all arms bound for the Middle East. But after two days, the administration rescinded the ban, prompting pro-Israel demonstrations along the Brooklyn waterfront. Congressional Democrats and Republicans demanded an investigation, and both Hoover and Dulles were called before the Senate Foreign Relations Committee.[13]

The congressional inquiry into the tank fiasco raised fundamental questions about the U.S.-Saudi relationship. Hoover took responsibility before the Senate committee for suspending, then reinstating, the export licenses, concealing the fact that the order had come from Eisenhower himself. Dulles fielded more difficult questions about the regime the U.S. was supplying with arms. Senator Wayne Morse (D-Oregon) asked whether Saudi Arabia was a "totalitarian government" and how the administration could justify arming such a regime while denying arms to "democratic" Israel. Hubert Humphrey (D-Minnesota) pressed the secretary about Saudi discrimination against Jewish Americans and expressed concerns that arms sent to Riyadh would be used against Israel. "The purpose, Senator, of the tanks," Dulles replied in a revealing admission, "is to maintain internal security." Morse concluded from Dulles's responses that "what we are doing is using the military support of the United States to keep down human rights and freedom." In private, however, committee chairman Senator Walter F. George (D-Georgia) conceded that Eisenhower would have to release the tanks. The president issued a public statement explaining the U.S. commitment to Saudi Arabia, and the tanks left Pier 29 in Brooklyn bound for the Saudi kingdom as planned.[14]

Neither the Anglo-American summit nor the tank controversy prompted a reconsideration of U.S.-Saudi relations. Aramco continued as the instrument of Washington's oil diplomacy, and official involvement in the Saudi kingdom remained restricted to supplying arms and maintaining the Dhahran airfield. Ironically, at the very time that George Allen was extolling to Shuckburgh the social benefits of corporate investment, a new labor disturbance was flaring up in Saudi Arabia's Eastern Province.[15] Administration officials nonetheless maintained their faith that private diplomacy could reconcile Western interests with Arab nationalism.

As concern increased about a Soviet-Arab alliance, Saudi Arabia assumed a central place in the Anglo-American political strategy in the Middle East. By March 1956, both Britain and the U.S. had abandoned attempts to court ʿAbd al-Nāṣir. On March 1, as Foreign Secretary Lloyd met with Nāṣir in Cairo, King Ḥusayn dismissed Sir John Bagot Glubb as commander of the Arab Legion. The British interpreted Glubb's dismissal as evidence of Nāṣir's growing influence, and Lloyd concluded from his meeting that Nāṣir sought to overthrow conservative regimes in Jordan and the Gulf states as well. Eden's government therefore reinforced its commitment to its Gulf clients and sought to deprive Egypt of financial support from King Saʿūd. "We should try to detach Saudi Arabia from Egypt," Lloyd told the cabinet, "by making plain to King Saud the nature of Nasser's ambitions." Eden sent Eisenhower a letter detailing Egyptian plans to subvert "the Saudis, as well as Iraq and Jordan."[16]

The president, meanwhile, was thinking along similar lines. A second mission to the Middle East by Robert Anderson failed to bring Nāṣir and Ben-Gurion any closer to agreement. Eisenhower now concurred that "our efforts should be directed toward separating the Saudi Arabians from the Egyptians," and that the U.S. should work to contain Nāṣir, whose foreign policy seemed increasingly friendly toward the Soviet Union. Washington and London organized a joint undertaking, known as Omega, to isolate Nāṣir, and central to this effort was the exploitation of what was assumed to be a natural tension between revolutionary Egypt and the oil-rich Saudi monarchy. President Eisenhower even suggested that King Saʿūd could be made into a pro-Western rival of Nāṣir. "Arabia is a country that contains the holy places of the Moslem world," wrote Eisenhower, who therefore reasoned that "the King could be built up as a spiritual leader."[17]

In discussing Eisenhower's alliance with Saʿūd, some scholars have justifiably criticized the president's naïveté about Islam and his failure to diagnose the king's incapacity for political leadership, but none has looked beyond Eisenhower himself for the origins of this policy.[18] Yet the president's gambit of building up Saʿūd can be understood only against the background of contemporary expertise regarding the assumed significance of Islam in Cold War politics. This context helps to reveal an important and overlooked facet of U.S. diplomacy in the Middle East.

Eisenhower's Islamic strategy did not emerge out of a vacuum, but instead reflected Western scholars' assumptions that religious faith was the essential, defining characteristic of Muslims and that a monolithic "Islam" could somehow be manipulated to shape the political future of the Middle East. Following World War Two, scholars of the Middle East eagerly volunteered their expertise on Cold War issues, especially the question of whether Middle Eastern societies were susceptible to communist expansion. The postwar years also witnessed the proliferation of near eastern area studies programs, reflecting an anxiety about the vulnerability of Islamic societies to Soviet influence, especially in the wake of a supposed crisis of faith caused by European expansion. "Westernization," wrote Albert Hourani, founding director of the Middle Eastern Studies Centre at St. Antony's College, Oxford, "was largely destructive" to the communal identities of Islamic societies. "Communism can spread among those on whom the inherited religion has lost its hold," Hourani warned, "and it can even spread within the framework of Islam." Professor Bernard Lewis of the University of London and later of Princeton was more optimistic that Islam could be a barrier to communism. "Pious Muslims—and most Muslims are pious—" he explained, "will not long tolerate an atheist creed, nor one that violates their traditional religious moral principles." The Soviets, moreover, should not be exempt from anti-colonial nationalism, because their empire encompassed the Muslim societies of central Asia. "[W]hy should this hatred include America," Lewis wrote, "which has never ruled any part of the Middle East, and exclude Russia, which still rules—not always gently—in such ancient Muslim, Asian cities as Samarkand and Bukhara, and many others besides?"[19]

Such considerations were not merely academic, but held implications for policy. The Eisenhower administration sponsored a conference in Washington of leading historians of the Middle East, including, among many others, the prominent Ottoman historian and later University of Chicago professor Halil Inalcik. National Security Council staffers routinely attended academic conferences and collected scholarly papers on the contemporary Middle East. In one notable example of Middle Eastern scholarship with Cold War ramifications, filed away in the NSC staff papers at the Eisenhower Library, Bernard Lewis explains how Naqshbandi Sufis living in the Caucasus region might be used as a fifth column inside the Soviet empire.[20]

The administration's reliance on this sort of Middle Eastern scholarship suggests important continuities in the relationship between knowledge and power as the U.S. inherited authority over the Middle East from Britain and France. In *Orientalism,* Edward Said traced the genealogy of a European literary tradition of writing about the Islamic world that constructed an Oriental "Other" with characteristics opposite and inferior to the qualities Europeans ascribed to themselves: Orientals were presumed to be as sensual, fanatical, and despotic as Europeans were rational and enlightened. As British and French imperial dominance in the Middle East peaked during the interwar mandate period, Orientalism transformed itself from a descriptive, literary form into a prescriptive expertise at the service of the colonial rulers. But Said is ambiguous about the degree to which the U.S. inherited Orientalism from the imperial powers. He contends that a generic, social science expertise, one disconnected from European traditions of writing about Islam, informed U.S. Cold War diplomacy in the Middle East. American policy makers relied on ideas that were Orientalist, he explains, but in only a fragmentary and "scarcely recognizable" form. Yet scholars who identified secularization as the dominant trend in the Arab Middle East reached this conclusion by focusing almost exclusively on Muslims energized by Arab nationalism and educated in Western-style teachers' colleges, army schools, and universities. These technocrats were the very elites whom modernization theorists and policy specialists regarded as the basis for a developed middle class. Middle Eastern historians' assumption that Western expansion had created a crisis of faith and ideological drift among Muslims therefore dovetailed nicely with modernization theorists' concern for middle-class economic and political development. The blending of Orientalist expertise with postwar social science did not reflect the waning of the tradition Said examines but was instead part of the long-term evolution of Orientalism "from being textual and contemplative into being administrative, economic, and even military." As Eisenhower's foreign policy suggests, this process spanned the decline of European empires and the dawn of U.S. power in the Middle East. Indeed, the recruiting of European talent for Mideast studies programs in the U.S. and official demand for work produced by such scholars illustrate Orientalism's resilience.[21]

The theme of Islam and the Cold War surfaced in American diplomacy apart from the Omega plan. The U.S. intervened in January to prevent Saudi Arabia, Jordan, and Syria from giving a Polish company a contract to study the reconstruction of the Hijaz railroad. This Ottoman-era railway, destroyed during the First World War, followed the old ḥajj route from Damascus to Medina and had been used to transport pilgrims. The U.S. prevailed on Saʿūd to grant the contract instead to the American IREX Corporation.[22] Wadsworth was encouraged when Saʿūd asked his ʿulamāʾ to draft a fatwā, based on the sūra al-Anfāl from the Qurʾān, proscribing aid from the communist bloc, a step the king probably took to convince Washington he was a natural Cold War ally and therefore a worthy recipient of American aid. Finally, the idea to find an anti-communist Islamic "spiritual leader" did not begin with Eisenhower. As early as 1951–52, intelligence analyst Miles Copeland reveals, Kermit Roosevelt and his staff had sought "a 'Moslem Billy Graham' to mobilize religious fervor . . . against Communism."[23] While Eisenhower badly misjudged Saʿūd, his assumptions about the importance of Islam in the Cold War were far from original and reflected trans-Atlantic continuities in Middle Eastern expertise just as the U.S. inherited regional power from its European allies.

Despite their collaboration with Washington on Omega, the British did not share Eisenhower's belief that the king, on the strength of his religious prestige, offered an alternative to Nāṣir. "I think that the United States are rather unrealistic," Lloyd wrote Eden, "in their assessment of the positive contribution which the Saudis could make." Cabinet Secretary Norman Brook observed more pointedly that Britain would be backing "a certain loser if we tried . . . to build up King Saud as the leader of the Arab world." Eden and his advisors did not rule out cultivating Islam as a bulwark against communism, but they were more intent on curtailing Saʿūd's support for Nāṣir than on enhancing the king's own stature. British concerns in this regard increased in April, when Saʿūd and Nāṣir offered financial aid to the imām of Yemen, who opposed British plans to form a protectorate over southwest Arabia based at Aden.[24]

London's desire for U.S. membership in the Baghdad Pact was an additional, ulterior motive behind the British campaign to break the Saudi-Egyptian alliance. Dividing the Saudis from Egypt and reconciling them to Hashemite Iraq, the British believed, would overcome a major obstacle to U.S. membership. Eden told the cabinet that American adherence "would be the greatest single contribution" Washington could make in the Middle East. Pressured to join by Defense Secretary Wilson and the Joint Chiefs, Eisenhower nevertheless sided with Dulles, who raised concerns about the Israeli reaction, Arab politics, and the drawbacks of a close association with Britain in the Middle East. Explaining that Mideast diplomacy was "a highly 'tangled skein'," Eisenhower promised to cooperate with the British in regional defense, but declined to join the Pact.[25]

Once again, Buraymī acted as a lightning rod for Anglo-American differences. Eisenhower's reliance on Saʿūd made him more interested than ever in extracting British concessions. Dulles told Ambassador Roger Makins that a prompt Buraymī settlement "was of vital importance" and that Britain "might have to pay a price to split the Saudis from the Egyptians." Attempts to reopen Anglo-Saudi negotiations on the basis of Eisenhower's territorial compromise showed early promise, then stalled. Following the Anglo-American summit, Harry Kern, a former *Newsweek* correspondent and globetrotting consultant for U.S. oil companies, brokered a meeting in New York between Lloyd and ʿAzzām Pasha. As a result of these talks, British envoy Arthur Dodds-Parker undertook a mission to the kingdom to discuss Buraymī, but Riyadh still insisted on British withdrawal from the oasis as a precondition for negotiations. Indeed, King Saʿūd maintained a *de facto* suspension of Anglo-Saudi relations by refusing to receive and accredit London's new ambassador, Roderick Parkes. The British, in turn, rejected Saudi demands and resisted U.S. pressures for compromise. Lloyd told Dulles on May 3 that the British hoped simply for "protracted negotiations which would keep [the] matter 'on ice'."[26]

In other ways, British and American policies seemed to be moving in opposite directions by the spring of 1956. On April 9, during consultations between Kim Roosevelt and Lloyd on Anglo-American covert operations, the British raised the possibility of organizing a coup against Saʿūd. The royal family was "brittle," observed one British official. Dulles told Eisenhower in a telephone conversation two days later that the British were "thinking in lines antagonistic to Saud" and had "some crazy ideas." At the same time, the U.S. was preparing to grant the Saudi kingdom military aid to ease renewal of the Dhahran lease. Whereas previously the administration had planned to offer the bare minimum necessary to ensure renewal, Dhahran was now linked to Eisenhower's hope of building up Saʿūd. The president told Dulles that the U.S. should offer a "substantial amount of armaments to the Saudis." Ambassador Wadsworth recommended that the U.S. also build a new air terminal at Dhahran and suggested that Eisenhower invite King Saʿūd to the U.S. Dulles, mindful of the uproar in February, postponed consideration of the last suggestion until after the election. But in contrast to the British, the Americans were interested in strengthening, not toppling, the Saudi leadership.[27]

The two allies, however, still shared mutual concerns about communist influence in the Middle East and Western Europe's oil supplies, and they grew alarmed by Nāṣir's increasingly friendly relations with the communist bloc. Egypt recognized communist China in May, and Nāṣir then invited Soviet foreign minister Dmitri Shepilov to ceremonies marking Britain's withdrawal from the Suez base, prompting the allies to rescind their offer to finance the Aswan Dam. Making matters worse, the Soviets had agreed to provide military and economic aid to Syria, whose territory was crossed by the two major pipelines, and skirmishes along Israel's borders threatened to escalate into a new war. A renewed Arab-Israeli conflict, according to one U.S. study, would jeopardize access to Mideast oil and would mean "serious dislocations of supplies for the West . . . [f]uel shortages, especially in Western Europe," and, worst of all, "[e]xtensive government controls" on oil consumption in the U.S. Dulles told Eisenhower that, deprived of Mideast oil, "Western Europe would collapse, industrially and militarily," and Shuckburgh reached the same conclusion. "Western Europe is *dependent* on the oil," he wrote, and "Nasser can stop it coming if he wants to, by closing the canal or the pipelines."[28]

The Americans and British did not agree on policy toward Saudi Arabia, and this difference had everything to do with the allies' distinct approaches in the Middle East. Washington remained committed to backing private oil diplomacy while arming the Saudi regime, a policy now subsumed under Eisenhower's initiative to build up Saʿūd. This informal American empire of corporate investment and military bases conflicted with the British colonial legacy of treaties and political advisors. London regarded Saudi support for ʿAbd al-Nāṣir as a threat to British oil supplies and to its imperial clients. The British were also baffled by Washington's refusal to engage directly in planning oil-funded development in the Gulf as Britain had. For separate reasons, however, preservation of the postwar petroleum order from the threat of Arab nationalism now appeared to leaders in both countries to depend on detaching Saʿūd from Nāṣir. Meanwhile, Arab nationalism was also fueling a crisis within the Saudi kingdom itself.

Labor unrest in the Saudi Eastern Province during January 1956 had been only a portent of further demonstrations and another general strike against Aramco later that year. As in 1953, Saudi workers, many of them members of the Shīʿa minority, protested not only Aramco's labor policies but also their government's close relationship with the United States. Inspired by ʿAbd al-Nāṣir and Arab nationalism, they rallied against the renewal of the American lease at the Dhahran airfield, and these disturbances, far more effectively than Anglo-American warnings, alerted King Saʿūd to the dangers for the Saudi regime of Nāṣir's pan-Arabism.

In May, demonstrators demanding expulsion of the U.S. from Dhahran and carrying banners reading "Down with American Imperialism" confronted Saʿūd when the king visited the Eastern Province. While Saʿūd ibn Jiluwī and local authorities quickly broke up the demonstration and arrested the leaders, agitation against renewal of the Dhahran lease continued. By summer, a petition opposing the presence of U.S. military personnel in the kingdom had reportedly gained 600 signatures. Wadsworth found himself "at a loss [to] understand this local opposition" in light of the benefits he felt the Saudis derived from the base.[29]

More serious was a general strike among the Aramco work force in June. The company had been reducing the number of its employees as it completed the basic infrastructure necessary for extracting Saudi oil. While Aramco made some progress in placing Saudi nationals in intermediate and middle-management jobs, the bulk of those it let go occupied the lower-skilled positions, classified by the company as "Grades 1–3." In 1952, Aramco had employed 10,960 such workers, but by 1956 that number had declined to 4,945. As they had three years earlier, workers struck over economic grievances, but this time, heightened Arab nationalism intensified the political overtones of the strike. Even more quickly than it had in 1953, the Saudi government broke up demonstrations, arrested leaders, and forced the strikers back to work. King Saʿūd issued a decree that forbade any worker from leaving his job as part of a conspiracy with other workers, threatened to imprison anyone instigating a demonstration or strike, and gave provincial governors special powers to deport any person suspected of subversion.[30]

Arab nationalism also threatened the Saudi regime from outside the kingdom. No less than Britain and the U.S., the Saudi government had reasons to fear the closure of the Suez Canal and the sabotage of Tapline. Cut off from its markets, Saudi Arabia would have to reduce production, which would mean less revenue for paying tribal subsidies and for the generous stipends that kept the peace within the royal family. As an NSC report explained, Saudi oil profits were devoted largely to such "uneconomic purposes" as "transfer payments to tribal groups as a price for loyalty" and "purchasing consumer goods by the royal family and its retinue." Unlike Iraq, which had invested royalties in development and therefore enjoyed a diversified economy, Saudi Arabia faced "complete economic collapse" if deprived of its oil revenue. Just as the Saudi state was the product of integration into the postwar petroleum order, disruption of those arrangements threatened the state's viability.[31]

The ambivalence toward Arab nationalism that had always characterized Saudi foreign policy now intensified, with King Saʿūd seeking to align with the West and Crown Prince Fayṣal sympathetic toward Nāṣirist goals. Saʿūd expressed his willingness to meet with Iraqi King Fayṣal in the Hijaz during the pilgrimage season or in the Gulf and to renew the Dhahran lease in exchange for U.S. support of his five-year plan. Conversely, in early June Prince Fayṣal demanded $250 million worth of American arms in exchange for renewing the lease, a proposal he must have known the U.S. would reject. At the same time, the Saudi foreign minister issued an ultimatum to Britain demanding the withdrawal of troops from Buraymī and neutral supervision over the oasis, conditions that were as unrealistic as his terms over Dhahran.

As domestic unrest and growing regional tensions threatened the stability of Saudi Arabia in the summer of 1956, divisions between Saʿūd and Fayṣal over how to address the danger spread to include junior princes and other members of the ruling family. A Lebanese newspaper reported that in July, seven younger princes presented Saʿūd with a petition critical of his policies. At the same time, the king sought to undermine the power-sharing compromise he had worked out earlier with his family members. Saʿūd appointed his son, Musāʿid, as head of the Royal Guard in an attempt to build the Guard into an institution that would both rival the kingdom's regular defense forces and provide exclusive loyalty to the king. Indeed, Saʿūd desired American military aid as part of this effort. Eisenhower's policies of absorbing Saudi revenues through weapons sales and cultivating the king as an alternative to Nāṣir unwittingly insinuated Washington into Saudi Arabia's ruling-family politics.[32]

Against the background of political instability in the Saudi kingdom and rising nationalist sentiment across the Arab world, Gamāl ʿAbd al-Nāṣir nationalized the Suez Canal Company. This discussion of Suez does not attempt to recount the details of a story that has been told many times elsewhere.[33] Rather, the objective here is to explain how the crisis affected relations among the U.S., Saudi Arabia, and Britain, the ways in which the Eisenhower administration struggled to preserve the postwar petroleum order, and the role that Washington assigned to Saudi Arabia during and after the crisis. Although Suez has been portrayed as a watershed in the Middle East, continuity characterized American, British, and Saudi foreign policies in the second half of 1956. For both the U.S. and Britain, Nāṣir's action made a split in the Saudi-Egyptian relationship more desirable, and officials in Washington and London regarded the seizure of the canal as an opportunity to drive a wedge between Saʿūd and Nāṣir. Eisenhower pursued his campaign to build up Saʿūd by attempting to negotiate a diplomatic solution to the Suez crisis through the king, while the British believed that nationalization of the canal, which connected Saudi oil fields to European markets, would finally open Saʿūd's eyes to the dangers of Nāṣirism. But the allies overestimated the degree to which Saʿūd was able or willing to distance himself from Nāṣir, whose prestige in the Arab world soared as a result of the Suez crisis. Contrary to Eisenhower's hopes, Arab politics during and after Suez were not conducive to a pro-Western coalition led by the Saudi king.

ʿAbd al-Nāṣir's momentous speech of July 26 lent urgency to Eisenhower's policy of building up King Saʿūd's stature as keeper of the Islamic holy places. The Egyptian president inspired revolutionary nationalist sentiment in many oil-producing and neutralist countries, which, officials immediately observed, were predominantly Muslim. "Nasser intends to make full use of the resources of the Arab world," wrote Dulles's special assistant Francis Russell, citing Nāṣir's *Philosophy of the Revolution,* "notably the Suez Canal and the oil . . . and the support of Muslims in Indonesia, China, Malaya, Siam, Burma and elsewhere, 'to wield a power without limit'." When Allen Dulles warned Eisenhower that military action against Nāṣir "would arouse the whole Arab world," the president interjected, "the whole Muslim world." The Joint Chiefs were similarly anxious about Nāṣir's growing influence among oil-producing states, "all Moslem countries and in neutralist and under-developed countries throughout the world."[34]

Consequently, the administration's Suez diplomacy included steps intended to strengthen U.S.-Saudi relations. Dulles suggested inviting Saudi Arabia to the London Conference on the canal, a proposal vetoed by Britain, and Washington redoubled efforts to negotiate renewal of the Dhahran lease. On July 31, Wadsworth held a two-and-a-half-hour conversation with Yāsīn, who insisted that $35 million worth of arms previously requested be shipped to Saudi Arabia in advance of payment. While the U.S. rejected this demand, the administration agreed at the end of August to build the $5 million air terminal earlier proposed by Wadsworth. Finally, on August 6, the American IREX Corporation signed a contract with Saudi Arabia, Jordan, and Syria to study the reconstruction of the Hijaz railroad, and the administration agreed to pick up the tab for the $500,000 project.[35]

Despite recent revelations of an administration "denial plan" to have Aramco sabotage its own installations if the Soviets invaded the Gulf, Arab nationalist revolution remained the more immediate danger that preoccupied national security planners. In the summer of 1956, U.S. officials took steps to ensure the security of the Saudi regime and Aramco oil assets against upheaval within the kingdom in the event of armed conflict over the canal. Treasury Secretary George Humphrey repeated to Dulles the remarks of a U.S. oil executive, who predicted that "Saudi Arabia could slide downhill fast if Nasser gained prestige." Similarly concerned about the Saudis, whose government he described as "feeble," Dulles agreed that "Nasser could take them over." Military leaders developed a contingency plan for deploying U.S. forces to Dhahran in the event of internal civilian revolt. The plan, involving 3,600 troops, was designed to protect Aramco oil fields and personnel from "local mob action and attempts at sabotage." Saʿūd's acquiescence in any American intervention was expected given the king's desire to maintain his income, and military intelligence concluded that the U.S. could count on Saʿūd's "effective banning of strikes and demonstrations." By focusing on the theoretical Soviet threat in the Gulf during the 1950s, analysis of the "denial plan" reinforces official claims that American policy was based on defending the region from communist aggression. But the strikes of 1953 and 1956 showed that the Arab nationalist threat to Aramco oil installations was far from hypothetical. The fact that U.S. military planners prepared to mobilize troops against nationalist agitation belies the administration's anti-colonial declarations and reveals that despite the split over Suez, the U.S. and Britain jointly opposed any indigenous political movements that might compromise Western control of Arab oil.[36]

In addition, Eisenhower sought Saʿūd's intercession with Nāṣir to broker a compromise over the canal. The president asked Robert Anderson to reprise his role as special envoy to the Middle East by traveling to Saudi Arabia in late August. According to CIA agent Wilbur Eveland, who accompanied Anderson, the idea came from Howard Page of Jersey Standard, but it was the administration that proposed Anderson's mission as an alternative to inviting a Saudi envoy to the White House, as Saʿūd had requested. Receiving a high-level Saudi delegation might have alienated the British and wrecked Dulles's efforts in London to find a solution to the crisis through international diplomacy. The approaching election also made a Saudi mission to the U.S. politically undesirable. For these reasons, Anderson undertook a secret mission first to meet Dulles in London, and then to the Saudi kingdom to open an Arab channel to Nāṣir.[37]

In conversations with Anderson, the king defended Nāṣir's action, revealing that American expectations of a break between Saʿūd and Nāṣir were unrealistic. Eveland blames Anderson's failure on a clumsy attempt to bluff the Saudi leadership into believing Europe would switch to nuclear power if the seizure of its oil lifeline went unchallenged. But Saʿūd appeared more concerned about the regional implications of a British attack on Egypt. Like American military planners, Saʿūd feared for the security of his own government in the event of such an attack, and he was also skeptical that Nāṣir would accept any form of international control over the canal. On this issue, Saʿūd was influenced by those around him less interested in cooperating with the U.S., including Prince Fayṣal, Yūsuf Yāsīn, and Royal Counselor Jamāl al-Ḥusaynī. Fayṣal argued that any international administration of the canal would constitute "intervention in the affairs of Egypt." Though Yāsīn subsequently prevailed on Nāṣir to meet the five-power delegation from the London Conference led by Australian prime minister Robert Menzies, no compromise resulted from Anderson's mission. The Eisenhower administration had assumed a divergence of interests between Saʿūd and Nāṣir and had ignored how domestic and Arab politics made it impossible for the king to pursue a more independent policy. As Anderson concluded after meeting with Saʿūd, the king refused to acknowledge "that his interests are diverse from Nasser's."[38]

While British officials similarly believed they could exploit clashing Egyptian-Saudi interests, they did not share Eisenhower's faith in Saʿūd as a mediator of the crisis. The Anderson mission did not remain secret. Australian prime minister Menzies accused Loy Henderson, the U.S. delegate to the London Conference, of "playing a separate game," and former journalist Harry Kern, who routinely apprised the Foreign Office of developments in U.S.-Saudi relations, personally told Selwyn Lloyd in September about Anderson's behind-the-scenes diplomacy. For his part, Eden was planning military action against Egypt and sought to ensure that when the attack came, Nāṣir would have as few Arab friends as possible. With this goal in mind, the British government renewed efforts to solve the Buraymī crisis and attempted to broker a rapprochement between the Saudis and Hashemite Iraq.[39]

On the eve of the Israeli invasion of Egypt, the British proposed a compromise over Buraymī and deliberately raised Saudi expectations for a settlement. Lloyd told the cabinet on July 26 that "the time had come to try to bring these negotiations to a head." Despite the British desire for compromise, however, the parties had remained frozen in their positions since Fayṣal's ultimatum demanding British withdrawal. British ambassador Parkes presented Fayṣal with new terms on July 29, offering to repatriate refugees chased out of the oasis during the British reoccupation and to assign Buraymī a higher priority on the agenda for new, comprehensive Anglo-Saudi talks. Although these concessions did not elicit substantive agreement, the British still hoped that they would improve the atmosphere in Anglo-Saudi relations and help to draw Saʿūd away from Nāṣir. "Today the attraction of a ride on the Egyptian band-wagon has largely passed" for Saʿūd, Parkes wrote Lloyd, and the king "would now gladly ease himself out of his link with Egypt."[40]

Through the autumn of 1956, Buraymī became linked to Suez in British foreign policy. As one Foreign Office official explained, "as long as the issue is in doubt, we believe that Saud will continue with the present negotiations and, should we eliminate Nasser, Saud might then thankfully put Buraimi into cold storage." As the Suez Canal Users' Association conference convened in London and as the British introduced the Suez issue at the U.N., Eden's government conducted a parallel diplomatic campaign to ease tensions over Buraymī. The Foreign Office warned the embassy in Jidda on October 22 that Lloyd does not "wish to do anything at present which might revive King Saud's hostility to us over Buraimi." On October 28, four days after Britain, Israel, and France finalized their plans at Sèvres to launch an attack against Egypt, and the day before the war began, Saʿūd agreed with Ambassador Parkes that the peaceful handling of Suez boded well for a Buraymī settlement. The king proposed new talks or reference of the dispute to the U.N., and Fayṣal asked for a British reply by November 10 so that Buraymī could be inscribed in the U.N. agenda for the current session.[41]

British policy makers were especially pleased with the apparent reconciliation between the Saudi and Iraqi ruling houses following King Saʿūd's meeting at the port of Dammam with Iraqi King Fayṣal. Despite their dynastic rivalry, Eden believed that as oil producers Riyadh and Baghdad shared a common opposition to Nāṣir's seizure of the canal. "There are some who doubt whether Saudi Arabia, Iraq and Kuwait," Eden wrote Eisenhower, "will be prepared even for a time to sacrifice their oil revenues for the sake of Nasser's ambitions." The British were optimistic that a Saudi-Iraqi rapprochement would end Saʿūd's subversion against British interests and foster Saudi acceptance of the Baghdad Pact. "King Saud's attitude towards Iraq and the Western Powers," exclaimed one Foreign Office official, "is developing even faster and more satisfactorily than could have been hoped."[42]

Fear of internal upheaval and pressure from within his own court, however, prevented King Saʿūd from playing the roles assigned him by both Washington and London. Days after meeting the Iraqi king, Saʿūd hastily invited Nāṣir and Quwwatlī to the kingdom for an Arab summit, a step British observers assumed Saʿūd took to appease Prince Fayṣal and Yāsīn. The king received a dramatic reminder of the popularity Nāṣir enjoyed in Saudi Arabia when thousands turned out to meet the three Arab leaders in Dammam. The crowds had obviously assembled to cheer the Egyptian president rather than their own sovereign, and as Nāṣir's motorcade made its way through the port city, a disturbance erupted that was only subdued by Saʿūd's baton-wielding *khuwiyya* bodyguards. Official accounts tried to put the best face on what can most accurately be described as a riot, explaining that the crowds were "rejoicing" in the spirit of Arabism. Despite the suppression of the June strike, labor agitation also remained a major concern. During an October visit to Beijing, the Saudi Workers' Committee, whose members now operated in exile and carried passports from other Arab states, attended an international labor conference sponsored by the communist Chinese government. Prince Musāʿid ibn ʿAbd al-Raḥmān, who headed the committee that investigated recent unrest in the Eastern Province, acknowledged the regime's concern over the labor movement in exile when he warned that any union within the kingdom would "inevitably be subject to control by outsiders."[43]

In the midst of the crisis, Saʿūd attempted to carve out his own role as a senior Arab diplomat by seeking a fair solution to the Suez issue without siding openly with the Western powers. The Saudi press regularly reprinted news stories from other Arab countries praising Saʿūd's statesmanship, and the king boasted to Eisenhower that it was only through his own good offices that Nāṣir was persuaded to receive the Menzies mission. The king told Ambassador Wadsworth that Nāṣir and Quwwatlī "came at my call" to Saudi Arabia to discuss the Suez crisis. In letters to the president in September and October, Saʿūd pledged to work for a "peaceful solution by means of negotiations aimed at guaranteeing freedom of passage through the Canal," though the king remained critical of the Suez Canal Users' Association, which he deemed incompatible with Egyptian sovereignty.[44]

Despite efforts to prevent it, war erupted on October 29 when Israel invaded the Sinai and drove toward the Suez Canal. As the parties had agreed at Sèvres, after delivering an ultimatum to Egypt and Israel the next day to clear the canal zone, Britain began bombing Egypt on October 31. Nāṣir responded by blocking the Suez Canal, and the Anglo-French invasion of Egypt followed on November 5. The Suez war disrupted the postwar petroleum order in tangible ways by obstructing the canal and prompting the sabotage of the Iraq Petroleum Company pipeline in Syria. Worse, it threatened to inflict irreparable damage to the relationships that constituted the postwar petroleum order. Saʿūd's position, already balanced precariously between Arab nationalism and cooperation with the West, threatened to become untenable. For the Western allies, the interruption in the flow of Mideast oil jeopardized the postwar system of multilateral relations characterized by more open economies, struck at one of the keys to Western European recovery, and removed the means by which Washington reconciled American responsibility for European defense with domestic prosperity. Furthermore, the conflict undermined U.S. attempts to forge a new relationship with oil-producing states based upon corporate investment and profit-sharing, and to overcome the legacy of colonialism.

These events confronted Saʿūd with a difficult choice. On the one hand, intense political pressures from the Arab world and within the king's own government demanded that he withhold oil from the European imperial powers waging war against an Arab state. On the other, such steps, coupled with the effects of the canal blockage, would reduce the government's revenue by about one third and threaten to cause a financial and political crisis. Out of political necessity, Saʿūd banned oil exports to Britain and France and staged a general mobilization of Saudi forces to demonstrate his solidarity with Nāṣir. The king continued in his role as senior Arab statesman, which *Al-Bilād al-Saʿūdiyya* documented by publishing his correspondence with other Arab leaders. Saʿūd also wrote Eisenhower on November 5 and 11, denouncing the tripartite attack as "aggression against all the Arabs and not against Egypt alone." By opting for such a policy, Saʿūd believed he could rely on Aramco to sustain his government through a budgetary shortfall as it had done so many times in the past. In an apparent vindication of the king's assumption, Aramco not only cushioned the economic impact of the Suez war on Saudi Arabia, but also cut off oil shipments to Britain, France, and the refinery at Bahrain as instructed by the king and fulfilled his request to provide Egypt with 150,000 tons of emergency oil.[45]

As Diane B. Kunz has shown, Eden's government gravely overestimated American willingness to offer economic support to Britain during the military operations, but British officials also erred when they assumed that Saudi oil would continue flowing. Projections first developed by the Ministry of Fuels and Power in joint studies with the U.S., and later incorporated into war plans by the cabinet's Egypt Committee, discounted the possibility of a Saudi embargo. "Assuming that supplies from the Persian Gulf and Saudi Arabia remained open," concluded the Egypt Committee on August 29, "and that the Americans will cooperate to the full and can provide a substantial increase in supplies from the Western Hemisphere . . . the limit on the supply of oil available here and in Europe would be set by the supply of tankers." Officials later conceded that this had been an important oversight. According to a report issued on November 15 by the Ministry of Fuels and Power, political restrictions imposed by Arab governments on their oil exports "were not foreseen in the joint planning studies." The restrictions were one reason that the oil shortfall in Europe following the attack on Egypt was forty million tons greater than planners had anticipated. This miscalculation reflected the British assumption that London had successfully broken the Saudi-Egyptian alliance.[46]

For the Americans, the Suez crisis posed a new and extreme version of the problem faced in Mideast oil diplomacy since 1945: how to preserve access to the petroleum resources necessary for Europe while avoiding association with the colonial powers. As it had during the Anglo-American oil talks in 1953, the Eisenhower administration sought to avoid open collaboration with Britain and relied on private interests as part of a strategy to manage Arab nationalism. Faced with disruption of the waterway through which two-thirds of Europe's oil passed, the administration organized the Middle East Emergency Committee (MEEC), a group of private oil companies, to coordinate an oil lift. Granted broad antitrust immunity, the MEEC was supervised by Eisenhower's director of the Office of Defense Mobilization, Arthur S. Flemming. Though the British had been consulted at the inception of the MEEC's plan of action beginning in August, one U.S. official wrote on October 30 that the war altered "many of the political and economic assumptions which were predominant at the time the Plan of Action was fashioned." Herbert Hoover Jr. instructed Flemming that the plan's readiness should be kept secret, and the administration refrained from activating it, which would have amounted to an economic mobilization in support of Anglo-French operations. Circumstances demanded, however, that the postwar petroleum order be restored. On November 7, the British government announced a mandatory 10 percent cut in the domestic consumption of petroleum products, and by mid-November, British hard currency reserves had fallen to the dangerously low level of just over $2 billion. Eisenhower sought a way to implement the MEEC plan without "getting the United States in a position, in the eyes of the Arab world, of bailing out the British and the French."[47]

The president looked to King Saʿūd to help prevent the implementation of the MEEC plan from alienating Nāṣir's Arab and Muslim supporters. "US relations with Saudi Arabia were very good," the president explained to congressional leaders, and the "US wanted to maintain these good relations, recognizing that we would have to be the ones to accomplish any restoration of western influence in the area." During meetings on November 19, 20, and 21, Eisenhower told officials that restoration of Europe's oil should be coordinated with Saʿūd, whom the U.S. should build up as "a great spiritual leader and keeper of the holy places." "We must face the question," Eisenhower declared, "what *must* we do in Europe and then the question, how do we square this with the Arabs?" He concluded that Saʿūd's acquiescence must be obtained, possibly through a Buraymī settlement favorable to Saudi Arabia, as an "ace in the hole."[48]

Though previously portrayed one-dimensionally as an advocate for U.S. oil companies and as an anti-British voice within the administration, Herbert Hoover Jr. played a leading role in Eisenhower's plan for restoring the postwar petroleum order. Historians have accepted the contemporary views of British officials such as Shuckburgh, who deeply distrusted Hoover. They have also suggested that Hoover's assumption of leadership at the State Department in place of an ill Dulles just as the Suez crisis descended into war led to a harsher U.S. reaction against London than would otherwise have been the case. Hoover's influence, they note, led Eisenhower to defer a meeting with Eden and French premier Guy Mollet until after Anglo-French military withdrawal.[49]

Such accounts, however, neglect that Hoover was committed to restoring Europe's oil supplies without jeopardizing the close U.S.-Saudi relationship, which Eisenhower had pursued since March and which was the basis for the president's efforts to preserve Western influence among Arab and Muslim countries. Eisenhower had asked Hoover in early October to maintain contacts with Saudi Arabia and other oil producers, and following the ceasefire, Hoover instructed Ambassador Wadworth to prepare Saʿūd for the implementation of the MEEC plan. Hoover told Wadsworth on November 18 that the growing economic crisis "necessitates implementation without delay" of the plan, but that Saʿūd's opposition could wreck U.S. efforts to resupply Europe. On November 23, Hoover explained to Eisenhower that the "oil situation is becoming very critical" and argued that "we should tell King Saud as the British take certain actions we feel that we should take certain measures of support." At Eisenhower's request, Hoover even began planning another Anderson mission to the Saudi kingdom to ensure King Saʿūd's cooperation. "We attach utmost importance," Hoover cabled Wadsworth, "to his understanding our policies and motivations."[50]

The administration successfully coordinated implementation of the MEEC plan with its Saudi diplomacy. Saʿūd pledged his cooperation to Wadsworth on November 23, provided Anglo-French withdrawal preceded the oil lift to Europe, a promise the king repeated to Aramco officials. Selwyn Lloyd announced the evacuation of British troops on December 3, the day Flemming had scheduled to reconvene the MEEC in New York, and on December 7, the oil companies began transferring western hemisphere oil to Europe.[51] The MEEC plan reconstituted the postwar petroleum order following the most serious challenge that set of relationships had yet weathered, and Eisenhower and other officials hoped that the way in which they had restored Europe's oil could prevent an Arab nationalist backlash and economic catastrophe.

From the reoccupation of Buraymī through the Suez crisis, the U.S. and Britain attempted to preserve the postwar petroleum order in sharply different ways. While the Eisenhower administration relied on private diplomacy to pacify oil-producing governments, Great Britain reinforced its colonial relationships in the Gulf and resorted to collusion and war to defend its economic interests. During the Suez crisis, these divergent approaches threatened to break the Anglo-American partnership, but Eisenhower's aggressive actions to restore Europe's oil supplies revealed his priorities in the Middle East and reflected the allies' common stake in the postwar petroleum order.

For the Saudis, Suez was both an international and a domestic crisis that accentuated the weaknesses of the Saudi state, and Saʿūd's economic and political vulnerabilities prevented the king from acting as a pro-Western, pan-Islamic leader, as Eisenhower wished. Nevertheless, the president emerged from the Suez crisis believing that Saʿūd could play precisely this role, and administration officials shaped post-Suez diplomacy partly on the basis of this assumption. The weakening of British influence in the Middle East also presented Eisenhower with an unprecedented opportunity to reshape the terms of the postwar petroleum order. What remained to be determined, however, was whether the American approach would look beyond corporate remuneration of producing governments and the arming of friendly regimes, and attempt to use the resources of the Gulf for the economic development of Middle Eastern societies.

1. Eisenhower listens to King Saʿūd's statement upon arriving for the first U.S.-Saudi summit in Washington, D.C., January 30, 1957. Courtesy Dwight D. Eisenhower Library and National Park Service.

2. King Saʿūd reviews troops at National Airport.
Courtesy Dwight D. Eisenhower Library and National Park Service.

3. Washington, D.C., welcomes the king.
Courtesy Dwight D. Eisenhower Library and National Park Service.

4. Saʿūd with entourage and Eisenhower at the White House prior to their summit.
Courtesy Dwight D. Eisenhower Library and National Park Service.

5. Eisenhower and the Custodian of the Two Holy Cities, Saʿūd ibn ʿAbd al-ʿAzīz, meet in the Oval Office. Courtesy Dwight D. Eisenhower Library and National Park Service.

6. Remaking the postwar petroleum order after Suez: Lloyd, Eisenhower, Macmillan, and Dulles at Bermuda, March 1957.
Courtesy Dwight D. Eisenhower Library and U.S. Naval Photographic Center.

7. Eisenhower dedicates the Islamic Center, June 28, 1957. Courtesy Dwight D. Eisenhower Library and National Park Service.

8. Eisenhower and Dulles meet with Saudi foreign minister Crown Prince Fayṣal, September 23, 1957. Fayṣal's absence from Saudi Arabia marked a short-lived political victory for King Saʿūd. Courtesy Dwight D. Eisenhower Library and National Park Service.

5

We Have Here an Opportunity: The Eisenhower Doctrine, January 1957–July 1958

FOLLOWING THE SINAI WAR, the Eisenhower administration sought to reduce the chance that the Soviet Union could exploit the crisis, and the administration struggled to prevent any further disruption of the postwar petroleum order. President Eisenhower also attempted to balance the restoration of the Anglo-American partnership in the Middle East with an accommodation of Arab nationalism, and he believed that as both an Arab leader who had played an important role in Suez diplomacy and as custodian of the Muslim holy places, King Saʿūd could be instrumental in reconciling these two objectives. Prior to opening talks with Britain on coordinating allied policy in the Middle East and the defense of the Gulf, Eisenhower hosted King Saʿūd at the White House, agreed to provide military and economic aid to Saudi Arabia, and undertook additional initiatives to curry favor with other Arab and Muslim states.

The centerpiece of the American policy was the Eisenhower Doctrine, a declaration by the president, supported by a congressional resolution, that promised assistance to any Middle Eastern country resisting communist aggression. Although the British continued to seek U.S. membership in the Baghdad Pact, the Eisenhower Doctrine offered aid on a bilateral basis to friendly Middle Eastern countries as an alternative to full U.S. participation in the Pact, which Eisenhower and Secretary Dulles had been reluctant to join even prior to the Suez crisis. Most significantly, Eisenhower and his advisors conceived their policy in broad terms that encompassed economic aid and directed oil revenues to raising living standards as a way of reducing the appeal of communism. Such a policy transcended the organizational constraints imposed upon American diplomacy by the U.S. political economy. Suez prompted Eisenhower to rethink the entrenched pattern of relationships that limited official U.S. involvement in the Middle East to military aid and diplomatic support for corporate investment, which officials had consistently regarded as the basis for smooth relations with oil-producing and oil-transit countries. The Eisenhower Doctrine represented the best opportunity since the beginning of the administration for restructuring American diplomacy toward the Middle East. Suez presented Eisenhower with a chance to rebuild the region's oil economy so that it benefited non-producing Arab states as well as Western corporations and consumers.

In its implementation, however, Eisenhower's policy devoted American resources mainly to supporting anti-communist regimes well-disposed toward the postwar petroleum order. The U.S. Congress was hesitant to fund economic development programs, and soon after the passage of the Eisenhower Doctrine resolution, the administration became preoccupied with crises first in Jordan and then in Syria, where the U.S. stood accused of trying to overthrow the regime. President Eisenhower appealed to King Saʿūd to lead an Arab campaign to install a pro-Western government in Damascus, but Saʿūd's response led officials to the realization that the king could not fulfill the role they had envisioned for him. By the end of 1957, these setbacks caused the administration to reconsider its policy of isolating Egyptian president ʿAbd al-Nāṣir and to entertain new proposals for funding development in the Middle East. But despite rhetoric favoring Arab self-determination and economic development, the U.S. and Britain dispatched troops to the Middle East in July 1958 to defend the postwar petroleum order.

Meanwhile, King Saʿūd faced serious challenges to his authority in Saudi Arabia, where he campaigned to marginalize his half-brother, Prince Fayṣal, and other royal family members. These efforts were the domestic counterpart of his attempts to make himself into a major Arab figure. After Saʿūd maneuvered to place his own sons in important positions in the defense establishment, Fayṣal registered his disapproval by taking an extended absence from the kingdom beginning in June 1957. Within a short time, however, Saudi Arabia faced an economic emergency caused by continued royal family extravagance and the shortfall in oil revenue created by the Suez crisis. By withholding royalty advances, Aramco deviated from the policy that had sustained the Saudi state since the time of ʿAbd al-ʿAzīz and triggered a bitter dispute within the ruling family over the kingdom's budget. As part of this conflict, Fayṣal and the younger princes forged an alliance against Saʿūd, whose alleged complicity in a plot against ʿAbd al-Nāṣir permitted Fayṣal to assume control of the government.

The crescendo of Arab nationalism and decline of British prestige in the Middle East confronted Eisenhower with a fateful choice. American hopes that the oil corporations themselves could palliate Arab nationalism met with disappointment during the Suez crisis. The U.S. would either have to adjust its policies to the reality of Arab nationalism and get behind development plans proposed by Arabs and non-Arabs for sharing the region's oil wealth, or assume the British mantle as enforcer of the postwar petroleum order. Eisenhower opted for the second alternative, and this decision proved much more important for defining the future U.S. role in the Middle East than his earlier one to halt the aggressors at Suez.

In the aftermath of the Suez crisis, the Eisenhower administration began work on short- and long-term plans to stabilize the Middle East while simultaneously conducting a wide-ranging review of U.S. aid policy toward the developing world. Burton I. Kaufman has shown that by early 1957, the administration had resolved "to reconsider old programs and devise new approaches to foreign economic development," which led to, among other programs, the Development Loan Fund. Soviet political initiatives in developing countries elicited an American response that involved a greater relative emphasis on governmental assistance and the availability of soft loans to complement private investment. In November 1956, Herbert Hoover Jr., who had orchestrated Eisenhower's oil diplomacy during the Suez crisis, informed the president of State Department policy proposals for the Middle East. These measures included securing a prompt withdrawal of British, French, and Israeli troops from Egypt and the rapid opening of the Suez Canal to tanker traffic. But Hoover also recommended the creation of a "regional economic organization among the Arab states" and proposed that oil producers fund development in non-petroleum-producing countries such as Syria and Jordan. "Strong emphasis is placed on economic and social progress," Hoover explained, "as paths to area stability and achievement of the legitimate aspirations of the peoples of the area."[1]

Although economic development had become a priority for Washington, the administration remained divided over the immediate question of political strategy in the Middle East. The Joint Chiefs insisted more forcefully than ever that the U.S. join the Baghdad Pact, but John Foster Dulles opposed adherence and characterized the Pact as "largely an instrument of U.K.-Arab politics." Re-establishing Anglo-American cooperation and securing the British position in the Gulf were crucial to the restoration of the postwar petroleum order after the Suez debacle, but open association with British colonialism undermined U.S. efforts to align American policy with the forces of progress in the Middle East. Consequently, the State Department proposed recruiting friendly governments, including Baghdad Pact members, for an independent organization, which Dulles suggested the U.S. could sponsor through a program "analogous to that of the Marshall Plan."[2]

Part of the reason for the administration's reluctance to join the Baghdad Pact was concern about antagonizing King Saʿūd, whom Eisenhower continued to regard as the basis for isolating ʿAbd al-Nāṣir and maintaining friendly relations with Arab and Muslim states. In fact, the State Department studied the possibility of Saudi leadership of a new Middle East charter organization, concluding on December 5 that "Saudi Arabia's attitude may well be the key factor in determining whether a new grouping can be established." Meanwhile, however, King Saʿūd had accepted an invitation for a summit meeting with Eisenhower to discuss the settlement of Suez issues and to negotiate renewal of the Dhahran base agreement in exchange for U.S. military and economic aid. Dulles favored postponing consideration of a Saudi-led organization until these issues were "buttoned up." On December 8, he put three alternatives before Eisenhower: adherence to the Baghdad Pact, sponsorship of a new organization, and a congressional resolution authorizing presidential action to oppose communism in the Middle East by offering assistance on a bilateral basis. The president selected the third option, while making clear his desire for a "package deal" that encompassed economic and social considerations.[3]

Conferring with British foreign secretary Selwyn Lloyd in Paris, Dulles expressed a desire for an Anglo-American rapprochement. He identified the three options under consideration by Washington without divulging Eisenhower's choice, but he did communicate both the administration's reluctance to join the Baghdad Pact and its intention to rely upon King Saʿūd to undermine Nāṣir. Eisenhower had cabled Dulles in Paris: "I continue to believe, as I think you do, that one of the measures that we must take is to build up an Arab rival of Nasser, and the natural choice would seem to be the man you and I have often talked about." Dulles echoed these sentiments when he told Lloyd that "Saudi Arabia in time could be built up as the best counter to Nasser" and that the success of the U.S.-led strategy to restore order to the Middle East depended partly upon an Anglo-Saudi compromise over Buraymī.[4]

Within six weeks of the cease-fire, the shape of post-Suez American diplomacy in the Middle East had materialized. Like U.S. foreign policy toward the Third World generally, it would emphasize economic development to counter Soviet initiatives, and in the Middle East this meant encouraging petroleum producers to devote oil revenues to raising living standards. Although the U.S. would refrain from joining the Baghdad Pact and would independently pursue bilateral relations with friendly states, Anglo-American cooperation remained the foundation of the postwar petroleum order. Significantly, the administration would place Saudi Arabia at the center of its diplomacy out of the belief that King Saʿūd could bind Arab and Muslim peoples to the West by virtue of his custodianship of the holy cities. At stake was the viability of the postwar petroleum order and the global economic system fashioned by the U.S. after 1945. Dulles remarked that "if we do not act, the Soviets are likely to take over the area, and they could thereby control Europe through the oil on which Europe is dependent." Eisenhower felt, however, that the new policy based upon bilateral ties of aid and his close cooperation with Saʿūd could address these challenges. "It seems to me," the president wrote Dulles, "we have here an opportunity."[5]

In a January 5 address to a joint session of Congress, President Eisenhower described the consequences for the West if it were denied inexpensive Middle Eastern oil, and he unveiled his plan for keeping the states of the region in the Western camp. America's European allies would be "subject to near strangulation" without Mideast oil. "Western Europe would be endangered just as though there had been no Marshall Plan, no North Atlantic Treaty Organization," the president warned. He therefore requested a resolution authorizing the administration to assist Middle Eastern countries economically, to provide them with military aid, and to use force if called upon to defend them from communist domination. Eisenhower stressed the need "economically to strengthen these countries," which he argued would "provide the greatest insurance against Communist inroads." Although he proposed no new appropriations for fiscal year 1957, he indicated his intention to seek $200 million in aid to Middle Eastern governments in each of the subsequent two budget cycles.[6]

Eisenhower's proposal met with a less-than-enthusiastic reception on Capitol Hill, where lawmakers resisted furnishing economic aid to a region rich in oil and took particular umbrage at funding development in the oil-producing states. Defending the administration's proposal before the Senate Foreign Relations Committee, Secretary Dulles explained that Middle Eastern countries' "most immediate and pressing concern is economic" and that the U.S. would have to offer economic aid to dispel Arab suspicions of Western imperialism and the view "that we think too exclusively in purely military terms." But Senator Hubert Humphrey spoke for the committee when he invoked Saudi Arabia as the embodiment of why states in the region were undeserving of American aid:

> I am not against economic assistance. But I want to know how much King Saud is going to get. I want to know how much these oil-rich countries are going to get. I think the American taxpayer has a right to know how much these countries that have fabulous resources of oil are going to get out of the American treasury.

Wayne Morse tacked on a rhetorical question: "Do you think that the aid and the military support that the resolution contemplates with Saudi Arabia is going to make Saudi Arabia more democratic?" Although the anti-communist thrust of the Eisenhower Doctrine received considerable support, congressional reluctance to fund economic programs meant that in order to pursue its foreign policy in the Middle East, the administration would have to supplement limited American aid with resources from international lending institutions such as the World Bank and from the oil-producing states themselves.[7]

This set of circumstances on the eve of the Saʿūd-Eisenhower summit ran directly counter to the expectations of the Saudi king, who sought substantial military and economic assistance from the U.S. as part of his attempt to achieve political supremacy at his brothers' expense and to address his country's escalating debt. In December, Saʿūd followed up the appointment of his son Musāʿid as head of the Royal Guard by naming his eldest son Fahd defense minister, and he planned to devote U.S. military aid to building up the Royal Guard forces in order to solidify his hold on the kingdom's defense establishment. At the same time, Saʿūd's government faced a debt of more than $200 million—closer to $300 million according to Aramco sources—that stemmed from the Suez crisis, Saʿūd's ambitious building campaign in Riyadh, and, above all, royal family expenses. Efforts early in Saʿūd's reign had failed to limit to $32,000 per male the yearly allowance paid to more than three hundred princes, and by 1957 these expenses reportedly constituted 40 to 60 percent of state expenditures. This spiraling debt was not simply the product of immoderate spending, but was driven as well by the organization of the Saudi state, which ceded the ruling family unrestrained access to oil royalties and made it the exclusive domain for political competition and patronage.[8]

A fracas surrounding Saʿūd's January 29 arrival in New York produced some awkward moments at the start of the summit, but ongoing disagreement over the shape of a post-Suez settlement and the amount of American aid to Saudi Arabia represented more substantive impediments to U.S.-Saudi cooperation. New York mayor Robert Wagner, protesting Saudi Arabia's discrimination against Jews and Catholics, created what the *New York Times* called a "minor international incident" by refusing to welcome Saʿūd prior to the king's appearance at the United Nations. But public sympathy for Saʿūd's young son, Mashhūr, who received treatment for a birth defect at Walter Reed Army Hospital, helped to improve the atmosphere somewhat once the royal party arrived in Washington on January 30. Saʿūd, accompanied by the new Defense Minister Prince Fahd, Deputy Foreign Minister Yūsuf Yāsīn, and other members of his circle, stayed in Washington during initial meetings with Eisenhower. King Saʿūd visited the Islamic Center and the Pentagon, and was Eisenhower's guest at a state dinner, which out of respect for the king's religion was a teetotaling affair. Officials completed negotiations surrounding U.S.-Saudi agreements on aid and other matters while Saʿūd retired to White Sulphur Springs, West Virginia, and the summit concluded with a final meeting at the White House between Saʿūd and the president on February 8.[9]

As he had during the Suez crisis, Saʿūd struck a careful balance between cooperation with the U.S. and his ambition to act as spokesman for the Arab states. The king arrived in Washington having just attended an Arab summit in Cairo, and he delivered to Eisenhower a communiqué that demanded the withdrawal of Israeli forces from the Sinai and Gaza. While expressing hope that the Eisenhower Doctrine "would greatly benefit the countries of the Middle East," Saʿūd also denied that Egypt or Syria was under Soviet control, and he lobbied against any recognition of Israel's right to remain in Gaza and the Gulf of Aqaba. This latter concern was particularly immediate to the Saudis, because the king's meeting with Eisenhower coincided with the introduction of an American resolution at the United Nations calling for an international force in Gaza and Sharm al-Shaykh. The king regarded the resolution as a concession to Israeli demands for security guarantees prior to evacuating Egyptian territory, and he worried that the timing of the American resolution would imply that he had given it his blessing. Yāsīn warned Dulles that if the resolution were introduced during Saʿūd's visit, the king's "influence in the Arab world would decline." Though Eisenhower privately dismissed Saʿūd's qualms over the resolution simply as a "question of pride," the controversy over the Gulf of Aqaba and other post-Suez matters reflected a serious disparity between the American conception of Saʿūd as an agent of pro-Western stability and the role in Arab politics to which the king himself aspired.[10]

More importantly, discussions of U.S. aid to Saudi Arabia illustrated the severe obstacles confronting the Eisenhower Doctrine policy of promoting development with oil revenues. Saʿūd brought with him a laundry list of specific programs he desired the U.S. to fund through grants, including upgrading of the Dammam and Jidda harbors, roads, railways, agricultural and mining projects, and broadcasting stations. In a private conversation with Eisenhower, the king explained that his government had exhausted its resources and needed "desperately to have economic assistance." The president offered only technical help, however, and stressed the importance of "small village and household industries" rather than impressive projects. During working-level talks, Deputy Undersecretary of State Robert Murphy reiterated the administration's preference to provide technical assistance and noted that because Saudi oil income would likely double within a decade, the kingdom could easily finance desired projects through loans from the World Bank and other sources. Saudi finance minister Muḥammad Surūr replied that Saudi Arabia, already deeply in debt, could not assume the additional loans necessary for "jumping from horseback to plane in one step."[11]

This dilemma over economic aid was inherent in the postwar petroleum order and reveals how those global arrangements affected the Saudi state. The U.S. had consistently encouraged Aramco to pay generous oil royalties to the Saudi ruling family as a way of promoting good relations and economic development. In practice, this policy had institutionalized runaway expenditures by fostering a political system in which largesse was distributed in ever-increasing amounts within the family as the price of containing discord and preserving the family's monopoly on power. But Suez had ushered in an era of relative austerity, and Saʿūd's government sought additional sources of support to sustain the political and economic status quo. Congressional opposition and budgetary constraints limited the direct assistance that the Eisenhower administration could provide. Yet if Riyadh relied on the World Bank and other international lenders, as the U.S. suggested, Saudi Arabia would be forced to bring its budget under control and to disrupt the very political arrangements within the royal family that had accompanied the kingdom's integration into the postwar petroleum order. During the summit, the Saudis agreed to join the IMF and the World Bank, but finding the means to reconcile fiscal discipline with the prevailing political system remained the major challenge facing Saʿūd's government.

Saʿūd was similarly disappointed in the amount of military aid offered by the U.S. as a quid pro quo for renewal of the Dhahran lease, but Eisenhower intervened to sweeten the military package because the king occupied such an important place in the administration's policy. In a memorandum to Eisenhower, Saʿūd requested help implementing his $100 million military development plan, which entailed equipment of thirteen regular infantry regiments plus a Royal Guard regiment, and expansion of the Saudi air force and navy. Defense Department officials had consented only to honor agreements from the previous summer to sell the Saudis equipment and to provide a $35 million, five-year military training program. As their subordinates conducted technical discussions, Saʿūd complained to Eisenhower on February 5 about the size of the aid package. Explaining that Saʿūd must not leave the summit empty-handed, the president instructed defense officials to revise U.S. offers upward to $50 million, which included the construction of a new $5 million air terminal at Dhahran.[12]

Despite Saʿūd's dissatisfaction with the amount of U.S. economic and military aid, Eisenhower regarded the summit as a success for his Middle East diplomacy. Having secured the Saudis' acceptance of a five-year renewal of the lease at Dhahran, Secretary Dulles likewise felt that the "Saudi thing came out pretty well." Eisenhower met subsequently with the Iraqi crown prince and Lebanese foreign minister Charles Malik as part of his effort to build a coalition of pro-Western Mideast leaders. Of these figures, however, the president regarded Saʿūd as the most important, given the king's role as custodian of the Muslim holy cities, and Eisenhower remained convinced that Islam held promise as a force for containing atheistic communism and for winning the Cold War in the Middle East.[13]

As he had since the spring of 1956, Eisenhower sought to build up Saʿūd as a regional leader on the basis of the king's religious prestige. This policy reflected what Western experts on the Middle East were writing, and it reflected the monolithic and determinist conception of Islam characteristic of their work. For both scholars and policy makers, the susceptibility of Islamic societies to radical secular ideologies was assumed to be a consequence of social fragmentation caused by the expansion of the West. In 1957, H. A. R. Gibb, the leading British Orientalist and later director of the Middle East Studies Center at Harvard, published the second volume of *Islamic Society and the West.* The study, co-written with Harold Bowen, described social, political, and religious institutions in the Muslim Middle East on the eve of Western encroachment and explained how the West had undermined those institutions. The authors placed particular emphasis on institutional Islam as "a vast corporation which included within itself all the other corporations, and formed the uniting link between them," yet this link was weakened by "the infiltration of Western ideas." They further explained that Islam "served in the minds of its adherents not for a body of religious beliefs only, but for a community which was animated by those beliefs." Though this analysis did not mention communism directly, it reflected Cold War preoccupations by associating a vague and general decline in Islamic religious belief with a dangerous ideological drift in Middle Eastern societies. Similar ideas found their way into statements by

U.S. officials, who worried that communism would flourish under such circumstances. A 1957 State Department policy paper began:

> The Near East, according to some scholars, has been in a state of political and cultural disequilibrium since the arrival of Napoleon in Egypt in 1798. The area's institutions and religions have steadily declined in vigor, as a result of the impact of Western culture, and native resistance to Communism per se has therefore been disappointing.

Eisenhower himself told the Congress in his State of the Union address that peoples living in traditional societies, in their "persistent search for the self-respect of authentic sovereignty . . . sever old ties; seek new alliances; experiment—sometimes dangerously—in their struggle to satisfy these human aspirations."[14]

Following the Saʿūd-Eisenhower summit, the administration continued to cultivate Islam as a bulwark against communism, and as part of this policy, it sought opportunities to overcome the supposed social fragmentation that afflicted the Middle East. In late January, the National Security Council staff established a working committee on Islamic organizations that compiled a list of Middle Eastern and North African social, cultural, and religious groups, such as Sufi brotherhoods, which the United States Information Agency could target with propaganda. In its report, the working committee warned that while Muslims shared "compatible values" with the United States, Islam had suffered "from the impact of the West and technology," and "unless a reconciliation is achieved between Islamic principles and current social and political trends, the spiritual values of Islam will be lost and the swing toward materialism will be hastened." Honoring earlier promises, Eisenhower also approved $500,000 in aid for Saudi Arabia to study the reconstruction of the Hijaz railroad that would carry pilgrims to the holy cities. Finally, in late June, the president delivered a speech at the dedication of a new Washington, D.C., Islamic Center, whose board of directors was chaired by the Saudi ambassador ʿAbdullah al-Khayyāl. After praising the cultural achievements of Islamic civilization, the president stressed the harmony between American and Islamic values, implicitly contrasting them with Soviet atheism:

> I should like to assure you, my Islamic friends, that under the American Constitution, under American tradition, and in American hearts, this Center, this place of worship, is just as welcome as could be a similar edifice of any other religion. Indeed, America would fight with her whole strength for your right to have here your own church and worship according to your own conscience.[15]

At the same time, King Saʿūd himself touted his role as custodian of the holy cities in the interest of raising his own stature within and outside Saudi Arabia, but certain implications of the king's policy were troubling to the Eisenhower administration. As part of his intensifying competition with the secular, nationalist ʿAbd al-Nāṣir, Saʿūd began discussing plans to host an all-Muslim conference. The king also directed his entrepreneur client Shaykh Muḥammad Bin Lādin to supervise a costly renovation of the Great Mosque in Mecca, which housed the Kaʿba, the holiest shrine in Islam. Saʿūd even engaged in Western-style public relations by inviting oil journalist Wanda M. Jablonski to Riyadh. Jablonski gushed in *Petroleum Week* that the king was "deeply religious—with no sham about it," that he liked having the Qurʾān read aloud, adhered conscientiously to Islamic strictures, and had "done much to help Islam's pilgrims."[16]

But to the dismay of U.S. officials, Saʿūd used his authority as guardian of the pilgrimage in a vocal public campaign against any Israeli maritime rights in the Gulf of Aqaba, which he portrayed as a threat to the ḥajj. Israel had conditioned its military withdrawal on U.S. assurances of free passage through the Gulf of Aqaba, which the U.S. offered in a February 11 aide-mémoire. Although it included language about protecting pilgrimage routes, the document embarrassed Saʿūd, who was scheduled shortly to attend an Arab summit where he had promised to defend U.S. anti-communist policies before Nāṣir and Syrian president Quwwatlī. The king told Eisenhower that Aqaba was a "matter of life and death," and he accused Israeli warships of menacing the Hijazi coast as part of a plot to seize Medina, site of "the tomb of the Prophet for whom hundreds of millions of the Moslems all over the world will sacrifice their wealth and soul."[17]

Despite Saʿūd's protests, the administration was unable to alter its policy because if it withheld assurances regarding Aqaba and imposed sanctions to compel Israeli evacuation, legislators sympathetic to Israel would obstruct the Eisenhower Doctrine. Indeed, Congress passed the president's Middle East resolution only after the administration conceded to Israeli conditions. For his part, King Saʿūd appeared more concerned over the implications of the Aqaba issue for Arab politics than with actually confronting the Israelis. The king worried that by accepting the U.S. position on Aqaba, he would forfeit any hope of using his guardianship of the ḥajj to increase his stature as an Arab leader, and ʿAbd al-Nāṣir's propaganda attempted to exploit the king's vulnerability on this issue. In an attempt to refute Egyptian charges that he condoned Israeli expansion, Saʿūd threatened to bring Aqaba before the U.N. Security Council, and, after the Israeli-chartered American ship *Kern Hills* navigated the Straits of Tiran, Saʿūd and King Ḥusayn of Jordan protested by jointly declaring the Gulf of Aqaba closed to pilgrim traffic. In the case of Aqaba, Saʿūd's own ambition within the Arab world interfered with the administration's policy of building up the king on the basis of presumed religious prestige, and the controversy provided another example of how American politics complicated Eisenhower's strategy in the Middle East.[18]

For Eisenhower, courting Saʿūd was not just a strategy for containing communism, but was also a way to render palatable to Arab and Muslim countries the Anglo-American rapprochement that was essential to restoring the postwar petroleum order. As Ritchie Ovendale has shown, the United States and Britain renewed their military partnership in the Middle East and coordinated defense strategy in the Gulf following the Bermuda Conference of March 1957.[19] Scholars have devoted insufficient attention, however, to the collaboration between the two countries on the problem of transporting Middle Eastern oil to Europe. The fact that the transportation infrastructure of the postwar petroleum order passed through Egypt and Syria, those states most affected by revolutionary Arab nationalism, had always been a basic structural weakness. Suez intensified this difficulty, and to address it the Eisenhower administration pursued a degree of cooperation with Britain that, in the interest of improving U.S.-Arab relations, it had previously avoided.

American officials regarded the Middle East Emergency Committee plan for supplying oil to western Europe as a temporary expedient, and following the Suez crisis, they sought structural reform of the postwar petroleum order to reduce the vulnerability of its transportation infrastructure. Within and outside of government, analysts debated whether construction of more and larger tankers or of new pipeline routes was the safest, most efficient way to supply Europe's energy needs. Major oil companies took the initiative by proposing a new pipeline connecting the northern Iraqi oil fields of Kirkuk to the Turkish Mediterranean port of Iskenderun. In the most grandiose version of the scheme, the main trunk would join feeder lines that extended to the Gulf and eastern Saudi Arabia. Such a route would circumvent Syria and Egypt and pass instead through Turkey, a non-Arab, NATO member. The new pipeline company, known as Metline, would be registered in the sterling area to prevent a further dollar shortage to Britain. As Jersey Standard director Howard Page explained to Herbert Hoover Jr., the success of Metline depended upon American and British agreement to sponsor a multilateral treaty system that would guarantee the integrity of the pipeline. Companies would be unwilling to bear the substantial construction cost, estimated at $800 million, in the absence of backing by the two governments. Hoover gave his blessing to Metline during a January 25 meeting with oil company executives, and he offered them suggestions for avoiding antitrust entanglements. By the eve of the Bermuda Conference, the administration had drawn up a joint policy paper with the British in which the allies agreed to explore ways of sponsoring Metline through "inter-governmental agreements," precisely the sort of commitments in oil diplomacy that Washington had resisted prior to Suez.[20]

Meanwhile, London sought to adjust to post-Suez realities by combining an overall reduction of obligations in the Middle East with the consolidation of its position in the Gulf. As part of the retrenchment, officials determined that Britain could no longer afford its subsidy to Jordan and in March granted King Ḥusayn's request to terminate the 1948 Anglo-Jordanian treaty. But given the importance of Gulf oil to the British economy, British military planners opted to retain a strong presence in the Gulf. A debate ensued over whether a greater U.S. role in the Gulf would promote British interests or undermine London's prestige among its clients. Bernard Burrows, political resident at Bahrain and an inveterate defender of Britain's traditional policy, shared the Bahraini ruler's apprehensions that U.S. interference in the Gulf would be "inconvenient and embarrassing." The Foreign Office also suspected Saudi ambitions in the Gulf, and officials felt that the Americans had encouraged these ambitions during the summit by promising Saʿūd military aid and by promoting Anglo-Saudi compromise over Buraymī. Moreover, the British continued to prefer strengthening the Baghdad Pact under Iraqi leadership to the American strategy of building up the Saudi king. Harold Beeley of the Foreign Office wrote the British embassy in Washington that "it would be an illusion to imagine that a sacrifice of our position . . . over Buraimi would strengthen the Western position in the Middle East," or that King Saʿūd, as guardian of the holy places, could rival the political popularity of ʿAbd al-Nāṣir.[21]

Nevertheless, during the Bermuda summit, the new British prime minister, Harold Macmillan, and President Eisenhower restored a close Anglo-American working relationship in the Middle East in the interest of salvaging the postwar petroleum order. Although the British resisted Eisenhower's exhortations to compromise with the Saudis on Buraymī, the two allies were of one mind on the need to maintain access to Middle Eastern oil. Both Macmillan and Foreign Secretary Lloyd stressed the importance of protecting oil-rich Kuwait from Arab nationalist agitation, and they called for an Anglo-American defense of Gulf petroleum. Eisenhower agreed to collaborate on a common "plan of battle," and the two sides endorsed Dulles's idea that a full Anglo-American review of Middle Eastern policy "should be linked primarily to oil."[22]

Following Bermuda, British and American representatives met in Washington to discuss what appeared to be ominous threats to Europe's oil supply. American staff studies pointed to the utter inadequacy of the existing transport infrastructure to accommodate the projected increase in European oil consumption and to the dire consequences if Western Europe were denied Middle Eastern oil altogether. Even if existing pipelines and the Suez Canal remained open, those conduits could transport only 40 percent of the oil that Europe would require by 1965. But British and American officials could not assume the continued availability of existing transport facilities, because they were situated in Egypt and Syria, "countries in which Soviet influence is most extensive, Arab nationalism most extreme and involvement in the Arab-Israel dispute currently most immediate." Should those countries interrupt the flow of oil, U.S. officials predicted that progress toward European integration "might suffer serious setbacks." Moreover, the West would become increasingly vulnerable to a crisis similar to Suez or the Anglo-Iranian dispute, because growing domestic demand prevented the U.S. from supplying Europe with western hemisphere petroleum unless Washington imposed rationing at home. During the Anglo-American talks, these concerns were uppermost in the minds of policy makers, who explored topics including Aqaba, Jordan, Syria, Buraymī, the Arab-Israeli dispute, and the role of ʿAbd al-Nāṣir, all under the heading, "Factors Affecting Access to Petroleum Resources of the Middle East."[23]

At this stage, a resurgence of rebel activity against the Sultan of Muscat and Oman underscored the tension within U.S. policy between cooperating with the British on the one hand and cultivating Saʿūd's prestige on the other. Meeting with British officials in June, American envoy Loy Henderson tried to head off renewed conflict over Oman by proposing direct talks between King Saʿūd and the sultan. But rebels who had taken refuge in Saudi Arabia following British military action in December 1955 returned to Oman and renewed their armed campaign to establish an independent state. In response, Britain sent additional forces to the Trucial Shaykhdoms and prepared to carry out air strikes against the rebels. Dulles expressed concern that the British action would give ʿAbd al-Nāṣir "a new chance to assert Arab leadership," and Eisenhower reminded Macmillan of the need for reconciliation between London and King Saʿūd, who represented "the best counterbalance" against Nāṣir. For his part, Saʿūd denied British accusations that he was arming the rebels, pointing the finger instead at the Indian government. But Aramco vice president James Terry Duce admitted that the Saudis had aided rebel forces, and the American military attaché at Dhahran later discovered that landmines used by the rebels bore serial numbers matching equipment sold to the Saudi government by Washington.[24]

Although the Omani rebellion complicated Anglo-American cooperation, it scarcely distracted the Eisenhower administration from its policy of defending Britain's position in the Gulf. When the U.S. refused to join Britain in opposing the Arab states' inscription of the Oman issue into the United Nations agenda, Macmillan warned Eisenhower against derailing the post-Suez rapprochement between their two countries. But Washington made no effort to obstruct British military deployment in the Gulf and abstained on the U.N. vote, which had the desired effect of defeating the measure without forcing the U.S. to take a public stand with Britain against the Arab states. Also, contemporary reports that portray the Oman conflict as an Anglo-American "oil war" by proxy ignore the fact that U.S. and British oil concessions in eastern Arabia were not coterminous with the territories of the mutually antagonistic Saudi and Omani rulers. The sultan had recently granted Cities Service, an independent American oil company, the concession for Dhufar on the southeastern coast of the Arabian peninsula. U.S. oil interests therefore operated on both sides of the disputed Saudi-Omani boundary. Finally, the long-term trend after Suez involved improved relations between the U.S. and Britain's Gulf clients. Indeed, the U.S. approached the sultan in June 1957 about a new trade and commercial treaty that was eventually signed over Saudi objections.[25]

By making Anglo-American defense of the postwar petroleum order his top priority, Eisenhower in several ways undermined his professed goal of raising living standards in the Middle East through economic assistance and the responsible use of oil revenues. First, the administration devoted its limited resources toward strategic support for pro-Western regimes and the Baghdad Pact. Dulles informed James P. Richards, Eisenhower's special envoy to the Middle East, that the litmus test for U.S. support of any development project was whether it would "reinforce the will and ability to resist international communism." Washington ceded Jordan $10 million in emergency aid to help King Ḥusayn defend his government from Arab nationalist opposition. After joining the military committee of the Baghdad Pact as a concession to Britain, the U.S. awarded $12.57 million to member countries, but earmarked the funds for highway, railroad, and communications projects intended to facilitate military cooperation.[26]

Second, if Metline were built as the administration envisioned, it would deny to the Arab transit countries, Jordan, Syria, Egypt, and Lebanon, the revenues that would accrue from increased canal and pipeline use as Europe consumed more Mideast oil. Even the large-capacity tankers that some analysts recommended as an alternative to Metline were intended to carry Middle Eastern oil to Europe via the Cape of Good Hope; some of these proposed vessels had drafts of greater than thirty-six feet, making them unable to navigate the Suez Canal. Bypassing the existing transit countries meant diminishing the already modest share of oil wealth enjoyed by the poorest of the Arab states, exactly the opposite of what the president and his advisors had in mind when they authored the Eisenhower Doctrine.[27]

Lastly, Eisenhower's indulgence of Saʿūd as part of the president's political strategy prevented reforms in the kingdom and undermined the contribution that Saudi Arabia could make toward development in the Arab world. For example, the administration had hoped that the Saudis could assume from Britain the burden of subsidizing the Jordanian government, thereby preventing Jordanian dependence upon Egypt and Syria. Both Eisenhower and the British were encouraged in this regard following Saʿūd's meeting with King Ḥusayn during the April crisis in Amman, when the Jordanian king purged Arab nationalists from his government. But faced with continued budget deficits, Riyadh suspended its support after making initial payments. Within the kingdom, the private structure of American oil diplomacy had fostered a pattern of domestic politics characterized by struggles within the royal family over oil royalties, rather than the systematic investment of those revenues. Instead of cutting spending, Saʿūd continued to demand economic assistance from the U.S., and the king rejected American offers he deemed insufficient. The $25 million that the Eisenhower administration had provided to expand the Dammam port, survey the Hijaz railway, and construct a new air terminal at Dhahran went unused by the end of the 1957 fiscal year. Ambassador Richards reported that compared with Iraq, Saudi Arabia devoted an "undue proportion" of its oil royalties to "showy edifices." Oil revenues, he observed, "seem to benefit principally and ostentatiously [the] royal family and its retainers while only trickling down" to the Saudi population.[28]

As Eisenhower's promise to promote economic development in the Middle East went unfulfilled, the administration faced a new Syrian crisis that piqued Anglo-American concerns about Arab nationalism in the transit states and finally convinced Eisenhower that his faith in Saʿūd was misplaced. As Patrick Seale first documented, the Syrian government, following the conclusion of an economic agreement with the Soviet Union in August, accused personnel attached to the American embassy in Damascus of plotting to overthrow the government and expelled them from the country. Eisenhower interpreted these actions as evidence of communist influence, though he and Dulles carefully avoided invoking the Middle East doctrine, lest they elicit a Soviet response. Instead, the president dispatched Loy Henderson to meet with President Menderes of Turkey,

Prime Minister Shamʿūn of Lebanon, King Ḥusayn of Jordan, and King Fayṣal of Iraq in the hope of encouraging regional states to intervene. The president also expedited arms deliveries promised to friendly Middle Eastern countries. Most importantly, in a test of the administration's strategy, Eisenhower appealed to Saʿūd in his capacity as "Keeper of the Holy Places of Islam" to use his influence so that "the atheistic creed of Communism will not become entrenched at a key position in the Moslem world."[29]

King Saʿūd continued to exalt his role as guardian of the holy places for the sake of his own ambitions, rather than in the interest of American objectives. The king remained preoccupied with his rivalry with ʿAbd al-Nāṣir, who was himself attempting to court Baʿthist supporters in the Syrian army and to undermine the influence of Khālid al-ʿAẓm and other Syrian figures interested in a more substantial Soviet role in the region. Days later, the king effectively rebuffed Eisenhower's entreaties and condemned a recent U.S. aide-mémoire on the Gulf of Aqaba controversy. To Eisenhower's disappointment, Saʿūd also traveled to Damascus on September 25 to exhibit his solidarity with the Syrian government as Turkish troops massed on the border, and, worst of all, the Saudi government announced on October 6 that it had never officially accepted the Eisenhower Doctrine.[30]

While the king cultivated his Arab nationalist credentials, Nāṣir hatched plans, in the words of historian David Lesch, to "steal Saʿūd's thunder." In a gesture timed to upstage the king, then at the Arab games in Beirut, Nāṣir dispatched Egyptian troops to the Syrian port of Latakia to help defend that Arab country from Western aggression. This action ratified ʿAbd al-Nāṣir's alliance with the Syrian military, confirmed him as the leading Arab nationalist figure, and profoundly embarrassed Saʿūd. The king's somewhat pathetic offer to mediate the conflict between Syria and Turkey fizzled, and the crisis faded amid mutual recriminations by the superpowers at the United Nations.[31]

Accounts by Lesch and others of the Syrian crisis stress its Cold War and Arab political aspects while neglecting the context of British and American efforts to address the oil transport problem. Months of Anglo-American study and discussions regarding Arab nationalism in the transit countries, Europe's economic dependence on Middle Eastern oil, and Metline had preceded the latest conflict with Damascus. Already alarmed by Syria's award of an oil refinery contract to a Czech firm, the British and Americans feared that the regime would sever the Iraq Petroleum Company (IPC) pipelines as it had during the Suez war. Indeed, just prior to Syria's treaty with the Soviets, the State Department forwarded a memo in support of both Metline and supertanker construction to the National Security Council, citing a "strong presumption that Syria will continue to use its position in the transport of Middle East petroleum for political purposes." As the administration attempted to persuade its Middle Eastern allies to topple the Syrian government, Secretary Dulles informed the council that "the situation in Syria indicated that there was a considerable hazard in the Middle East area which could involve another interruption of the flow of Middle Eastern oil to the Free World." At the request of the British, Eisenhower agreed if necessary to reconstitute the Middle East Emergency Committee to supply Europe with petroleum. Disruption in the flow of oil was considered detrimental not only to consumers in Europe, but also to the producing states. A national intelligence estimate in early October noted that attacks on the IPC pipelines in Syria could deprive Iraq of the revenue necessary for implementing its "well coordinated" development plans.[32]

Eisenhower administration officials concluded that Syria was likely to sever the pipelines if confronted with armed intervention by Turkey or by a Western power, and this belief increased their desire for King Saʿūd to spearhead an Arab solution to the crisis. On August 24, Dulles received a confidential message from his brother, who had met in Rome with Loy Henderson, then en route to Turkey. Allen Dulles surmised that the U.S. could count on Syria's neighbors to apply economic pressure on Damascus and observed that if Syria sabotaged the Trans-Arabian and IPC pipelines, it would seriously alienate both the Saudis and Iraqis. In the event of outside intervention, however, "we must reckon that both lines would go." Secretary Dulles immediately shared with British embassy officials his concern that Syria might sever the IPC pipelines, and on August 27 he warned Macmillan that any action against Syria "should come from within the area and be led by an Arab state or states, not Turkey." The administration regarded the Saudi king as the logical choice to lead the charge against Syria, not only because of his supposed religious influence, but also because it believed it could exploit a rift between oil-producing and oil-transit states. As the British had during Suez, American officials erroneously assumed that King Saʿūd would be motivated more by sheer economic self-interest than by the politics of Arab nationalism.[33]

At no time were conditions more favorable than during the months following the Syrian crisis for the Eisenhower administration to accommodate Arab nationalism and address the challenges of economic development in the Middle East. Indeed, observers within and outside of the administration began to consider ways of cooperating with ʿAbd al-Nāṣir, both because Nāṣir's recent actions indicated his concern about Soviet influence in the Middle East and because some Americans thought it possible, even necessary, to accept Arab nationalism as a way of preserving the postwar petroleum order. The crisis had also demonstrated the uselessness of relying on King Saʿūd to isolate Egypt, the administration's strategy since the spring of 1956. Though the king was still an important U.S. ally, the Americans no longer regarded him as a "Moslem pope," and they found Saʿūd increasingly distracted by serious political and economic problems at home.[34] At the same time, U.S. policy makers, American allies, and the Arab states themselves advanced proposals for using oil revenues and other sources to fund economic development in the region. Unreceptive to these plans, the administration persevered in collaborating with the British to defend the postwar petroleum order, even when such a policy led to the sort of military intervention that Eisenhower had opposed at Suez.

As part of a Mideast policy review, the administration re-examined its attitude toward Arab nationalism, and both Secretary Dulles and President Eisenhower expressed interest in a cautious overture to ʿAbd al-Nāṣir. National Security Council planning board chairman Robert Cutler called for "a new, fresh look" at U.S. policy, and the board considered U.S. sponsorship of a "sensible plan of Arab unity" and regional economic organization. Dulles investigated the possibilities for improving relations with Egypt, and the secretary instructed Ambassador Wadsworth to ascertain King Saʿūd's opinion about a change in U.S. policy toward Nāṣir.[35]

Eisenhower entertained an opening to Egypt after his close personal friend, W. Alton "Pete" Jones, held a two-hour *tour d'horizon* with Nāṣir in October. A regular member of Eisenhower's card-playing gang and a career oilman, Jones was the president of Cities Service, the American petroleum company that had obtained prospecting rights for Dhufar in Oman, and he stopped in Cairo while in the Middle East inspecting his firm's new concession. Jones found Nāṣir "more mellow than before" the Suez war, and he urged Eisenhower to improve relations with Egypt, a suggestion the president passed along to Dulles with instructions to have the State Department consult Jones. A few days after Jones again prevailed on Eisenhower "to win over Egypt and Nasser to our side," the president asked Dulles: "Do you think there would be any percentage in initiating a drive to attempt to bring back Nasser to our side?" Dulles cautioned the president, however, about Nāṣir's ambition to dominate his Arab neighbors and about the risks of alienating the conservative Arab allies Saudi Arabia, Jordan, Lebanon, and Iraq.[36]

Meanwhile, concern over disparities in wealth within the Arab world spawned myriad plans for funding economic development in the Middle

East. Inside the administration, Eisenhower's most trusted oil advisors Herbert Hoover Jr. and Robert Anderson discussed a regional development organization funded by a 10 percent tax on oil revenues. Though the Arab states themselves wrangled over the agenda for an oil summit scheduled to meet in Cairo, even the oil producers publicly subscribed to the idea that all Arabs should benefit from Arab petroleum resources. To demonstrate their commitment to this principle, Iraqi officials vetoed Metline, and Iraqi finance minister ʿAlī Mumtāz al-Daftarī proposed an Arab development fund financed by the oil-producing states. Another especially innovative plan came from Italian foreign minister Giuseppe Pella, who in September 1957 proposed a "triangular system" in which European countries, in lieu of repaying Marshall Plan loans to the U.S., would deposit local-currency equivalents of those debts into a Middle Eastern development fund. Finally, U.N. Secretary-General Dag Hammarskjöld sent Dulles and Lloyd a proposal for a Middle East development fund managed by the Arab states, the World Bank, and the U.N. Although the oil companies would at first provide credits to the poor Arab countries, Hammarskjöld explained that eventually the oil-producing Arab "haves" could support projects in the "have not" countries, thereby promoting Arab unity, fostering balanced economic development among the Arab states, and even addressing the Palestinian refugee crisis.[37]

Central to administration attitudes toward these proposals were the oil corporations' increasingly antagonistic relationships with the producing and transit countries. For its part, Saudi Arabia demanded more than $100 million from Aramco in retroactive Tapline fees, as well as the appointment of Saudis to the company's board of directors. In addition, the Saudi petroleum minister ʿAbdullah al-Ṭāriqī, a University of Texas graduate and veteran Texaco geologist, insisted that Aramco maximize the Saudi government's income by becoming a fully "integrated" company encompassing the transportation, refining, and marketing of Saudi oil, a proposal that both Aramco and the administration opposed. Of equal concern was an offshore concession deal between Iran and Enrico Mattei of the Italian AGIP corporation that assigned Iran a 75 percent share of profits. The AGIP deal precipitated other breaches in the fifty-fifty standard, which Aramco had pioneered and which the U.S. and Britain had mutually pledged to defend.[38]

These challenges to the oil companies' concessions hardened official resolve to preserve the status quo. According to the State Department, Aramco-Saudi relations ought to remain "on a purely commercial basis," and the administration should be willing to intervene "when there is a clear threat to American interests." By backing the corporations, department analysts assumed the same hold-the-line attitude in oil diplomacy for which they had criticized their British counterparts years earlier. More significantly, officials' determination to uphold the private structure of American oil diplomacy precluded a regional development body of the type proposed by Hammarskjöld. Dulles told John J. McCloy, president of Chase Manhattan, where several of the major oil corporations did their banking, that by fostering Arab unity, Hammarskjöld's plan "may make it more difficult for the oil companies to maintain a decent position" in the Middle East. During a meeting with Lloyd, the secretary conveyed McCloy's sense that the plan contained "inherent dangers for the oil companies," and Lloyd agreed that the U.S. and Britain should obstruct the proposal without seeming to oppose it.[39]

Similarly, the administration discarded plans for improving relations with ʿAbd al-Nāṣir in favor of backing regimes well-disposed toward the postwar petroleum order. This policy became more pronounced once the establishment of the United Arab Republic by Syria and Egypt put Nāṣir in control of Syrian oil transit facilities and Yemen's affiliation with the UAR threatened to give him a foothold on the Arabian peninsula. Since October, the U.S. had sought restoration of Anglo-Saudi relations and an increase in King Saʿūd's influence in Yemen in order to obstruct Egyptian and Soviet influence in Arabia and the Gulf. Moreover, the administration's new policy paper on the Middle East, NSC 5801, couched U.S. support for Arab unity in terms of "strengthening of the ties among Saudi Arabia, Jordan and Iraq" and bolstering these "more moderate Arab states" against Egypt. Speaking in opposition to the Hammarskjöld plan, Dulles reiterated his anxiety that consolidation of the Arab states "might make Western Europe's situation with respect to oil even more serious than it now was." In response to the UAR, proclaimed on February 1 while Dulles met in Ankara with representatives of the Baghdad Pact countries, the administration encouraged Saudi involvement in an Iraqi-Jordanian Arab union. But King Saʿūd insisted that Iraq first secede from the Baghdad Pact, and the Saudi government declared its inability to subsidize Jordan, the non-oil-producing member of the grouping promoted by the State Department. Predicting that the Arab monarchies would in fact recognize the UAR, Dulles discerned "little or no evidence that our Arab friends are able or willing to formulate common action," and Eisenhower likewise found Saʿūd "unenthusiastic" about confronting ʿAbd al-Nāṣir's brand of revolutionary Arab nationalism.[40]

Just as Washington faced the new problem of the UAR, King Saʿūd abandoned his well-publicized Arab diplomacy in order to address his country's financial problems and challenges to his authority from within the ruling family. Saʿūd's powers in the kingdom had reached a high water mark in June 1957, when his son Khālid became head of the National Guard, Prince Fayṣal left the country ostensibly for medical treatment, and the cabinet, which provided the royal family with a check on Saʿūd's authority, ceased its meetings. But the multifaceted economic crisis quickly eroded King Saʿūd's position. Aramco chairman Fred Davies told British officials in September that his company would curtail advances to the king to promote a "more responsible" approach to spending revenues, and two months later, Saʿūd accepted austerity measures recommended by the International Monetary Fund to bolster the sagging riyal and to reduce the kingdom's debt, which had ballooned to $480 million. The resulting budget, published in *Al-Bilād al-Saʿūdiyya* on January 14, elicited strong dissent from younger members of the royal family, who opposed reductions in their allowances, and they struck an anti-Saʿūd alliance with Fayṣal when the crown prince returned to Saudi Arabia in February.[41]

In the midst of this financial and political crisis, the UAR published sensational accusations on March 5 that King Saʿūd had paid Syrian intelligence chief ʿAbd al-Ḥamīd al-Sarrāj 1.7 million Australian guineas to arrange ʿAbd al-Nāṣir's murder, a charge al-Sarrāj substantiated by producing what he claimed were checks drawn on the Arab Bank of Riyadh. This scandal crystallized the anti-Saʿūd alliance in the kingdom and forced the king to announce on March 22 that he would cede power over both domestic and foreign policy to Prince Fayṣal. As Ghassan Salamé suggests, the episode also punctuated Saʿūd's alienation from the prevailing nationalist currents in Arab politics; the charges were widely believed in the Arab world precisely because the king was considered an ally of Washington. Hostility toward the Eisenhower Doctrine, Salamé writes, "was transferred to the Arab spokesman for it."[42]

Historians and other observers have advanced various theories regarding the origins of the accusations against King Saʿūd. By far the most intriguing is Sarah Yizraeli's suggestion that John Foster Dulles, in consultation with both Aramco and Fayṣal, engineered Saʿūd's downfall to ensure the success of reforms in the kingdom. Lacking direct proof, Yizraeli cites Dulles's interest in Fayṣal's movements while the crown prince was in the U.S. and the fact that State Department officials in Washington appeared to recognize the implications of Saʿūd's transfer of power to Fayṣal sooner than did American diplomats in Saudi Arabia. Significant countervailing evidence, however, casts doubt on Yizraeli's claims. First, Eisenhower continued to support Saʿūd and even raised the possibility of sending troops to strengthen the king during the March crisis. Undermining Saʿūd would therefore have involved defiance by

Dulles of the president's authority, a scenario incompatible with revisionists' understanding of the relationship between Eisenhower and his secretary of state. Second, State Department officials gave no indication of realizing prior to the March 22 royal decree that Fayṣal would take control of the Saudi government. Assistant Secretary William Rountree wrote Dulles on March 14 that it was unlikely al-Sarrāj's charges would have sufficient impact "to threaten seriously the King's present position," and the State Department shared this view with British ambassador Harold Caccia. Finally, when the department received information on March 3 from Saʿūd's keeper of the privy purse ʿAbdullah Tubayshī about an imminent coup in Syria, Secretary Dulles approved a reply stating that there was currently "little organized opposition" in Damascus on which to base such an undertaking. Indeed, Allen Dulles told the National Security Council that the U.S. had sought to dissuade King Saʿūd from any moves in Syria and to warn him that "he was falling into a trap."[43]

It is more fruitful in any event to situate the March crisis in the context of the postwar petroleum order and of Saudi state building than to fixate on intrigues and plots. By encouraging generous corporate subsidies for the royal family, Washington had helped to preserve the patrimonial nature of ʿAbd al-ʿAzīz's state, even as oil exports connected the kingdom to international markets. Aramco's advances on oil royalties and its role in supervising development projects not only excused the Saudi government from having to operate according to an annual budget, but also enabled the kingdom to get along without political mechanisms for deciding how to apportion fixed revenues. Despite the creation of the cabinet and the short-lived compromise between Saʿūd and Fayṣal after their father's death, no institutional arrangements existed for defusing conflict within the royal family other than distributing allowances, a practice responsible for the kingdom's financial problems, let alone for sharing power with groups outside the family. The withholding of advances by Aramco had been the main catalyst for the revolt against Saʿūd, who could not sustain his drive for political dominance without resources sufficient to pacify the younger princes. In this way, the political economy of American oil diplomacy had both set the stage for the March crisis and had been an important factor in shaping the Saudi state.

The consolidation of the UAR and King Saʿūd's surrender of power fostered an escalating sense of crisis in London and Washington that culminated in Anglo-American military intervention to safeguard the postwar petroleum order. This action was the consummation not only of the Eisenhower administration's support for conservative Arab states against ʿAbd al-Nāṣir, but also of allied collaboration since the Bermuda conference on the defense of the Gulf and oil-transit issues. On March 24, Dulles received an assessment prepared by State, Defense, and CIA officials on the situation in the Middle East. With the formation of the UAR and the scandal involving Saʿūd, the report argued, Nāṣir had "reduced or neutralized" most U.S. assets in the region and advanced the cause of radical Arab nationalism, which threatened to place access to petroleum "in constant jeopardy." Director of Central Intelligence Allen Dulles conveyed to the National Security Council in April the "very gloomy" predictions of certain intelligence reports that "foresaw the nationalization of Aramco and also a take-over of Saudi Arabia by President Nasser."[44]

Within two weeks, civil war erupted in Lebanon, terminus of both Tapline and two of the Iraq Petroleum Company's five outlet lines to the Mediterranean, and the Anglo-American response mirrored shared concerns about protecting oil production and transportation. At Eisenhower's behest, Dulles made explicit on May 13 the U.S. willingness to intervene militarily in support of President Shamʿūn of Lebanon, who faced violent opposition to his bid for another term in office. This guarantee came one day after an Anglo-American study group established following the Bermuda conference finalized its report on the oil-transit crisis. The group concluded that even with the present surplus of tankers capable of plying the Cape route, closure of the Suez Canal and Mideast pipelines would deprive Europe of about a third of its oil and, until at least 1960, European countries would have to make up the shortfall during an emergency by purchasing western hemisphere petroleum. Such steps could involve hard currency losses to Europe of $1 billion annually, "of which over three-quarters would fall on the U.K."[45]

Following the July 14 revolution that overturned Britain's client regime in Baghdad, the Americans and British dispatched troops to the transit states of Lebanon and Jordan respectively, as well as to the Gulf to protect the key oil-producing regions of the Saudi Eastern Province and Kuwait. Described in such terms, the Anglo-American intervention can best be understood from the panoramic vantage of the postwar petroleum order, yet historians of these events have instead pitched their analyses at the national level and have focused on the allies' division of labor in Jordan and Lebanon. Whereas Douglas Little contends with justification that Washington viewed Lebanon in particular as a test case for U.S. credibility, Nigel John Ashton argues less convincingly that American suspicions of British motives prevented Eisenhower from supporting intervention in Jordan.[46]

Offering the most sophisticated interpretation of U.S. policy toward Beirut, Irene Gendzier insists that the American landings in Lebanon were not a response to the Iraq coup but rather a direct consequence of the pervasive U.S. influence in Lebanon's politics, economy, and society. In debunking the "myth of the surrogate intervention," however, she loses sight of the regional petroleum economy into which Lebanon had become integrated, a concept that suffuses her study but which is curiously absent from her account of July 1958. She also speculates that U.S. officials declined to support action in Iraq so that American companies could profit at the expense of Britain and the Iraq Petroleum Company. Such a conjecture misses that American policy makers thought about the Middle East not as an arena for competition with Britain, but in terms of the multilateral arrangements established for the sake of the European economy. It also misrepresents the transnational character of the oil industry, epitomized by the fact that two of the largest American companies, Socony-Mobil and Jersey Standard, were each shareholders in IPC.[47]

Indeed, only two factors seemed to constrain Eisenhower as he cooperated with the British to uphold the postwar petroleum order. First, the administration ruled out direct action against the UAR or Iraq, which could have prompted the Soviets to send "volunteers" to the Middle East as they had during the Suez crisis. Second, the president faced congressional opposition to military action outside of Lebanon, especially in the absence of meaningful evidence that Lebanese instability was the result of subversion from without. On July 14, Eisenhower consequently rejected Macmillan's suggestion of American participation in a "big operation," which would go "far beyond anything I have the power to do constitutionally," and the president told Foreign Secretary Lloyd that political factors necessitated an allied division of labor in the Middle East. The allied partnership included coordinating the British defense of Kuwait with the offshore deployment of U.S. Marines in the Gulf and Washington's supplying of British troops in Amman. With military operations underway, John Foster Dulles consistently reminded the president of the economic importance of Gulf oil to the U.K. Dulles told Eisenhower on July 23 that Britain would be "badly hurt" if deprived of cheap sterling oil from the region, and Dulles's comments the next day to the National Security Council underscored this point. "If the oil fields of Iraq and Kuwait fell under hostile control and if the conditions for the sale of oil were altered (that is if oil prices were increased)," Dulles warned, "the financial impact on the United Kingdom might be catastrophic."[48]

While Washington collaborated with Britain, American relations with Saudi Arabia became bifurcated as U.S. officials maintained separate channels to King Saʿūd and Crown Prince Fayṣal and as deep divisions emerged within the kingdom over the Anglo-American intervention. Since March,

Saʿūd had continued through his envoy ʿAzzām Pasha to angle for U.S. aid to bolster his political position, and he had warned American officials about ʿAbd al-Nāṣir's cooperation with the Soviets and his ambition to annex Lebanon to the UAR. Following the Iraqi coup, Saʿūd vocally backed allied military action, telling Eisenhower that "if the United States and the United Kingdom do not act now they are finished as powers in the Mid-East." By contrast, Fayṣal, who had declared in April that Saudi Arabia would follow a neutral foreign policy, opposed the intervention, refused to allow the U.S. to supply British troops from Saudi territory, and insisted that the American flag not be flown at the Dhahran airfield. Such conflicting attitudes were reflected in the various constituencies within the kingdom that supported either Saʿūd or Fayṣal in their domestic power struggle. While Saʿūd retained backing from the Royal Guard and elite Nejdi families, opposition to the intervention was strongest in Fayṣal's power base of the Hijaz, where leaflets denouncing Aramco and the Western powers appeared days after the revolution in Baghdad.[49] Taken together, the king's surrender of authority and the Anglo-American intervention marked a shift away from Saʿūd's efforts to gain advantage over Fayṣal through regional diplomacy and an alliance with Washington, and toward a period during which Riyadh turned its attention inward and foreign policy became one of several issues tied to internal reform. Saʿūd's high-profile role in Arab politics was therefore at an end, but Fayṣal's campaign to reconcile modern state building with continued family rule in Saudi Arabia had only just begun.

At its inception, the Eisenhower Doctrine raised the possibility of a new approach toward American foreign policy in the Middle East that made economic development of the region a higher priority, attempted to address the tremendous disparities in wealth among the Arab states, and, significantly, indicated a willingness to depart from an oil diplomacy based mostly on supporting private investment. Yet U.S. officials, concerned that Arab nationalism would jeopardize access to petroleum, missed this opportunity to reconfigure American foreign oil policy and opted instead to work with Britain to defend the existing relationships among the oil companies, oil-producing states, and transit countries. Despite American officials' consistent desire to protect the postwar petroleum order, they recognized that generous compensation of Arab governments by the oil corporations was no longer sufficient to preserve regional stability. Eisenhower and Dulles admitted as much when, after first seeking to use King Saʿūd to isolate ʿAbd al-Nāṣir, a strategy whose weaknesses the Syrian crisis exposed, they then coordinated oil diplomacy with Britain in a way they had previously avoided, and finally resorted to Anglo-American military intervention. The Eisenhower Doctrine therefore set the U.S. on the path to replace Britain as custodian of the Gulf and its oil resources.

For members of the Saudi ruling family, the period following the Suez war marked a watershed of a different sort: the beginning of a process of political and economic reform that laid the foundations of the modern Saudi state. This process unfolded in a context determined by American corporate investment and the kingdom's integration into the postwar petroleum order. Financial constraints made it impossible for Saʿūd to rule in the imperious manner of his father and still retain the family's support. Having gained control of the government, Fayṣal faced the challenge of reforming the kingdom's finances and administration without alienating the younger princes who had backed him against Saʿūd. Trends toward greater production and lower prices in global oil markets during the late 1950s would only make the crown prince's task more difficult.

6

We Might as Well Believe in Arab Nationalism: OPEC and the Modern Saudi State, August 1958–December 1960

An exquisite irony of American Mideast foreign policy during the 1950s is that just when the destruction of the Iraqi monarchy appeared to hand ʿAbd al-Nāṣir his greatest triumph, political and economic forces suddenly converged to weaken the Arab nationalist threat to the postwar petroleum order. Although American officials initially regarded the Iraqi revolution as a victory for Nāṣirism, the Iraqi leader, ʿAbd al-Karīm Qāsim, emerged as a bitter rival of Nāṣir in the Arab world. Qāsim's alliance with the communists in Iraq and his sympathy toward those in the United Arab Republic, as well as his friendliness toward the Soviet Union, prompted Nāṣir to seek a rapprochement with both the U.S. and conservative Arab states such as Saudi Arabia.

At the same time conflict between Cairo and Baghdad divided the Arab world, a sea-change in the global oil industry undermined the political leverage that Arab oil-producing states commanded in their relations with major oil companies and Western consumers. By the late 1950s, persistent efforts by the U.S. and its allies to secure sufficient oil to fuel postwar reconstruction and Cold War defense had fostered a supply of petroleum that outstripped demand. In response, Arab oil states cooperated in an attempt to stabilize prices, but instead of formulating their demands in an Arab nationalist context, Saudi Arabia and other Arab producers sought collaboration with the non-Arab petroleum-producing countries Venezuela and Iran to obtain more favorable prices on the global market. This campaign, which led to the establishment of the Organization of Petroleum Exporting Countries (OPEC), reflected the diminished stature of producing governments in an era of oil overabundance and a drastic political retreat from the Arab nationalist agenda of the early 1950s.

Pressured by falling oil prices to control the kingdom's budget, Crown Prince Fayṣal encountered opposition to his reform campaign from two sources within the ruling family. First, King Saʿūd doggedly sought to return to power by patronizing leading tribal families, courting opponents of Fayṣal's fiscal austerity, and quietly seeking support from the U.S. Second, a faction known as the "Free Princes," led by Ṭalāl ibn ʿAbd al-ʿAzīz, pushed for reforms more drastic than those pursued by Fayṣal, including a constitution and a representative national assembly. Promising to transform the Saudi state in major ways and drawing inspiration from ʿAbd al-Nāṣir, the Free Princes envisioned a constitutional monarchy in which the distribution of oil revenues would become part of a political process, rather than the exclusive privilege of senior ruling family members.

In an unexpected reversal of the alignments that had followed the March 1958 crisis, Saʿūd assumed control of the government in December 1960 by siding with the Free Princes, and the king even expressed sympathy for their proposed constitution. Saʿūd's alliance was only a tactical maneuver, however, and upon regaining power, the king quickly withdrew his support for the constitution, dismissed Ṭalāl months later from the government, and consented under family pressure to an uneasy reconciliation with Fayṣal. Saʿūd was therefore unsuccessful in his bid to establish the same personal authority his father had commanded over the ruling family. Saudi Arabia retained a patrimonial system of government, however, instead of developing a constitutional one. Fayṣal's achievement in forcing the king to submit to a budget maintained family rule in Saudi Arabia and the dynasty's stake in the postwar petroleum order.

By 1960, Arab nationalism had failed to achieve its most radical vision of redistributing oil wealth from producing to non-producing Arab countries. By creating OPEC, Saudi Arabia and other Arab oil states finally repudiated their poorer Arab brethren in the way that British and American officials had long predicted and hoped they would. A similar process occurred within the Saudi kingdom itself, as Fayṣal's reforms pre-empted the demands of Arab nationalist opponents for more profound political and economic change and preserved the royal family's authority over the country's oil riches. The postwar petroleum order was therefore secure following a decade of severe challenges from Arab nationalism, but it was falling prices and Arab antagonism, rather than Anglo-American diplomacy, that finally fulfilled American and British goals.

Although Anglo-American military operations in July 1958 preserved Lebanon's pro-Western orientation and the Hashemite monarchy in Jordan, the intervention also stoked Arab nationalist resentment against the Western powers and appeared only to reinforce the popularity of ʿAbd al-Nāṣir. While the U.S. was powerless to contain Arab nationalism, accommodation of revolutionary Arab politics implied abandoning conservative allies such as Saudi Arabia and Jordan, relinquishing Western oil assets and military bases in the Middle East, and endorsing Nāṣir's regional ambitions. A National Security Council planning board paper captured this dilemma by explaining on the one hand that the U.S. "must adapt to Arab nationalism . . . if we are to retain more than a steadily declining influence in the Arab world," while suggesting on the other that "the United States cannot afford to accommodate to it" if such acceptance meant surrendering Western interests. For his part, Secretary Dulles remained intensely concerned that Nāṣir might jeopardize access to the oil crucial to the economy of Western Europe. Control of Middle Eastern oil, Dulles told the National Security Council, would permit the UAR president "to blackmail Western Europe and threaten the solvency of the United Kingdom." Eisenhower, however, believed that the U.S. should seek opportunities to demonstrate support for Arab economic development and self-determination when the costs of doing so were not unacceptable. "Since we are about to get thrown out of the area," the president remarked with apparent sarcasm, "we might as well believe in Arab nationalism."[1]

As the U.S. withdrew troops from Lebanon during the late summer and early fall of 1958, administration officials acknowledged the need for qualified acceptance of Arab nationalism but resisted recognizing ʿAbd al-Nāṣir as leader of the Arab world. In early August, Eisenhower expressed support before the United Nations for an Arab development bank and for the right of Arab peoples to choose their own leaders. Deputy Undersecretary of State Robert Murphy, following a tour of the Middle East, circulated a paper proposing a multilateral treaty to neutralize the region and ensure Western access to Arab oil, but Murphy offered no specific recommendations concerning Nāṣir, whom he described as a "difficult personality." Dulles dismissed Murphy's proposal for an arms limitation treaty for the Middle East and hoped that, instead of relying on formal agreements, the U.S. and Britain could exploit "selfish and competitive interests" among oil-producing states to undermine the effectiveness of any price-fixing or embargo. As for Nāṣir, Dulles advocated flexibility in relations with the UAR president, whom the secretary reluctantly acknowledged as the "dominant power" in the Arab world. Following intense debate, the administration struck a compromise between the State Department, which backed Dulles's pragmatism, and those officials in Defense and Treasury who opposed any compromise with Nāṣir. NSC 5820, the paper on Middle East policy completed in November, endorsed cooperation with ʿAbd al-

Nāṣir as head of the UAR but not as paramount Arab leader. It also stated that the U.S. should continue to deny the area to the Soviets, secure Gulf oil resources in cooperation with Britain, and establish a "working relationship" with Arab nationalism while "seeking . . . to contain its outward thrust."[2]

Shifts in Arab politics rapidly overtook U.S. policy, however, and the development of what Malcolm Kerr has called an "Arab Cold War" between Cairo and Baghdad contradicted American assumptions that ʿAbd al-Nāṣir enjoyed unchallenged prestige as leader of the Arab world. Far from an unambiguous Nāṣirist victory, the July Revolution in Baghdad triggered a power struggle among Iraqi factions that had opposed the monarchy, including Kurds, Shīʿites, nationalists both sympathetic and hostile toward Nāṣir, and communists. Out of this confusion, Major-General ʿAbd al-Karīm Qāsim, son of a Sunni Arab father and Shīʿite Kurdish mother, emerged as prime minister with substantial support from Iraqi communists, and the premier immediately alienated Nāṣir by publicly denouncing him and by prosecuting advocates of union with the UAR. The policies of the communist-aligned Qāsim threatened Nāṣir's already tenuous hold on Syria, where communists such as Khālid Baqdash had begun to denounce Cairo's heavy-handed rule and had defied Nāṣir's campaign to eliminate all political groups except those under his control. In response, ʿAbd al-Nāṣir arrested communist dissidents, angering his erstwhile Soviet ally. At the same time, he also sought to improve relations with conservative Arab states, a policy he had initiated during an August 1958 summit meeting with Saudi Crown Prince Fayṣal, who appeared eager to reduce tensions with the UAR in exchange for pursuing a neutral foreign policy. Finally, Nāṣir indicated a desire to cooperate with the United States.[3]

Senior U.S. officials fully grasped the significance of the Nāṣir-Qāsim hostility only after Assistant Secretary of State William Rountree returned in December 1958 from the Middle East, where he had met separately with both Arab leaders. Rountree reported to the National Security Council that he had encountered violent communist demonstrations in Baghdad and that Nāṣir had expressed concern about Arab communism. More candidly, the assistant secretary divulged in a private meeting with Eisenhower and Acting Secretary Christian Herter that Nāṣir feared Qāsim and had requested a reconciliation with Washington. "Nasser desires to work with us on Iraq," Rountree stated, and is "much concerned over Communist influence with Qasim." Eisenhower noted that although it would be difficult to back Nāṣir openly without provoking Israel and its supporters, the UAR president could prove to be the most effective opponent of communism in the Middle East. Following Rountree's return, the administration, which had already awarded the UAR aid in the form of surplus agricultural goods, concluded that Cairo's burgeoning antagonism toward Baghdad represented a positive development in the American campaign to manage Arab nationalism and contain communism. Policy makers therefore refrained from any major new initiative that might galvanize Arab opinion against the West and lessen the rivalries within the Arab world that Washington hoped to exploit.[4]

As part of this strategy, the U.S. accepted Prince Fayṣal's neutral foreign policy, which not only helped to ease the Nāṣirist threat against Saudi Arabia but also permitted Fayṣal to concentrate on economic reforms regarded by the administration as crucial to the regime's survival. Since assuming power, Fayṣal had implemented International Monetary Fund recommendations for stabilizing the budget and the Saudi riyal and had imposed import restrictions to curtail the loss of hard currency stemming largely from the purchase of foreign luxury goods by the royal family. In January 1959, Fayṣal's government published the kingdom's first balanced budget and, in the words of Sarah Yizraeli, the crown prince "took pains to carry it out to the letter." To assist in these efforts, the United States granted Riyadh a second one-year moratorium on debts owed on military equipment since fiscal year 1957 and absorbed the loss when the Saudis defaulted on their subsidy to the U.S. military training mission. Nāṣir's rivalry with Qāsim and the resulting *détente* with the Arab monarchies, U.S. officials believed, both lessened Saudi Arabia's vulnerability to external subversion and facilitated reforms that enhanced internal stability.[5]

Anglo-American cooperation remained basic to U.S. policy in the Middle East, and joint planning proceeded to defend Gulf oil by force if necessary. Throughout 1959, British military planners continued to consult with their American counterparts on Mideast defense, as they had since the Bermuda conference, and even sought to involve U.S. officials directly in contingency planning for intervention in Kuwait. Despite this cooperation, however, the allies diverged in their responses to the "Arab Cold War." During a March 1959 summit meeting between Eisenhower and Prime Minister Macmillan, it became apparent that, unlike the Americans, the British were concerned more by ʿAbd al-Nāṣir's continuing popularity in the Arab world and his influence in the oil-producing Gulf states than by Qāsim's cooperation with Iraqi communists and potential alliance with the Soviet Union. In part, the British attitude was the consequence of growing Arab nationalism in Kuwait, where Nāṣirist demonstrations had erupted on February 1, and whose ruler had recently decided to adhere to the Arab League against the advice of London's political resident. While Eisenhower recommended that the U.S. and Britain seek to intensify ʿAbd al-Nāṣir's feud with Arab communists and the Soviet Union, Macmillan was wary of precipitating the very Soviet-Iraqi partnership that Washington feared, and the British remained categorically opposed to cooperation with Nāṣir. "Dining with the devil," declared Foreign Secretary Selwyn Lloyd, "called for a long spoon."[6]

Unwilling to jeopardize Britain's ties with its Gulf clients, officials in London also refused to make the compromises regarding Buraymī that Fayṣal held out as preconditions for restoring Anglo-Saudi relations. State Department officials sought a rapprochement between Britain and Saudi Arabia and believed that in light of the threat Iraq posed in the Gulf, the British should "reduce to the greatest extent possible other pressures upon their position in this area." Prior to the Eisenhower-Macmillan summit, London opened contacts with the Saudis through U.N. Secretary-General Dag Hammarskjöld, an initiative that continued without success into June 1959. For his part, Fayṣal insisted that agreement on eastern Arabia precede restoration of diplomatic relations, and evidence suggests that the crown prince stalled to avoid endangering his *modus vivendi* with Nāṣir, who was himself locked in a series of disputes with Britain related to the Suez crisis. The situation therefore closely resembled that of July 1954, when the Saudis had delayed the Buraymī arbitration agreement until the ink had dried on the Anglo-Egyptian treaty.[7]

Both the U.S. and Britain remained intent on preserving access to the inexpensive petroleum of the Gulf, though the turmoil in Arab politics led the allies to separate conclusions about whether Iraq or the UAR posed the more dire threat to the postwar petroleum order. Focused on Cold War priorities, the Eisenhower administration pursued tactical cooperation with ʿAbd al-Nāṣir in order to isolate the communist-aligned government of ʿAbd al-Karīm Qāsim. By contrast, the British struggled to preserve the ruling dynasties in Kuwait and the other Gulf protectorates against Arab nationalism, and from London's perspective, Nāṣir continued to represent the most serious threat to the oil crucial to Britain's economy. Meanwhile, the cumulative effect of changes in the global oil industry suggested that the Western allies could successfully preserve the postwar petroleum order through means short of force.

A mentality of scarcity and fear of nationalist expropriation on the part of Western officials and oil company executives had pervaded the creation of the postwar petroleum order, but by the late 1950s, an abundant oil supply had altered the terms of trade in favor of consumers and severely compromised the political leverage of producing countries. Interest in the oil resources of eastern Arabia and the Gulf intensified during World War Two, when wartime demand resurrected fears of an oil shortage, and such concerns persisted into the era of the Marshall Plan, the Korean War, and the Cold War remilitarization of Western Europe. During the same period, Western officials and industry leaders faced a series of nationalist crises, including the Arab-Israeli War of 1948, Musaddiq's seizure of the Anglo-Iranian Oil Company, and the Suez crisis, that threatened the supply of oil essential for civilian sector reconstruction and military rearmament.

Following Suez, however, several factors helped to foster a global oil surplus and shift concerns from securing adequate supply to finding sufficient markets and bolstering prices. First, companies other than the major Anglo-American firms, including Japanese and Italian interests, won oil concessions from Middle Eastern countries eager to augment their oil revenues, and this proliferation of concessions increased production among existing oil states. Second, at the behest of the British and American governments, the major corporations began exploration in north African countries such as Libya and even war-torn Algeria, whose location west of the Mideast oil-transit facilities made them potentially more secure sources of petroleum than the Gulf countries. Finally, the Soviet Union began selling large amounts of central Asian crude to European buyers at rates significantly below the prevailing price. Although demand continued to surge, increasing by about 6 percent among "free world" countries during 1959, supplies grew even faster, and the rate at which existing global capacity surpassed demand more than doubled during the second half of the decade. As a result of these trends, the industry crossed a Rubicon in February 1959 when British Petroleum became the first major corporation to lower the per-barrel prices of all grades of oil it exported from the Middle East.[8]

Already, the growing surplus had affected the Eisenhower administration's oil policy, which had been geared toward supporting the major oil companies' overseas operations but became increasingly attuned to domestic producers' concerns about cheap, imported petroleum. Although restricting imports contradicted Eisenhower's promotion of freer trade, the president relented under political pressure from congressmen representing coal- and oil-producing states. In 1957, the administration established voluntary controls limiting imports to 10 percent of domestic consumption and, two years later, made these restrictions mandatory. Eisenhower expressed regret about constraining free trade and limiting the amount of dollars sent abroad but justified the restrictions on the basis of national security. It was necessary to offer domestic producers "some kind of assurance that they are not to be eliminated as productive industries," Eisenhower wrote, "if for no other reason than in the event of emergency we shall need their facilities operating at an increasing tempo." While stabilizing domestic prices, the import restrictions only exacerbated the glut on the global market, however, by excluding foreign producers from the United States, the richest oil market in the world, and by forcing them to compete for customers in markets already saturated with inexpensive oil from the Middle East, the USSR, and the Caribbean.[9]

In response to the decline in oil prices, the Arab states planned an oil congress for spring 1959 in Cairo, a step that alarmed oil company executives and Western officials. Representatives from Jersey Standard warned Christian Herter, who had replaced an ill Dulles as secretary of state in April, that the congress would be an opportunity for producers "to enunciate highly detrimental national policies with respect to petroleum." Company executives were particularly concerned that the conference would become a platform for the combative Saudi petroleum minister ʿAbdullah al-Ṭāriqī. Controversy also surrounded a scheduled presentation by oil lawyer Frank Hendryx, a consultant to the Saudi government, whose paper, "A Sovereign Nation's Legal Ability to Make and Abide by a Petroleum Concession Contract," argued that under some circumstances, a producing country could unilaterally alter the terms of an oil concession agreement. Indeed, the mere fact that the congress was convening in Cairo under the auspices of ʿAbd al-Nāṣir's government suggested that Arab nationalism would define the conference's agenda. Aramco management was so concerned about this possibility that Vice President James Terry Duce traveled to Cairo in February to sound out UAR and Arab League oil officials.[10]

Though it raised concerns in Western capitals and oil company boardrooms, the congress proved less of an Arab nationalist rally than a forum for businesslike cooperation among Arab and non-Arab oil-producing countries. In March 1959, Nāṣir's government had backed an anti-Qāsim uprising in the Iraqi city of Mosul, and for this reason, Iraq refused to send official representatives to the Cairo conference. Not only did the "Arab Cold War" prevent a united Arab front in oil policy, but congress participants also included observers from the non-Arab oil-producing states of Venezuela and even Iran, a country that maintained diplomatic relations with Israel. Ṭāriqī's innocuous proposal for a new, Arab-managed pipeline set a tone of moderation, while, according to British intelligence reports, Hendryx's thesis "made little headway within the Congress," and delegates recognized that falling oil prices made it impossible "to draw up an 'Arab policy.'" ʿAbd al-Nāṣir himself, who years earlier had called on

Arabs to exploit their control of oil for political purposes, acknowledged that producers had to cooperate with the West in order to secure adequate markets. "Arabs know," Nāṣir explained, "that their oil has to go to the customer before it has any value." The congress was important, however, in bringing together for the first time Ṭāriqī and the Venezuelan observer, Petroleum Minister Juan Pablo Pérez Alfonzo, who joined with representatives from other oil-producing countries to sign an unofficial gentlemen's agreement pledging mutual cooperation to defend prices. From the Cairo oil congress, Arab oil states therefore subordinated an Arab nationalist agenda that included the destruction of Israel, Arab unity, and the economic development of resource-poor Arab countries to a limited sort of collaboration with non-Arab oil producers focused on securing the best possible terms within the postwar petroleum order.[11]

By pressuring Aramco to increase Saudi Arabia's income, and even calling for the "arabization" of the company, Petroleum Minister ʿAbdullah al-Ṭāriqī emerged as the principal antagonist of American oilmen. Both U.S. officials and Aramco board chairman Norman Hardy criticized Ṭāriqī's "ignorance" of the oil industry, his penchant for "fanatically obeying political and ideological motives," and "irrational hostility toward ARAMCO." Further straining Saudi-Aramco relations, the overproduction crisis coincided with a generational turnover in Aramco management, marked by the retirements of long-time Vice President James Terry Duce and Chairman Fred A. Davies, and the promotion of Hardy as chairman and geologist Tom Barger as president. These younger executives, charged with sustaining company revenues under adverse circumstances, lacked the personal friendships that their predecessors had enjoyed with Saudi ministers during the early years of expanding markets, production, and profits.[12]

Despite contempt for Ṭāriqī on the part of Aramco management, the Saudi petroleum minister tenaciously bargained to increase Saudi revenues within the context of the kingdom's existing relationship with Aramco. In fact, the major Saudi-Aramco controversy in 1959 and 1960 basically involved how to market Saudi oil most profitably in a glutted market. Aramco proposed that its parents create third-party trading companies, which would aggressively seek new customers by offering discounted prices. Such a policy would preserve both the parents' monopoly on the marketing of Saudi oil and Aramco's U.S. tax deduction on royalties. For his part, Ṭāriqī still backed the "integration" of Aramco to include marketing and Saudi participation in the company's profits in shipping, refining, and retail sales, proposals management opposed because they would involve Aramco in competition for markets with its own parent companies. Aramco sought to assuage Ṭāriqī in other ways, however, by appointing him and Ḥāfiẓ Wahba, the veteran Saudi diplomat, to the company board. Executives told British officials that by giving the Saudi petroleum minister a role in company policy making, they hoped to blunt his demands, and, indeed, that Ṭāriqī was a "model of respectability" at the 1959 board meeting in San Francisco.[13]

Following a new Arab League initiative among oil-producing members to coordinate pricing strategy, British officials submitted an aide-mémoire to the State Department on February 26, 1960, arguing the benefits of increasing production in Iran at the expense of Iraq and other Arab oil exporters. Oil overproduction, they pointed out, fostered strong competition for markets among existing producers, and there were "cogent political reasons" for exploiting this competition and for backing Iran against the Arab states. For instance, Iran was a member of the Central Treaty Organization, the Western-sponsored alliance that had succeeded the Baghdad Pact. London therefore planned secretly to ask British companies to "take account of the political considerations" in apportioning production and to include their American partners in these decisions. British officials urged the Eisenhower administration to lobby U.S. corporations for a similar policy. As reflected in their attitude toward the "Arab Cold War," the British continued to regard Arab nationalism as the major threat in the Middle East, and Macmillan's government consequently sought any opportunity to prevent an effective combination of Arab oil states.[14]

American policy makers, however, believed it possible to revert to diplomatic support for private industry as the Arab nationalist threat to the postwar petroleum order diminished and as cooperation among oil-producing states proceeded on a basis other than Arab nationalism. For example, the State Department again intervened to forestall antitrust action against Aramco that threatened the company's position in its ongoing disputes with Ṭāriqī and Saudi Arabia. As Lewis Jones, assistant secretary for near eastern affairs, explained, prosecution "would provide substantial support to elements in that country which have been pressing for Arabization of the company on integrated lines." In March 1960, the administration also named Cornelius Dwyer as its first at-large petroleum officer and assigned him to monitor company-government relations in the Middle East. Meanwhile, the State Department's Bureau of Economic Affairs determined that the British approach was unnecessary because the oil surplus had already enhanced the companies' bargaining position with host governments, and a departmental paper on oil concessions in the Middle East noted that Arab nationalism had failed to foster unity among producing and non-producing Arab countries. Instead, Arab oil states recognized that they lacked the expertise to run their industries without the Western corporations and "have begun to see that it might be profitable for them to cooperate with non-Arab oil producing countries in achieving a more favorable position vis-a-vis the companies" on pricing, production, and revenues.[15]

By focusing either on celebrities such as Ṭāriqī and Pérez Alfonzo, or on the minutiae of oil pricing, analysts of OPEC's birth have neglected how economic forces compelled Saudi Arabia and other Arab producers to forsake broader nationalist goals in favor of pragmatic cooperation with non-Arab oil states. For all of his rhetoric about "arabization," Ṭāriqī's oil diplomacy was remarkable for its non-Arab character, and his most important initiative involved ongoing cooperation with his Venezuelan counterpart, whom he visited in Caracas in May to work out a plan for prorationing global production. This plan was the precursor to OPEC, which the oil ministers unveiled after Exxon's decision in August to lower the posted price that was the basis for determining producing countries' royalties. Crown Prince Fayṣal and Ṭāriqī protested Exxon's unilateral action, but demanded only that companies consult producing countries on pricing decisions. In addition, the signatories to the Cairo gentlemen's agreement responded to the price cuts by assembling in Baghdad for a producers' meeting from which the UAR, still engaged in a bitter feud with Iraq, was excluded.[16]

American officials recognized that the oil states were simply trying to extract more favorable terms from the corporations, and for this reason did not place OPEC in the same category as previous threats to U.S. petroleum interests, such as the Suez, Syrian, and Lebanese crises. OPEC's confrontation with the major companies was limited to pricing, an arena in which overproduction gave the corporations a distinct advantage. The desire for increased revenue and competition for markets also gave OPEC members strong incentives to exceed production ceilings and to renege on prorationing agreements. As far as "the Middle Eastern countries in the new Organization were concerned," Eisenhower told the National Security Council, "anyone could break up the Organization by offering five cents more per barrel for the oil of one of the countries."[17]

Significantly, analysts writing in the wake of the 1973 embargo, confronted by evidence of OPEC's power to dictate prices and determined to blame the crisis on corporate and government policies, did not recognize how the formation of a producers' cartel in 1960 deprived Arab nationalism of its most potentially radical implications. Arab League members envisioned an oil policy that benefited non-producing Arab states economically and that promised a transfer of wealth from the industrialized, consuming nations to resource-poor Arab countries. Though serious differences had divided oil and non-oil Arab states since the late 1940s,

King Saʿūd, for example, repeatedly acted against his economic self-interest to demonstrate solidarity with Arab nationalism.

Yet OPEC eclipsed the League as the Arab producers' most important consultative forum, while the UAR and other non-producing Arab states became marginalized in oil diplomacy as producers set policies according to their domestic requirements, pursued price-stabilizing strategies detrimental to Arab consumers, and invested more of their revenues at home and in the developed economies over the long term than in the poorest Arab countries. According to one economist, Arab producers devoted only about 6 percent of the post-embargo bonanza to official aid programs within and outside the Arab world during the years 1974–81.[18] For the Arab oil states, in other words, the decision to work within the postwar petroleum order meant renouncing what Western governments and companies found most threatening about Arab nationalism.

As Arab oil producers foreclosed redistributive possibilities by abandoning Arab nationalist goals, a strikingly similar process was underway within Saudi Arabia, where, between 1958 and 1960, Fayṣal's reforms helped to set the mold for the modern Saudi state. Though Fayṣal earned plaudits from U.S. officials, Aramco management, and IMF economists for his fiscal austerity, such measures antagonized elements within and outside the royal family. Not surprisingly, Saʿūd sought to reverse the March 1958 transfer of power by courting Fayṣal's opponents, but more importantly, the Free Princes' faction led by Ṭalāl criticized Fayṣal for the limited nature of his reforms and promoted a constitutional monarchy aligned with ʿAbd al-Nāṣir. When Saʿūd successfully regained control of the government by allying with the Free Princes, it briefly appeared that their Arab nationalist agenda would change the Saudi state from a patrimonial government to one in which the ruling family consulted ʿulamāʾ, tribal leaders, and even elected officials. But to the Princes' dismay, Saʿūd had never intended to share political power, or control over oil revenues, in the manner desired by his junior partners.

In seeking to subvert Fayṣal's authority, Saʿūd demonstrated a sophistication that was absent during the early years of the king's reign, when he had recklessly pursued political supremacy at the cost of alienating members of his own family. Saʿūd recognized that he was not in a position to challenge Fayṣal directly, especially after the family sided with the crown prince during a May 1959 dispute in which Fayṣal refused to pay royal debts out of the state treasury. Instead, the king appealed to his existing supporters, the Nejdi tribes, and to groups harmed by Fayṣal's reforms, such as Hijazi merchants who profited from the import trade. According to

British reports, in the Hijaz, Saʿūd "made a royal progress in style, distributing largesse and building himself up as the open-handed father of the Arabs on the old lines," and the king garnered support in Nejd and elsewhere by granting favors "in response to the lightest petition, and otherwise making free with the privy purse." Saʿūd also sought backing outside the kingdom through an awkward overture to Macmillan in April 1959, which the prime minister politely rebuffed, and even by meeting ʿAbd al-Nāṣir in Cairo five months later. In addition, the king petitioned the U.S. embassy in Jidda for financial and military aid, but the State Department withheld such assistance in the belief that Saʿūd would use it to undermine Fayṣal's reforms, and the State Department warned Ambassador Heath to restrict his dealings with the king. Saʿūd should be given the "absolute minimum of encouragement," the department instructed the embassy, "in any projects which would appear [to] run counter [to] efforts by Faisal and [the] IMF [to] stabilize Saudi finances."[19]

Of greater potential significance for the Saudi state than the king's maneuvering was the rise of the Free Princes' faction led by Ṭalāl ibn ʿAbd al-ʿAzīz. He had served as the political spokesman for the generation of Saudi princes born after 1930 since becoming the first among them to receive a cabinet portfolio early in Saʿūd's reign. Given the ban on political activity outside the royal family, the Free Princes wielded important influence both by controlling the balance of power between Saʿūd and Fayṣal and by filtering Arab nationalist ideas into ruling family politics. Ṭalāl and other younger princes such as Nawwāf and Badr had signed the July 1956 petition critical of Saʿūd's pro-Western foreign policy, and the Free Princes had given Fayṣal crucial support during the March 1958 crisis. They subsequently backed Fayṣal's budgetary retrenchment by voluntarily refusing their princes' stipends, and they also hoped that economic reforms would open the door to greater consultation within the ruling family as well as mechanisms for power sharing with non-royal groups. By some accounts, Ṭalāl had conditioned his endorsement of Fayṣal on the crown prince's willingness to establish a "legitimate legislative council" composed of one-third appointed members and the rest government-approved candidates elected by provincial bodies. Once in power, however, Fayṣal pursued fiscal solvency and efficient bureaucracy without implementing the Free Princes' proposals for greater political openness. The crown prince further alienated his younger supporters by following IMF recommendations that included modest agricultural and irrigation projects, but no program for harnessing oil revenues to economic development. Whereas the Free Princes regarded economic reforms as only the beginning of a more far-reaching transformation of the Saudi state into a constitutional monarchy,

Fayṣal reorganized the kingdom's finances and administration chiefly in order to preserve the royal family's monopoly on political power.[20]

Exclusive focus on the personal rivalry between Fayṣal and Saʿūd neglects the ways in which the Saudi-Aramco relationship predetermined the nature of the crown prince's political reforms. Fayṣal's major contributions were controlling the budget and creating a bureaucracy distinct from, but not independent of, the royal family. Such measures marked the beginning of a transition in Saudi fiscal policy from the extraction of taxes to the distribution of oil revenues. In other words, Saudi Arabia became a rentier state, or one in which government machinery exists to distribute revenues as a way of pre-empting demands for political participation. Though this state-building pattern developed in other Gulf oil monarchies, it occurred later in Saudi Arabia as the direct result of the private structure of American oil diplomacy and because Aramco had functioned for years as the surrogate for a Saudi state bureaucracy. Scholars who study Saudi state building have been reluctant to acknowledge this fact. Kiren Aziz Chaudhry, for example, understates Aramco's importance by describing it as merely "the biggest taxpayer in the kingdom" and argues that the lack of a colonial legacy in Saudi Arabia makes possible a historical analysis of state and market formation in isolation from the international economy. As the history of Fayṣal's reforms makes clear, however, any discussion of Saudi state building apart from the postwar petroleum order is impossible. More importantly, though Saudi Arabia lacked a history of European colonialism, the legacy of America's informal empire was a major factor in the kingdom's development.[21]

During Fayṣal's cabinet, the highest priority for the ruling family, the U.S. government, and Aramco was not ensuring the success of government reforms *per se,* but preserving the set of relationships that had been so mutually profitable. Though the State Department had kept Saʿūd at a distance while supporting Fayṣal's reforms, the embassy contacted the king in the summer of 1960 to share evidence of a coup planned by Saudi military officers. For their part, Aramco executives, in contrast to the administration, were even willing to countenance Saʿūd's return to power if it meant that ʿAbdullah al-Ṭāriqī would forfeit control over the kingdom's oil diplomacy and lose the ability to disrupt the existing terms of the company-government relationship. William Eddy, consultant to Aramco and former U.S. minister to the Saudi kingdom, quietly discussed this possibility with Saʿūd during a June 1960 mission. Given the overriding consideration of sustaining the Saudi-Aramco association, the likelihood that the Free Princes or non-royal activists could change the nature of the Saudi regime was at best remote.[22]

Indeed, although Saʿūd temporarily regained control of the government through an alliance of convenience with the Free Princes, his veto of Ṭalāl's political agenda effectively frustrated reformers' hopes for a constitutional monarchy. Saʿūd's appeal to reformist elements began in November 1959, when he appointed ʿAbd al-ʿAzīz Muʿammar to his royal dīwān, or council. Muʿammar, the scion of an elite Nejdi family allied to the Saudi dynasty, had nevertheless gained a reputation as a radical leader during the Aramco labor violence of 1953. Saʿūd found Muʿammar useful as a liaison to Ṭalāl's Free Princes, to Arab nationalists in the Hijaz, and to government bureaucrats and intellectuals who formed the group Nejd al-Fatīy (Young Nejd) to agitate for political reform. According to Aramco accounts, Saʿūd charged Muʿammar with instituting "some form of representative government," a plan Fayṣal warned could trigger an "avalanche" of political disorder. It appeared that Saʿūd intended to implement the Free Princes' agenda when the king forced Fayṣal's resignation over a budget crisis in December 1960, formed a new government in which Ṭalāl and Badr held cabinet posts, and announced over Radio Mecca the formation of a constitutional committee. But Saʿūd's public repudiation of the proposed constitution on December 29, scarcely a week after regaining power, reflected the cynical and ephemeral nature of the king's partnership with the Free Princes.[23]

Most importantly, through his subsequent policies Saʿūd gradually acknowledged that the king would have to govern in consultation with elder members of the dynasty if the ruling family was to resist Arab nationalist pressures and continue to enjoy the spoils of the postwar petroleum order. In fact, the king reversed himself on the constitution partly in response to family protests, and he confirmed Fayṣal's status as crown prince according to the wishes of the king's brothers Muḥammad and Khālid. By adopting Fayṣal's strict 1961 budget, which had precipitated the most recent political crisis, Saʿūd also surrendered the sort of resources that would permit the king to sustain a power base outside the family among tribal leaders and other constituents. Finally, Saʿūd acceded to the family's capital demand in September 1961 by dismissing Ṭalāl from the government for airing family disputes to a Lebanese newspaper. As Sarah Yizraeli has noted, the collapse that same month of the UAR, which ʿAbd al-Nāṣir blamed on Arab "reactionaries" and which abruptly ended his *détente* with the Arab monarchies, made it necessary for Saʿūd to reconcile with Fayṣal, who became acting prime minister in November. Sharing a transcendent concern for their family's place in the postwar petroleum order, Saʿūd and Fayṣal could set aside their rivalry for a time and rally to the defense of the dynasty when it was threatened by Arab radicalism within or outside the kingdom. Saudi Arabia therefore became neither the absolute monarchy Saʿūd had sought since the death of his father, nor the constitutional regime desired by the Free Princes, but instead a family-ruled state in which the dynasty distributed oil revenues only insofar as it was necessary to preserve its unchallenged authority.[24]

During the last years of the Eisenhower administration, the postwar petroleum order was more secure than at any time since its creation, but this development was the result of factors other than Western diplomacy. A "Cold War" between the self-described revolutionary Arab regimes in Cairo and Baghdad changed the nature of the superpowers' Cold War in the Middle East by distancing ʿAbd al-Nāṣir from the Soviet Union and by promoting a temporary truce between the UAR and conservative Arab states aligned with Washington. At the same time, Arab oil producers responded to weakening petroleum prices through a common strategy with non-Arab exporters, and this approach relocated oil politics from the arena of Arab nationalism to the domain of company-government bargaining.

The post-Suez surfeit of oil acted as the catalyst not only for OPEC, but also for the establishment within Saudi Arabia of a rentier-state economy administered by senior members of the ruling family. Fayṣal intended his financial and administrative reforms to preserve the kingdom's place in the postwar petroleum order and to preserve the benefits derived by the dynasty from an intimate relationship with U.S. oil corporations. This basic fact precluded the establishment of the constitutional monarchy advocated by the Free Princes. Fayṣal's reform cabinet ensured on the one hand that within the ruling family the king would be first among equals, and on the other that the dynasty would dispense oil wealth in a limited way as an alternative to sharing political power. This twofold compromise defined modern Saudi Arabia by reconciling the patrimonial nature of the state carved out by ʿAbd al-ʿAzīz in the years before oil exports with his kingdom's subsequent integration into the global economy.

Conclusion

For the Anglo-American allies, crises such as Buraymī and Suez were "symptoms of a general difference of approach to Middle East questions and of views about the merits and defects of imperialism," recalled Bernard Burrows, former British resident at Bahrain, "and on the best methods of exerting influence from the West on the turbulent Middle East scene."[1] Just as American officials pursued a foreign oil policy based upon private enterprise and the experience of domestic capitalist development, their counterparts in London inherited a century-old imperial presence in the Gulf. The changing of the guard in the Gulf during the second half of the twentieth century, from British hegemony to an American capitalist order, involved a transition between two different kinds of empire. Exploring U.S. relations with Saudi Arabia, the focus of the emerging postwar American presence in the Middle East, provides a way of understanding this transition and the historic change behind America's leading role in the Gulf War of 1990–91.

The transfer of power from London to Washington was a cooperative process because a common conception of the postwar European economy determined the nature of Anglo-American relations in the Middle East. By the time of Eisenhower's presidency, the two allies had reached a working compromise that permitted freer and more open European economies while recognizing Britain's special intermediary position between the U.S. and Europe as head of the sterling area. As both British and American policy makers believed, the U.K. could sustain this bargain only through continued access to the sterling oil of the Middle East and maintenance of its authority over the ruling dynasties of the Gulf. Britain and the U.S. therefore shared an interest in preserving the relationships among themselves, oil-producing and oil-transit states, and the major petroleum companies established for the sake of the European economy. This set of economic and political relationships, known as the postwar petroleum order, also enabled the U.S. to reconcile domestic consumer demand for oil with new Cold War responsibilities overseas. For these reasons, inexpensive Mideast oil was the life's blood of the global economy after 1945, and in order to keep it flowing, the Anglo-American allies jointly pursued strategic planning, a solution to the oil transit crisis, and military intervention.

Yet the allies' efforts to secure the region's petroleum met resistance as revolutionary nationalism mobilized growing segments of Arab societies against Western colonialism, the state of Israel, and political leaders who had inherited their status from the Ottoman era. Throughout his two terms as president, Eisenhower faced the dilemma of trying to accommodate the new Arab politics while cooperating with Great Britain. Though Washington's support for Israel and its partnership with Britain posed serious obstacles to assuaging Arab nationalism, Eisenhower and other officials initially assumed that limited offers of arms and private investment in the petroleum producing states could prevent radical political forces from threatening oil supplies. As Arab nationalism intensified in the oil transit countries and the Soviets established ties with ʿAbd al-Nāṣir, however, Eisenhower first looked to Saʿūd in a misguided attempt to exploit the king's supposed religious prestige, and then resorted to military intervention with Britain to defend the postwar petroleum order. Pursuit of this primary objective caused the administration to miss an opportunity after Suez to reconfigure the political economy of its foreign oil policy. Instead of designing a development program to raise living standards in the Middle East through Western contributions and the investment of oil revenues, Eisenhower chose instead to assume the responsibility from Britain as guardian of the region's oil. This decision shaped the future of the U.S. role in the Middle East.

But the failure of Arab nationalism to distribute resources more equitably within the Arab world was not simply the consequence of Washington's priorities. By 1960, the Arab nationalist threat to the industrialized economies had diminished for reasons that had less to do with U.S. policy than with the decision by oil-producing Arab states to form a price-lobbying cartel with non-Arab producers. By participating in OPEC, Arab oil exporters sought to protect their own incomes first rather than establish institutional mechanisms for sharing oil wealth and funding development in the Arab transit states. Rejection of the most radical aspects of the Arab nationalist agenda by Saudi Arabia and other Arab exporters in 1960 meant that windfall revenues generated by the oil embargo and price hike thirteen years later went mostly into the pockets of the Gulf's ruling families and their clients. The embargo against the U.S. was short-lived if economically disruptive, and the oil crisis of 1973–74 ultimately came down to a dispute between producers and consumers over *prices*. In the 1970s, Arab oil states did not question the idea that their resources existed essentially to fuel the developed economies, because their earlier decision to operate within the terms of the postwar petroleum order had already closed the book on this issue. At the time of the Egyptian revolution, Nāṣir and other Arab leaders had envisioned marshaling the oil resources of the Gulf to serve Arab nationalist goals, such as the destruction of Israel and the development of poor Arab countries. Events two decades later reversed this logic, when the October War served as the occasion for a dramatic increase in oil prices that principally benefited producing governments. The ruling families of the Gulf retained control over how much oil wealth they would share with the other Arab states, and the largest source of redistribution has come in the form of remittances from Arab migrant laborers working in the producers' oil industries.[2]

As this study has argued, the private structure of America's informal empire also held implications for state building in modern Saudi Arabia, the peculiar outgrowth of American corporate investment grafted onto ʿAbd al-ʿAzīz's pre-petroleum state. The late king left his heirs no elaborate plan for governing the kingdom following his death, in large measure because Aramco's pervasive role in finance, construction, education, and public health rendered an extensive state machinery unnecessary. While the company employed the techniques of welfare capitalism and bureaucratic management, the U.S. government played a part in Saudi oil development circumscribed by the contours of the American political economy. This role entailed supporting Aramco through generous indulgence on corporate taxes and in antitrust matters, thwarting challenges to Aramco interests such as Onassis's tanker company, and maintaining a military presence at Dhahran. As Arab nationalism intensified and the Cold War came to the Middle East, Washington militarized the postwar petroleum order by arming Riyadh. The Saudi government, in turn, exploited American fears of communism to bargain for the military aid necessary to defend itself from Arab nationalists at home and abroad. Eisenhower's decision in 1956 to "absorb" Saudi oil revenues through arms sales set a precedent that helped make the kingdom a leading consumer of American weapons.[3]

Just as the formation of OPEC foreclosed chances for redistributing oil wealth in the Arab world, reforms within Saudi Arabia kept control of petroleum revenues in the hands of the ruling family. Saʿūd and Fayṣal, despite their personal rivalry, shared the common goal of defending their dynasty's stake in the postwar petroleum order from Arab nationalism, and their determination severely limited the possibilities for political reform even when the initiative originated within the ruling family, as in the case of the Free Princes. Only when compelled by financial necessity in the form of falling oil prices, a change in Aramco policy, and the Suez crisis, which tore a gaping hole in Saudi revenues, did the royal family accept a political compromise that both capped the budget and limited the power of the king. As a result of Fayṣal's reforms, Saudi Arabia assumed the features of a rentier state and subsequently became more methodical in the public investment of oil revenues, though hardly more democratic, by establishing a development board and implementing a series of five-year economic plans.

Indeed, compromises struck during Fayṣal's cabinet established the basis of the modern Saudi state. In 1964, Fayṣal deposed Saʿūd as king in consultation with the ruling family and the ʿulamāʾ, a move consistent with the reforms that had made the Saudi monarch first among equals. During the 1970s, the growth of the Saudi state bureaucracy coincided with the friendly purchase of Aramco by the Saudi government, a process not completed until March 1980. The Arabian-American consortium formed by U.S. corporations in the 1940s was no longer necessary, not only because the basic infrastructure for extracting Saudi petroleum was in place, but also because the Saudi state had evolved to assume functions previously fulfilled by the Western oil companies. While the trajectory of Saudi development corresponded to the postwar experiences of other oil-producing Gulf states, the political economy of U.S. foreign policy shaped the unique circumstances of Saudi state building and enabled the ruling family to postpone crucial decisions about the division of power and wealth in the kingdom. Aramco's policies of enlightened self-interest, including the advances on royalties it paid to the Saudi government and the company's economic development programs, made it possible for a modern oil economy to emerge in Saudi Arabia without overturning family rule.[4]

Eisenhower and other Americans, both government officials and corporate leaders, exuded an almost boundless optimism about the stabilizing potential of corporate investment in the Middle East, and they made a conscious choice to use private enterprise as a strategy to distinguish expanding U.S. power from European imperialism. Their approach enabled Americans to carve out an informal empire in the name of anti-colonialism. Nevertheless, the most striking change in America's Mideast foreign policy during the 1950s is the way in which the U.S. role came increasingly to resemble the one Britain had played since the nineteenth century. This shift occurred in both subtle and not-so-subtle ways. Eisenhower's bid to build up Saʿūd on the basis of essentialist notions about Islam borrowed from British Orientalism and connected American foreign policy to European traditions of studying, and dominating, the Middle East. More overt was the growing U.S. military role that included sponsoring regional defense schemes, maintaining bases, engaging in joint plans with Britain for defense of the Gulf, and, most of all, intervening in July 1958 to protect the postwar petroleum order. Yet falling oil prices and the retreat of the Arab nationalist threat to Western oil supplies prolonged this transfer of power until new dangers, such as the Iranian revolution and Ṣaddām Ḥusayn's ambitions, made it necessary for the U.S. to take greater initiative in the region. Only now, looking backward a decade after the Gulf War, is it possible to understand how Americans stepped into the shoes of the British, and the ways in which the Anglo-American transfer of power shaped the historical development of Saudi Arabia and the Gulf.

Abbreviations

ACW	Dwight D. Eisenhower, Papers as President of the United States (Ann C. Whitman File)
CAB	Cabinet Papers
CAH	Christian A. Herter Papers
DDEL	Dwight D. Eisenhower Library
FO	Foreign Office
FRUS	Foreign Relations of the United States
JFD	John Foster Dulles Papers
NSC	National Security Council
POWE	Ministry of Fuels and Power
PPP	Public Papers of the Presidents of the United States
PREM	Prime Minister's Papers
PRO	British Public Record Office
RG	Record Group, National Archives and Records Administration
WEM	William E. Mulligan Papers

Notes

Introduction

1. Raymond Hare, Oral History Transcript, OH-189, p. 51, DDEL; "Address to the Nation Announcing the Deployment of United States Armed Forces to Saudi Arabia," August 8, 1990, PPP, *George Bush, 1990,* Book II, 1108–1109. On U.S.-Saudi security relations and the Gulf War, see F. Gregory Gause III, "From 'Over the Horizon' to 'Into the Backyard': The U.S.-Saudi Relationship and the Gulf War," in *The Middle East and the United States: A Historical and Political Reassessment,* ed. David Lesch, 2nd ed. (Boulder, Colo.: Westview Press, 1999), 341–53.

2. See Aaron David Miller, *Search for Security: Saudi Arabian Oil and American Foreign Policy, 1933–1949* (Chapel Hill: University of North Carolina Press, 1980); Irvine Anderson, "Lend-Lease for Saudi Arabia: A Comment on Alternative Conceptualizations," *Diplomatic History* 3 (Fall 1979): 413–23, and *Aramco, the United States, and Saudi Arabia: A Study of the Dynamics of Foreign Oil Policy, 1933–1950* (Princeton, N.J.: Princeton University Press, 1981); and James L. Gormly, "Keeping the Door Open in Saudi Arabia: The United States and the Dhahran Airfield, 1945–46," *Diplomatic History* 4 (Spring 1980): 189–205. On FDR's meeting with ʿAbd al-ʿAzīz, see memorandum of conversation by Eddy, February 14, 1945, *FRUS, 1945,* 8: 2–3; and William A. Eddy, *F.D.R. Meets Ibn Saud* (New York: American Friends of the Middle East, 1954). On the mythology surrounding U.S. oil development in Saudi Arabia, see Robert Vitalis, "The Closing of the Arabian Oil Frontier and the Future of Saudi-American Relations," *Middle East Report* 27 (July–September 1997): 15–25, and "Crossing Exceptionalism's Frontiers to Discover America's Kingdom," *Arab Studies Journal* 6 (Spring 1998): 10–31.

3. For the company's account of the Saudi concession, see Arabian-American Oil Company, *The Aramco Handbook* (1960), 131–36. For sympathetic historical treatments based on company sources, see Anderson, *Aramco, the United States, and Saudi Arabia;* and Anthony Cave Brown, *Oil, God, and Gold: The Story of Aramco and the Saudi Kings* (Boston: Houghton Mifflin, 1999).

4. The geographic term "Middle East" (and the adjectives "Middle Eastern" and "Mideast") generally refer to the region between the Oxus and Nile Rivers east-to-west, and from Anatolia to the Arabian Peninsula north-to-south. I use "Persian Gulf" because it is more familiar to Americans than "Arab Gulf," though I recognize that Arabs use the latter designation. I try to avoid this controversy when convenient by simply referring to "the Gulf."

On naval strategy in the Gulf and the Anglo-American changing of the guard, see Michael A. Palmer, *Guardians of the Gulf: A History of America's Expanding Role in the Persian Gulf, 1833–1992* (New York: The Free Press, 1992). Americans never "naively expected to supplant the British commercially" without taking on military and strategic burdens, as Palmer argues. In fact, the U.S. sought to preserve British authority in the Gulf after World War Two while it simultaneously used Aramco's private activities as part of a strategy to manage Arab nationalism. See Palmer, *Guardians of the Gulf*, 243.

5. Parker T. Hart, *Saudi Arabia and the United States: Birth of a Security Partnership* (Bloomington: Indiana University Press, 1998), 5.

6. See Anderson, *Aramco, the United States, and Saudi Arabia;* Miller, *Search for Security;* David S. Painter, *Oil and the American Century: The Political Economy of U.S. Foreign Oil Policy, 1941–1954* (Baltimore: Johns Hopkins University Press, 1986); Douglas Little, "Pipeline Politics: America, TAPLINE and the Arabs," *Business History Review* 64 (Summer 1990): 255–85; Rex J. Casillas, *Oil and Diplomacy: The Evolution of American Foreign Policy in Saudi Arabia, 1933–1945* (New York: Garland, 1987); Michael B. Stoff, *Oil, War and American Security: The Search for a National Policy on Foreign Oil, 1941–1947* (New Haven, Conn.: Yale University Press, 1980); and Stephen J. Randall, *United States Foreign Oil Policy, 1919–1948: For Profits and Security* (Kingston: McGill-Queen's University Press, 1985).

7. See Painter, *Oil and the American Century.* On U.S. foreign oil policy during the 1920s, see Michael J. Hogan, *Informal Entente: The Private Structure of Cooperation in Anglo-American Economic Diplomacy, 1918–1928* (Columbia: University of Missouri Press, 1977), 159–85. See also idem, *The Marshall Plan: America, Britain, and the Reconstruction of Western Europe, 1947–1952* (New York: Cambridge University Press, 1987).

8. Daniel Yergin, *The Prize: The Epic Quest for Oil, Money, and Power* (New York: Simon and Schuster, 1992), 409–430.

9. On Middle Eastern oil, U.S. demand, and European reconstruction, see David Painter, "Oil and the Marshall Plan," *Business History Review* 58 (Autumn 1984): 359–83; and idem, *Oil and the American Century,* 96–102. On the fifty-fifty deal, see Yergin, *The Prize,* 409–10, 445–49; Painter, *Oil and the American Century,* 165–71; Anderson, *Aramco, the United States, and Saudi Arabia,* 187–97; and Miller, *Search for Security,* 213.

10. Irvine Anderson, *The Standard-Vacuum Oil Company and United States East Asian Policy, 1933–1941* (Princeton, N.J.: Princeton University Press, 1975); Hogan, *Informal Entente;* and William Stivers, *Supremacy and Oil: Iraq, Turkey, and the Anglo-American World Order, 1918–1930* (Ithaca, N.Y.: Cornell University Press, 1982).

11. On the Red Line, see William Stivers, "A Note on the Red Line Agreement," *Diplomatic History* 7 (Winter 1979): 23–34; Hogan, *Informal Entente,* 159–85; and Yergin, *The Prize,* 203–206. On the 1944 agreement, see Painter, *Oil and the American Century,* 59–74; Anderson, *Aramco, the United States, and Saudi Arabia,* 86–107; Miller, *Search for Security,* 100–106; and Yergin, *The Prize,* 402–403.

12. On Anglo-American tensions over Mideast oil, see Anderson, "Lend-Lease for Saudi Arabia: A Comment on Alternative Conceptualizations"; and Simon Davis, "Keeping the Americans in Line? Britain, the United States and Saudi Arabia, 1939–45: Inter-Allied Rivalry in the Middle East Revisited," *Diplomacy & Statecraft* 8 (March 1997): 96–136. On revision of the "Red Line," see Yergin, *The Prize,* 413–19, and Miller, *Search for Security,* 158–60.

On Anglo-American conflict in the Middle East, see William Roger Louis, *The British Empire in the Middle East, 1945–1951: Arab Nationalism, the United States, and Postwar*

Imperialism (New York: Oxford University Press, 1984); Gormly, "Keeping the Door Open in Saudi Arabia"; John DeNovo, "The Culbertson Economic Mission and Anglo-American Tensions in the Middle East, 1944–1945," *Journal of American History* 63 (March 1977): 913–36; and Robert Vitalis, "The 'New Deal' in Egypt: The Rise of Anglo-American Commercial Competition in World War II and the Fall of Neocolonialism," *Diplomatic History* 20 (Spring 1996): 211–39.

13. On the importance of Middle Eastern oil to U.S. strategic interests in Europe, see Painter, "Oil and the Marshall Plan," and *Oil and the American Century,* 153–60; and Melvyn P. Leffler, *A Preponderance of Power: National Security, the Truman Administration, and the Cold War* (Stanford, Calif.: Stanford University Press, 1992), 237–39.

For reinterpretations of Anglo-American diplomacy in Egypt, see Peter L. Hahn, *The United States, Great Britain, and Egypt, 1945–1956: Strategy and Diplomacy in the Early Cold War* (Chapel Hill: University of North Carolina Press, 1991); Nigel John Ashton, *Eisenhower, Macmillan, and the Problem of Nasser: Anglo-American Relations and Arab Nationalism, 1955–59* (New York: St. Martin's Press, 1996); and Ray Takeyh, *The Origins of the Eisenhower Doctrine: The U.S., Britain, and Nasser's Egypt, 1953–1957* (New York: St. Martin's Press, 2000). On Iran, see Mark Gasiorowski, *U.S. Foreign Policy and the Shah: Building a Client State in Iran* (Ithaca, N.Y.: Cornell University Press, 1991); and Mary Ann Heiss, *Empire and Nationhood: The United States, Great Britain, and Iranian Oil, 1950–1954* (New York: Columbia University Press, 1997). See also Ritchie Ovendale, *Britain, the United States, and the Transfer of Power in the Middle East, 1945–1962* (New York: Leicester University Press, 1996).

On Arabia and the Gulf, see John B. Kelly, *Eastern Arabian Frontiers* (London: Faber and Faber, 1964), and *Arabia, the Gulf, and the West* (London: Weidenfeld and Nicolson, 1980); Edward Peter Fitzgerald, "The Iraq Petroleum Company, Standard Oil of California, and the Contest for Eastern Arabia, 1930–1933," *International History Review* 13 (August 1991): 441–65; Tore Tingvold Petersen, "Anglo-American Rivalry in the Middle East: The Struggle for the Buraimi Oasis, 1952–1957," *International History Review* 14 (February 1992): 71–91; John Bulloch, *The Gulf: A Portrait of Kuwait, Qatar, Bahrain and the UAE* (London: Century Publishing, 1984); and B. R. Pridham, ed., *The Arab Gulf and the West* (London: Croom Helm, 1985). For an account that acknowledges U.S. support for British hegemony in the Gulf, see Miriam Joyce, "Washington and Treaty-Making with the Sultan of Muscat and Oman," *Middle Eastern Studies* 30 (January 1994): 145–54.

14. For an example of new scholarship that emphasizes Anglo-American competition for Mideast oil, see Tore Tingvold Petersen, *The Middle East between the Great Powers: Anglo-American Conflict and Cooperation, 1952–7* (New York: St. Martin's Press, 2000).

15. On oil and the "dollar drain," see Painter, *Oil and the American Century,* 160–65; Anderson, *Aramco, the United States, and Saudi Arabia,* 184–86; Yergin, *The Prize,* 422–25; Edward W. Chester, *United States Oil Policy and Diplomacy: A Twentieth-Century Overview* (Westport, Conn.: Greenwood Press, 1983), 96–97; and John G. Clark, *The Political Economy of World Energy: A Twentieth-Century Perspective* (Chapel Hill: University of North Carolina Press, 1991), 106–107.

16. For a summary of the literature on Arab nationalism, see Rashid Khalidi, "Arab Nationalism: Historical Problems in the Literature," *American Historical Review* 96 (December 1991): 1363–73. On notables, economic change, and the Ottoman *Tanzimat,* see Albert Hourani, "Ottoman Reform and the Politics of Notables," in *The Beginnings of Modernization in the Middle East,* ed. W. R. Polk and R. L. Chambers (Chicago: University of Chicago Press, 1968), 41–68; Donald Quataert, "The Age of Reforms, 1812–1914,"

in *An Economic and Social History of the Ottoman Empire, 1300–1914,* ed. Halil Inalcik and Donald Quataert (Cambridge: Cambridge University Press, 1994), 761–933; Moshe Ma'oz, *Ottoman Reform in Syria and Palestine, 1840–1861: The Impact of the Tanzimat on Politics and Society* (Oxford: Clarendon Press, 1968); and Philip Khoury, *Urban Notables and Arab Nationalism: The Politics of Damascus, 1860–1920* (Cambridge: Cambridge University Press, 1983). On the intellectual origins of Arab nationalism, see Albert Hourani, *Arabic Thought in the Liberal Age, 1798–1939* (London: Oxford University Press, 1962).

For the Ottoman legacy in the politics of the successor states and their relations with the imperial powers, see Hanna Batatu, *The Old Social Classes and the Revolutionary Movements of Iraq* (Princeton, N.J.: Princeton University Press, 1978); C. Ernest Dawn, *From Ottomanism to Arabism: Essays on the Origins of Arab Nationalism* (Urbana: University of Illinois Press, 1973); Philip Khoury, *Syria and the French Mandate: The Politics of Arab Nationalism, 1920–1945* (Princeton, N.J.: Princeton University Press, 1987); Afaf Lutfi al-Sayyid Marsot, *Egypt's Liberal Experiment, 1922–1936* (Berkeley: University of California Press, 1977); Peter Sluglett, *Britain in Iraq, 1914–1932* (London: Ithaca Press, 1976); and Mary C. Wilson, *King Abdullah, Britain, and the Making of Jordan* (New York: Cambridge University Press, 1987). Recent literature on the Ottoman legacy is anthologized in L. Carl Brown, ed., *Imperial Legacy: The Ottoman Imprint on the Balkans and the Middle East* (New York: Columbia University Press, 1996) and Albert Hourani, Philip Khoury, and Mary C. Wilson, eds. *The Modern Middle East: A Reader* (Berkeley: University of California Press, 1993). For the Ottoman legacy in the Gulf, see Frederick F. Anscombe, *The Ottoman Gulf: The Creation of Kuwait, Saudi Arabia, and Qatar* (New York: Columbia University Press, 1997).

17. See Mary C. Wilson's introduction and the section on the Middle East after 1945 in *The Modern Middle East: A Reader,* 529–687. Yehoshua Porath, *In Search of Arab Unity, 1930–1945* (London: Frank Cass, 1986), 162–96; Khoury, *Syria and the French Mandate,* 397ff.; John F. Devlin, *The Baʿth Party: A History from Its Origins to 1966* (Stanford, Calif.: Stanford University Press, 1966); and Patrick Seale, *The Struggle for Syria: A Study of Post-War Arab Politics, 1945–1958,* 2nd ed. (New Haven, Conn.: Yale University Press, 1986), 24–45. See also Derek Hopwood, *Egypt: Politics and Society, 1945–1981* (London: Allen and Unwin, 1982), 20–32; and Israel Gershoni and James P. Jankowski, *Redefining the Egyptian Nation, 1930–1945* (Cambridge: Cambridge University Press, 1995).

18. Anderson, *Aramco, the United States, and Saudi Arabia,* 177. See also Painter, *Oil and the American Century,* 116–20; Yergin, *The Prize,* 425–27; Miller, *Search for Security,* 173–203; and Ghassan Salamé, *Al-siyāsa al-khārjiyya al-Saʿūdiyya mundhu ʿām 19Ɛ0: dirāsa fī al-ʿalāqa al-dawliyya* [Saudi Foreign Policy since 1945: A Study in International Relations] (Beirut: Mahad al-Inmāʾ al-ʿArabī, 1980), 546–48.

19. Hourani, "Ottoman Reform and the Politics of Notables," 52; Christine Moss Helms, *The Cohesion of Saudi Arabia: Evolution of Political Identity* (London: Croom Helm, 1981), 19–20, 58.

20. Dale F. Eickelman, *The Middle East: An Anthropological Approach,* 2nd ed. (Englewood Cliffs, N.J.: Prentice Hall, 1988), 78.

21. Ibn Khaldūn, *The Muqaddimah,* trans. Franz Rosenthal, ed. N.J. Dawood (Princeton, N.J.: Princeton University Press, 1967); see Helms, *The Cohesion of Saudi Arabia,* 54; Joseph Kostiner, *The Making of Saudi Arabia, 1916–1936: From Chieftancy to Monarchical State* (New York: Oxford University Press, 1993); and David Holden and Richard Johns, *The House of Saud* (London: Sidgwick and Johnson, 1981), 18–19.

22. Nadav Safran, *Saudi Arabia: The Ceaseless Quest for Security* (Ithaca, N.Y.: Cornell University Press, 1985), 9–27; Helen Lackner, *A House Built on Sand: A Political Economy of Saudi Arabia* (London: Ithaca Press, 1978), 10–13; Alexei Vassiliev, *The History of Saudi Arabia* (London: Saqi Books, 1998), 29–209; P.M. Holt, *Egypt and the Fertile Crescent, 1516–1922: A Political History* (Ithaca, N.Y.: Cornell University Press, 1966), 149–55, 179–80; Anscombe, *Ottoman Gulf,* 34–90; and Robert G. Landen, "The Changing Pattern of Political Relations between the Arab Gulf and the Arab Provinces of the Ottoman Empire," in *The Arab Gulf and the Arab World,* ed. B. R. Pridham (London: Croom Helm, 1988), 41–66.

23. The origins of modern Saudi Arabia and the events of ʿAbd al-ʿAzīz's life have been mythologized by certain authors and, above all, by Aramco itself. See, for example, Leslie McLoughlin, *Ibn Saud: Founder of a Kingdom* (New York: St. Martin's Press, 1993); Arabian-American Oil Company, *Aramco Handbook,* 57–73; and James Parry, "A Man for Our Century," *Aramco World* 50 (January–February 1999) [A Commemoration of Saudi Arabia's Centennial]: 4–11. For less celebratory works, see Robert Lacey, *The Kingdom: Arabia and the House of Saud* (New York: Avon, 1981); and Johns and Holden, *The House of Saud.*

For scholarly accounts, see Vassiliev, *History of Saudi Arabia,* 210–86; Kostiner, *The Making of Saudi Arabia;* idem, "Transforming Dualities: Tribe and State Formation in Saudi Arabia," in *Tribes and State Formation in the Middle East,* ed. Philip S. Khoury and Joseph Kostiner (Berkeley: University of California Press, 1990), 226–51; idem, "On Instruments and Their Designers: The Ikhwan of Najd and the Emergence of the Saudi State," *Middle Eastern Studies* 21 (July 1985): 298–323; Helms, *The Cohesion of Saudi Arabia,* 227–45; and Mordechai Abir, "The Consolidation of the Ruling Class and the New Elites in Saudi Arabia," *Middle Eastern Studies* 23 (April 1987): 150–71.

Other recent literature examines how the Saudis sought to harness Wahhābism as an instrument of state power. See Ayman al-Yassini, *Religion and State in the Kingdom of Saudi Arabia* (Boulder, Colo.: Westview Press, 1985); Joseph Nevo, "Religion and National Identity in Saudi Arabia," *Middle Eastern Studies* 34 (July 1998): 34–53; and Ghassan Salamé, "Islam and Politics in Saudi Arabia," *Arab Studies Quarterly* 9 (Summer 1987): 306–25.

24. For Kostiner, British patronage was decisive in the consolidation of the Saudi state. See Kostiner, "Transforming Dualities: Tribe and State Formation in Saudi Arabia," 228–29 and *The Making of Saudi Arabia,* 6; see also Jacob Goldberg, *The Foreign Policy of Saudi Arabia: The Formative Years, 1902–18* (Cambridge, Mass.: Harvard University Press, 1986).

25. For post-1945 Saudi history, see Mordechai Abir, *Saudi Arabia: Government, Society and the Gulf Crisis* (London: Routledge, 1993); Willard A. Beiling, ed., *King Faisal and the Modernisation of Saudi Arabia* (London: Croom Helm, 1980); Salamé, "Islam and Politics in Saudi Arabia," and idem, *Al-siyāsa al-khārjiyya al-Saʿūdiyya* [Saudi Foreign Policy]; Lackner, *A House Built on Sand;* Tim Niblock, ed., *State, Society and Economy in Saudi Arabia* (London: Croom Helm, 1982); and Michel G. Nehme, "Saudi Arabia, 1950–1980: Between Nationalism and Religion," *Middle Eastern Studies* 30 (October 1994): 930–43.

26. Simon Bromley, *American Hegemony and World Oil: The Industry, the State System and the World Economy* (University Park, Pa.: Pennsylvania State University Press, 1991), 246, 47–48. On foreign embassies in Saudi Arabia and Soviet-Saudi relations, see Vassiliev, *History of Saudi Arabia,* 296; and Lacey, *The Kingdom,* 240–41. On oil and the Cold War, see Diane B. Kunz, *Butter and Guns: America's Cold War Economic*

Diplomacy (New York: The Free Press, 1997), 223–52. On the post–Cold War continuities in U.S. policy, see Atif A. Kubursi and Salim Mansur, "Oil and the Gulf War: An 'American Century' or a 'New World Order,'" *Arab Studies Quarterly* 15 (Fall 1993): 1–17.

27. "Eisenhower Revisionism," associated with such scholars as Robert Divine and Stephen Ambrose, has been integrated into the literature on Eisenhower's Mideast foreign policy. See, for example, Hahn, *The United States, Great Britain, and Egypt,* 155–56; Ashton, *Eisenhower, Macmillan, and the Problem of Nasser,* 3–4, 6–7; and Isaac Alteras, *Eisenhower and Israel: U.S.-Israeli Relations, 1953–1960* (Gainesville: University Press of Florida, 1993), 21. While acknowledging that Eisenhower played a more active role in policy making than initially believed, some scholars have criticized his failure to come to terms with revolutionary nationalism. See Robert J. McMahon, "Eisenhower and Third World Nationalism: A Critique of the Revisionists," *Political Science Quarterly* 101 (Fall 1986): 453–73. For a restatement of this criticism of Eisenhower with respect to Arab nationalism, see David Lesch, *Syria and the United States: Eisenhower's Cold War in the Middle East* (Boulder, Colo.: Westview Press, 1992), 5–6. For other, "postrevisionist" perspectives, see Richard Immerman, "Confessions of an Eisenhower Revisionist: An Agonizing Reappraisal," *Diplomatic History* 14 (Summer 1990): 319–42; and Chester J. Pach Jr. and Elmo Richardson, *The Presidency of Dwight D. Eisenhower* (Lawrence: University Press of Kansas, 1991).

On John Foster Dulles, see *John Foster Dulles and the Diplomacy of the Cold War,* ed. Richard H. Immerman (Princeton, N.J.: Princeton University Press, 1990); Frederick W. Marks, *Power and Peace: The Diplomacy of John Foster Dulles* (New York: Praeger, 1993); and Leonard Mosley, *Dulles: A Biography of Eleanor, Allen, and John Foster Dulles and Their Family Network* (New York: Dial Press, 1978).

28. See Robert H. Wiebe, *The Search for Order, 1877–1920* (New York: Hill and Wang, 1967); Ellis W. Hawley, "Herbert Hoover, the Commerce Secretariat, and the Vision of an 'Associative State,' 1921–1928," *Journal of American History* 61 (June 1974): 116–40; idem, *The Great War and the Search for a Modern Order: A History of the American People and Their Institutions, 1917–1933* (New York: St. Martin's Press, 1979); and Alfred D. Chandler Jr., *The Visible Hand: The Managerial Revolution in American Business* (Cambridge, Mass.: Belknap Press, 1977).

29. Key works in the development of the corporatist synthesis include: Carl Parrini, *Heir to Empire: United States Economic Diplomacy, 1916–1923* (Pittsburgh: University of Pittsburgh Press, 1969); Joan Hoff, *American Business and Foreign Policy, 1920–1933* (Lexington: University Press of Kentucky, 1971); Hogan, *Informal Entente* and *The Marshall Plan;* Melvyn P. Leffler, *The Elusive Quest: The American Pursuit of European Stability and French Security, 1919–1933* (Chapel Hill: University of North Carolina Press, 1979); Emily S. Rosenberg, *Spreading the American Dream: American Economic and Cultural Expansion, 1890–1945* (New York: Hill and Wang, 1982); and Frank Costigliola, *Awkward Dominion: American Political, Economic, and Cultural Relations with Europe, 1919–1933* (Ithaca, N.Y.: Cornell University Press, 1984). See also Michael J. Hogan, "Corporatism," in *Explaining the History of American Foreign Relations,* ed. Michael J. Hogan and Thomas G. Paterson (New York: Cambridge University Press, 1991), 226–36; and Charles S. Maier, "American Visions and British Interests: Hogan's Marshall Plan," *Reviews in American History* 18 (March 1990): 102–11.

30. See Anderson, *Aramco, the United States, and Saudi Arabia;* Painter, *Oil and the American Century;* Stivers, *Supremacy and Oil;* Stoff, *Oil, War, and American Security;* Randall, *United States Foreign Oil Policy;* and Miller, *Search for Security.* By contrast, recent scholarship on U.S. relations with Latin America attempts to draw conclusions

about the consequences of corporate investment. See, for example, Elizabeth A. Cobbs, *The Rich Neighbor Policy: Rockefeller and Kaiser in Brazil* (New Haven, Conn.: Yale University Press, 1992); and Paul J. Dosal, *Doing Business with the Dictators: A Political History of United Fruit in Guatemala, 1899–1944* (Wilmington, Del.: SR Books, 1993).

31. See Sarah Yizraeli, *The Remaking of Saudi Arabia: The Struggle between King Saʿūd and Crown Prince Fayṣal, 1953–1962* (Tel Aviv: Moshe Dayan Center for Middle Eastern and African Studies, 1997); Ayman al-Yassini, *Religion and State in the Kingdom of Saudi Arabia;* Mark Heller and Nadav Safran, "The New Middle Class and Regime Stability in Saudi Arabia," Harvard Middle East Papers, No. 3, Center for Middle Eastern Studies, 1985; Mordechai Abir, "The Consolidation of the Ruling Class and the New Elites in Saudi Arabia"; idem, *Government, Society and the Gulf Crisis,* 27–50; Lackner, *A House Built on Sand,* 57–64, 93–109; Gary S. Samore, "Royal Family Politics in Saudi Arabia, 1953–1983" (Ph.D. diss., Harvard University, 1983); and Saad Eddin Ibrahim, *The New Arab Social Order: A Study of the Social Impact of Oil Wealth* (Boulder, Colo.: Westview Press, 1982): 95–122. On the changing roles of so-called "traditional" constituencies in modern state politics, see F. Gregory Gause III, *Oil Monarchies: Domestic and Security Challenges in the Arab Gulf States* (New York: Council on Foreign Relations Press, 1994).

32. See Paul W. T. Kingston, *Britain and the Politics of Modernization in the Middle East, 1945–1958* (Cambridge: Cambridge University Press, 1996); Gerwin Gerke, "The Iraq Development Board and British Policy, 1945–1950," *Middle Eastern Studies* 27 (April 1991): 231–55; Frauke Heard-Bey, *From Trucial States to United Arab Emirates: A Society in Transition,* 2nd ed. (London: Longman, 1996), 319–35; and Jill Crystal, *Oil and Politics in the Gulf: Rulers and Merchants in Kuwait and Qatar,* 2nd ed. (Cambridge: Cambridge University Press, 1995). For documentation on the U.S. Export-Import loan to Saudi Arabia, see *FRUS, 1950,* 5: 1167, 1181–82.

33. Kingston, *Britain and the Politics of Modernization,* 109–10; Crystal, *Oil and Politics in the Gulf,* 66–111. Aramco's corporate attitude toward its mission in Saudi Arabia is summarized in the *Aramco Handbook,* 208–21.

34. Vitalis's comparison between the North American mining frontier of the nineteenth century and the eastern Arabian oil frontier of the twentieth obscures the ways in which American capitalism evolved over the intervening decades. See Vitalis, "Crossing Exceptionalism's Frontiers to Discover America's Kingdom."

35. See Khoury and Kostiner, eds., *Tribes and State Formation in the Middle East.*

1. A Dutch Uncle

1. See Aramco vice president James Terry Duce to Parker T. Hart and attached memo, "Developments in al-Buraimi, August 1952," September 16, 1952, 780.022, RG 59; Gifford to the Department of State, September 12, 1952, *FRUS, 1952–1954,* 9: 2470–71, n2. See also Tore Tingvold Petersen, "Anglo-American Rivalry in the Middle East: The Struggle for the Buraimi Oasis, 1952–1957," *International History Review* 14 (February 1992): 71–91; idem, *The Middle East between the Great Powers: Anglo-American Conflict and Cooperation, 1952–7* (New York: St. Martin's Press, 2000), 36–47; John B. Kelly, *Eastern Arabian Frontiers* (London: Faber and Faber, 1964), 158–64, and *Arabia, the Gulf and the West* (London: Weidenfeld and Nicolson, 1980), 69–71; Frauke Heard-Bey, *From Trucial*

States to United Arab Emirates: A Society in Transition, 2nd ed. (London: Longman, 1996), 302–305; Bernard Burrows, *Footnotes in the Sand: The Gulf in Transition* (Wilton, Salisbury, England: Michael Russell, 1990), 87–111; and John C. Wilkinson, *The Imamate Tradition of Oman* (Cambridge: Cambridge University Press, 1987), 294–95. David Holden and Richard Johns, *The House of Saud* (London: Sidgwick and Johnson, 1981), 147, incorrectly gives September 20 as the date of Turkī's expedition, but reports about the Saudi occupation of Ḥamāsā reached the State Department by September 3.

2. See Kelly, *Eastern Arabian Frontiers,* 51–106; Jeremy Black, *Maps and Politics* (Chicago: University of Chicago Press, 1997), 139–41; and John C. Wilkinson, *Arabia's Frontiers: The Story of Britain's Boundary Drawing in the Desert* (New York: St. Martin's Press, 1991). See Ibn Khaldūn, *The Muqaddimah,* trans. Franz Rosenthal, ed. N. J. Dawood (Princeton, N.J.: Princeton University Press, 1967). For recent scholarship, see *Tribes and State Formation in the Middle East,* ed. Philip Khoury and Joseph Kostiner (Berkeley: University of California Press, 1990).

3. Kelly, *Eastern Arabian Frontiers,* 33–35.

4. See Kelly, *Eastern Arabian Frontiers,* 17–24; and idem, *Arabia, the Gulf and the West,* 60–74. On the early petroleum concessions in eastern Arabia, see Edward Peter Fitzgerald, "The Iraq Petroleum Company, Standard Oil of California, and the Contest for Eastern Arabia, 1930–1933," *International History Review* 13 (August 1991): 441–65.

5. For an account of interviews of Saudi tax collectors conducted by Aramco's Arabian Affairs Division, see the monthly report for January 1949 in Folder 14, "ART, AAD, etc., 1949," Box 2, WEM. See also Robert Lacey, *The Kingdom: Arabia and the House of Saud* (New York: Avon Books, 1981), 290–93; Holden and Johns, *House of Saud,* 146–47; and Kelly, *Eastern Arabian Frontiers,* 212.

6. See David Roberts, "The Consequences of the Exclusive Treaties: A British View," and Husain M. Al-Baharna, "The Consequences of Britain's Exclusive Treaties: A Gulf View, in *The Arab Gulf and the West,* ed. B. R. Pridham (London: Croom Helm, 1985), 1–37; Frederick F. Anscombe, *The Ottoman Gulf: The Creation of Kuwait, Saudi Arabia, and Qatar* (New York: Columbia University Press, 1997), 14–15; Burrows, *Footnotes in the Sand,* 9–27; and Kelly, *Arabia, the Gulf, and the West,* 51–52. For the economic importance of Middle East oil to Great Britain and the determination of the Churchill government to remain in the Gulf, see Ritchie Ovendale, *Britain, the United States and the Transfer of Power in the Middle East, 1945–1962* (New York: Leicester University Press, 1996), 18, 63–64, 84–89; Nigel John Ashton, *Eisenhower, Macmillan, and the Problem of Nasser: Anglo-American Relations and Arab Nationalism, 1955–59* (New York: St. Martin's Press, 1996), 10–12; and George Philip, *The Political Economy of International Oil* (Edinburgh: Edinburgh University Press, 1994), 115–116, 123–26. See also Kelly, *Eastern Arabian Frontiers,* 142–43.

7. On the negotiations for the renewal of the Dhahran airfield lease and military aid to Saudi Arabia, see *FRUS, 1951,* 5: 1017–24, 1042–56. See also Peter L. Hahn, "Containment and Egyptian Nationalism: The Unsuccessful Effort to Establish the Middle East Command, 1950–1953," *Diplomatic History* 11 (Winter 1987): 23–40; and David R. Devereux, *The Formulation of British Defence Policy towards the Middle East, 1948–56* (London: Macmillan, 1990), 19–24, 43–74.

8. Foreign Office minutes, March 27, 1952, by P. E. Ramsbotham and April 3, 1952 by Roger Makins, FO 371/99191, PRO. See also Ovendale, *Transfer of Power in the Middle East,* 18; and Mary Ann Heiss, *Empire and Nationhood: The United States, Great Britain, and Iranian Oil, 1950–1954* (New York: Columbia University Press, 1997).

9. "Middle East Oil Policy," June 19, 1952, FO 371/99191, PRO.

10. Pelham to Bowker, April 15, 1952, and Foreign Office minute by W. P. Cranston, June 15, 1952, FO 371/98828, PRO. See Ovendale, *Transfer of Power in the Middle East,* 84–85.

11. See Petersen, "Anglo-American Rivalry in the Middle East," 89, and *Middle East between the Great Powers,* 36–47.

12. For Bevin's policy in the Middle East, see William Roger Louis, *The British Empire in the Middle East: Arab Nationalism, the United States, and Postwar Imperialism* (New York: Oxford University Press, 1984); Alan Bullock, *Ernest Bevin, Foreign Secretary, 1945–1951* (New York: Norton, 1983); and Nadav Safran, *Saudi Arabia: The Ceaseless Quest for Security* (Ithaca, N.Y.: Cornell University Press, 1985), 62–63. The origins of the Fertile Crescent plan are discussed in Yehoshua Porath, *In Search of Arab Unity: 1930–1945* (London: Frank Cass, 1986).

13. Truman to ʿAbd al-ʿAzīz, October 31, 1950, *FRUS, 1950,* 5: 1190–91. See Nadav Safran, *Ceaseless Quest for Security,* 67; Patrick Seale, *The Struggle for Syria: A Study of Post-War Arab Politics, 1945–1958,* 2nd ed. (New Haven, Conn.: Yale University Press, 1986), 47; and George McGhee, *Envoy to the Middle World: Adventures in Diplomacy* (New York: Harper and Row, 1983), 186.

14. See Louis, *The British Empire in the Middle East,* 18–19, 105–27, 307–10, 313–14, 331–36; Daniel Silverfarb, *The Twilight of British Ascendancy in the Middle East: A Case Study of Iraq, 1941–1950* (New York: St. Martin's Press, 1994), 125–55; *The End of the Palestine Mandate,* ed. William Roger Louis and Robert Stookey (Austin: University of Texas Press, 1986); and Michael J. Cohen, *Palestine and the Great Powers, 1945–1948* (Princeton, N.J.: Princeton University Press, 1982).

15. On Anglo-Egyptian relations, see Louis, *British Empire in the Middle East,* 226–64; Hahn, "Containment and Egyptian Nationalism"; idem, *The United States, Great Britain, and Egypt, 1945–1956: Strategy and Diplomacy in the Early Cold War* (Chapel Hill: University of North Carolina Press, 1991), 38–147. For analysis of Churchill's foreign policy, see John Young, ed., *The Foreign Policy of Churchill's Peacetime Administration, 1951–1955* (Leicester, England: University of Leicester Press, 1988); and Ovendale, *Transfer of Power in the Middle East,* 58–83.

16. Kelly, *Eastern Arabian Frontiers,* 107–14.

17. On early Saudi diplomacy, see Jacob Goldberg, *The Foreign Policy of Saudi Arabia: The Formative Years, 1902–1918* (Cambridge, Mass.: Harvard University Press, 1986).

18. On ʿAbd al-ʿAzīz's concerns regarding "encirclement," see statement by the United States and United Kingdom groups, November 22, 1949, and editorial note, *FRUS, 1949,* 6: 88–9, 1624; U.S. aide-mémoire to U.K., April 7, 1952, and Pelham to Foreign Office, April 9, 1952, FO 371/98828, PRO. See Kelly, *Eastern Arabian Frontiers,* 124–41; and Wilkinson, *Imamate Tradition of Oman,* 288.

19. Memoranda of conversations by Awalt, March 19, 1951, June 20, 1951, and September 25, 1951, *FRUS, 1951,* 5: 286–87, 318–21, 330–32; On the Dammam Conference, see editorial note, *FRUS 1952–1954,* 9: 2458–59; see telegrams from Hare to Department of State, March 10, 1952, and March 11, 1952, *FRUS, 1952–1954,* 9: 2459–62. See Kelly, *Eastern Arabian Frontiers,* 142–58.

20. On Saudi objectives in eastern Arabia, see Ghassan Salamé, *Al-siyāsa al-khārajiyya al-Saʿūdiyya mundhu ʿam 19Ɛ0: dirāsa fī al-ʿalāqa al-dawliyya* [Saudi Foreign Policy since 1945: A Study in International Relations] (Beirut: Mahad al-Inmāʾ al-ʿArabī, 1980), 19, 505.

21. Foreign Office minute by Archibald Ross, April 26, 1952, FO 371/98828, PRO; Ross to Burrows, June 5, 1952, FO 371/98828, PRO. On the American and British military

missions, see William Elliot to Gen. Hoyt Vandenberg, October 2, 1951, *Records of the Joint Chiefs of Staff, 1946–1953,* part 2: *The Middle East* (Washington, D.C.: University Publications Microfilm, 1978), reel 2, Frames 1203–1204.

22. Acheson to Gifford, March 24, 1952, *FRUS, 1952–1954,* 9: 2462–63.

23. See Kelly, *Eastern Arabian Frontiers,* 159–63; and Petersen, "Anglo-American Rivalry in the Middle East," 74.

24. Abbey to Department of State, September 20, 1952, *FRUS, 1952–1954,* 9: 2474–75.

25. Secretary of State to the embassy in Saudi Arabia, September 19, 1952, *FRUS, 1952–1954,* 9: 2473–74.

26. Memorandum of conversation by Sturgill, September 18, 1952, *FRUS, 1952–1954,* 9: 2471–72.

27. Hare to Department of State, September 28, 1952, *FRUS, 1952–1954,* 9: 2475–76; see note 2, p. 2475.

28. Memorandum of conversation by Sturgill, September 29, 1952, *FRUS, 1952–1954,* 9: 2477–78.

29. Memorandum of conversation by Hart, September 30, 1952, *FRUS, 1952–1954,* 9: 2478–80.

30. Department of State to U.S. embassy in Jidda, October 2, 1952, 780.022, RG 59.

31. Hare to the Department of State, October 6, 1952, *FRUS, 1952–1954,* 9: 2480–81.

32. Jernegan to Bruce, October 6, 1952, 780.022, RG 59.

33. Memorandum of conversation by Hart, October 6, 1952, *FRUS, 1952–1954,* 9: 2482–85.

34. Department of State to Hare, October 8, 1952, *FRUS, 1952–1954,* 9: 2485–86. Gifford to the Department of State, October 8, 1952, 780.022, RG 59. See also CAB 128/25, October 7, 1952, CC(84)5, PRO.

35. Hare to Department of State, October 8, 1952, 780.022, RG 59; secretary of state to embassy in United Kingdom, October 10, 1952, *FRUS, 1952–1954,* 9: 2486–87. See also Gifford to Department of State, October 11, 1952, 780.022, RG 59; and Hare to Department of State, October 14, 1952, *FRUS, 1952–1954,* 9: 2487–88. The Saudi press disingenuously reported that the British had blockaded Buraymī unprovoked, and that the Saudi government had learned of Muscati claims on the oasis for the first time in September. See *Al-Bilād al-Saʿūdiyya,* October 12, 1952 and *Umm al-Qurā,* October 17, 1952.

36. Sarrell to U.S. embassy, October 15, 1952, FO 371/98833, PRO; Bruce to embassy in the United Kingdom, *FRUS, 1952–1954,* 9: 2489–90; memo by the foreign secretary, November 4, 1952, CAB 129/56, C(52)383. See Kelly, *Eastern Arabian Frontiers,* 164–66.

37. Byroade to Bruce, October 17, 1952, Saudi Arabia (June–December 1952), Box 19, Subject Files Relating to the Arabian Peninsula, 1952–1960, Lot 61, D 260, RG 59; Hare to Department of State, October 26, 1952, 780.022, RG 59.

38. Hare to Department of State, October 28, 1952, *FRUS, 1952–1954,* 9: 2491. See also Pelham to Foreign Office, October 24, 1952, FO 371/98833, PRO; and Kelly, *Eastern Arabian Frontiers,* 163.

39. Berry to Acheson, April 1, 1952, 786A.5-MSP, RG 59; Acheson to Lovett, April 16, 1952, *FRUS, 1952–1954,* 9: 2413–14.

40. Foster to secretary of state, June 13, 1952, and memoranda of conversations by Sturgill, August 19, 1952, and September 19, 1952, *FRUS, 1952–1954,* 9: 2415–16, 2419–21, 2422–25. See also Martin to Jernegan, August 13, 1952, 786.5-MSP, RG 59.

41. See editorial notes, *FRUS, 1952–1954,* 9: 2421–22, 2425–26.

42. Memorandum of conversation by Sturgill, August 19, 1952, *FRUS, 1952–1954,* 9: 2420; Hare, Oral History Transcript, OH-189, p. 56, DDEL. For Hare's comments regarding Saudi concerns during the 1951 negotiations on Dhahran, see Hare to Department of State, January 18, 1951, *FRUS, 1951,* 5: 1022–25.

43. *United States Treaties and Other International Agreements* (Washington, D.C.: Government Printing Office, 1952), 1474–82. See also Bruce to Hare, November 26, 1952, and Hare's reply, December 10, 1952, *FRUS, 1952–1954,* 9: 2429–31.

44. Bruce to embassy in Saudi Arabia, November 1, 1952, *FRUS, 1952–1954,* 9: 2492–93. See memo by foreign secretary, November 4, 1952, CAB 129/56, C(52)383, PRO.

45. Gifford to Department of State, November 1, 1952, 780.022, RG 59; Hare to Department of State, November 4, 1952, *FRUS, 1952–1954,* 9: 2493–95.

46. Bruce to embassy in Saudi Arabia, November 11, 1952, *FRUS, 1952–1954,* 9: 2496–97. See also Hare to Department of State, November 25, 1952, ibid., 2426–28; Pelham to Foreign Office, November 1, 1952, FO 371/98833, PRO.

47. Memoranda of conversations by Plitt, December 2 and 4, 1952, *FRUS, 1952–1954,* 9: 2498–2503.

48. Bruce to embassy in Saudi Arabia, December 17, 1952; Hare to Department of State, December 18, 1952, *FRUS, 1952–1954,* 9: 2506–2508; see also "Negotiating Paper—The Buraimi Dispute," December 8, 1952, and Hart to Sturgill, December 22, 1952, Saudi Arabia (June–December 1952), Box 19, Subject Files Relating to the Arabian Peninsula, 1952–1960, Lot 61, D 260, RG 59.

49. Evelyn Shuckburgh, *Descent to Suez: Diaries, 1951–56* (New York: W.W. Norton and Company, 1986), 63, 67; memo by Eden, December 19, 1952, CAB 129/57, C(52)450; Pelham to Eden, December 17, 1952, FO 371/98828, PRO; see also CAB 128/25, December 22, 1952, CC(107)1.

50. "Note for Saudi Arabia File," December 30, 1952, and Eisenhower to Dulles, January 5, 1953, Saudi Arabia (2), Box 46, International File, ACW, DDEL; see editorial note, *FRUS, 1952–1954,* 9: 2512–13.

51. Hare to Department of State, January 4, 1953, 780.022, RG 59; secretary of state to embassy in Saudi Arabia, January 10, 1953, *FRUS, 1952–1954,* 9: 2513–14.

52. Foreign service despatch from Hare to Department of State, January 10, 1953, 786A.5MSP, RG 59; Fritzlan to Hare, January 16, 1953, *FRUS, 1952–1954,* 9: 2431–33. See Hahn, *The United States, Britain, and Egypt,* 147–53.

2. Old Soldiers

1. On Eisenhower's foreign policy in the Middle East, see Peter L. Hahn, *The United States, Great Britain, and Egypt, 1945–1956: Strategy and Diplomacy in the Early Cold War* (Chapel Hill: University of North Carolina Press, 1991), 156ff.; Malik Mufti, "The United States and Nasserist Pan-Arabism," in *The Middle East and the United States: A Historical and Political Reassessment,* ed. David Lesch, 2nd ed. (Boulder, Colo.: Westview Press, 1999), 163–82; and Peter L. Hahn, "National Security Concerns in U.S. Policy toward Egypt, 1949–1956," in *The Middle East and the United States,* ed. Lesch, 89–99; Burton I. Kaufman, *The Arab Middle East and the United States: Inter-Arab Rivalry and Superpower Diplomacy* (New York: Twayne Publishers, 1996), 17–29; George Lenczowski, *American Presidents and the Middle East* (Durham, N.C.: Duke University Press,

1990), 30–66; and William Stivers, "Eisenhower and the Middle East," in *Reevaluating Eisenhower: American Foreign Policy in the 1950s,* ed. Richard A. Melanson and David Mayers (Urbana: University of Illinois Press, 1987), 192–219.

2. On U.S.-Egyptian relations, see Sayed-Ahmed Abd al-Wahab, *Nasser and American Foreign Policy, 1952–1956* (London: LAAM, 1989); Geoffrey Aronson, *From Sideshow to Center Stage: U.S. Policy toward Egypt, 1946–1956* (Boulder, Colo.: Lynne Rienner, 1986); Nigel John Ashton, *Eisenhower, Macmillan and the Problem of Nasser: Anglo-American Relations and Arab Nationalism, 1955–59* (New York: St. Martin's Press, 1996); Hahn, *The United States, Great Britain, and Egypt;* Matthew Holland, *America and Egypt: From Roosevelt to Eisenhower* (New York: Praeger, 1996); Gail E. Meyer, *Egypt and the United States: The Formative Years* (Rutherford, N.J.: Fairleigh Dickinson University Press, 1980); Laila Amin Morsey, "The Role of the United States in the Anglo-Egyptian Agreement of 1954," *Middle Eastern Studies* 29 (July 1993): 526–58; and Barry Rubin, "America and the Egyptian Revolution, 1950–1957," *Political Science Quarterly* 97 (Spring 1982): 73–90.

On the U.S. and Suez, see Steven Z. Freiberger, *Dawn over Suez: The Rise of American Power in the Middle East, 1953–1957* (Chicago: Ivan R. Dee, 1992); Diane B. Kunz, *The Economic Diplomacy of the Suez Crisis* (Chapel Hill: University of North Carolina Press, 1991); William Roger Louis and Roger Owen, eds., *Suez 1956: The Crisis and Its Consequences* (Oxford: Clarendon Press, 1989); W. Scott Lucas, *Divided We Stand: Britain, the United States and the Suez Crisis* (London: Hodder & Stoughton, 1991); and Donald Neff, *Warriors at Suez: Eisenhower Takes America into the Middle East* (New York: Linden Press/Simon and Schuster, 1981).

3. Accounts by American officials differ on whether the U.S. maintained close relations with the Free Officers in Egypt before the July Revolution. See Miles Copeland, *The Game of Nations: The Amorality of Power Politics* (New York: Simon and Schuster, 1969), 52–74; and Wilbur Crane Eveland, *Ropes of Sand: America's Failure in the Middle East* (New York: W.W. Norton & Co., 1980), 96–97. On this issue, see Hahn, *The United States, Great Britain, and Egypt,* 145–47, and Holland, *America and Egypt,* 22–23. See also Joel Gordon, *Nasser's Blessed Movement: Egypt's Free Officers and the July Revolution* (New York: Oxford University Press, 1991), 162–65; and Jon B. Alterman, "American Aid to Egypt in the 1950s: From Hope to Hostility," *Middle East Journal* 52 (Winter 1998): 51–69.

4. Gamal Abd al-Nasser, *Philosophy of the Revolution* (Buffalo, N.Y.: Smith, Keynes and Marshall, 1959), 61; Hashim S. H. Behbehani, *The Soviet Union and Arab Nationalism, 1917–1966* (London: KPI, 1986), 112–13.

5. Eisenhower's diary entry for January 6, 1953, is published in *The Eisenhower Diaries,* ed. Robert H. Ferrell (New York: Norton, 1981), 222–24.

6. Abba Eban, *Personal Witness: Israel through My Eyes* (New York: Putnam, 1992), 225, 233; *Al-Bilād al-Saʿūdiyya,* November 13, 1952; "Memorandum of Discussion at Special Meeting of the National Security Council," March 31, 1953, Box 4, NSC Series, ACW, DDEL. On Eisenhower's Israel policy see Isaac Alteras, *Eisenhower and Israel: U.S.-Israeli Relations, 1953–1960* (Gainesville: University Press of Florida, 1993), 21–51; Steven Spiegel, *The Other Arab-Israeli Conflict: Making America's Middle East Policy, from Truman to Reagan* (Chicago: University of Chicago Press, 1985), 50–93; and Ray Takeyh, *The Origins of the Eisenhower Doctrine: The U.S., Britain, and Nasser's Egypt, 1953–1957* (New York: St. Martin's Press, 2000), 24. On Arab expectations for the Eisenhower administration, see David Lesch, *Syria and the United States: Eisenhower's Cold War in the Middle East* (Boulder, Colo.: Westview Press, 1992), 29. For a reinterpretation

of Eisenhower's policy toward the Jewish state, see Abraham Ben-Zvi, *Decade of Transition: Eisenhower, Kennedy, and the Origins of the American-Israeli Alliance* (New York: Columbia University Press, 1998).

7. PPP, *Dwight D. Eisenhower, 1953,* 4.

8. Robert Griffith, "Eisenhower and the Corporate Commonwealth," *American Historical Review* 87 (February 1982): 87–122. See also Burton I. Kaufman, *Trade and Aid: Eisenhower's Foreign Economic Policy, 1953–1961* (Baltimore: Johns Hopkins University Press, 1982).

9. "Memorandum of discussion at the 139th Meeting of the National Security Council," April 8, 1953, Box 4, NSC Series, ACW, DDEL. On the government's case against the petroleum companies, see Burton I. Kaufman, *The Oil Cartel Case: A Documentary Study of Antitrust Activity in the Cold War Era* (Westport, Conn.: Greenwood Press, 1978).

10. "Security and International Issues Arising From the Current Situation in Petroleum," January 6, 1953, *FRUS, 1952–1954,* 9: 641; "Time Lapse Study of NSC Projects," February 16, 1953, NSC Organization and Function, February 1953 (5), Box 6, White House Office, Records of the Office of the Special Assistant for National Security Affairs, 1952–61, DDEL; Byroade to Hare, February 20, 1953, Saudi Arabia, Boundaries, Buraimi (January–June 1953), Box 19, Subject Files Relating to the Arabian Peninsula, 1952–1960, Lot 61, D 260, RG 59. See David R. Devereux, *The Formulation of British Defence Policy towards the Middle East, 1948–1956* (New York: Macmillan, 1990), 110–12.

11. Arabian-American Oil Company, "Report of Operations to the Government of Saudi Arabia," Dhahran, April 15, 1956, p. 7. The crude petroleum export figures for 1952 do not include the more than eight million tons refined in the kingdom's eastern province at the Ras Tanura facility. See Table 6, "Production, Trade and Apparent Supply of Crude Petroleum and Refinery Capacity," in United Nations, Department of Economic and Social Affairs, Statistical Office, *World Energy Supplies, 1950–1974* (New York: United Nations, 1976), 211–12. See also Mark Gasiorowski, *U.S. Foreign Policy and the Shah: Building a Client State in Iran* (Ithaca, N.Y.: Cornell University Press, 1991), 81.

12. Hare to Department of State, February 14, 1953, *FRUS, 1952–1954,* 9: 2434–35. See also Jernegan to Dulles, February 26, 1953, 786A.5MSP, RG 59; Smith to Stassen, February 27, 1953, *FRUS, 1952–1954,* 9: 2435–38; Stassen to secretary of state and attached memorandum from Eisenhower, March 14, 1953, and memorandum by the president to Stassen, March 14, 1953, *FRUS, 1952–1954,* 9: 2018–19, 2438. See Hahn, *The United States, Great Britain, and Egypt,* 159–60.

13. Hare to Department of State, February 3, 1953, 780.022, RG 59.

14. Memoranda of conversations by Fritzlan, March 2, 1953, *FRUS, 1952–1954,* 9: 2516–17, 2518–19. See also Dulles to Eisenhower, January 29, 1953, December 1952–January 1953 (1), Box 1, Chronological Series, JFD, DDEL; memorandum for the president, February 28, 1953, Department of State through September 1953 (1), Box 67, Confidential File, White House Central File, DDEL.

15. Memoranda of conversations by Fritzlan, March 2 and 3, 1953, *FRUS, 1952–1954,* 9: 2520–22.

16. Memorandum of conversation by Fritzlan, March 16, 1953, and secretary of state to embassy in Saudi Arabia, March 27, 1953, *FRUS, 1952–1954,* 9: 2523–26; Eden telegram to Foreign Office for Churchill, March 6, 1953, PREM 11/698, PRO; see also Hare to Department of State, March 19, 1953, 786A.5MSP, RG 59.

17. Memo by the foreign secretary, March 16, 1953, CAB 129/60, C(53)103, PRO; see also CAB 128/26, March 17, 1953, CC(20)9, PRO; and John Barrett Kelly, *Eastern Arabian Frontiers* (London: Faber and Faber, 1964), 168.

18. Churchill to ʿAbd al-ʿAzīz, March 30, 1953; ʿAbd al-ʿAzīz to Churchill, April 21, 1953; Pelham to Churchill, April 28, 1953, PREM 11/698, PRO. See also Parliamentary Debates (Commons), 1952–53, April 2, 1953, 513: 1369–71; note by cabinet secretary, April 10, 1953, CAB 129/60, C(53)123, PRO; Harc to Department of State, April 12, 1953, 780.022, RG 59; memo by minister of defense, April 17, 1953, CAB 129/60, C(53)128, PRO; and Pelham to Foreign Office, April 21, 1953, PREM 11/698, PRO. See Kelly, *Eastern Arabian Frontiers,* 168–71.

19. Churchill to Lloyd, May 1, 1953, PREM 11/698, PRO. See also Lloyd to Churchill, April 20, 1953; and Dixon to Churchill, May 2, 1953, ibid.

20. Memorandum of conversation by Fritzlan, April 3, 1953, *FRUS, 1952–1954,* 9: 2533–35. See also Byroade to Dulles, March 24, 1953, 786A.11, RG 59; secretary of state to the embassy in Saudi Arabia, April 2, 1953, *FRUS, 1952–1954,* 9: 2531–32.

21. For documentation on the Dulles-Stassen mission to the Middle East, see *FRUS, 1952–1954,* 9: 1–167.

22. See Gerald DeGaury, *Faisal, King of Saudi Arabia* (New York: Praeger, 1966); Robert Lacey, *The Kingdom: Arabia and the House of Saud* (New York: Avon Books, 1981), 153–57, 250, 288–89; and David Holden and Richard Johns, *The House of Saud* (London: Sidgwick and Johnson, 1981), 74–75, 102, 128–29, 143–44, 179–80.

23. On the deputy foreign minister's role in negotiations concerning the Dhahran base, see *FRUS, 1951,* 5: 1017–25, 1053–55. On Yāsīn, see Lacey, *The Kingdom,* 197; Holden and Johns, *House of Saud,* 106, 132, 145–46, 148, 160; J. E. Peterson, *Historical Dictionary of Saudi Arabia* (London: Scarecrow Press, Inc., 1993), 183; and Patrick Seale, *The Struggle for Syria: A Study of Post-War Arab Politics, 1945–1958,* 2nd ed. (New Haven, Conn.: Yale University Press, 1986), 26, 140.

24. Memoranda of conversations prepared by the embassy in Saudi Arabia, May 18–19, 1953, *FRUS, 1952–1954,* 9: 96–112.

25. Aldrich to Department of State, May 22, 1953, CF 156, Dulles-Stassen Trip to Near East, May 1953 (2), Box 24, Executive Secretariat Conference Files, 1949–63, RG 59; Coleville to Strang, May 22, 1953, PREM 11/698, PRO; Churchill to minister of state, May 24, 1953, PREM 11/698, PRO. See Tore Tingvold Petersen, "Anglo-American Rivalry in the Middle East: The Struggle for the Buraimi Oasis, 1952–1957," *International History Review* 14 (February 1992): 76.

26. Foreign Office to embassy in Jidda, June 2, 1953, PREM 11/698, PRO. See also memo to the prime minister, May 29, 1953; and Lloyd to Churchill, May 29, 1953, ibid.

27. "Memorandum of discussion at the 147th meeting of the National Security Council," June 1, 1953, Box 4, NSC Series, ACW, DDEL.

28. Dulles to Eisenhower, June 8, 1953, June 1953 (7), Box 3, Chronological Series, John Foster Dulles Papers, DDEL; see editorial note, and President Eisenhower to King Ibn Saud, June 15, 1953, *FRUS, 1952–1954,* 9: 2540–42.

29. On U.S. aid to Iraq and the "northern tier," see NSC 155, "United States Objectives and Policies with Respect to the Near East," July 14, 1953, and Dulles to Wilson, September 8, 1953, *FRUS, 1952–1954,* 9: 399–406, 416–17; memorandum of conversation by Barrow, September 3, 1953, *FRUS, 1952–1954,* 9: 2356–60; and Jernegan to Henderson, November 9, 1953, *FRUS, 1952–1954,* 9: 424–28. See also Dulles's report to the National Security Council cited in note 27.

On the origins of the "northern tier" defense concept and the Baghdad Pact, see Ashton, *Eisenhower, Macmillan, and the Problem of Nasser,* 37–60; Ayesha Jalal, "Towards the Baghdad Pact: South Asia and Middle East Defence in the Cold War, 1947–1955," *International History Review* 11 (August 1989): 409–33; Ara Sanjian, "The Formulation of the

Baghdad Pact," *Middle Eastern Studies* 33 (April 1997): 226–66; Magnus Persson, *Great Britain, the United States, and the Security of the Middle East: The Formation of the Baghdad Pact* [Lund Studies in International History 35] (Lund, Sweden: Lund University Press, 1998); and Takeyh, *The Origins of the Eisenhower Doctrine,* 56–65. On the Dulles tour, see Alteras, *Eisenhower and Israel,* 52–81; Devereux, *The Formulation of British Defence Policy toward the Middle East,* 65; Freiberger, *Dawn over Suez,* 50–54; Hahn, *The United States, Egypt, and Great Britain,* 156–65; Lucas, *Divided We Stand,* 25–26; and Niẓām Sharābī, *Amrīka wa al ʿArab: al-sīyāsa al-Amrīkiyya fī al-waṭan al-Arabī fī al-qarn al-ʿashrīn* [America and the Arabs: American Policy in the Arab World in the Twentieth Century] (London: Riad al-Rayyes Books, 1990), 89–91.

30. ʿAbd al-ʿAzīz to Eisenhower, June 28, 1953; Hare to Department of State, June 29, 1953; Bishop to Department of State, June 30, 1953; secretary of state to the consulate general at Dhahran, July 4, 1953, *FRUS, 1952–1954,* 9: 2544–50; Dulles to Eisenhower, June 30 and July 7, 1953, Saudi Arabia—King Saud 1952–56 (4), Box 46, International Series, ACW, DDEL.

31. "Suggested Approach to British Ambassador Concerning Buraimi Dispute," June 30, 1953, 780.022, RG 59.

32. Foreign Office to embassy in Washington, July 2, 1953, PREM 11/698, PRO; memorandum of conversation by Fritzlan, July 11, 1953, *FRUS, 1952–1954,* 9: 2556–58.

33. Salisbury to Foreign Office, July 14, 1953, PREM 11/698, PRO. See also Dulles to Eisenhower, July 15, 1953, Saudi Arabia—King Saud 1952–56 (1), Box 46, International Series, ACW, DDEL; secretary of state to embassy in the United Kingdom, July 16, 1953, *FRUS, 1952–1954,* 9: 2558; Makins to Foreign Office, July 11, 1953, PREM 11/698, PRO; see also CAB 128/26, July 16, 1953, CC(43)5, PRO.

34. CAB 128/26, July 21, 1953, CC(44)5, PRO; Evelyn Shuckburgh, *Descent to Suez: Diaries 1951–56* (New York: W. W. Norton and Company, 1986), 99; Salisbury to Dulles, July 27, 1953, *FRUS, 1952–1954,* 9: 2559–60.

35. See James A. Bill, *The Eagle and the Lion: The Tragedy of American-Iranian Relations* (New Haven, Conn.: Yale University Press, 1988), 51–97; idem, "America, Iran, and the Politics of Intervention, 1951–1953" in *Musaddiq, Iranian Nationalism, and Oil,* ed. James A. Bill and William Roger Louis (London: I. B. Tauris & Co., 1988), 261–95; Mark Gasiorowski, "The 1953 *Coup D'Etat* in Iran," *International Journal of Middle East Studies* 19 (1987): 261–86; James F. Goode, *The United States and Iran: In the Shadow of Musaddiq* (New York: St. Martin's Press, 1997), 109–24; Mary Ann Heiss, *Empire and Nationhood: The United States, Great Britain, and Iranian Oil, 1950–1954* (New York: Columbia University Press, 1997), 167–86; and Louis, "Musaddiq and the Dilemmas of British Imperialism," in *Musaddiq, Iranian Nationalism, and Oil,* 228–60.

36. British frustration regarding U.S. antitrust law was evident following a meeting between Fred A. Davies of Aramco and Sir Horace Gibson of IPC. See Foreign Office (Belgrave) to Beeley at the embassy in Washington, August 13, 1953, FO 371/104878, PRO. See also Gasiorowski, *U.S. Foreign Policy and the Shah,* 81–84; Mary Ann Heiss, "The United States, Great Britain, and the Creation of the Iranian Oil Consortium 1953–1954," *International History Review* 16 (August 1994): 511–35; idem, *Empire and Nationhood,* 187–220; and Kaufman, *Oil Cartel Case,* 50–63.

37. For documentation on Saudi-Aramco and Tapline negotiations during 1953, see *FRUS, 1952–1954,* 9: 677–79, 693–701, 745–47.

38. Foreign Office to embassy in Washington, July 25, 1953 and July 30, 1953, FO 371/104878, PRO; Foreign Office minutes by Bowker, July 29, 1953 and Belgrave, August 4, 1953, FO 371/104878, PRO.

39. Memorandum of conversation by Jernegan, August 17, 1953, *FRUS 1952–1954* 9: 705.

40. Funkhouser to Hart, July 3, 1953 (revised September 10, 1953), *FRUS, 1952–1954,* 9: 679–87 [This memo also appears as "Appendix F" in Kaufman, *Oil Cartel Case,* 161–70]; memorandum of conversation by Robertson, August 26, 1953, *FRUS, 1952–1954,* 9: 709–13.

41. Memoranda by Robertson of Anglo-American oil talks, August 27–October 1, 1953, are printed in *FRUS, 1952–1954,* 9: 713–24, 728–45 [Beeley's remark appears on p. 714]; and memorandum of conversation by Eakens, September 1, 1953, *FRUS, 1952–1954,* 9: 724–27.

42. See Jill Crystal, *Oil and Politics in the Gulf: Rulers and Merchants in Kuwait and Qatar,* 2nd ed. (Cambridge: Cambridge University Press, 1995): 62–111; and Bernard Burrows, *Footnotes in the Sand: The Gulf in Transition, 1953–1958* (Wilton, Salisbury, England: Michael Russell, 1990), 22–23.

43. For O'Keefe's report, see *FRUS, 1950,* 5: 1112–20. On SAMA, see Sarah Yizraeli, *The Remaking of Saudi Arabia: The Struggle between King Saʿūd and Crown Prince Fayṣal, 1953–1962* (Tel Aviv: Moshe Dayan Center for Middle Eastern and African Studies, 1997), 124–27; Johns and Holden, *House of Saud,* 165–67; and Rodney Wilson, "The Evolution of the Saudi Banking System and its Relationship with Bahrain," in *State, Society and Economy in Saudi Arabia,* ed. Tim Niblock (London: Croom Helm, 1982), 278–300.

44. Hill to Department of State, February 10, 1950, *FRUS, 1950,* 5: 23–25. See Johns and Holden, *House of Saud,* 148–49, 151, 156, 167–68; and Lacey, *The Kingdom,* 291–92.

45. Michael Sheldon Cheney, *Big Oil Man from Arabia* (New York: Ballantine Books, 1958), 1–3; Barger to Henry, June 30, 1955, and attached report, "Local Government Relations Department Program" [quotation on p. 2 of report], Folder 19, "Barger 1955 Paper," Box 4, WEM. See also Arabian-American Oil Company, *Aramco Handbook* (1960), 148, 189–221.

46. Cheney, *Big Oil Man from Arabia,* 19; Said K. Aburīsh, *The Rise, Corruption, and Coming Fall of the House of Saud* (New York: St. Martin's Press, 1995), 287; Helen Lackner, *A House Built on Sand: A Political Economy of Saudi Arabia* (London: Ithaca Press, 1978), 95.

47. Mordechai Abir, *Saudi Arabia in the Oil Era: Regime and Elites; Conflict and Collaboration* (Boulder, Colo.: Westview Press, 1988), 72. See also idem, *Saudi Arabia, Government, Society and the Gulf Crisis* (London: Routledge, 1993), 32–7; Lackner, *A House Built on Sand,* 95–97; Johns and Holden, *House of Saud,* 168–69; see Tables, "Nationality of Aramco Employees in Saudi Arabia," and "Composition of Aramco Work Force in Saudi Arabia," *Aramco Handbook,* 161, 211; Table, "Development of a Skilled Arab Work Force," Arabian-American Oil Company, "Report of Operations to the Government of Saudi Arabia," Dhahran, April 15, 1961, p. 24.

48. For contemporary accounts of the strike, see U.S. consul general at Dhahran (Bishop) to Department of State, October 13, 16, and 17, 1953, 886A.06, 886A.062, RG 59; U.S. consul at Dhahran (Hackler) to Department of State, October 20, October 21, October 22, October 24, November 3, November 4, November 5, and November 14, 1953, 886A.062, RG 59; Counselor at the embassy in Saudi Arabia (Jones) to Department of State, October 21, 1953, 886A.062, RG 59; Burrows to Foreign Office, October 16, October 19, and October 23, 1953; Phillips to Foreign Office, October 20, 1953, FO 371/104882, PRO; and Cheney, *Big Oil Man From Arabia,* 226–39. See also editorial note, *FRUS, 1952–1954,* 9: 747–48.

49. Hackler to Department of State, "Labor Disturbances in Eastern Saudi Arabia," November 4, 1953, 886A.062, RG 59; "Memorandum of Discussion at the 168th Meeting of the National Security Council," October 29, 1953, Box 4, NSC Series, ACW, DDEL; Phillips to Greenhill, October 27, 1953, FO 371/104882, PRO.

50. Foreign Office to embassy in Washington, October 13, 1953, PREM 11/698, PRO; Penfield to Department of State, October 13, 1953, and Jones to Department of State, October 18, 1953, *FRUS, 1952–1954,* 9: 2569–70; Aldrich to Department of State, October 22, 1953, 780.022, RG 59. See Kelly, *Eastern Arabian Frontiers,* 171.

51. Pelham to Foreign Office, September 6, 1953, PREM 11/698, PRO. See also Shuckburgh, *Descent to Suez,* 105; Eden to Churchill, October 14, 1953, PREM 11/698, PRO; Eisenhower to ʿAbd al-ʿAzīz, October 27, 1953, and editorial note, *FRUS, 1952–1954,* 9: 2571–72, 2574; and Aldrich to Department of State, October 29 and November 12, 1953, 780.022, RG 59. Ovendale notes the divergence between the views of Pelham and Burrows on Anglo-American cooperation in the Gulf as early as November 1952, when the latter served as counselor at the embassy in Washington. See Ritchie Ovendale, *Britain, the United States and the Transfer of Power in the Middle East, 1945–1962* (New York: Leicester University Press, 1996), 86–9.

52. On Saʿūd's appointment as head of the Council of Ministers, see *Al-Bilād al-Saʿūdiyya,* October 11 and October 25, 1953. On ʿAbd al-ʿAzīz's death, see Lacey, *The Kingdom,* 297–98; Johns and Holden, *House of Saud,* 171–75; Alexander Bligh, *From Prince to King: Royal Succession in the House of Saud in the Twentieth Century* (New York: New York University Press, 1984), 56–57. See also Tim Niblock, "Social Structure and the Development of the Saudi Arabian Political System," in *State, Society and Economy in Saudi Arabia,* 75–105. On the role of the ʿulamāʾ, or religious leadership, in Saudi Arabia, see Ghassan Salamé, "Islam and Politics in Saudi Arabia," *Arab Studies Quarterly* 9 (Summer 1987): 306–25 [esp. 321–24].

53. "Message on the Death of King Ibn Saud of Saudi Arabia," PPP, *Dwight D. Eisenhower, 1953,* 766–67; "Memorandum of Discussion at the 170th Meeting of the National Security Council," November 12, 1953, Box 4, NSC Series, ACW, DDEL. See also Jones to Department of State, November 10, 1953, *FRUS, 1952–1954,* 9: 2447–48 (and note 3, p. 2447).

54. Alteras, *Eisenhower and Israel,* 99.

3. Reaching a Crossroads

1. See Sarah Yizraeli, *The Remaking of Saudi Arabia: The Struggle between King Saʿūd and Crown Prince Fayṣal, 1953–1962* (Tel Aviv: Moshe Dayan Center for Middle Eastern and North African Studies, 1997); David Holden and Richard Johns, *The House of Saud* (London: Sidgwick and Johnson, 1981), 176–83; Robert Lacey, *The Kingdom: Arabia and the House of Saud* (New York: Avon Books, 1981), 299–302; Tim Niblock, "Social Structure and the Development of the Saudi Arabian Political System," in *State, Society and Economy in Saudi Arabia,* ed. Tim Niblock (London: Croom Helm, 1982), 95–99; and Mordechai Abir, *Saudi Arabia in the Oil Era: Regime and Elites, Conflict and Collaboration* (Boulder, Colo.: Westview Press, 1988), 66–67. For a basic chronicle of Saʿūd's early reign, see Amīn Saʿīd, *Taʾrīkh al-dawla al-Saʿūdiyya* [History of the Saudi State], vol. 3: *ʿahd Saʿūd ibn ʿAbd al-ʿAzīz* [The Reign of Saʿūd] (Beirut: dar al-kātib al-ʿArabī, 1970), 15–21, 46–57.

2. Yizraeli, *Remaking of Saudi Arabia,* 52–4; Helen Lackner, *A House Built on Sand: A Political Economy of Saudi Arabia* (London: Ithaca Press, 1978), 59–60; Niblock, "Social Structure and the Development of the Saudi Arabian Political System," 95; Holden and Johns, *House of Saud,* 178–79; Gary S. Samore, "Royal Family Politics in Saudi Arabia, 1953–1983" (Ph.D. diss., Harvard University, 1983), 74–93; and Saʿīd, *ʿahd Saʿūd ibn ʿAbd al-ʿAzīz* [The Reign of Saʿūd], 40–41.

3. On ʿAlī Riḍā and Onassis, see Lacey, *The Kingdom,* 188, 303–304; Holden and Johns, *House of Saud,* 180–81. On the Saudi-Onassis tanker deal, see Nathan J. Citino, "Defending the 'Postwar Petroleum Order': The US, Britain, and the 1954 Saudi-Onassis Tanker Deal," *Diplomacy & Statecraft* 11 (July 2000): 137–60. See also Peter Evans, *Ari: The Life and Times of Aristotle Socrates Onassis* (London: Jonathan Cape, 1986), 116–19; and Nicholas Fraser et al., *Aristotle Onassis* (New York: J.B. Lippincott Company, 1977), 132–53. For biographical information on the ʿAlī Riḍā family, see "The Alireza or Zainal Family," Folder 70, "Arabs—Miscellaneous Biographies," Box 1, WEM.

4. See Evans, *Ari;* Fraser et al., *Aristotle Onassis.* See also "The Man Who Bought the Bank," *Time,* January 19, 1953, 85–86.

5. See Pelham to Fry, February 2, 1954, FO 371/110122; Foreign Office memo by R.C. Blackham, November 12, 1954, FO 371/110124, PRO. On Schacht's role as economic advisor to Iran, Egypt, and Syria, see John Weitz, *Hitler's Banker: Hjalmar Horace Greeley Schacht* (Boston: Little, Brown and Co., 1997), 335–37.

6. Aramco cable McDonald to Chapman, February 5, 1954, "Oil—Onassis 1954," Box 14, Records of the Office of Near Eastern Affairs, Subject File, 1941–1954, Lot 57 D 298, RG 59; see also Rathbone to Byroade, February 19, 1954; Follis to Byroade, February 24, 1954; Long to Dulles, March 2, 1954, 886A.2553, RG 59; "Discrimination in Shipping Saudi Arabian Oil?" *Petroleum Press Service,* June 1954, 203–204; "The Saudi Arabia-Onassis Agreement," ibid., July 1954, 241–42.

7. On Wadsworth, see Dulles to Eisenhower and attached biographical summary, September 3, 1953, Department of State through September 1953 (11), Box 67, Subject Series, Confidential File, White House Central File, DDEL; undated biographical summary, 8–F Wadsworth, George, Box 165, Official File, White House Central File, DDEL. See also Parker T. Hart, *Saudi Arabia and the United States: Birth of a Security Partnership* (Bloomington: Indiana University Press, 1998), 41–42.

8. Wilson to Dulles, April 16, 1954, and enclosed letter from Anderson, March 18, 1954, *FRUS, 1952–1954,* 9: 809–11. See also Wadsworth to Department of State, February 6, 1954; Department of State to Wadsworth, February 12, 1954, *FRUS, 1952–1954,* 9: 786–88.

9. Memorandum of conversation by Dorsey, March 16, 1954, *FRUS, 1952–1954,* 9: 795–96. See also Evans, *Ari,* 151–52; Fraser, et al., *Aristotle Onassis,* 138–39.

10. Wadsworth to Department of State, May 1, 1954; memorandum of conversation by Hart, May 26, 1954; memorandum of conversation by Fritzlan, May 27, 1954, *FRUS, 1952–1954,* 9: 813–15, 819–23.

11. Wadsworth to Department of State, February 6, 1954; memorandum of conversation by Fritzlan, May 12, 1954, *FRUS, 1952–1954,* 9: 786–87, 815–16; Pelly to Foreign Office, May 26, 1954; Burrows to Foreign Office, May 26, 1954, FO 371/109914, PRO; memorandum of conversation at the Foreign Office, June 2, 1954, FO 371/110122, PRO; memorandum of conversation at the Foreign Office, June 2, 1954, FO 371/109914, PRO. See also *Parliamentary Debates,* 1953–54, 529: 23–24.

12. Foreign Office minute by Fry, May 19, 1954; Brook to Beckett, May 28, 1954, FO 371/110122, PRO. See also Logan to Biggs, May 24, 1954; Samuel to Dickinson,

July 7, 1954, FO 371/110122, PRO; Foster to Dodds-Parker, June 26, 1954; Brook to Butler, June 28, 1954; Foreign Office minute by Wilson, July 1, 1954; Lloyd to chancellor of the exchequer, July 15, 1954; Bailey to Foreign Office, July 20, 1954; Maudling (Treasury) to Lloyd, July 28, 1954; and Foreign Office minute by Belgrave, July 28, 1954; FO 371/110123, PRO.

13. Wadsworth to Department of State, July 7, 1954, RG 59, 886A.2553; memorandum of conversation by Hallett, July 12, 1954, *FRUS, 1952–1954,* 9: 826–27; Byroade to Murphy, July 15, 1954, 886A.2553, RG 59; memorandum of conversation by Gay, July 16, 1954; Department of State to Wadsworth, July 16, 1954, *FRUS, 1952–1954,* 9: 829–33. See also Evans, *Ari,* 132–33; Fraser et al., *Aristotle Onassis,* 141–42; and Lacey, *The Kingdom,* 304–305.

14. Memorandum of conversation by Dorsey, July 15, 1954, *FRUS, 1952–1954,* 9: 827–29; NSC 5428, July 23, 1954, *FRUS, 1952–1954,* 9: 525–36 [quoted portion on pp. 529–30]. See also "Memorandum of Discussion at the 207th Meeting of the National Security Council," July 22, 1954, Box 5, NSC Series, ACW, DDEL; and Wadsworth to Department of State, July 30, 1954, *FRUS, 1952–1954,* 9: 840–42.

15. Fritzlan to Hart, January 20, 1954, 786A.5MSP, RG 59; Wadsworth to Department of State, January 18, 1954, *FRUS, 1952–1954,* 9: 2450–51; foreign service despatch by Wadsworth, February 8, 1954, 786A.5MSP, RG 59. See also memorandum of conversation, January 5, 1954, Staff Notes January–December 1954, Box 4, DDE Diary Series, ACW, DDEL; Smith to Wilson, November 12, 1953; Wilson to Smith, January 29, 1954, *FRUS, 1952–1954,* 9: 428–30, 476–77.

16. Foreign service despatch by Caffery, May 26, 1954, 786A.00, RG 59; *Al-Bilād Al-Saʿūdiyya,* February 22, 1954, April 27, 1954. See also Wadsworth to Department of State, June 1, 1954, *FRUS, 1952–1954,* 9: 2452–53; Wadsworth to Department of State, June 4, 1954, 611.86A, RG 59; Wadsworth to Department of State, June 28, 1954, 886A.00–TA, RG 59; Lacey, *The Kingdom,* 310–11; Johns and Holden, *House of Saud,* 184–85; and Joel Gordon, *Nasser's Blessed Movement: Egypt's Free Officers and the July Revolution* (New York: Oxford University Press, 1992), 127–43.

17. Wadsworth to Department of State, June 1, 1954, *FRUS, 1952–1954,* 9: 2452–53; Wadsworth to Department of State, June 4, 1954, 786A.5MSP, RG 59. See also paper prepared by the Operations Coordinating Board, July 29, 1954, *FRUS, 1952–1954,* 9: 537–39; and Nadav Safran, *Saudi Arabia: The Ceaseless Quest for Security* (Ithaca, N.Y.: Cornell University Press, 1985), 80.

18. Eden to cabinet, January 7, 1954, PREM 11/718, PRO. See also Burrows to Foreign Office, December 1, 1953; Pelham to Foreign Office, December 3, 1954, PREM 11/698, PRO; Tore Tingvold Petersen, "Anglo-American Rivalry in the Middle East: The Struggle for the Buraimi Oasis, 1952–1957" *International History Review* 14 (February 1992): 71–91 [see p. 77]. Rumors of an oil discovery in Abu Dhabi reached Aramco management as early as September 30, 1953. See Mulligan, memo to file, October 7, 1953, Folder 33, "ARD, Chronological Files, October 1953," Box 2, WEM.

19. Kirkpatrick to Burrows, January 29, 1954, FO 371/109828, PRO; Lloyd to Eden, February 11, 1954, FO 371/109829, PRO. See also Burrows to Kirkpatrick, February 6, 1954; Foreign Office Draft Instruction, February 11, 1954; and Eden to Lloyd, February 12, 1954, FO 371/109829, PRO.

20. British aide-mémoire, "Saudi Arabia Frontier Dispute," not dated; Department of State to Wadsworth, February 16, 1954, *FRUS, 1952–1954,* 9: 2576–77, 2580.

21. Memoranda of conversations by Fritzlan, March 10 and March 23, 1954, *FRUS, 1952–1954,* 9: 2583–87, 2593–95. See also Wadsworth to Department of State, March 9,

1954; Department of State to Wadsworth, March 17, 1954; Wadsworth to Department of State, March 19, 1954, *FRUS, 1952–1954,* 9: 2581–83, 2590–91, 2592–93; Byroade to Smith, April 1, 1954, Saudi Arabia—Boundaries (Buraimi) January–June 30, 1954, Box 19, Subject Files Relating to the Arabian Peninsula, 1952–1960, Lot 61 D 260, RG 59.

22. Burrows to Foreign Office, May 2, 1954, FO 371/109831, PRO; editorial note, *FRUS, 1952–1954,* 9: 2604–2605. For Yāsīn's request for Aramco maps prior to his trip to Bahrain, see Rentz to Yāsīn, February 27, 1954, Folder 37, "ARD Chronological Files, February 1954," Box 2; and memorandum by Mulligan, April 29, 1954, Folder 40, "ARD Chronological Files, April 1954," Box 2, WEM. See also Wadsworth to Department of State, March 9, 1954; memorandum of conversation by Fritzlan, March 10, 1954, *FRUS, 1952–1954,* 9: 2581–82, 2583–87; Aramco cable, March 26, 1954, Saudi Arabia—Boundaries (Buraimi) January–June 30, 1954, Box 19, Subject Files Relating to the Arabian Peninsula, 1952–1960, Lot 61 D 260, RG 59; Record of Chiefs of Mission Conference in Istanbul, May 11–14, 1954, OCB 091.4 Near East File #1(1) May 1954–March 1955, Box 77, OCB Central Files Series, NSC Staff Papers, DDEL; Pelham to Foreign Office, April 15, 1954; Beeley to Fry, April 15, 1954, FO 371/109831, PRO; Foreign Office to Pelham, May 6, 1954; Pelham to Foreign Office, May 15, 1954, FO 371/109832, PRO; and Pelham to Eden, May 22, 1954, FO 371/109834, PRO.

23. Foreign Office minute by Lloyd, May 25, 1954, FO 371/109833, PRO; memo by minister of state, May 28, 1954, CAB 129/68, C(54)179, PRO. See also Wadsworth to Department of State, March 9, 1954; Department of State to Wadsworth and Byroade at Chiefs of Mission Conference in Istanbul, May 14, 1954; Department of State to embassy in London, May 22, 1954; Aldrich to Department of State, May 24, 1954; Wadsworth to Department of State, May 31, 1954, *FRUS, 1952–1954,* 9: 2581–82, 2605–11; Makins to Foreign Office, May 23, May 25, May 27, 1954; Foreign Office minute by Kirkpatrick, May 24, 1954; and Foreign Office to Makins, May 26, 1954, FO 371/109833, PRO.

24. Petersen, "The Struggle for the Buraimi Oasis," 82; Churchill to Lloyd, June 2, 1954, FO 371/109834, PRO. See also Foreign Office minute by Lloyd, May 25, 1954; Makins to Foreign Office, May 27, 1954; Foreign Office to Bahrain, May 27, 1954; Churchill to Eden, May 28, 1954; Pelham to Foreign Office, May 29, 1954; Foreign Office to Bahrain, May 31, 1954, FO 371/109833, PRO; Lloyd to Churchill, June 2, 1954, FO 371/109834, PRO; CAB 128/27, June 5, 1954, CC(39)4, PRO.

25. Evelyn Shuckburgh, *Descent to Suez: Diaries, 1951–56* (New York: W.W. Norton and Co., 1986), 217; Wadsworth to Department of State, June 6, 1954, *FRUS, 1952–1954,* 9: 2611–12; Churchill to Lloyd, June 12, 1954, FO 371/109835, PRO. See also Lloyd to Churchill, June 9, and June 14, 1954, FO 371/109835, PRO; and Rentz to Cypher, July 7, 1954, Folder 42, "ARD Chronological Files, July 1954," Box 2, WEM.

26. "Memorandum of Discussion at the 199th Meeting of the National Security Council," May 28, 1954, Box 5, NSC Series, ACW, DDEL.

27. Pelham to Foreign Office, July 11, 1954, FO 371/109836, PRO; unsigned memorandum of conversation, June 27, 1954, Churchill Visit June 1954 (1), Box 20, International Series, ACW, DDEL. See also Foreign Office to Jidda, June 12, 1954, FO 371/109835, PRO; Foreign Office minute by Shuckburgh, June 28, 1954; Foreign Office to Pelham, July 14, 1954, FO 371/109836, PRO; Foreign Office draft of arbitration proposal, July 13, 1954, FO 371/109837, PRO; editorial notes and Wadsworth to Department of State, July 31, 1954, *FRUS, 1952–1954,* 9: 2613–15; Shuckburgh, *Descent to Suez,* 235–36; Ritchie Ovendale, *Britain, the United States and the Transfer of Power in the Middle East, 1945–1962* (New York: Leicester University Press, 1996), 91; and Mary Ann

Heiss, *Empire and Nationhood: The United States, Great Britain, and Iranian Oil, 1950–1954* (New York: Columbia University Press, 1997), 187–220.

28. Richards to Samuel, August 19, 1954, FO 371/109839, PRO. See also Pelham to Foreign Office, July 16, 1954, and successive drafts of agreement, FO 371/109837, PRO; Pelham to Foreign Office, July 27, 1954, FO 371/109838, PRO.

29. Memorandum of conversation by Awalt, August 31, 1954, 611.86A, RG 59; memorandum of conversation by Gay, August 16, 1954; memorandum of conversation by Jernegan, September 24, 1954, *FRUS, 1952–1954,* 9: 846–47, 858–59. See also Bailey to Samuel, August 13, 1954, FO 371/100110, PRO; memorandum of conversation by Jernegan, September 6, 1954, *FRUS, 1952–1954,* 9: 855–56.

30. Niarchos to Hopwood, September 21, 1954, and enclosed photostat copies of Catapodis documents; Foreign Office minute by Samuel, September 27, 1954; Foreign Office minute by Blackham, November 12, 1954; Samuel to Fry, November 12, 1954, FO 371/110124, PRO. See also Fraser, et al., *Aristotle Onassis,* 147–48, which gives the incorrect date of September 24 for the Catapodis deposition; and Evans, *Ari,* 135–36, which lists the equally erroneous date of September 27. Catapodis must have given his deposition no later than September 21.

31. Memorandum of conversation by Jernegan, September 24, 1954, *FRUS, 1952–1954,* 9: 856–58. See also Fraser, et al., *Aristotle Onassis,* 146–50; and Evans, *Ari,* 137.

32. Phillips to Eastern Department, October 3, 1954, FO 371/110124, PRO. On Aramco payments to Saudi Arabia, see Davies to Surūr, October 3, 1954, "Basic Agreements and Selected Documents," 1958, pp. 60–61, Folder 20, Box 4, WEM. See also Phillips to Foreign Office, August 31, 1954, FO 371/110124, PRO; Wadsworth to Department of State, October 1, 1954, *FRUS, 1952–1954,* 9: 2455–57; Dorsey to Murphy, October 4, 1954, 786A.2553, RG 59; memorandum of conversation by Eakens, October 15, 1954, 886A.2553, RG 59; Evans, *Ari,* 137–38; Fraser, et al., *Aristotle Onassis,* 149–53; Anthony Cave Brown, *Oil, God, and Gold: The Story of Aramco and the Saudi Kings* (Boston: Houghton Mifflin, 1999), 227–29; and Lacey, *The Kingdom,* 307.

33. Wadsworth to Department of State, October 25, 1954, *FRUS, 1952–1954,* 9: 859–60; Phillips to Eastern Department, November 13, 1954, FO 371/110124, PRO; Wadsworth to Department of State, December 18, 1954, *FRUS, 1952–1954,* 9: 870–71. See also Wadsworth to Department of State, November 4, 1954; Department of State to embassy in Jidda, November 27, 1954; memorandum of conversation by Wadsworth, November 29, 1954; Department of State to embassy in Jidda, December 27, 1954, *FRUS, 1952–1954,* 9: 862–63, 865–69, 874; Phillips to Foreign Office, November 8 and December 16, 1954, FO 371/110124, PRO; Brook to Beckett (Ministry of Fuels and Power), December 20, 1954, FO 371/114897, PRO.

34. Murphy to acting secretary, November 9, 1955, 886A.2553, RG 59. See also Rogers to Hoover, September 29, 1955; Phleger to acting undersecretary, October 3, 1955, 886A.2553, RG 59; memorandum of telephone conversation, Brownell and Dulles, October 7, 1955, Telephone Conversations—General September 1–December 30 1955(4), Box 4, Telephone Calls Series, JFD, DDEL; unsigned memorandum of conversation, October 11, 1955; Newsom to Wilkins, October 18, 1955; memorandum of telephone conversation, Burger and Murphy, October 24, 1955; Allen to acting secretary, November 4, 1955; and Brownell to Dulles, January 3, 1956, 886A.2553, RG 59. On the Ship Sales case, see Evans, *Ari,* 114–15, 120–24, 152–53.

35. On Alpha, see Peter L. Hahn, *The United States, Britain, and Egypt, 1945–56: Strategy and Diplomacy in the Early Cold War* (Chapel Hill: University of North Carolina Press, 1991), 186–94; W. Scott Lucas, *Divided We Stand: Britain, the U.S., and the Suez*

Crisis (London: Hodder and Stoughton, 1991), 46–69; Ovendale, *Transfer of Power in the Middle East,* 115–17; Nigel John Ashton, *Eisenhower, Macmillan and the Problem of Nasser: Anglo-American Relations and Arab Nationalism, 1955–59* (New York: St. Martin's Press, 1996), 49, 51, 54, 57–9; Isaac Alteras, *Eisenhower and Israel: U.S.-Israeli Relations, 1953–1960* (Gainesville: University Press of Florida, 1993), 128–31; Steven Z. Freiberger, *Dawn over Suez: The Rise of American Power in the Middle East, 1953–1957* (Chicago: Ivan R. Dee, 1992), 99; and Shuckburgh, *Descent to Suez,* 242–67.

36. See Ovendale, *Transfer of Power in the Middle East,* 111–14; David Dutton, *Anthony Eden: A Life and Reputation* (London: Arnold, 1997), 366–67; Ashton, *Eisenhower, Macmillan, and the Problem of Nasser,* 37–60; Ara Sanjian, "The Formulation of the Baghdad Pact," *Middle Eastern Studies* 33 (April 1997): 226–66; Hahn, *The United States, Great Britain, and Egypt,* 186; and Lucas, *Divided We Stand,* 45–46.

37. Safran, *Ceaseless Quest for Security,* 78; *Al-Bilād al-Saʿūdiyya,* February 10, 1955. See also *Umm al-Qurā,* February 11 and March 11, 1955; and *Al-Bilād,* February 16 and March 4, 1955. See also Patrick Seale, *The Struggle for Syria: A Study of Post-War Arab Politics, 1945–1958,* 2nd ed. (New Haven, Conn.: Yale University Press, 1986), 223–24.

38. *Al-Bilād al-Saʿūdiyya,* April 15 and April 4, 1955. For coverage of Bandung, see *Al-Bilād,* March 31, April 17–23, 25–26, and May 1, 1955. See also Saʿīd, *ʿahd Saʿūd ibn ʿAbd al-ʿAzīz* [The Reign of Saʿūd], 79–102.

39. Department of State to embassy in Jidda, March 5, 1955; memorandum of conversation by Fritzlan, March 7, 1955, *FRUS, 1955–1957,* 13: 254–56, 257–59. See also Ashton, *Eisenhower, Macmillan, and the Problem of Nasser,* 53.

40. Quoted in *Al-Bilād al-Saʿūdiyya,* March 4, 1955. See also Ghassan Salamé, *Al-siyāsa al-khārjiyya al-Saʿūdiyya mundhu ʿām 19Ɛ0: dirāsa fī al-ʿalāqa al-dawliyya* [Saudi Foreign Policy since 1945: A Study in International Relations] (Beirut: Mahad al-Inmāʾ al-ʿArabī, 1980), 279–82; Safran, *Ceaseless Quest for Security,* 78–80; Seale, *Struggle for Syria,* 224; and David Lesch, *Syria and the United States: Eisenhower's Cold War in the Middle East* (Boulder, Colo.: Westview Press, 1992), 74.

41. Lackner, *House Built on Sand,* 96–97, 103–104; Mordechai Abir, *Saudi Arabia: Government, Society, and the Gulf Crisis* (London: Routledge, 1993), 34–37. See also memorandum of conversation by Fritzlan, November 24, 1953, 886A.06, RG 59; foreign service despatch by Carrigan, May 20, 1954, 886A.062, RG 59; foreign service despatch by Jenkins, May 12, 1955, 886A.43, RG 59; foreign service despatch by consul general, Dhahran, June 1, 1955, 786A.00, RG 59. See also Safran, *Ceaseless Quest for Security,* 80–81; Michael Sheldon Cheney, *Big Oil Man from Arabia* (New York: Ballantine Books, 1958), 248; Gary S. Samore, "Royal Family Politics in Saudi Arabia," 94–95; Yizraeli, *Remaking of Saudi Arabia,* 155; and Alexei Vassiliev, *The History of Saudi Arabia* (London: Saqi Books, 1998), 337–41.

42. See Holden and Johns, *House of Saud,* 180; Niblock, "The Saudi Arabian Political System," 93–99; Abir, *Saudi Arabia: Government, Society and the Gulf Crisis,* 16, 27–39; Saad Eddin Ibrahim, *The New Arab Social Order: A Study of the Social Impact of Oil Wealth* (Boulder, Colo.: Westview Press, 1982): 105–106; Lackner, *House Built on Sand,* 107; and Yizraeli, *The Remaking of Saudi Arabia,* 21, 136–38.

43. NRF manifesto quoted in Vassiliev, *History of Saudi Arabia,* 339. On the rise of the Saudi opposition and royal corruption, see Pelham's 1954 Report on Saudi Arabia, January 6, 1955, FO 371/114872, PRO; and Pelham to Eden, February 21, 1955, FO 371/114874, PRO. On the growing "internal security problem" in the kingdom, see Wadsworth's report to the Chiefs of Mission Conference in Istanbul, May 11–14, 1954, OCB

091.4 Near East File #1 (1), May 1954–March 1955, Box 77, OCB Central Files Series, NSC Staff Papers, DDEL. For a recent critique of the Saudi regime and American support for the royal family, see Said K. Aburīsh, *The Rise, Corruption, and Coming Fall of the House of Saud* (New York: St. Martin's Press, 1995).

44. Wadsworth to Department of State, May 22, 1955, 786A.561, RG 59. See also Department of State to embassy in Jidda, May 6, 1955, *FRUS, 1955–1957,* 13: 259–61.

45. Memorandum of conversation by Matthews, June 23, 1955, *FRUS, 1955–1957,* 12: 103–11. See also memorandum of conversation by Matthews, June 24, 1955, *FRUS, 1955–1957,* 12: 112–22; and Ovendale, *Transfer of Power in the Middle East,* 121–24.

46. Hoover to Dulles, July 11, 1955, *FRUS, 1955–1957,* 12: 132–33; editorial note, *FRUS, 1955–1957,* 14: 301–302. See also memorandum of conversation by Shuckburgh, July 14, 1955; Anderson to Hoover, July 26, 1955; unsigned memorandum of conversation, July 27, 1955, *FRUS, 1955–1957,* 14: 295–98, 320–25; memorandum by Dulles of conversation with the president, August 5, 1955, August 1955 (7), Box 12, Chronological Series, JFD, DDEL; Ovendale, *Transfer of Power in the Middle East,* 123–24; and Dutton, *Anthony Eden,* 368.

47. Hoover to Dulles, July 11, 1955, *FRUS, 1955–1957,* 12: 132–33; Wadsworth to Department of State, August 30, 1955, *FRUS, 1955–1957,* 14: 422–23. See also Phillips to Shuckburgh, August 31, 1955, FO 371/114876, PRO; Hahn, *United States, Great Britain, and Egypt,* 192–93; Ashton, *Eisenhower Macmillan, and the Problem of Nasser,* 53–54; and Alteras, *Eisenhower and Israel,* 132–34.

48. Chapin to Department of State, August 11, 1955; Department of State to embassy in Tehran, August 8, 1955, 786A.11, RG 59. See also Wadsworth to Department of State, July 25, 1955; Department of State to embassy in Jidda, July 25, 1955, *FRUS, 1955–1957,* 13: 261–64; Cabell to Dulles, August 25, 1955; Armstrong to Dulles, September 23, 1955, *FRUS, 1955–1957,* 14: 395–96, 507–508; "Memorandum of Discussion at the 260th Meeting of the National Security Council," October 6, 1955, *FRUS, 1955–1957,* 12: 158–68; Phillips to Foreign Office, August 16, 1955; Foreign Office minute for the record, August 19, 1955, FO 371/114876, PRO; Foreign Office minute by Fry, August 20, 1955, FO 371/114561, PRO; Foreign Office to embassy in Washington, August 22, 1955; and Scott to Foreign Office, August 26, 1955, PREM 11/943, PRO.

49. Department of State to embassy in Jidda, July 25, 1955, *FRUS, 1955–1957,* 13: 263–64. See also Department of State to embassy in Jidda, September 14, 1955; Wadsworth to Department of State, September 15, 1955; Department of State to embassy in Jidda, September 30, 1955, *FRUS, 1955–1957,* 13: 267–71, 273–74. On the Saudi delegation to Prague, see Yizraeli, *Remaking of Saudi Arabia,* 169.

50. Eden quoted in Macmillan's report to the cabinet, October 4, 1955, CAB 128/29 CC 34(8), PRO. See also Department of State to embassy in Jidda, September 3, 1955; Department of State to embassy in Jidda, October 10, 1955, *FRUS, 1955–1957,* 13: 265–66, 278–79; Wadsworth to Department of State, September 8, 1955, 611.86A, RG 59; memorandum of conversation by Newsom, October 14, 1955, 786A.5, RG 59; unsigned memorandum of conversation, September 26, 1955; memorandum of conversation by Russell, October 6, 1955, *FRUS, 1955–1957,* 14: 516–19, 558–62.

51. On the organization of the Geneva arbitration tribunal, see Foreign Office minute by Bullard, January 24, 1955; deVisscher to Simpson, January 28, 1955, FO 371/114608, PRO. Documents related to the British "memorial," or legal brief in support of the Gulf clients' claims at Buraymī, can be found in FO 371/114609, PRO. See also Eastern Department to Chancery at British embassy in Cairo, April 15, 1955, FO 371/114610, PRO; Cairo Chancery to Foreign Office, April 22, 1955, FO 371/114611, PRO; Fry to Bullard, July 1,

1955, FO 371/114615, PRO; and memorandum of conversation at the Foreign Office, August 24, 1955, FO 371/114616, PRO. On the Ḥamāsā fire, see resident at Bahrain to Foreign Office, July 14, 1955; Phillips to Foreign Office, July 19, 1955, FO 371/114636, PRO; Little to Foreign Office, August 2, 1955, FO 371/114616, PRO; Phillips to Foreign Office, August 9, 1955, FO 371/114877, PRO. See also foreign service despatch, July 22, 1955; Wadsworth to Department of State, August 13, 1955, 780.022, RG 59; and *Umm al-Qurā,* July 28 and August 12, 1955.

52. See Bullard's statement quoted in "Breakdown of Arbitration Over Buraimi," London *Times,* September 17, 1955, p. 6. See also "Bribery by Saudi Arabia in Buraimi Oasis Dispute," ibid., October 5, 1955, p. 7; Simpson to Shawcross and attached memo on Saudi bribery, August 31, 1955; minutes of arbitration tribunal meeting, September 5, 1955, FO 371/114618, PRO; Memo by Broad, September 8, 1955; Delegation at Geneva to Foreign Office, September 10 and 12, 1955, FO 371/114617, PRO; transcript of arbitration tribunal hearing, September 11–15, 1955, FO 371/114619, PRO; Simpson to de-Visscher, September 22, 1955, FO 371/114620, PRO; and Shuckburgh, *Descent to Suez,* 278. See also Duce to Wilkins, September 17, 1955; Aldrich to Department of State, October 5, 1955, 780.022, RG 59.

53. On captured Saudi correspondence and funds, see Foreign Office to embassy in Washington, November 1, 1955, FO 371/114624, PRO; Burrows to Foreign Office, November 2 and 6, 1955, FO 371/114626, PRO; Foreign Office minute by Riches, November 9, 1955, FO 371/114629, PRO; Burrows to Foreign Office, December 6 and 12, 1955, FO 371/114632, PRO. Additional documentation related to Saudi bribery and the Ibn Jiluwī correspondence can be found in FO 371/114633, PRO. The most complete set of the original Arabic-language correspondence can be found in Folder 9, "Al-Buraimi Documents, 1952," Box 10, WEM. On the British decision not to pursue allegations surrounding Dr. Hasan, see Foreign Office minutes by Samuel, September 22, 26, 28, 1955, FO 371/114625, PRO; Pickard (Commonwealth Relations Office) to Broad, October 15, 1955; Shuckburgh to Clark (Commonwealth Relations Office), October 17, 1955; Foreign Office minute by Fitzmaurice, FO 371/114621, PRO; Macmillan to Hancock, October 20, 1955, FO 371/114622, PRO. On Dr. Hasan's notes, see Rentz to Yāsīn, March 22, 1955, Folder 46, "ARD Chronological Files, March 1955," Box 2, WEM. For official Saudi reaction to British charges, see *Umm al-Qurā,* September 16, 1955; and *Al-Bilād al-Saʿūdiyya,* September 8 and 15, 1955.

54. Lucas, *Divided We Stand,* 71; Ovendale, *Transfer of Power in the Middle East,* 125. See Leonard Mosley, *Dulles: A Biography of Eleanor, Allen, and John Foster Dulles and Their Family Network* (New York: Dial Press, 1978), 348–53; and idem, *Power Play: Oil in the Middle East* (New York: Random House, 1973), 235–46.

55. Burrows to Shuckburgh, March 20, 1955, FO 371/114610, PRO; Simpson to Samuel, September 15, 1955, FO 371/114620, PRO; Foreign Office minute by Shuckburgh, September 16, 1955, FO 371/114618, PRO. See also Shuckburgh to Caccia, September 17, 1955, FO 371/114618, PRO.

56. Foreign Office minute by Samuel, September 24, 1955; memorandum of conversation by Shuckburgh, September 29, 1955; Shuckburgh to Caccia, October 1, 1955; Foreign Office minute by Samuel, September 30, 1955, FO 371/114621, PRO.

57. Memo by Macmillan, October 15, 1955, CAB 129/78, C(55)153, PRO; Eden's statement quoted in "Buraimi Oasis Taken Over by Former Occupants," London *Times,* October 27, 1955, p. 10. See also Shuckburgh to Kirkpatrick, October 11, 1955, FO 371/114625, PRO; Gault to Foreign Office, October 13, 1955, FO 371/114624, PRO; Foreign Office minute by Shuckburgh, October 19, 1955, FO 371/114624, PRO; Foreign Office minute by

Shuckburgh, October 22, 1955, FO 371/114625, PRO; Shuckburgh, *Descent to Suez,* 291–93. On the British decision not to give the U.S. advance warning of military action at Buraymī, see Foreign Office minute by Riches, October 25, 1955, FO 371/114625, PRO; Makins to Shuckburgh, October 25, 1955; Foreign Office to embassy in Washington, October 25, 1955, FO 371/114622, PRO; brief for secretary of state, October 26, 1955, FO 371/114624, PRO. On the Riyadh Line as basis for the new boundary in eastern Arabia, see Foreign Office to Jidda, October 25, 1955, FO 371/114622, PRO. For reports on events in Buraymī, see Bahrain to Foreign Office, October 26 and 27, 1955, FO 371/114623, PRO. Petersen incorrectly gives October 16 as the date of the British reoccupation of Buraymī. See Petersen, "Struggle for the Buraimi Oasis," 84.

58. Undated memo from Allen W. Dulles to John Foster Dulles, *FRUS, 1955–1957,* 13: 281–82; memorandum of conversation by Newsom, October 31, 1955, 780.022, RG 59. See also editorial note and Carrigan to State Department, October 30, 1955, *FRUS, 1955–1957,* 13: 282–85; Wadsworth to Department of State, October 31, 1955, 780.022, RG 59; Foreign Office minute by Brook, October 31, 1955, FO 371/114628, PRO. For Saudi reaction, see "Saudi Arabian Protest," London *Times,* October 27, 1955, p. 10; *Umm al-Qurā,* November 4, 1955; *Al-Bilād al-Saʿūdiyya,* October 28, 30, 31, 1955.

59. Memorandum of conversation by Russell, October 28, 1955, *FRUS, 1955–1957* 14: 670–72; Macmillan to the Foreign Office, October 28, 1955, FO 371/114624, PRO; "Memorandum of Discussion at the 263rd Meeting of the National Security Council," October 28, 1955, Box 7, NSC Series, ACW, DDEL; Makins to the Foreign Office, October 27, 1955, FO 371/114623, PRO; "Memorandum of Discussion at the 267th Meeting of the National Security Council," November 22, 1955, Box 7, NSC Series, ACW, DDEL. See also Makins to Foreign Office, October 26, 1955, FO 371/114623, PRO; Goodpaster to Eisenhower, October 31, 1955, October 1955, Box 6, Dulles-Herter Series, ACW, DDEL.

60. See Department of State to embassy in Jidda, October 29, 1955, 780.022, RG 59.

4. A Tangled Skein

1. Wadsworth to Department of State, November 30, 1955, *FRUS, 1955–1957,* 13: 294–95; Parkes to Foreign Office, November 9, 1955, PREM 11/1471, PRO. See also Parkes to Riches, December 7, 1955, FO 371/114632, PRO; and memorandum of conversation forwarded to file by Bailey, December 8, 1955, FO 371/114559, PRO.

2. Mathews to Bowie, December 13, 1955, *FRUS, 1955–1957,* 12: 212–13. See also memo by the Chief of Staff, United States Air Force to the Joint Chiefs, October 18, 1955, *Records of the Joint Chiefs of Staff, 1946–1953,* part 2: *The Middle East* (Washington, D.C.: University Publications Microfilm, 1978), Reel 2, Frames 1295–98; Department of State to embassy in Jidda, November 23, 1955, 786A.5MSP, RG 59; Department of State to embassy in Jidda, December 8, 1955, *FRUS, 1955–1957,* 13: 296–97; and memorandum of conversation by Rountree, December 2, 1955, November–December 1955, Box 4, Secretary-Undersecretary Memcons, Lot 64 D 199, RG 59.

3. Foreign Office minute by Shuckburgh, November 14, 1955, FO 371/114630, PRO. See also Foreign Office minute by Nutting, November 10, 1955, FO 371/114628, PRO; Trevelyan to Foreign Office, November 9, 1955, FO 371/114627, PRO; Foreign Office minutes by Riches, November 11 and 12, 1955, FO 371/114630, PRO.

4. See Foreign Office memo, January 10, 1956, FO 371/120755, PRO; David Lesch, *Syria and the United States: Eisenhower's Cold War in the Middle East* (Boulder, Colo.: Westview Press, 1992), 54–55, 88–89; and Patrick Seale, *The Struggle for Syria: A Study of Post-War Arab Politics, 1945–1958,* 2nd ed. (New Haven, Conn.: Yale University Press, 1986), 160–62, 178–79, 186–237.

5. Macmillan to Eden, November 25, 1955, PREM 11/1448, PRO; and Evelyn Shuckburgh, *Descent to Suez: Diaries, 1951–56* (New York: W.W. Norton and Co., 1986), 313–14. See also Shuckburgh, *Descent to Suez,* 304–305; Samuel to Bailey, November 16, 1955, FO 371/114628, PRO; memorandum of conversation, November 20, 1955; Foreign Office to embassy in Washington, November 25, 1955; Duke to Foreign Office, December 9, 1955, PREM 11/1448, PRO. On the Templer mission, see Ritchie Ovendale, *Britain, the United States and the Transfer of Power in the Middle East, 1945–1962* (New York: Leicester University Press, 1996), 134; and Nigel John Ashton, *Eisenhower, Macmillan and the Problem of Nasser: Anglo-American Relations and Arab Nationalism, 1955–59* (New York: St. Martin's Press, 1996), 66–67.

6. See Macmillan to Eden, November 17, 1955, PREM 11/1471, PRO; Department of State to embassy in London, December 13, 1955, *FRUS, 1955–1957,* 13: 222–23; Shuckburgh, *Descent to Suez,* 309; "Desert Drive by Forces of Sultan," London *Times,* December 16, 1955, p. 8; and "End of Desert 'Campaign,'" ibid., December 17, 1955, p. 6. See also John C. Wilkinson, *The Imamate Tradition of Oman* (Cambridge: Cambridge University Press, 1987), 299–315. In a series of December 1955 meetings, Saudi deputy foreign minister Yāsīn and Egyptian military officials sought Aramco support for the imām's forces. See memo by Mueller, "Protection of Southern Borders," February 7, 1956, Folder 50, "ARD Chronological Files, January–March 1956," Box 2, WEM.

7. Dulles to embassy in London, December 13, 1955, *FRUS, 1955–1957,* 13: 301–302; Shuckburgh, *Descent to Suez,* 311; and Kirkpatrick to Shuckburgh, December 15, 1955, FO 371/114559, PRO. See also Macmillan to Eden, November 25, 1955, PREM 11/1448, PRO; Barbour to Dulles, December 15, 1955, *FRUS, 1955–1957,* 13: 223–25; Foreign Office to embassy in Washington, December 15, 1955; Riches to Shuckburgh, December 15, 1955; Shuckburgh to Kirkpatrick, December 16, 1955, FO 371/114559, PRO; Foreign Office to embassy in Washington, December 16, 1955, PREM 11/1471, PRO; Makins to Foreign Office, December 16, 1955; Foreign Office to embassy in Washington, FO 371/114632, PRO; Jebb to Kirkpatrick, December 28, 1955, FO 371/120525, PRO; and Hoover to Dulles, December 20, 1955, *FRUS, 1955–1957,* 13: 303–304.

8. See Dulles to the embassy in London, December 23, 1955, *FRUS, 1955–1957,* 13: 305–306; Foreign Office to embassy in Washington, December 15, 1955, FO 371/114559, PRO; Bailey to Riches, December 23, 1955, FO 371/114633, PRO; memorandum of conversation by Caccia, December 29, 1955, PREM 11/1471, PRO; Foreign Office to embassy in Washington, January 7, 1956, FO 371/120578, PRO. On the Aswan Dam, see Peter L. Hahn, *The United States, Great Britain, and Egypt, 1945–1956: Strategy and Diplomacy in the Early Cold War* (Chapel Hill: University of North Carolina Press, 1991), 193–94.

9. Memorandum of conversation by Geren, January 13, 1956, *FRUS, 1955–1957,* 12: 216–28; Makins to the Foreign Office, January 19, 1956, PREM 11/1471, PRO; and Shuckburgh, *Descent to Suez,* 321–22. See also Allen to Hoover, January 17, 1955, *FRUS, 1955–1957,* 13: 314–16; memorandum of conversation by Dixon, January 18, 1956, *FRUS, 1955–1957,* 12: 234–39; memorandum of conversation by Wilkins, January 19, 1956, *FRUS, 1955–1957,* 13: 317–21; Shuckburgh to Foreign Office, January 16, 1956; Kirkpatrick to Shuckburgh, January 17, 1956, FO 371/120578, PRO; Makins to Foreign

Office, January 19, 1956, PREM 11/1471, PRO; and Foreign Office memo by Riches, January 20, 1956, FO 371/120579, PRO.

10. Eden to Eisenhower, January 16, 1956, *FRUS, 1955–1957,* 13: 313–14; editorial note, *FRUS, 1955–1957,* 13: 324; memorandum of conversation by Dulles, January 19, 1956, Memos of Conversations, E-I (3), Box 1, General Correspondence and Memcon Series, JFD, DDEL. See also memo by secretary of state, "Buraimi," CAB 129/79, C(56)9, January 9, 1956, PRO; and CAB 128/30, CC(3)5, January 11, 1956, PRO.

11. Memorandum of conversation by Goodpaster, February 2, 1956, January 1956—Goodpaster, Box 12, DDE Diary Series, ACW, DDEL. See also unsigned memoranda of Eden talks, January 30–31, 1956, *FRUS, 1955–1957,* 13: 327–37; and *FRUS, 1955–1957,* 12: 240–44; memorandum of conversation, January 31, 1956, PREM 11/1448, PRO; secretary of state to Foreign Office, February 1, 1956; Foreign Office to embassy in Washington, February 1, 1956, FO 371/120580, PRO.

12. Samuel to Riches, February 3, 1956, FO 371/120776, PRO; and CAB 128/30, CC(10)1, February 9, 1956, PRO. See also memorandum of conversation by Newsom, February 2, 1956; memorandum of conversation by Wilkins, February 3, 1956, *FRUS, 1955–1957,* 13: 338–41; memo by secretary of state, "Buraimi," February 24, 1956, CAB 129/80, C(56)52, PRO; CAB 128/30, CC(17)2, February 28, 1956, PRO. On McCloy's mission, see Kai Bird, *The Chairman: John J. McCloy, the Making of the American Establishment* (New York: Simon and Schuster, 1992), 441–45; and Wilbur Crane Eveland, *Ropes of Sand: America's Failure in the Middle East* (New York: W.W. Norton and Co., 1980), 141–43. On the Anderson mission, see Isaac Alteras, *Eisenhower and Israel: U.S.-Israeli Relations, 1953–1960* (Gainesville: University Press of Florida, 1993), 148; and Hahn, *The United States, Great Britain, and Egypt,* 195–97.

13. See Department of State to consulate in Dhahran, February 8, 1956; Department of State to embassy in Jidda, February 17, 1956, 786A.561, RG 59; Philip Klutznick of B'nai B'rith to Eisenhower, February 17, 1956, Saudi Arabia Kingdom of, Box 886, White House Central File, Official File, DDEL; embassy in Jidda to Department of State, February 18, 1956, 786A.561, RG 59; Makins to Foreign Office, February 18, 1956, FO 371/120776, PRO; Shuckburgh, *Descent to Suez,* 334; Allen Dulles to John Foster Dulles, February 20, 1956, *FRUS, 1955–1957* 15: 193–94; and memorandum for the record by Hoover, February 21, 1956, *FRUS, 1955–1957,* 13: 341–43. See also "U.S. Bars Tanks for Saudi Arabia," and "18 U.S. Tanks Remain on Barges Alongside Freighter in Brooklyn," *New York Times,* February 17, 1956, p. 1, 3; "George Requests Inquiry on Tanks for Saudi Arabia," ibid., February 18, 1956, p. 1, 3; and "U.S. Lifts Its Ban on Mideast Arms; Frees Arab Tanks," ibid., February 19, 1956, p. 1, 3.

14. Congress, Senate, Committee on Foreign Relations, *Situation in the Middle East,* 84th Cong., 2nd sess., February 24, 1956. See also memorandum of conversation by Dulles, March 2, 1956, *FRUS, 1955–1957,* 15: 275–76.

15. See foreign service despatch by McClanahan, January 14, 1956, 886A.2553, RG 59.

16. CAB 128/30, CC(25)5, March 21, 1956, PRO; Eden to Eisenhower, March 15, 1956, *FRUS, 1955–1957,* 15: 364–65. See also Shuckburgh, *Descent to Suez,* 346; CAB 128/30, CC(18)2, March 5, 1956, PRO; CAB 128/30, CC(19)1, March 6, 1956, PRO. On Glubb's dismissal, see Ovendale, *Transfer of Power in the Middle East,* 147; and Ashton, *Eisenhower, Macmillan, and the Problem of Nasser,* 61, 70–71.

17. Diary entries by the president, March 8 and 28, 1956, *FRUS, 1955–1957* 15: 326–27, 425. See also Hoover to Dulles, March 12, 1956; diary entry by the president, March 13, 1956; memo by Wilkins, March 14, 1956, *FRUS, 1955–1957* 15: 341–43, 352–57; memorandum of conversation by Goodpaster, March 15, 1956, *FRUS, 1955–1957,*

12: 258–59; Hoover to Dulles, March 16, 1956; memorandum of conversation by Wilson, March 21, 1956; Makins to Dulles, March 21, 1956, *FRUS, 1955–1957,* 15: 370–71, 383–87, 389–92; and editorial note, *FRUS, 1955–1957,* 12: 264.

18. See, for example, Ovendale, *Transfer of Power in the Middle* East, 149; Ashton, *Eisenhower, Macmillan and the Problem of Nasser,* 60, 78, 106, 111–12, 119; Lesch, *Syria and the United States,* 89; Salim Yaqub, "The King and Ike: U.S.-Saudi Relations, 1956–1958," paper presented at the annual meeting of the Society for Historians of American Foreign Relations, Georgetown University, June 1997; Fawaz Gerges, *The Superpowers and the Middle East: Regional and International Politics, 1955–1967* (Boulder, Colo.: Westview Press, 1994), 52; Ray Takeyh, *The Origins of the Eisenhower Doctrine: The U.S., Britain, and Nasser's Egypt, 1953–1957* (New York: St. Martin's Press, 2000), 113; and Ghassan Salamé, *Al-siyāsa al-khārjiyya al-Saʿūdiyya mundhu ʿām 19Ɛ0: dirāsa fi al-ʿalāqa al-dawliyya* [Saudi Foreign Policy since 1945: A Study in International Relations] (Beirut: Mahad al-Inmāʾ al-ʿArabī, 1980), 629. See also Raymond Hare, Oral History Interview, OH-189, DDEL, p. 58–59.

19. Albert Hourani, "The Decline of the West in the Middle East—I," *International Affairs* 29 (January 1953): 22–42; Bernard Lewis, "Communism and Islam," *International Affairs* 30 (January 1954): 1–12; and Bernard Lewis, *The Middle East and the West* (Bloomington: Indiana University Press, 1961), 134–35. See also "Middle Eastern Studies on the Campus, 1956–1957," *Middle Eastern Affairs* 7 (November 1956): 423–24; Albert Hourani, "The Decline of the West in the Middle East—II," *International Affairs* 29 (April 1953): 156–83; Stephen Longrigg, "The Decline of the West in the Middle East: An Alternative View," *International Affairs* 29 (July 1953): 326–39; Bernard Lewis, "Democracy in the Middle East—Its State and Prospects," *Middle Eastern Affairs* 6 (April 1955): 101–108; and Edward Said, *Orientalism* (New York: Vintage Books, 1978), 275–76.

20. See OCB 091.4 (Near East) May 1954–March 1956, Box 77, OCB Central Files, NSC Staff Papers, DDEL. For Lewis's work, see folder #3. See also 144–B-4 Islamic and Moslem Religion, Box 737, Official File, White House Central File, DDEL.

21. Said, *Orientalism,* 290, 210; see also idem, *Covering Islam: How the Media and the Experts Determine How We See the Rest of the World* (New York: Pantheon Books, 1981), 11–16. On modernization theory and the Middle East, see Samuel P. Huntington, *Political Order in Changing Societies* (New Haven, Conn.: Yale University Press, 1968), 33, 65, 289; *The Beginnings of Modernization in the Middle East,* ed. W. R. Polk and R. L. Chambers (Chicago: University of Chicago Press, 1968); Philip K. Hitti, *Islam and the West: A Historical Cultural Survey* (Princeton, N.J.: D. Van Nostrand Co., 1962), 86–94; and *The Modernization of the Arab World,* ed. Jack H. Thompson and Robert D. Reischauer (Princeton, N.J.: D. Van Nostrand Co., 1966). On the recruiting of European talent for Middle Eastern studies centers in the U.S., see Said, *Orientalism,* 296. On Orientalism and American foreign relations, see Andrew J. Rotter, "Saidism without Said: *Orientalism* and U.S. Diplomatic History," *American Historical Review* 105 (October 2000): 1205–17.

22. On the Hijaz railroad, see embassy in Amman to Department of State, January 4, 1956, 986A.712, RG 59; embassy in Jidda to Department of State, January 7, 1956, *FRUS, 1955–1957,* 13: 310–12; embassy in Jidda to Department of State, April 8, 1956, 986A.712, RG 59; King Saʿūd to Eisenhower, April 10, 1956, Saudi Arabia, King Saud, 1952–1956 (1), Box 46, International Series, ACW, DDEL; Progress Report on Omega, April 23, 1956, "Omega vol. 3," Box 54, Lot 61 D 417, Records of the Secretary, Undersecretary, and Executive Secretariat, Meeting Summaries and Project Files, 1951–1959, RG 59; and Hollister to Dulles, April 25, 1956, 986A.712, RG 59. See also F. E. Peters,

The Hajj: The Muslim Pilgrimage to Mecca and the Holy Places (Princeton, N.J.: Princeton University Press, 1994), 316–21.

23. Miles Copeland, *The Game of Nations: The Amorality of Power Politics* (New York: Simon and Schuster, 1969), 58. On the anti-Communist fatwā, see Phillips to Foreign Office, April 5, 1956, FO 371/120755, PRO. The Qurʾānic passage in question (8:59–60) reads: "The infidels should not think/that they can bypass (the law of God). / Surely they cannot get away. / Prepare against them whatever arms and cavalry / you can muster, that you may strike terror / in (the hearts of) the enemies of God and your own, / and others besides them not known to you, / but known to God. / Whatever you spend in the way of God / will be paid back to you in full, / and no wrong will be done to you." See *Al-Qurʾān,* trans. Ahmed Ali, rev. ed. (Princeton, N.J.: Princeton University Press, 1984), 159.

24. Lloyd to Eden, April 6, 1956, PREM 11/1471, PRO; Brook to Eden, April 14, 1956, PREM 11/1457, PRO. See also Phillips to Foreign Office, April 11, 1956, FO 371/120587, PRO; Phillips to Foreign Office, April 11, 1956, FO 371/120755, PRO; Foreign Office to embassy in Washington, April 14, 1956; Foreign Office minute by Samuel, April 14, 1956, FO 371/120765, PRO; Trevelyan to Foreign Office, April 21, 1956, FO 371/120759, PRO; Phillips to Foreign Office, April 22, 1956, PREM 11/1472, PRO; and memorandum of conversation by Lloyd, April 23, 1956, FO 371/120766, PRO.

25. CAB 128/30, CC(19)1, March 6, 1956, PRO; memorandum of conversation by Goodpaster, April 3, 1956, *FRUS, 1955–1957* 15: 46–48. See also Eden to Eisenhower, *FRUS, 1955–1957,* 12: 249; memorandum of conversation by Goodpaster, March 15, 1956, *FRUS, 1955–1957,* 12: 258–59; joint chiefs of staff to Wilson, March 23, 1956, *FRUS, 1955–1957,* 12: 261; Wilson to National Security Council, April 5, 1956, President's Papers 1956 (5), Box 3, Presidential Subseries, Special Assistant Series, White House Office, Records of the Office of the Special Assistant for National Security Affairs, 1952–1961, DDEL; memorandum of telephone conversation, April 7, 1956, *FRUS, 1955–1957,* 12: 270; and memorandum of conversation by MacArthur, April 9, 1956, *FRUS, 1955–1957,* 12: 275–76.

26. Memorandum of conversation by MacArthur, April 1, 1956, *FRUS, 1955–1957,* 15: 435–45; editorial note, *FRUS, 1955–1957,* 13: 365–66. On Foreign Office contacts with Harry Kern, see FO 371/120587, PRO; Shuckburgh to Kirkpatrick, April 18, 1956 [and documents related to Dodds-Parker mission], FO 371/120766, PRO; Dodds-Parker to Foreign Office, April 29 and 30, May 1 and 2, 1956; Parkes to Foreign Office, April 30, 1956, FO 371/120767, PRO; Saʿūd to Eden, April 30, 1956, PREM 11/1472, PRO; Report by Dodds-Parker, May 9, 1956, FO 371/120768, PRO; Lloyd to Eden, May 14, 1956, PREM 11/1472, PRO; and Shuckburgh, *Descent to Suez,* 355.

27. Memorandum of conversation by Rountree, April 24, 1956, "Omega vol. 3," Box 54, Records of the Secretary, Undersecretary, and Executive Secretariat, Meeting Summaries and Project Files, 1951–1959, Lot 61 D 417, RG 59; memorandum of telephone conversation, April 11, 1956, Memo Tel. Conv. with White House January 3–August 31, 1956 (4), Box 11, Telephone Conversations Series, JFD, DDEL; memorandum of conversation with the president, May 9, 1956, Meetings with the President January–July 1956 (3), Box 4, White House Memo Series, JFD, DDEL. See also memorandum by Wadsworth, May 9, 1956, Saudi Arabia, King Saud 1952–1956 (2), Box 46, International Series, ACW, DDEL; Summary of Saudi Five-Year Plan, May 10, 1956, Saudi Arabia, King Saud 1952–1956 (1), Box 46, International Series, ACW, DDEL; Rountree to Dulles, May 21, 1956, *FRUS, 1955–1957,* 13: 374–75; memorandum for the record, May 25, 1956, "Omega vol. 5," Box 55, Records of the Secretary, Undersecretary, and Executive Secretariat, Meeting

Summaries and Project Files, 1951–1959, Lot 61 D 417, RG 59; and Stephen Dorril, *MI6: Inside the Covert World of Her Majesty's Secret Intelligence Service* (New York: Free Press, 2000), 615.

28. Armstrong to Hoover, May 4, 1956, "Omega vol. 4," Box 54, Records of the Secretary, Undersecretary, and Executive Secretariat, Meeting Summaries and Project Files, 1951–1959, Lot 61 D 417, RG 59; Dulles to Eisenhower, May 18, 1956, May 1956, Box 7, Dulles-Herter Series, ACW, DDEL; Shuckburgh, *Descent to Suez,* 352. On Egyptian recognition of China and relations with the Soviets, see Hahn, *United States, Great Britain, and Egypt,* 200–206; and Ovendale, *Transfer of Power in the Middle East,* 150–51. On Soviet aid to Syria, see Seale, *Struggle for Syria,* 255–56; and Lesch, *Syria and the United States,* 92–93. On violence along the Gaza frontier, see Alteras, *Eisenhower and Israel,* 179–80.

29. Helen Lackner, *A House Built on Sand: A Political Economy of Saudi Arabia* (London: Ithaca Press, 1978), 97–98; and Wadsworth to Department of State, July 11, 1956, *FRUS, 1955–1957,* 13: 389–91. See also Mordechai Abir, *Saudi Arabia: Government, Society and the Gulf Crisis* (London: Routledge, 1993), 37–38; and Nadav Safran, *Saudi Arabia: The Ceaseless Quest for Security* (Ithaca, N.Y.: Cornell University Press, 1985), 81.

30. See Table, "Composition of Aramco Work Force in Saudi Arabia," in Arabian-American Oil Company, *Aramco Handbook,* 1960, p. 211. King Saʿūd's royal decree is published in *Al-Bilād al-Saʿūdiyya,* June 22, 1956, p. 1.

31. See report by Economic Intelligence Committee's Ad Hoc Working Group on Middle East Oil, May 3, 1956, Near and Middle East Oil, 1956–1960, Box 14, Briefing Notes Subseries, NSC Series, White House Office, Records of the Office of Special Assistant for National Security Affairs, 1952–1961, DDEL.

32. See Department of State to embassies in London, Baghdad, and Jidda, May 23, 1956, "Omega vol. 5," Box 55, Records of the Secretary, Undersecretary, and Executive Secretariat, Meeting Summaries and Project Files, 1951–1959, Lot 61 D 417, RG 59; editorial note, and Department of State to embassy in Jidda, July 11, 1956, *FRUS, 1955–1957,* 13: 373–74, 389–91. On Fayṣal's ultimatum to Britain, see Parkes to Foreign Office, June 14, 1956; Parkes to Lloyd, June 17, 1956; Foreign Office minute by Riches, June 18, 1956, FO 371/120769, PRO; Memo by secretary of state, "Buraimi," July 24, 1956, CAB 129/82, C(56)190, PRO. On royal family politics, see Sarah Yizraeli, *The Remaking of Saudi Arabia: The Struggle between King Saʿūd and Crown Prince Fayṣal, 1953–1962* (Tel Aviv: Moshe Dayan Center for Middle Eastern and African Studies, 1997), 55–56; Alexander Bligh, *From Prince to King: Royal Succession in the House of Saud in the Twentieth Century* (New York: New York University Press, 1984), 61; and Gary S. Samore, "Royal Family Politics in Saudi Arabia, 1953–1983" (Ph.D. diss., Harvard University, 1983), 96.

33. The literature on Suez is summarized in Tore Tingvold Petersen, *The Middle East between the Great Powers: Anglo-American Conflict and Cooperation, 1952–7* (New York: St. Martin's Press, 2000), 65–75. For basic accounts of Suez, see Kennett Love, *Suez: The Twice-Fought War* (New York: McGraw-Hill, 1969); and Donald Neff, *Warriors at Suez: Eisenhower Takes America into the Middle East* (New York: Linden Press/Simon and Schuster, 1981). Since the thirty-year anniversary and the opening of British documents on the crisis, numerous works on Suez have been published. See William Roger Louis and Roger Owen, eds., *Suez 1956: The Crisis and Its Consequences* (Oxford: Clarendon Press, 1989); Keith Kyle, *Suez* (New York: St. Martin's Press, 1991); W. Scott Lucas, *Divided We Stand: Britain, the U.S. and the Suez Crisis* (London: Hodder and

Stoughton, 1991); Diane B. Kunz, *The Economic Diplomacy of the Suez Crisis* (Chapel Hill: University of North Carolina Press, 1991); Steven Z. Freiberger, *Dawn over Suez: The Rise of American Power in the Middle East, 1953–1957* (Chicago: Ivan R. Dee, 1992); and Takeyh, *The Origins of the Eisenhower Doctrine,* 124–41. For Arabic-language accounts of the crisis, see Muhammed Hasanayn Haykal, *miliffāt al-Sūways: ḥarb al-thalāthīn sina* [The Suez Files: The Thirty-Years War] (Cairo: markaz al-harām lil tarjama wa al-nashr, 1986); and Ḥasan al-Badrī and Fatīn Aḥmed Farīd, *ḥarb al-tawāṭū' al-thalāthī* [The War of Triple Collusion] (Cairo: al-maktaba al-akādīmīa, 1997).

34. Paper by Russell, August 4, 1956, *FRUS, 1955–1957,* 16: 140–41; memorandum of conversation by Goodpaster, July 31, 1956, ibid., 62–68; and Wilson to National Security Council with enclosed memo from Joint Chiefs, August 7, 1956, ibid., 153–56.

35. See Dulles to Department of State, August 2 and 3, 1956; and Tripartite Statement issued at London, August 2, 1956, *FRUS, 1955–1957,* 16: 111–16, 126–27, 119–24. On the Dhahran airfield, see Department of State to embassy in Jidda, August 8 and 31, 1956, *FRUS, 1955–1957,* 13: 395–99. On the Hijaz railroad, see Department of State to Embassies in Jidda, Amman, and Damascus, August 10, 1956, 986A.712, RG 59.

36. Memorandum of telephone conversation, August 9, 1956, Memo of Telephone Conversations—General July 12–September 29, 1956 (3), Box 5, Telephone Calls Series, JFD, DDEL; Commander in Chief, U.S. Naval Forces, Eastern Atlantic and Mediterranean to Chief of Naval Operations, August 22 and 29, 1956, CCS. 381 Saudi Arabia (2–7–45) Sec. 11, Box 32, Geographic File, 1954–1956, Records of the U.S. Joint Chiefs of Staff, RG 218. See also Joint Chiefs to Boone, August 15, 1956; and Memorandum of Conversation by Bennett, August 31, 1956, *FRUS, 1955–1957,* 16: 200, 342–44. On the oil "denial plan," see Steve Everly, "Cold War Deal Saved Big Oil," *Kansas City Star,* June 27, 2001.

37. On the origins of the Anderson mission, see memorandum of telephone call, July 28, 1956, July 1956—Phone Calls, Box 16, DDE Diary Series, ACW, DDEL; Hanes to Rountree, August 16, 1956, August 1956 (2), Box 10, Special Assistant Chronological Series, JFD, DDEL; Department of State to Dulles, August 17 and 18, 1956, *FRUS, 1955–1957,* 16: 220, 230–31; editorial note and Eisenhower to Sa'ūd, August 20, 1956, *FRUS, 1955–1957,* 16: 246–47, 275–76. For Eveland's account, see Eveland, *Ropes of Sand,* 209–13.

38. Unsigned memorandum of conversation, August 24, 1956, *FRUS, 1955–1957,* 16: 287–94; and Anderson to Department of State, August 23, 1956, *FRUS, 1955–1957,* 16: 273–75. See also Sa'ūd to Eisenhower, August 24, 1956; Anderson to Department of State, August 24, 1956; Wadsworth to Byroade, August 26, 1956; editorial note; Byroade to Department of State, August 28, 1956; memorandum of conversation by Dulles, August 29, 1956; memorandum of telephone conversations between the president and secretary of state, August 31, 1956, *FRUS, 1955–1957,* 16: 294–97, 299–303, 310–11, 314–15, 340–41; "Summary of Special Mission to King Saud," undated; Department of State to embassy in Jidda, August 30, 1956, Saudi Arabia—King Saud, 1952–1956 (3), Box 46, International Series, ACW, DDEL; and Dulles to Eisenhower with enclosed memo by Anderson, August 31, 1956, August 1956 (1), Box 7, Dulles-Herter Series, ACW, DDEL. See also Salamé, *Al-siyāsa al-khārjiyya al-Sa'ūdiyya* [Saudi Foreign Policy], 628–29.

39. Memorandum of telephone conversation between president and secretary of state, September 7, 1956, *FRUS, 1955–1957,* 16: 418–19. For Kern's discussion with Lloyd regarding the Anderson mission, see memorandum of conversation, September 25, 1956, FO 371/120771, PRO.

40. CAB 128/30 CC(53)6, July 26, 1956, PRO; Parkes to Lloyd, August 11, 1956, FO 371/120759, PRO. See also Parkes to Prince Fayṣal, July 29, 1956, FO 371/120771, PRO.

41. Foreign Office minute by Pirie-Gordon, August 30, 1956, FO 371/120589, PRO; and Foreign Office to embassy in Jidda, October 22, 1956, FO 371/120771, PRO. See also Lloyd to Foreign Office, October 19, 1956; FO 371/120771, PRO; and Parkes to Foreign Office, October 28, 1956 [two cables on that date], FO 371/120589, PRO.

42. Eden to Eisenhower, September 6, 1956, *FRUS, 1955–1957,* 16: 400–403; and Foreign Office minute by Walmsley, September 17, 1956, FO 371/120757, PRO. On the Saudi-Iraqi summit, see Wright to Foreign Office, September 3, 14, 15, and 23, 1956, FO 371/120756, PRO; and Wadsworth to Department of State, September 22, 1956, September 1956 (1), Box 7, Dulles-Herter Series, ACW, DDEL.

43. See the account in *Al-Bilād al-Sa'ūdiyya,* September 24, 1956, p. 1. Prince Musā'id quoted in biographical sketch, Folder 69, "Arabs—Miscellaneous Biographies," Box 1, WEM. See also Report Prepared in the Executive Secretariat of the Department of State, September 27, 1956, *FRUS, 1955–1957,* 16: 592–93; Parkes to Foreign Office, September 22 and October 2, 1956, FO 371/120757, PRO; and memo by Parkes, October 3, 1956, FO 371/120758, PRO. On the Saudi labor delegation in Beijing, see chancery Jidda to Foreign Office, October 13, 1956; and political advisor Hong Kong (Ledward) to embassy in Jidda, December 4, 1956, FO 371/120792, PRO. See also Safran, *Ceaseless Quest for Security,* 81; and Robert Lacey, *The Kingdom: Arabia and the House of Saud* (New York: Avon Books, 1981), 314.

44. Despatch from Wadsworth to Department of State, October 4, 1956, Saudi Arabia-King Saud 1952–1956 (2), Box 46, International Series, ACW, DDEL; Sa'ūd to Eisenhower, September 17, 1956, Saudi Arabia-King Saud 1952–1956 (2), Box 46, International Series, ACW, DDEL. For praise of Sa'ūd's statesmanship, see *Al-Bilād al-Sa'ūdiyya,* September 9 and 10, 1956.

45. Sa'ūd to Eisenhower, November 5 and 11, 1956, Saudi Arabia-King Saud 1952–1956 (2), Box 46, International Series, ACW, DDEL. See also Sa'ūd to Eisenhower, October 30, 1956, Saudi Arabia-King Saud 1952–1956 (2), Box 46, International Series, ACW, DDEL; Staff Notes #47, November 30, 1956, November 1956—Diary Staff Notes, Box 19, DDE Diary Series, ACW, DDEL; "Memorandum of Discussion at the 303rd Meeting of the National Security Council," November 8, 1956, *FRUS, 1955–1957,* 16: 1070–86; foreign service despatch from embassy in Jidda, November 20, 1956, 786A.00, RG 59; and *Al-Bilād al-Sa'ūdiyya,* November 1 and 7, 1956. On the economic effects of the Suez crisis on Saudi Arabia, see undated Reference Papers, "Aramco-Saudi Arabian Relations," and "Saudi Arabia's Finances," King Saud Visit Briefing Book, vol. II, CF 832, Box 123, Executive Secretariat Conference Files, 1949–1963, RG 59.

46. Minutes of Cabinet Egypt Committee (1956) 35, August 29, 1956; and "Oil Supplies for Europe and the United Kingdom," Memo prepared by the Ministry of Fuels and Power for the Economic Sterling Committee Sub-Committee on Economic Measures, November 15, 1956, PREM 11/2014, PRO. See also Interim Report of Working Committee, August 2, 1956; Draft of Memo for Ministers on Restriction of Oil Consumption in the U.K., August 16, 1956; and Secret Data on U.K. Oil Consumption, November 2, 1956, POWE 28/279, PRO. See also Kunz, *Economic Diplomacy of the Suez Crisis,* 133–52.

47. Vaughn to Toner, October 30, 1956, Suez Canal Crisis (1), Box 82, Subject Series, Confidential File, White House Central File, DDEL; and "Memorandum of Discussion at the 303rd Meeting of the National Security Council," November 8, 1956, *FRUS, 1955–1957,* 16: 1070–86 [quotation on p. 1073].

On the MEEC plan, see memorandum of conversation with the president by Goodpaster and attached memo, September 11, 1956, September 1956 Diary—Staff Memos, Box 17, DDE Diary Series, ACW, DDEL; "Memorandum—Responsibilities of Office of Oil and

Gas," October 1956, Oil to Europe (1), Box 21, Ewald Research File Series, Fred A. Seaton Papers, DDEL; Vaughn to Toner, September 10, 1956, Suez Crisis (1), Box 82, Subject File Series, Confidential File, White House Central File, DDEL; unsigned memorandum of conversation, November 25, 1956, *FRUS, 1956,* 16: 1195–96; and Arthur S. Flemming, Oral History Interview, OH-504, pp. 1–10, DDEL. See also Kunz, *The Economic Diplomacy of the Suez Crisis,* 87–88, 102, 141, 181–83.

On Britain's cut in oil consumption and dire economic straits, see Gregory to all Whitehall Departments, November 7, 1956, POWE 28/279, PRO; Elbrick and Kalijarvi to Hoover, November 17, 1956, *FRUS, 1956* 16: 1145–47; and Kunz, *The Economic Diplomacy of the Suez Crisis,* 133–38, 150–52.

48. Memorandum of conversation by Minnich, November 9, 1956, November 1956—Miscellaneous (3), Box 20, DDE Diary Series, ACW, DDEL; MacArthur to Hoover, November 20, 1956, *FRUS, 1956* 16: 1165; memorandum of conversation by Goodpaster, November 21, 1956, *FRUS, 1956,* 12: 340–42. See also memorandum of conversation by Goodpaster, November 19, 1956, *FRUS, 1956,* 16: 1153; memorandum of conversation by Goodpaster, November 20, 1956, *FRUS, 1956,* 16: 1166–69; and "Memorandum of Discussion at the 304th Meeting of the National Security Council," November 15, 1956, *FRUS, 1956,* 16: 1127–32.

49. On Hoover, see Shuckburgh, *Descent to Suez,* 323. For accounts of Hoover's role during the Suez crisis, see Freiberger, *Dawn over Suez,* 193; Lucas, *Divided We Stand,* 71–72, 282; Ashton, *Macmillan, Eisenhower and the Problem of Nasser,* 98; and Ovendale, *Transfer of Power in the Middle East,* 246.

50. Hoover to Wadsworth, November 18, 1956; memorandum of conversation by Goodpaster, November 23, 1956; and Hoover to Wadsworth, November 29, 1956, *FRUS, 1956,* 16: 1147–48, 1178–80, and 1212–13. See also memo by Hoover, October 10, 1956, October 1956 (2), Box 7, Dulles-Herter Series, ACW, DDEL; Hoover to Eisenhower, November 21, 1956, *FRUS, 1956,* 12: 343–51; unsigned memorandum of conversation, November 25, 1956, *FRUS, 1956,* 16: 1195–96; and Hoover to Wadsworth, November 26, 1956, Department of State, November 1956 (2), Box 72, Subject Series, Confidential File, White House Central File, DDEL.

51. See Wadsworth to Department of State, November 26, 1956, *FRUS, 1956,* 16: 1200; and press release, November 30, 1956, Oil to Europe (2), Box 21, Ewald Research File Series, Fred A. Seaton Papers, DDEL. See also Kyle, *Suez,* 514, and Kunz, *The Economic Diplomacy of the Suez Crisis,* 181–82.

5. We Have Here an Opportunity

1. Burton I. Kaufman, *Trade and Aid: Eisenhower's Foreign Economic Policy, 1953–1961* (Baltimore: Johns Hopkins University Press, 1982), 96; undated memo to the president by Hoover and attachment, November 1956 (1), Box 8, Dulles-Herter Series, ACW, DDEL.

2. Memorandum by Dulles, November 16, 1956, *FRUS, 1955–1957,* 12: 330–31; memorandum of conversation by Greene, December 3, 1956, ibid., 366–67. See also Wilson to acting secretary, November 14, 1956, ibid., 324–25; memorandum of conversation by Finn, November 16, 1956, ibid., 327–30; Murphy to Radford, November 17, 1956, Near and Middle East (2), Box 109, Policy Planning Staff Office Files 1956, Miscellaneous Lot Files, Lot 66 D 487, RG 59; Rountree to Acting Secretary, November 18,

1956, *FRUS, 1955–1957,* 12: 331–37; Radford to Wilson, November 30, 1956, ibid., 361–63; Wilson to Eisenhower, December 4, 1956, ibid., 372–76; memorandum of telephone conversation, Hoover and Dulles, December 8, 1956, Memoranda of Telephone Conversations with the White House, September 4–December 31 1956 (1), Box 11, Telephone Calls Series, JFD, DDEL; Hoover to Murphy, December 10, 1956, *FRUS, 1955–1957,* 12: 398.

3. Rountree to Dulles and attachment, December 5, 1956, *FRUS, 1955–1957,* 12: 376–82; memorandum of conversation by Greene, December 7, 1956, ibid., 393–95; memorandum of telephone conversation, Dulles and Eisenhower, December 8, 1956, ibid., 395–96. See also Eisenhower to Saʿūd, November 16, 1956, *FRUS, 1955–1957,* 16: 1137–39; Department of State to Jidda, November 26, 1956, Department of State November 1956 (2), Box 72, Subject Series, Confidential File, White House Central File, DDEL; Wadsworth to Department of State, November 26, 1956, *FRUS, 1955–1957,* 13: 405–406; Murphy to Rountree and Burdett, December 3, 1956, *FRUS, 1955–1957,* 12: 368–69; Henderson to Dulles, December 6, 1956, ibid., 387–89; memorandum of telephone conversation, Dulles and Eisenhower, December 6, 1956, ibid., 390.

4. Eisenhower to Dulles, December 12, 1956, December 1956 Miscellaneous (3), Box 20, DDE Diary Series, ACW, DDEL; memorandum of conversation by Macomber, *FRUS, 1955–1957,* 12: 399–401. See also Dulles memorandum of conversation with Caccia, December 24, 1956, Memoranda of Conversations—General, A-D (3), Box 1, General Conversation and Memo Series, JFD, DDEL.

5. Memorandum of conversation by Goodpaster, December 20, 1956, *FRUS, 1955–1957,* 12: 415–17; Eisenhower to Dulles, December 19, 1956, December 1956, miscellaneous (2), Box 20, DDE Diary Series, ACW, DDEL.

6. "Special Message to the Congress on the Situation in the Middle East," January 5, 1957, PPP *Dwight D. Eisenhower, 1957,* 8, 15.

7. Congress, Senate, Committee on Foreign Relations and the Committee on Armed Services, *The President's Proposal on the Middle East,* Part 1, 85th Cong., 1st Sess., January 15, 1957, p. 153; ibid., January 24, 1957, pp. 243, 260.

8. See undated reference paper, "Saudi Arabia's Finances," King Saud Visit Briefing Book, volume II, CF 832, Box 123, Executive Secretariat Conference Files, 1949–1963, RG 59; Nadav Safran, *Saudi Arabia: The Ceaseless Quest for Security* (Ithaca, N.Y.: Cornell University Press, 1988), 104–105; and Sarah Yizraeli, *The Remaking of Saudi Arabia: The Struggle between King Saʿūd and Crown Prince Fayṣal, 1953–1962* (Tel Aviv: Moshe Dayan Center for Middle Eastern and African Studies, 1997), 56–57, 122.

9. "Mayor Bars Fete for Saud, Here Today on State Visit," *New York Times,* January 29, 1956, pp. 1, 4. See also memo by Dulles, January 15, 1957, White House Correspondence—General 1957 (8), Box 5, White House Memo Series, JFD, DDEL; Itinerary for King Saud's Visit, January 25, 1957, Department of State January–February 1957 (2), Box 72, Subject Series, Confidential File, White House Central File, DDEL; memorandum of conversation by Goodpaster, January 30, 1957, January 1957 Diary—Staff Memos, Box 21, DDE Diary Series, ACW, DDEL; editorial note, *FRUS, 1955–1957,* 13: 413–14; and Wilbur Crane Eveland, *Ropes of Sand: America's Failure in the Middle East* (New York: W.W. Norton and Company, 1980), 242–43. On Prince Mashhūr, see "President's Hospital Suite Assigned to Saudi Prince," *New York Times,* February 1, 1957, p. 3; "Saud Visits Young Son in the Hospital," ibid., February 2, 1957, p. 3; and "Saudi Prince Showered with Gifts," ibid., February 5, 1957, p. 1. See also Amīn Saʿīd, *Taʾrīkh al-dawla al-Saʿūdiyya* [History of the Saudi State], vol. 3: *ʿahd Saʿūd ibn ʿAbd al-ʿAzīz* [The Reign of Saʿūd] (Beirut: dar al-kātib al-ʿArabī, 1970), 176–81.

10. Unsigned memorandum of conversation at the White House, January 30, 1957, *FRUS, 1955–1957,* 13: 417–23; memorandum of conversation by Dulles, February 1, 1957, February 1957 (2), Box 14, Chronological File, JFD, DDEL; memorandum of telephone conversation, Dulles and Lodge, February 1, 1957, February 1957 Phone Calls, Box 21, DDE Diary Series, ACW, DDEL. See also memorandum of telephone conversation Dulles and Lodge, January 31, 1957, Memos of Telephone Conversations—General January–February 28, 1957 (3), Box 6, Telephone Calls Series, JFD, DDEL; and unsigned memorandum of conversation between Eisenhower and Saʿūd, February 1, 1957, Saudi Arabia (1), Box 46, International Series, ACW, DDEL.

11. Memorandum of conversation by Eisenhower, January 30, 1957, *FRUS, 1955–1957,* 13: 423–30; memorandum of conversation by Gay, February 4, 1957, ibid., 456–61. See also memorandum of conversation by Stoltzfus, January 31, 1957, ibid., 431–44.

12. Saʿūd to Eisenhower, January 18, 1957, Visit of King Saud January 30–February 9, 1957, Box 5, Subject Series, JFD, DDEL; Saʿūd to Eisenhower, February 5, 1957, King Saud 1957 (1), Box 46, International Series, ACW, DDEL; Murphy to Dulles, February 5, 1957, *FRUS, 1955–1957,* 13: 464–65; Eisenhower to Saʿūd, February 5, 1957, King Saud 1957 (3), Box 46, International Series, ACW, DDEL; memoranda of Eisenhower's telephone calls with Robertson and Dulles, February 5, 1957, February 1957 phone calls, Box 21, DDE Diary Series, ACW, DDEL. On U.S. military aid to Saudi Arabia, see also Wilson to Dulles, January 29, 1957, *FRUS, 1955–1957,* 13: 416; memorandum of telephone conversation, Eisenhower and Dulles, January 30, 1957, Memoranda of Telephone Conversations with the White House January–February 28 1957 (2), Box 11, Telephone Calls Series, JFD, DDEL; Cannon to Radford, February 1, 1957, .091 Saudia [*sic*] Arabia, Box 17, Chairman's File, Admiral Radford, 1953–1957, Records of the U.S. Joint Chiefs of Staff, RG 218; memorandum of conversation by Sherwood and Stoltzfus, *FRUS, 1955–1957,* 13: 449–53; memorandum of conversation by Stoltzfus, February 7, 1957, ibid., 468–77; and notes by Dulles, February 8, 1957, Meetings with the President 1957 (7), Box 6, White House Memo Series, JFD, DDEL.

13. Memorandum of telephone conversation, John Foster Dulles and Allen W. Dulles, February 8, 1957, Telephone Calls—General January 1957–February 28, 1957 (3), Box 6, Telephone Calls Series, JFD, DDEL. See also memorandum of conversation by John Foster Dulles, February 5, 1957, Memoranda of Conversations, E-I (3), Box 1, General Conversation and Memo Series, JFD, DDEL; memorandum of telephone conversation, Eisenhower and Dulles, February 6, 1957, Memos of Telephone Conversations with the White House, Box 11, Telephone Calls Series, JFD, DDEL; memorandum of telephone conversation, Eisenhower and Dulles, February 7, 1957, February 1957 Phone Calls, Box 21, DDE Diary Series, ACW, DDEL; and editorial note, *FRUS, 1955–1957,* 13: 488–89.

14. H. A. R. Gibb and Harold Bowen, *Islamic Society and the West: A Study of the Impact of Western Civilization on Moslem Culture in the Near East,* 2 vols. (London: Oxford University Press, 1950, 1957), 1: 10–11; ibid., 2: 70; Staff Study Prepared in the Department of State, October 30, 1957, *FRUS, 1955–1957,* 12: 619–47 [quotation on p. 622]; State of the Union Address, January 10, 1957, PPP, *Dwight D. Eisenhower 1957,* 18.

15. "Inventory of U.S. Government and Private Organization Activity Regarding Islamic Organizations as an Aspect of Overseas Policy," May 3, 1957, OCB 000.3 (Religion) File #2 (4) January–May 1957, Box 2, OCB Central File Series, White House Office, NSC Staff Papers, DDEL; "Remarks at Ceremonies Opening the Islamic Center," June 28, 1957, PPP, *Dwight D. Eisenhower, 1957,* 509–10. See also Gustin to Staats, February 1, 1957, OCB 091.4 Near East File #4 (5) December 1956–June 1957, Box 79, OCB Central Files, NSC Staff Papers, DDEL; and memo by Gustin, April 25, 1957,

Islamic Organizations, OCB Secretariat Series, Box 4, NSC Staff Papers, DDEL. On the Hijaz railroad, see memo to Herter, March 29, 1957, April 1957 (4), Box 1, Chronological File, CAH, DDEL; Herter to Hollister, May 6, 1957, May 1957 (4), Box 1, Chronological File, CAH, DDEL; and Department of State to embassy in Jidda, May 24, 1957, 986A.712, RG 59. On the Islamic Center, see Herter to Shanley, May 6, 1957, May 1957 (4), Box 1, Chronological File, CAH, DDEL; Rountree to Herter, May 8, 1957, May 1957 (3), Box 1, Chronological File, CAH, DDEL; and documents related to Islamic Center dedication, July 1, 1957, 144-B-4 Islamic and Moslem Religion, Box 737, Official File, White House Central File, DDEL.

16. "This Is No 'Arabian Nights' Potentate," *Petroleum Week,* February 8, 1957, pp. 16–18. See Jablonski's other dispatches from Saudi Arabia in ibid., January 18, 25, and February 8, 15, and 22, 1957. See also memorandum of conversation by Wilkins, May 16, 1957, 786A.11, RG 59; Report by Bureau of Near Eastern, South Asian, and African Affairs, May 20, 1957, "Suez Canal—UN Efforts for Settlement of Canal Problems," Box 68, Records Relating to Suez Canal 1956–1960, Lot 69 D 488, RG 59. On the refurbishment of the Great Mosque, see "al-mashrūʿ al-ʿimlāq," April 12, 1957, *Al-Bilād al-Saʿūdiyya,* p. 1, as well as the series of articles on the project in ibid., May 15, 20, and 24, 1957; and F. E. Peters, *The Hajj: The Muslim Pilgrimage to Mecca and the Holy Places* (Princeton, N.J.: Princeton University Press, 1994), 69.

17. Telegram from embassy in Madrid to Department of State with text of Saʿūd's message to Eisenhower, February 17, 1957, Saudi Arabia, King Saud 1957 (1), Box 46, International Series, ACW, DDEL. See also aide-mémoire from the Department of State to the Israeli embassy, February 11, 1957, *FRUS, 1955–1957,* 17: 132–34; U.S. Mission at the United Nations to Department of State, February 11, 1957, ibid., 141–42; memorandum of telephone call, Dulles and Eisenhower, February 13, 1957, memos of telephone conversations with the White House January–February 28 1957 (2), Box 11, Telephone Calls Series, JFD, DDEL; memorandum of telephone call, Dulles and Eisenhower, February 14, 1957, Memos of Telephone Conversations with the White House January–February 28 1957 (1), Box 11, Telephone Calls Series, JFD, DDEL; Department of State to embassy in Jidda, with text of Eisenhower message to Saʿūd, February 14, 1957, Saudi Arabia, King Saud 1957 (3), Box 46, International Series, ACW, DDEL; Department of State to embassy in Jidda with text of Eisenhower message to Saʿūd, February 28, 1957, ibid; and telegram from Dhahran to Department of State with text of Saʿūd's message to Eisenhower, April 8, 1957, Saudi Arabia, King Saud 1957 (1), Box 46, International Series, ACW, DDEL.

18. See memorandum of conversation by Sherwood, May 9, 1957, *FRUS, 1955–1957,* 17: 605–608; Rountree to Dulles, May 10, 1957, ibid., 614–16; Wilcox to Dulles, May 16, 1957, "Suez Canal—UN—Israeli Withdrawal—Rights in Gaza—Gulf of Aqaba," Box 68, Records Relating to Suez Canal 1956–1960, Lot 69 D 488, RG 59; Saʿūd to Eisenhower, May 25, 1957, Saudi Arabia, King Saud 1957 (2), Box 46, International Series, ACW, DDEL; and memorandum of conversation by Bergus, June 14, 1957, *FRUS, 1955–1957,* 17: 642–45. Additional documentation regarding Saudi Arabia and the Aqaba controversy can be found in ibid., 625–26, 634–42, 648, 656–61, 679–91. On congressional politics, Israeli withdrawal, and passage of the Eisenhower Doctrine resolution, see Isaac Alteras, *Eisenhower and Israel: U.S.-Israeli Relations, 1953–1960* (Gainesville: University Press of Florida, 1993), 260–86; and Zach Levey, *Israel and the Western Powers, 1952–1960* (Chapel Hill: University of North Carolina Press, 1997), 81–82.

19. See Ritchie Ovendale, *Britain, the United States and the Transfer of Power in the Middle East, 1945–1962* (New York: Leicester University Press, 1996), 184–86.

20. "Guarantees for Maintenance of Flow of Middle East Oil through Pipelines (Agreed U.S.-U.K. Paper)," March 16, 1957, *FRUS, 1955–1957,* 12: 460–61. On Metline, see also memorandum of conversation by Rountree and Waggoner, December 20, 1956, ibid., 417–19; and memorandum of conversation by Williams, January 25, 1957, ibid., 443–44. See also Daniel Yergin, *The Prize: The Epic Quest for Oil, Money, and Power* (New York: Simon and Schuster, 1992), 496–97.

21. Burrows to Riches, March 29, 1957, FO 371/126910, PRO; Beeley to Coulson, January 19, 1957, FO 371/127155, PRO. See also documents related to review of British strategic policy in the Gulf, December 29, 1956, FO 371/126854, PRO; Caccia to Foreign Office, January 28, 1957, FO 371/127152, PRO; Riches to Burrows, February 8, 1957, FO 371/126910, PRO; Caccia to Lloyd, February 19, 1957; and Morris to Walmsley, February 27, 1957, FO 371/127155, PRO. See also Ovendale, *Transfer of Power in the Middle East,* 180–82, 185.

22. Unsigned memorandum of conversation, March 21, 1957, Bermuda (1957) chronologies Thursday, March 21, 1957, Box 2, International Trips and Meetings Series, White House Office of the Staff Secretary Records, DDEL. See also Dulles to embassy in Jidda, March 22, 1957, Bermuda (1957) chronologies Thursday, March 21 1957 (2), Box 2, International Trips and Meetings Series, White House Office of the Staff Secretary Records, DDEL.

23. Undated Briefing Paper for U.S. Bermuda Delegation, "Boycott of Suez Canal Assessment of Probable Economic Effects," CF 856 Bermuda Meetings Briefing and Position Papers vol. II, Box 127, Executive Secretariat Conference Files, 1949–1963, RG 59; Rountree to Herter with attachment, April 13, 1957, *FRUS, 1955–1957,* 12: 496–503. See also "U.S. Views on Middle East Problems Bearing Upon the Supply of Oil to the Free World," April 11, 1957, "Near and ME 1957," Box 154, Records of the Policy Planning Staff, 1957–1961, Lot 67 D 548, RG 59; memoranda of Anglo-American talks by Newsom, April 17–18, 1957, *FRUS, 1955–1957,* 12: 504–15; and minute for the prime minister, "Working Party on the Transport of Oil from the Middle East," April 3, 1957, PREM 11/2014, PRO.

24. Editorial note, *FRUS, 1955–1957,* 13: 236; Department of State to embassy in United Kingdom, July 24, 1957, ibid., 230–31. See also Gault to Lloyd, June 20, 1957; Lloyd to Macmillan, June 24, 1957, PREM 11/1944, PRO; CAB 128/31, July 18, 1957, CC(54)5, Part 2, PRO; Foreign Office to embassy in Washington, July 18 and 21, 1957, PREM 11/1944, PRO; Macmillan to Eisenhower, July 22, 1957, PREM 11/1944, PRO; CAB 128/31, July 23, 1957, CC(56)1, Part 2, PRO; and editorial note, *FRUS, 1955–1957,* 13: 232–33. On Saudi charges of Indian involvement in Oman, see memorandum by Lloyd of conversation with Dulles, July 31, 1957, PREM 11/1944, PRO; memorandum of telephone call, Allen W. Dulles and Herter, July 29, 1957, CAH Telephone Calls March 8–August 14, 1957 (1), Box 10, CAH, DDEL; Jidda to Department of State, July 29, 1957, July 1957, Box 9, Dulles-Herter Series, ACW, DDEL; and Howe to John Eisenhower with attached cable, August 3, 1957, State Department, August–October 1957 (1), Box 2, State Department Subseries, Subject Series, White House Office of the Staff Secretary Records, DDEL. For evidence of Saudi support for the Omani rebels, see Cumming to Dulles, August 1, 1957, *FRUS, 1955–1957,* 13: 234–35; memorandum of conversation by Newsom, September 19, 1957, 886A.2553, RG 59; Hart to acting secretary, December 17, 1958, December 1958 (1), Chronological File, Box 6, CAH, DDEL; Herter to Caccia, December 17, 1958; and Department of State to Jidda, December 17, 1958, 786A.58, RG 59.

25. See Macmillan to Eisenhower, August 17, 1957, *FRUS, 1955–1957,* 13: 240–41, and other documentation regarding the inscription of Oman into the United Nations agenda,

ibid., 237–47. On the Anglo-American "oil war," see Cumming to Dulles, July 24, 1957, July 1957, Box 9, Dulles-Herter Series, ACW, DDEL; and Burrows to Foreign Office, August 21, 1957, PREM 11/1948, PRO. On the Cities Service concession, see Whetsel to Rockwell, February 4, 1957, 886A.2553, RG 59. On the U.S.-Omani treaty, see copy of Saudi aide-mémoire to U.S. embassy, August 12, 1960; Weir to Walmsley, October 28, 1960, FO 371/148926, PRO; and Miriam Joyce, "Washington and Treaty-Making with the Sultan of Muscat and Oman," *Middle Eastern Studies* 30 (January 1994): 145–54.

26. Dulles to Richards, March 9, 1957, *FRUS, 1955–1957,* 12: 454–57. See also Rountree to Dulles, April 16, 1957, ibid., 494–95; and Department of State to embassy in Jordan, May 7 and 17, 1957, *FRUS, 1955–1957,* 13: 129–30, 132–33.

27. On supertankers and the canal, see D.A. Farnie, *East and West of Suez: The Suez Canal in History, 1854–1956* (Oxford: Clarendon Press, 1969), 737–38. On the oil companies' plans regarding Metline, see State Department to Dulles, March 22, 1957, CF 863 Bermuda Talks 1957 Dulte-Tedul-Tels, Box 128, Executive Secretariat Conference Files, 1949–1963, RG 59; memorandum of conversation by Dillon, April 4, 1957, *FRUS, 1955–1957,* 12: 482–84; and "Summary of Middle East Pipeline Project," June 5, 1957, ibid., 545–46.

28. Richards to Department of State, April 11, 1957, *FRUS, 1955–1957,* 13: 491–94. See also briefing paper on Jordan, March 20, 1957, CF 856, Bermuda Mtgs Briefing and Position Papers vol. II, Box 127, Executive Secretariat Conference Files, 1949–1963, RG 59; memorandum of telephone call, Dulles and Eisenhower, April 27, 1957, April 1957 phone calls, Box 23, DDE Diary Series, ACW, DDEL; and Johnson to Foreign Office, April 27, 1957, FO 371/127156, PRO.

29. Department of State to embassy in Saudi Arabia, August 21, 1957, *FRUS, 1955–1957,* 13: 645–46. See also Patrick Seale, *The Struggle for Syria: A Study of Post-War Arab Politics, 1945–1958,* 2nd ed. (New Haven, Conn.: Yale University Press, 1986), 283–306; David W. Lesch, "The Saudi Role in the American-Syrian Crisis of 1957," *Middle East Policy* 1 (Spring 1992): 33–48; idem, *Syria and the United States: Eisenhower's Cold War in the Middle East* (Boulder, Colo.: Westview Press, 1992), 138–72; and Nigel John Ashton, *Eisenhower, Macmillan and the Problem of Nasser: Anglo-American Relations and Arab Nationalism, 1955–59* (New York: St. Martin's Press, 1996), 122–39.

30. Saʿūd to Eisenhower, August 25, 1957, Saudi Arabia, King Saud 1957 (2), Box 46, International Series, ACW, DDEL. On Saʿūd's mission to Syria, see "al-bayān al-malakī al-tārīkhī," *Al-Bilād al-Saʿūdiyya,* September 29, 1957, p. 1. For the Saudi statement on the Eisenhower Doctrine, see ibid., October 6, 1957, p. 1; Denson to Morris, October 14, 1957, and Morris's reply, October 26, 1957, FO 371/127155, PRO.

31. Lesch, "The Saudi Role in the American-Syrian Crisis," 46. See also idem, *Syria and the United States,* 173–89.

32. Bowie to Cutler with attached State Department paper, "Significance of a New Middle East Pipeline System," August 1, 1957, *FRUS, 1955–1957,* 12: 563–72 [quotation on p. 569]; "Memorandum of Discussion at the 336th Meeting of the National Security Council," September 13, 1957, Box 9, NSC Series, ACW, DDEL; National Intelligence Estimate, October 8, 1957, *FRUS, 1955–1957,* 12: 594–611 [quotation on p. 603]. See also National Security Council Report, "Construction of a New Middle East Petroleum Pipeline System," September 30, 1957, ibid., 587–94.

33. Unsigned letter to Dulles, August 24, 1957, *FRUS, 1955–1957,* 13: 652–53; Dulles to Macmillan, August 27, 1957, August 1957 (1), Box 15, Chronological File, JFD, DDEL. Although the signature has been withheld from the letter to Dulles as it appears in

FRUS, William Rountree told the secretary's staff that while in Rome, Henderson had met with Allen W. Dulles. See memo by Howe of secretary's staff meeting, August 23, 1957, Secretary's Staff Meeting Minutes, June 3, 1957–December 30, 1957, Box 7, Minutes and Notes of the Secretary's Staff Meetings, 1952–1961, Lot 63, D 75, RG 59. I am grateful to Salim Yaqub for this document. See also memorandum of conversation by Rountree, August 26, 1957, *FRUS, 1955–1957,* 12: 575–76.

34. Both Ambassador George Wadsworth and Ambassador Raymond Hare used the term "pope" in reference to King Saʿūd. See Wadsworth's testimony in Congress, Senate, Committee on Foreign Relations and the Committee on Armed Services, *The President's Proposal on the Middle East,* Part 2, 85th Cong., 1st Sess., February 6, 1957, p. 651. Years later, Hare criticized the "amateurish" strategy to make Saʿūd into a "Moslem pope." See Raymond Hare, Oral History Transcript, OH-189, Interview #2, DDEL, pp. 59–60.

35. Editorial note, *FRUS, 1955–1957,* 12: 651; memorandum presented to the National Security Council Planning Board, November 4, 1957, ibid., 649–51. See also "United States Objectives and Policies with Respect to the Near East," October 30, 1957, ibid., 619–47; Rountree to Dulles, November 4, 1957, *FRUS 1955–1957,* 17: 785–88; memorandum of telephone call, Dulles to Rockwell, November 20, 1957, Memos of Telephone Conversations—General Nov 1–Dec 27 1957 (2), Box 7, Telephone Calls Series, JFD, DDEL; Department of State to Jidda, November 20, 1957, *FRUS, 1955–1957,* 17: 805–806; and Wadsworth to Department of State, November 28, 1957, ibid., 827–28.

36. Undated letter, Jones to Eisenhower, Jones, W. Alton (Pete) (3) [Middle East], Box 20, Name Series, ACW, DDEL; Jones to Eisenhower, November 9, 1957, ibid.; and Eisenhower to Dulles, November 13, 1957, *FRUS, 1955–1957,* 17: 795. See also memo for the record by Dulles, November 15, 1957, ibid., 796. On Jones's suggestions for U.S. policy toward ʿAbd al-Nāṣir, see memorandum of conversation by Dulles, October 28, 1957, Meetings with the President 1957 (2), Box 5, White House Memo Series, JFD, DDEL; and memorandum of telephone conversation, Jones and Herter, November 21, 1957, Aug 1–Dec 31 1957 (1), Box 11, CAH Telephone Calls, CAH, DDEL. On Eisenhower's relationship with Jones, see Stephen E. Ambrose, *Eisenhower,* vol. 2, *The President* (New York: Simon and Schuster, 1984), 28, 109, 198, 366, 604, 610, 646.

37. Memorandum of conversation by Engle, December 6, 1957, *FRUS, 1955–1957,* 12: 663–66; editorial note, *FRUS, 1958–1960,* 12: 1–2. On administration discussion of oil-funded development, see memo by Dulles, October 21, 1957, *FRUS, 1955–1957,* 12: 618. On the Pella plan, see memorandum of conversation by Torbert, September 25, 1957, *FRUS, 1955–1957,* 12: 584–85; Department of State to embassy in Rome, November 22, 1957, ibid., 661–62; memorandum of conversation by Long, December 6, 1957, ibid., 666–68; and, for a reference to a later version of the Pella plan, see Kaufman, *Trade and Aid,* 183. On the Iraqi proposal, the demise of Metline, and oil politics among the Arab states, see memoranda of conversations by Newsom, September 25, 1957, *FRUS, 1955–1957,* 12: 585–87; Rountree to Dulles, October 9, 1957, ibid., 617–18; embassy in London to Department of State, November 13, 1957, ibid., 656; Ministry of Fuels and Power memorandum, September 30, 1957, PREM 11/1948, PRO; and "Cairo Oil Congress Worries Producers," *Petroleum Week,* September 6, 1957, p. 44.

38. See memorandum of conversation by Sherwood, August 29, 1957, *FRUS, 1955–1957,* 13: 503–505; memorandum of conversation by Newsom, September 19, 1957, 886A.2553, RG 59; and memorandum of conversation by Shaw, December 17, 1957, *FRUS, 1955–1957,* 12: 670–73. For the Anglo-American commitment to defend the fifty-fifty standard, see Rountree to Dulles, May 14, 1957, with attachment, "Review of Middle East Problems Bearing Upon the Supply of Oil to the Free World," *FRUS, 1955–1957,*

10: 680–89 [esp. p. 686]. See also Yergin, *The Prize,* 501–507, 513–14; and Wanda M. Jablonski, "How Could Aramco Compete against Its Owners?" *Petroleum Week,* October 18, 1957, pp. 20–22.

39. "United States Objectives and Policies with Respect to the Near East," October 30, 1957, *FRUS, 1955–1957,* 12: 619–47 [quotation on p. 637]; editorial note, *FRUS, 1958–1960,* 12: 1–2; and memorandum of conversation by Reinhardt, January 30, 1958, ibid., 35.

40. National Security Council Report, NSC 5801/1, January 24, 1958, *FRUS, 1958–1960,* 12: 17–32 [quotation on p. 29]; "Memorandum of Discussion at the 352nd Meeting of the National Security Council" with attachment, January 22, 1958, ibid., 6–16 [quotation on p. 9]; Dulles to Eisenhower, February 8, 1958, State Department February–April 1958 (1), Box 2, State Department Subseries, Subject Series, White House Office of the Staff Secretary Papers, DDEL; Dwight D. Eisenhower, *Waging Peace, 1956–1961* (Garden City, N.Y.: Doubleday and Company, 1965), 263. On U.S. policy toward the Arabian peninsula, see undated background paper, October 1957, State Department October 1957 Briefing Book, Macmillan Visit, Box 74, Subject Series, Confidential File, White House Central File, DDEL; and "United States Objectives and Policies with Respect to the Near East," October 30, 1957, *FRUS, 1955–1957,* 12: 619–47 [esp. pp. 638–39]. On the Arab Union and Saudi reservations, see Herter to Eisenhower, January 30, 1958, January 1958 (1), Box 3 Chronological File, CAH, DDEL; Dulles to embassy in Jidda, February 1, 1958, Saudi Arabia-King Saud 1958–60, Box 46, International Series, ACW, DDEL; embassy in Jordan to Department of State, February 3, 1958, *FRUS, 1958–1960,* 11: 270–72; and embassy in Jidda to Department of State, February 7, 1958, Saudi Arabia—King Saud 1958–60, Box 46, International Series, ACW, DDEL.

41. Memo by Paul Gore-Booth, September 25, 1957, PREM 11/1948, PRO. See also *al-Bilād al-Saʿūdiyya,* January 14, 1958, p. 1–2; and Yizraeli, *Remaking of Saudi Arabia,* 57–58, 123.

42. Ghassan Salamé, *Al-siyāsa al-khārjiyya al-Saʿūdiyya mundhu ʿām 19Ɛ0: dirāsa fī al-ʿalāqa al-dawliyya* [Saudi Foreign Policy since 1945: A Study in International Relations] (Beirut: Mahad al-Inmāʾ al-ʿArabī, 1980), 632–33. See also Yizraeli, *Remaking of Saudi Arabia,* 63–74; Amīn Saʿīd, *Taʾrīkh al-dawla al-Saʿūdiyya,* 3: 239–40; Gary Samore, "Royal Family Politics in Saudi Arabia, 1953–1983" (Ph.D. diss., Harvard University, 1983), 112–17; and Jubrān Shāmiyya, *Āl Saʿūd: māḍīhim wa mustaqbaluhum* [The Saudi Dynasty: Its Past and Future] (Beirut: dār al-abḥāth wa al-nashr, 1986), 270. For the text of ʿAbd al-Nāṣir's speech exposing the plot, see "aghra min al-khayāl," *Al-Ahrām,* March 6, 1958, pp. 1, 3. For public Saudi denials of the charges, see *Al-Bilād al-Saʿūdiyya,* March 7, 1958, p. 1. The royal decree ceding Fayṣal power is published in ibid., March 22, 1958, p. 1.

43. Rountree to Dulles, March 14, 1958, *FRUS, 1958–1960,* 12: 719; Department of State to embassy in Jidda, March 3, 1958, ibid., 714; "Memorandum of Discussion at the 357th Meeting of the National Security Council," March 6, 1958, Box 9, NSC Series, ACW, DDEL. See also "Memorandum of Discussion at the 358th Meeting of the National Security Council," March 13, 1958, *FRUS, 1958–1960,* 12: 46–47; Caccia to Foreign Office, March 15, 1958, PREM 11/5068, PRO; Yizraeli, *Remaking of Saudi Arabia,* 65–67; and Eveland, *Ropes of Sand,* 273.

44. Rountree to Dulles with attachments, March 24, 1958, *FRUS, 1958–1960,* 12: 48–54 [quotations on pp. 53, 54]; "Memorandum of Discussion at the 363rd Meeting of the National Security Council," April 24, 1958, Box 10, NSC Series, ACW, DDEL.

45. Dillon to Herter, June 30, 1958, and attachment, "Transport of Oil from the Middle East (Joint Report by US-UK Officials)," May 12, 1958, *FRUS, 1958–1960,* 12: 64–71 [quotation on p. 69]. See also memorandum of conversation by Rountree, May 13, 1958; telegram from the Department of State to the embassy in Lebanon, May 13, 1958, *FRUS, 1958–1960,* 11: 45–50.

46. See Douglas Little, "His Finest Hour? Eisenhower, Lebanon, and the 1958 Middle East Crisis," *Diplomatic History* 20 (Winter 1996): 27–54; and Ashton, *Eisenhower, Macmillan and the Problem of Nasser,* 165–89. For an account that emphasizes Anglo-American cooperation, see Ovendale, *Transfer of Power in the Middle East,* 198–215.

47. Irene Gendzier, *Notes from the Minefield: United States Intervention in Lebanon and the Middle East, 1945–1958* (New York: Columbia University Press, 1997), 11–15, 295–304. Gendzier offers no evidence for her claim other than Wilbur Eveland's observations. See ibid., 413 n. 25.

48. Memorandum of telephone call, Eisenhower and Macmillan, July 14, Telephone Calls July 1958, Box 34, DDE Diary Series, ACW, DDEL; memorandum of conversation by Goodpaster, July 23, 1958, *FRUS, 1958–1960,* 12: 98–100; and "Memorandum of Discussion at the 373rd Meeting of the National Security Council," July 24, 1958, ibid., 100–109 [quotation on p. 102] . See also memorandum of conversation by Goodpaster, July 16, 1958, ibid., 72–75; memorandum of conversation by Reinhardt, July 17, 1958, ibid., 76–77; and CAB 128/32 [see record of Macmillan's call to Dulles during the cabinet meeting], July 16, 1958, Part 2, CC(59), PRO.

49. Memorandum of conversation by Goodpaster, July 14, 1958, *FRUS, 1958–1960,* 12: 211–15. On Saʿūd's relations with the U.S. since March, see memorandum of conversation by Newsom, March 26, 1958, ibid., 720–23; Department of State to embassy in Jidda, April 1, 1958, ibid., 724–25; and Department of State to embassy in Jidda, June 6, 1958, ibid., 729–30. On Fayṣal's foreign policy, see Heath to Department of State, April 20, 1958, 686A.00, RG 59. On Fayṣal's stance during the Anglo-American intervention, see Dulles to Eisenhower, July 17, 1958, Saudi Arabia (1), Box 46, International Series, ACW, DDEL; Middle East Situation Report #8, JCS vol. II (1) July 19–22 1958, Box 4, DOD Subseries, Subject Series, White House Office of the Staff Secretary Papers, DDEL; "Synopsis of Presidential Reports on the Middle East, July 14–19," July 19, 1958, Mideast July 1958 (1), Box 40, International Series, ACW, DDEL; "balāgh rasmī min raʾīs majlis al-wuzarāʾ," *Al-Bilād al-Saʿūdiyya,* July 20, 1958, p. 1; Heath to Department of State, July 25, 1958, *FRUS, 1958–1960,* 12: 730–33; foreign service despatch, fortnightly review from embassy in Jidda, July 31, 1958, 786A.00, RG 59; and Eisenhower, *Waging Peace,* 277–80. On divisions within Saudi Arabia over the intervention, see Situation Report on Lebanon Number 2, July 16, 1958, JCS vol II (1) July 16–18 1958, Box 4, DOD Subseries, Subject Series, White House Office of the Staff Secretary Papers, DDEL; and Heath to Department of State, July 30, 1958, 786A.00, RG 59.

6. We Might As Well Believe in Arab Nationalism

1. "Issues Arising Out of the Situation in the Near East," July 29, 1958, *FRUS, 1958–1960,* 12: 114–24 [quotations on pp. 116–17]; "Memorandum of Discussion at the 374th Meeting of the National Security Council," July 31, 1958, ibid., 124–34 [quotations on pp. 128 and 132].

2. Murphy to Herter with attachment, August 15, 1958, *FRUS, 1958–1960,* 12: 143–45; paper by Dulles, August 23, 1958, ibid., 157–58; NSC 5820/1, November 4, 1958, ibid.,

187–99 [quotation on p. 190]. For the debate within the administration on ʿAbd al-Nāṣir, see ibid., 136, 145–54,162–66. For the text of Eisenhower's U.N. speech, see "Address at the Third Special Emergency Session of the General Assembly of the United Nations," August 13, 1958, PPP *Dwight D. Eisenhower, 1958,* 606–16; and see also memorandum by Goodpaster of conference with the president, August 11, 1958, State Department 1958 (May–August) (5), Box 3, State Department Subseries, Subject Series, White House Office of the Staff Secretary Papers, DDEL.

3. See Malcolm Kerr, *The Arab Cold War: Gamal ʿAbd al-Nasir and His Rivals, 1958–1970,* rev. ed. (New York: Oxford University Press, 1971), 1–25; Charles Tripp, *A History of Iraq* (Cambridge: Cambridge University Press, 2000), 148–67; and Peter Sluglett and Marion Farouk-Sluglett, *Iraq since 1958: From Revolution to Dictatorship* (London: KPI, 1987), 47–66. On Nāṣir's meeting with Fayṣal, see Heath to Department of State, August 12, 1958, 786A.11, RG 59; Heath to Department of State, August 20 and 23, 1958, 686A.86B, RG 59; and Johnston to Foreign Office, August 23, 1958, FO 371/132658, PRO.

4. Memorandum by Goodpaster of conference with the president, December 23, 1958, State Department (September 1958–January 1959) (4), Box 3, State Department Subseries, Subject Series, White House Office of the Staff Secretary Papers, DDEL. See also Rountree to Dulles, December 27, 1958, *FRUS, 1958–1960,* 12: 200–204. On the U.S. *modus vivendi* with Nāṣir, see Jeffrey A. Lefebvre, "The United States and Egypt: Confrontation and Accommodation in Northeast Africa, 1956–1960," *Middle Eastern Studies* 29 (April 1993): 321–38.

5. Sarah Yizraeli, *The Remaking of Saudi Arabia: The Struggle between King Saʿūd and Crown Prince Fayṣal, 1953–1962* (Tel Aviv: Moshe Dayan Center for Middle Eastern and African Studies, 1997), 128–29. On U.S. measures in support of Fayṣal's reforms, see Bell to Dillon, February 3, 1959; and Heath to Rountree, February 9, 1959, *FRUS, 1958–1960,* 12: 739–45.

6. Memorandum of conversation by Reinhardt, March 22, 1959, *FRUS, 1958–1960,* 12: 217–18. See also editorial notes, ibid., 216, 218–19; Briefing Book, Macmillan Visit (March 20–22, 1959) (5), Box 24, International Series, ACW, DDEL; "US-UK—The Problem of the Use of Military Force to Maintain Access to Middle East Oil, Ramsey's Commission," April 7, 1959, Box 23, Records of the Component Offices of the Bureau of Economic Affairs, 1941–1963, Lot 64 D 69, RG 59; State Department report, April 15, 1959, Iraq, March–April, 1959, Box 8, International Series, ACW, DDEL; minute by foreign secretary, May 5, 1959, CAB 128/33, CC(28)4, PRO; and Dennison to McElroy, June 29, 1959, *FRUS, 1958–1960,* 12: 224–26. On Anglo-American attitudes toward the "Arab Cold War," joint military planning, and British concerns about Kuwait, see Ritchie Ovendale, *Britain, the United States and the Transfer of Power in the Middle East, 1945–1962* (New York: Leicester University Press, 1996), 216–241; Nigel John Ashton, *Eisenhower, Macmillan and the Problem of Nasser: Anglo-American Relations and Arab Nationalism, 1955–59* (New York: St. Martin's Press, 1996), 199–207; and Miriam Joyce, *Kuwait, 1945–1996: An Anglo-American Perspective* (London: Frank Cass, 1998), 51–60.

7. Rountree to Murphy, December 22, 1958, *FRUS, 1958–1960,* 12: 736–38. For the British initiative involving the U.N. secretary-general, see Dixon to Foreign Office, January 15, 1959; and Foreign Office to Dixon, January 31, 1959, FO 371/140361, PRO; memorandum of conversation between Hammarskjöld and Lloyd, May 10, 1959; Hammarskjöld to Lloyd, May 19, 1959; Lloyd to Macmillan, May 24, 1959; Zulueta to Macmillan, May 25, 1959; Zulueta to Acland, May 26, 1959; Macmillan to Lloyd, June 12, 1959; Lloyd to Macmillan, June 15, 1959, PREM 11/4446, PRO; notes by Dixon, June 2, 1959,

FO 371/140365, PRO; and documents related to Hammarskjöld's mediation between Britain and Saudi Arabia, FO 371/140366, PRO. On Saudi reluctance to resume relations with London, see Beeley to Stevens, November 30, 1959; and Weir to Walmsley, December 1, 1959, FO 371/140368, PRO.

8. See Daniel Yergin, *The Prize: The Epic Quest for Oil, Money, and Power* (New York: Simon and Schuster, 1992), 499–508, 514–15; "Mideast Crude Prices Cut Sharply," *Petroleum Week,* February 20, 1959, pp. 19–20; and Wanda M. Jablonski, "A Look Ahead: Too Much, for Much Too Long," ibid., May 27, 1960, pp. 20–21.

9. Robert H. Ferrell, ed., *The Eisenhower Diaries* (New York: W.W. Norton and Company, 1981), 361–62. See also Burton I. Kaufman, *Trade and Aid: Eisenhower's Foreign Economic Policy, 1953–1961* (Baltimore: Johns Hopkins University Press, 1982), 88–91; Stephen G. Rabe, *The Road to OPEC: United States Relations with Venezuela, 1919–1976* (Austin: University of Texas Press, 1982), 157–58; and Yergin, *The Prize,* 535–40.

10. Memorandum of conversation by Rountree, March 18, 1959, *FRUS, 1958–1960,* 12: 214–15. See also memorandum of telephone conversation, Holman and Herter, March 17, 1959, January 1–April 27 1959 (1), CAH Phone Calls, Box 12, CAH, DDEL; Copy of Hendryx paper, "A Sovereign Nation's Legal Ability to Make and Abide by a Petroleum Concession Contract," FO 371/141209, PRO; and "Venezuela Slates Big Turnout in Cairo," *Petroleum Week,* April 3, 1959, p. 58. On Duce's mission to Cairo, see memo for file by Rentz, March 29, 1959, Folder 50, "Rentz, George S., Correspondence, 1948–1959," Box 1, WEM.

11. Intelligence Report No. 48, April 8, 1959, FO 371/141207, PRO; Ministry of Fuels and Power note to prime minister, May 4, 1959, FO 371/141208, PRO; Wanda M. Jablonski, "Nasser Speaks Up on Oil for the First Time," *Petroleum Week,* May 1, 1959, p. 18. On the Mosul uprising, see Sluglett, *Iraq since 1958,* 66–70. See also "Cairo Congress: A Note of Stability," *Petroleum Week,* May 8, 1959, p. 15; "Cairo Forum," *Petroleum Press Service,* May 1959, pp. 168–70; and Yergin, *The Prize,* 516–18.

12. Heath to Department of State, August 28, 1959, 886A.2553, RG 59. See also foreign service despatch by Heath, October 19, 1959, 886A.2553, RG 59. On management changes within Aramco, see foreign service despatch by Schwinn, October 23, 1958, 886A.2553, RG 59; the Arabian-American Oil Company, *Aramco Handbook* (1960), 139, 145; and the Arabian-American Oil Company, Report to the Saudi Arab Government, Dhahran, April 15, 1960.

13. Weir to Walmsley, June 17, 1959, FO 371/140378, PRO. See also Foreign Office minute by Walker, July 16, 1959, FO 371/140357, PRO; foreign service despatch by Heath, November 25, 1959, 886A.2553, RG 59; Heath to Department of State, November 26, 1959, *FRUS, 1958–1960,* 12: 749–50; foreign service despatch by Heath, January 24, 1960, ibid., 752–54; foreign service despatches by Heath, May 3 and 10 [with attached letter from Saudi government to Aramco], 1960, 886A.2553, RG 59; memorandum of conversation by Crawford, May 11, 1960, 886A.2553, RG 59; and foreign service despatch by Dwyer, July 27, 1960, 880.2553, RG 59.

14. Memorandum of conversation by Jones, February 26, 1960, 880.2553, RG 59. The author obtained the attached British aide-mémoire through the Freedom of Information Act.

15. Jones to Hager, April 20, 1960, *FRUS, 1958–1960,* 12: 251–53; "Middle East Oil Concession Problems," May 11, 1960, "US-UK—The Problem of the Use of Military Force to Maintain Access to Middle East Oil, Ramsey's Commission," Box 23, Records of the Component Offices of the Bureau of Economic Affairs, 1941–1963, Lot 64 D 69, RG 59. See also Herter to various missions, March 11, 1960, 880.2553, RG 59; Martin to

Merchant, May 3, 1960, *FRUS, 1958–1960,* 12: 255–57; and Heath to Department of State, May 3, 1960, 886A.2553, RG 59.

16. On the origins of OPEC, see Yergin, *The Prize,* 519–23; John G. Clark, *The Political Economy of World Energy: A Twentieth-Century Perspective* (Chapel Hill: University of North Carolina Press, 1991), 124–27; Rabe, *The Road to OPEC,* 159–61; Ian Skeet, *Opec: Twenty-five Years of Prices and Politics* (Cambridge: Cambridge University Press, 1988), 1–34; Dankwart A. Rustow, *Oil and Turmoil: America Faces OPEC and the Middle East* (New York: W.W. Norton, 1982), 108–12; Anthony Sampson, *The Seven Sisters: The Great Oil Companies and the World They Shaped* (New York: Viking, 1975), 156–66; Pierre Terzian, *OPEC: The Inside Story,* trans. Michael Pallis (Avon: Bath Press, 1985), 65–97; Leonard Mosley, *Power Play: Oil in the Middle East* (New York: Random House, 1973), 289–99; and Mana Saeed al-Otaiba, *OPEC and the Petroleum Industry* (New York: John Wiley and Sons, 1975), 47–55. See also "Tariki: Export Nations Should Prorate to Market Demand, Based on Reserves," *Petroleum Week,* May 6, 1960, pp. 15–16; and "Tariki & Perez: Oil Nations Could End Crude Surplus," ibid., May 20, 1960, pp. 12–13. On the Saudi reaction to the price cuts, see Heath to Department of State, August 12, 1960, 886A.2553, RG 59; and Schwinn to Department of State, August 13, 1960, 880.2553, RG 59.

17. "Memorandum of Discussion at the 460th Meeting of the National Security Council," September 21, 1960, *FRUS, 1958–1960,* 12: 275–77. See also "Current Major Oil Issues in the Middle East," October 5, 1960, ME (General) 1959–60 Petroleum, Box 22, Records of the Component Offices of the Bureau of Economic Affairs, 1941–63, Lot 64 D 69, RG 59; and National Intelligence Estimate 30–60, Middle East Oil, Petroleum 1960, Box 14, Briefing Notes Subseries, NSC Series, White House Office, Office of the Special Assistant for National Security Affairs Papers, 1952–1961, DDEL. On oil company executives' concerns about OPEC, see memorandum of conversation by Beckner, October 19, 1960, *FRUS, 1958–1960,* 12: 277–80; and memorandum of conversation by Dillon, November 3, 1960, ibid., 285.

18. See Abbas Alnasrawi, *Arab Nationalism, Oil, and the Political Economy of Dependency* (Westport, Conn.: Greenwood Press, 1991), 103–104. On Saudi Arabia's external investment of oil revenues following the embargo, see Hossein Askari, *Saudi Arabia's Economy: Oil and the Search for Economic Development* [Contemporary Studies in Economic and Financial Analysis, vol. 67, ed. Robert J. Thornton and J. Richard Aronson] (Greenwich, Conn.: JAI Press, 1990), 55–65. See also Mohammed Imady, "Patterns of Arab Economic Aid to Third World Countries," *Arab Studies Quarterly* 6 (Winter/Spring 1984): 70–91.

19. Foreign Office minute by Riches, February 2, 1959; and Weir to Walmsley, April 8, 1959, FO 371/140357, PRO; Department of State to embassy in Jidda, March 4, 1959, *FRUS, 1958–1960,* 12: 745–47. See also Herter to embassy in Jidda, February 21, 1959, 786A.00, RG 59. On the dispute over Saʿūd's debts, see editorial note, *FRUS, 1958–1960,* 12: 748; Caccia to Foreign Office, May 12, 1959; and memorandum of conversation, Lloyd and Herter, May 13, 1959, FO 371/140357, PRO. On Saʿūd's overture to London, see Middleton to Foreign Office [with text of Saʿūd's message], April 1, 1959; memorandum of conversation, Lloyd and Herter, April 4, 1959; Caccia to Foreign Office, April 6, 1959; Crosthwaite to Foreign Office, April 18, 1959; and Macmillan to Saʿūd, April 22, 1959, PREM 11/4446, PRO. On the king's meeting with ʿAbd al-Nāṣir, see editorial note, *FRUS, 1958–1960,* 12: 749; Crowe to Foreign Office, September 5, 1959; and Crowe to Lloyd, September 8, 1959, FO 371/140359, PRO. See also Yizraeli, *Remaking of Saudi Arabia,* 73–83.

20. See Sweeney to Department of State, April 22, 1959, 786A.00, RG 59. See also Yizraeli, *Remaking of Saudi Arabia,* 63–64, 68–70, 112–14, 139–40; Gary S. Samore, "Royal Family Politics in Saudi Arabia, 1953–1983" (Ph.D. diss., Harvard University, 1983), 136–37; and Fahd al-Qaḥṭānī, *ṣirāʿ al-ajnaḥ fī al-ʿāʾila al-Saʿūdiyya: dirāsa fī al-niẓām al-siyāsī wa taʾsus al-dawla* [Factional Conflict within the Saudi Dynasty: A Study of the Political Structure and Foundation of the State] (London: al-ṣafā al-nashr wa al-tawzīʿ, 1988), 91–92.

21. See Kiren Aziz Chaudhry, *The Price of Wealth: Economies and Institutions in the Middle East* (Ithaca, N.Y.: Cornell University Press, 1997), 81. For comparative perspective on rentier states in the Gulf, see Jill Crystal, *Oil and Politics in the Gulf: Rulers and Merchants in Kuwait and Qatar,* 2nd ed. (Cambridge: Cambridge University Press, 1995); F. Gregory Gause, III, *Oil Monarchies: Domestic and Security Challenges in the Arab Gulf States* (New York: Council on Foreign Relations Press, 1994); and Jacqueline S. Ismael, *Kuwait: Dependency and Class in a Rentier State* (Gainesville: University Press of Florida, 1993). See also Hazem Beblawi and Giacomo Luciani, eds., *The Rentier State* [Nation, State and Integration in the Arab World, vol. 2] (London: Croom Helm, 1987).

22. On the coup plot, see Department of State to embassy in Jidda, July 22 and 26, 1960, *FRUS, 1958–1960,* 12: 762–64; Heath to Department of State, August 1, 1960; Schwinn to Department of State, August 2, 1960; Department of State to embassy in Jidda and consulate in Dhahran, August 17, 1960, 786A.00, RG 59; and Department of State to embassy in Jidda, August 18, 1960, *FRUS, 1958–1960,* 12: 765. On Eddy's mission, see Smith to Department of State [signed by Heath], June 17, 1960, 786A.00, RG 59. For Aramco interest in Saʿūd's return to power, see memorandum of conversation by Brewer, July 14, 1960, 886A.2553, RG 59; Schwinn to Department of State, December 22, 1960, 880.2553, RG 59; and Schwinn to Department of State, December 26, 1960, 886A.2553, RG 59.

23. Heath to Department of State, March 23, 1960, 886A.2553, RG 59. On Muʿammar, see Heath to Department of State, January 10, 1960, 786A.00, RG 59; Heath to Department of State, January 15, 1960, 886A.2553, RG 59; Weir to Walmsley, January 12, May 9, and June 15, 1960, FO 371/149233, PRO. On Saʿud's return to power, see Cumming to Herter, December 22, 1960, *FRUS, 1958–1960,* 12: 769–70; Meyer to Jones, December 23, 1960, ibid., 771–73; and Caccia to Foreign Office, December 22, 1960, FO 371/149234, PRO. On Fayṣal's opposition to Muʿammar's idea for representative government, see Mulligan to Mandis, February 8, 1960, Folder 64, "AAD Chronological Files, January–April 1960," Box 2, WEM. See alsoYizraeli, *Remaking of Saudi Arabia,* 113–14; al-Qaḥṭānī, *ṣirāʿ al-ajnaḥ fī al-ʿāʾila al-Saʿūdiyya* [Factional Conflict within the Saudi Dynasty], 100–102; Samore, "Royal Family Politics in Saudi Arabia," 139–51; and Robert Lacey, *The Kingdom: Arabia and the House of Saud* (New York: Avon Books, 1981), 336.

24. See Yizraeli, *Remaking of Saudi Arabia,* 85–93, 185–97.

Conclusion

1. Bernard Burrows, *Footnotes in the Sand: The Gulf in Transition, 1953–1958* (Wilton, Salisbury, England: Michael Russell, 1990), 110.

2. On the October War and embargo, see Daniel Yergin, *The Prize: The Epic Quest for Oil, Money, and Power* (New York: Simon and Schuster, 1992), 588–632; and Nadav Safran, *Saudi Arabia: The Ceaseless Quest for Security* (Ithaca, N.Y.: Cornell University

Press, 1985), 151–79. On oil revenues, remittances, and the Middle Eastern economy, see Roger Owen and Şevket Pamuk, *A History of Middle East Economies in the Twentieth Century* (Cambridge, Mass.: Harvard University Press, 1999), 222–24; and Kiren Aziz Chaudhry, *The Price of Wealth: Economies and Institutions in the Middle East* (Ithaca, N.Y.: Cornell University Press, 1997). On economic inequalities within the Arab world, see *The Least Developed and the Oil-Rich Arab Countries: Dependence, Interdependence, or Patronage?,* ed. Kunibert Raffer and M.A. Mohamed Salih (New York: St. Martin's Press, 1992). See also Yusif A. Sayigh, *Arab Oil Policies in the 1970s: Opportunity and Responsibility* (London: Croom Helm, 1983).

3. On U.S. arms sales to Saudi Arabia, see Safran, *Saudi Arabia,* 180–214, 420–47; and Anthony Cordesman, *Saudi Arabia: Guarding the Desert Kingdom* (Boulder, Colo.: Westview Press, 1997), 108–11.

4. On Fayṣal's accession and policies, see Parker T. Hart, *Saudi Arabia and the United States: Birth of a Security Partnership* (Bloomington: Indiana University Press, 1998), 237–47; Alexei Vassiliev, *The History of Saudi Arabia* (London: Saqi Books, 1998), 366–68; Robert Lacey, *The Kingdom: Arabia and the House of Saud* (New York: Avon Books, 1981), 343–57; Alexander Bligh, *From Prince to King: Royal Succession in the House of Saud in the Twentieth Century* (New York: New York University Press, 1984), 70–79, 84–90; and Joseph Kostiner and Joshua Teitelbaum, "State Formation and the Saudi Monarchy," in *Middle East Monarchies: The Challenge of Modernity,* ed. Joseph Kostiner (Boulder, Colo.: Lynne Rienner Publishers, 2000), 131–49. On Aramco's nationalization, see Vassiliev, *History of Saudi Arabia,* 389–90; Robert Vitalis, "The Closing of the Arabian Oil Frontier and the Future of Saudi-American Relations," *Middle East Report* 27 (July–September 1997): 15–25; and Lacey, *The Kingdom,* 492. On oil and the Saudi state, see Simon Bromley, *Rethinking Middle East Politics* (Austin: University of Texas Press, 1994), 142–47. For Saudi state building in comparative perspective, see F. Gregory Gause III, "The Persistence of Monarchy in the Arabian Peninsula: A Comparative Analysis," in Kostiner, ed., *Middle East Monarchies,* 167–86.

Bibliography

Primary Sources

Government Archives

Dwight D. Eisenhower Presidential Library, Abilene, Kansas
- John Foster Dulles Papers
- Dwight D. Eisenhower, Papers as President of the United States, 1953–1961 (Ann C. Whitman File)
  - DDE Diaries Series
  - Dulles-Herter Series
  - International Series
  - Name Series
  - National Security Council Series
- Christian A. Herter Papers
- Fred A. Seaton Papers
- White House Central Files, 1953–1961
  - Confidential File
  - Official File
- White House Office
  - National Security Council Staff Papers, 1948–1961
  - Office of the Special Assistant for National Security Affairs, Records 1952–61
  - Office of the Staff Secretary, Records 1952–1961
- Oral Histories
  - Winthrop Aldrich
  - George V. Allen
  - Arthur S. Flemming
  - Raymond Hare
  - Loy Henderson
  - Robert Murphy

National Archives and Records Administration, College Park, Maryland
Record Group 59, General Records of the Department of State
Record Group 218, Records of the Joint Chiefs of Staff
Record Group 48, Records of the Office of the Secretary of the Interior

British Public Record Office, Kew, England
Political Correspondence of the Foreign Office (FO 371)
Records of the Cabinet Office (CAB 128, 129)
Records of the Ministry of Fuels and Power (POWE 28)
Records of the Prime Minister's Office (PREM 11)

Private Manuscript Collections

William E. Mulligan Papers. Special Collections Division, Lauinger Library, Georgetown University, Washington, D.C.

Published Primary Sources

Abd al-Nasser, Gamal. *Philosophy of the Revolution.* Buffalo, N.Y.: Smith, Keynes and Marshall, 1959.

Arabian-American Oil Company. Annual Reports of Operations to the Government of Saudi Arabia, 1952–1961.

———. *The Aramco Handbook.* 1960.

The Eisenhower Diaries. Edited by Robert H. Ferrell. New York: W.W. Norton and Co., 1981.

Hansard. *Parliamentary Debates,* 1952–1960.

Ibn Khaldūn, ʿAbd al-Raḥmān Abū Zayid ibn Muḥammad. *The Muqaddimah.* Translated by Franz Rosenthal, edited by N. J. Dawood. Princeton, N.J.: Princeton University Press, 1967.

Al-Qurʾān. Translated by Ahmed Ali. Rev. ed. Princeton, N.J.: Princeton University Press, 1984.

United Nations. Statistical Office. Department of Economic and Social Affairs. *World Energy Supplies, 1950–1974.* 1976.

U.S. Congress. *Congressional Record,* 1954–1960.

———. Senate. Senate Foreign Relations Committee. *Multinational Corporations and United States Foreign Policy.* 93rd Cong., 1st Sess., 1975.

———. Senate. Senate Foreign Relations Committee. *Multinational Corporations and United States Foreign Policy.* 93rd Cong., 2nd Sess., 1975.

———. Senate. Executive Session of the Senate Foreign Relations Committee, Joint Sessions with the Senate Armed Services Committee. *The President's Proposal on the Middle East.* Part 2. 85th Cong., 1st Sess., 1957.

———. Senate. Senate Foreign Relations Committee. Hearings. *The Situation in the Middle East.* 84th Cong., 2nd Sess., 1956.

U.S. Department of Defense. Joint Chiefs of Staff. *Records of the Joint Chiefs of Staff, Part 2, 1946–1953: The Middle East.* Washington, D.C.: University Publications Microfilm, 1978.

U.S. Department of State. *Bulletin.* 1950–1961.

———. *Foreign Relations of the United States.* Washington D.C.: U.S. Government Printing Office, 1986–1993.

———. *United States Treaties and Other International Agreements.* Washington, D.C.: Government Printing Office, 1952.

U.S. Office of the Federal Register. *Public Papers of the Presidents of the United States: Dwight D. Eisenhower, 1953–1960.* Washington, D.C.: Government Printing Office.

———. *Public Papers of the Presidents of the United States: George Bush, 1989–1992.* Washington, D.C.: Government Printing Office.

Periodicals

Al-Ahrām
Aramco World
Al-Bilād al-Saʿūdiyya
International Affairs
Middle Eastern Affairs
New York Times
Petroleum Press Service
Petroleum Week
Times of London
Time
Umm al-Qurā

Memoirs

Burrows, Bernard. *Footnotes in the Sand: The Gulf in Transition, 1953–1958.* Wilton, Salisbury, England: Michael Russell, 1990.

Cheney, Michael Sheldon. *Big Oil Man from Arabia.* New York: Ballantine Books, 1958.

Copeland, Miles. *The Game of Nations: The Amorality of Power Politics.* New York: Simon and Schuster, 1969.

Eban, Abba. *Personal Witness: Israel Through My Eyes.* New York: Putnam, 1992.

Eddy, William A. *F.D.R. Meets Ibn Saud.* New York: American Friends of the Middle East, 1954.

Eden, Anthony. *Full Circle: The Memoirs of Anthony Eden.* London: Cassell, 1960.

Eisenhower, Dwight D. *Mandate for Change, 1953–56.* Garden City, N.Y.: Doubleday, 1963.

———. *Waging Peace, 1956–61.* Garden City, N.Y.: Doubleday, 1965.

Eveland, Wilbur Crane. *Ropes of Sand: America's Failure in the Middle East.* New York: W.W. Norton and Co., 1980.

Hart, Parker T. *Saudi Arabia and the United States: Birth of a Security Partnership.* Bloomington: Indiana University Press, 1998.

Haykal, Muhammad Hasanayn. *miliffāt al-Sūways: ḥarb al-thalāthīn sina* [The Suez Files: The Thirty-Years War]. Cairo: markaz al-Ḥarām lil tarjama wa al-nashr, 1986.

Lloyd, Selwyn. *Suez 1956: A Personal Account.* London: Jonathan Cape, 1978.

Macmillan, Harold. *Riding the Storm, 1956–59.* London: Macmillan, 1971.

McGhee, George. *Envoy to the Middle World: Adventures in Diplomacy.* New York: Harper and Row, 1983.

Murphy, Robert. *A Diplomat among Warriors.* Garden City, N.Y.: Doubleday, 1964.

Nutting, Anthony. *No End of a Lesson: The Story of Suez.* London: Constable, 1967.

Philby, Harry St. John. *Arabian Jubilee.* London: Robert Hale, 1952.

Shuckburgh, Evelyn. *Descent to Suez: Diaries, 1951–56.* New York: W.W. Norton and Co., 1986.

Secondary Sources

Unpublished Theses, Papers

Samore, Gary S. "Royal Family Politics in Saudi Arabia, 1953–1983." Ph.D. diss., Harvard University, 1983.

Yaqub, Salim. "The King and Ike: U.S.-Saudi Relations, 1956–1958." Paper presented at the annual meeting of the Society for Historians of American Foreign Relations, Georgetown University, June 1997.

Articles, Published Papers

Abir, Mordechai. "The Consolidation of the Ruling Class and the New Elites in Saudi Arabia." *Middle Eastern Studies* 23 (April 1987): 150–71.

Alterman, Jon B. "American Aid to Egypt in the 1950s: From Hope to Hostility." *Middle East Journal* 52 (Winter 1998): 51–69.

Anderson, Irvine. "Lend-Lease for Saudi Arabia: A Comment on Alternative Conceptualizations." *Diplomatic History* 3 (Fall 1979): 413–23.

Brands, H. W. "The Cairo-Teheran Connection in Anglo-American Rivalry in the Middle East, 1951–1953." *International History Review* 11 (August 1989): 434–56.

Citino, Nathan J. "Defending the 'Postwar Petroleum Order': The US, Britain, and the 1954 Saudi-Onassis Tanker Deal." *Diplomacy & Statecraft* 11 (July 2000): 137–60.

Davis, Simon. "Keeping the Americans in Line? Britain, the United States and Saudi Arabia, 1939–1945: Inter-Allied Rivalry in the Middle East Revisited." *Diplomacy & Statecraft* 8 (March 1997): 96–136.

DeNovo, John. "The Culbertson Economic Mission and Anglo-American Tensions in the Middle East, 1944–1945." *Journal of American History* 63 (March 1977): 913–36.

Everly, Steve. "Cold War Deal Saved Big Oil." *Kansas City Star,* June 27, 2001.

Fitzgerald, Edward Peter. "The Iraq Petroleum Company, Standard Oil of California, and the Contest for Eastern Arabia, 1930–1933." *International History Review* 13 (August 1991): 441–65.

Gasiorowski, Mark. "The 1953 *Coup D'Etat* in Iran." *International Journal of Middle East Studies* 19 (1987): 261–86.

Gerke, Gerwin. "The Iraq Development Board and British Policy, 1945–1950." *Middle Eastern Studies* 27 (April 1991): 231–55.

Gormly, James L. "Keeping the Door Open in Saudi Arabia: The United States and the Dhahran Airfield, 1945–46." *Diplomatic History* 4 (Spring 1980): 189–205.

Griffith, Robert. "Eisenhower and the Corporate Commonwealth." *American Historical Review* 87 (February 1982): 87–122.

Hahn, Peter L. "Containment and Egyptian Nationalism: The Unsuccessful Effort to Establish the Middle East Command, 1950–53." *Diplomatic History* 11 (Winter 1987): 23–40.

Harrison, R. Martin. "Saudi Arabia's Foreign Policy: Relations with the Superpowers." Durham University, Center for Middle Eastern and Islamic Studies. CMEIS Occasional Paper no. 46. University of Durham, 1995.

Hawley, Ellis W. "Herbert Hoover, the Commerce Secretariat, and the Vision of an 'Associative State,' 1921–1928." *Journal of American History* 61 (June 1974): 116–40.

Heiss, Mary Ann. "The United States, Great Britain, and the Creation of the Iranian Oil Consortium, 1953–1954." *International History Review* 16 (August 1994): 511–35.

Heller, Mark, and Nadav Safran. "The New Middle Class and Regime Stability in Saudi Arabia." Harvard Middle East Papers, No. 3. Center for Middle Eastern Studies, 1985.

Imady, Mohammed. "Patterns of Arab Economic Aid to Third World Countries." *Arab Studies Quarterly* 6 (Winter/Spring 1984): 70–91.

Immerman, Richard. "Confessions of an Eisenhower Revisionist: An Agonizing Reappraisal." *Diplomatic History* 14 (Summer 1990): 319–42.

Jalal, Ayesha. "Towards the Baghdad Pact: South Asia and Middle East Defence in the Cold War, 1947–1955." *International History Review* 11 (August 1989): 409–33.

Jasse, Richard. "The Baghdad Pact: Cold War or Colonialism?" *Middle Eastern Studies* 27 (January 1991): 140–56.

Joyce, Miriam. "Washington and Treaty-Making with the Sultan of Muscat and Oman." *Middle Eastern Studies* 30 (January 1994): 145–54.

Khalidi, Rashid. "Arab Nationalism: Historical Problems in the Literature." *American Historical Review* 96 (December 1991): 1363–73.

Kostiner, Joseph. "On Instruments and Their Designers: The Ikhwan of Najd and the Emergence of the Saudi State." *Middle Eastern Studies* 21 (July 1985): 298–323.

Kubursi, Atif A. and Salim Mansur. "Oil and the Gulf War: An 'American Century' or a 'New World Order.'" *Arab Studies Quarterly* 15 (Fall 1993): 1–17.

Lefebvre, Jeffrey A. "The United States and Egypt: Confrontation and Accommodation in Northeast Africa, 1956–60." *Middle Eastern Studies* 29 (April 1993): 321–38.

Lesch, David W. "The Saudi Role in the American-Syrian Crisis of 1957." *Middle East Policy* 1 (1992): 33–48.

Little, Douglas. "Cold War and Covert Action: The United States and Syria, 1945–1958." *Middle East Journal* 44 (Winter 1990): 51–75.

———. "His Finest Hour? Eisenhower, Lebanon, and the 1958 Middle East Crisis." *Diplomatic History* 20 (Winter 1996): 27–54.

———. "Pipeline Politics: America, TAPLINE, and the Arabs." *Business History Review* 64 (Summer 1990): 255–85.

Maier, Charles S. "American Visions and British Interests: Hogan's Marshall Plan." *Reviews in American History* 18 (March 1990): 102–11.

McMahon, Robert J. "Eisenhower and Third World Nationalism: A Critique of the Revisionists." *Political Science Quarterly* 101 (Fall 1986): 453–73.

Morsey, Leila Amin. "The Role of the United States in the Anglo-Egyptian Agreement of 1954." *Middle Eastern Studies* 29 (July 1993): 526–58.

Nehme, Michel G. "Saudi Arabia, 1950–80: Between Nationalism and Religion." *Middle Eastern Studies* 30 (October 1994): 930–43.

Nevo, Joseph. "Religion and National Identity in Saudi Arabia." *Middle Eastern Studies* 34 (July 1998): 34–53.

Ovendale, Ritchie. "Great Britain and the Anglo-American Invasion of Jordan and Lebanon in 1958." *International History Review* 14 (February 1994): 284–303.

Painter, David. "Oil and the Marshall Plan." *Business History Review* 58 (Autumn 1984): 359–83.

Petersen, Tore Tingvold. "Anglo-American Rivalry in the Middle East: The Struggle for the Buraimi Oasis, 1952–1957." *International History Review* 14 (February 1992): 71–91.

Rotter, Andrew J. "Saidism without Said: *Orientalism* and U.S. Diplomatic History," *American Historical Review* 105 (October 2000): 1205–17.

Rubin, Barry. "America and the Egyptian Revolution, 1950–1957." *Political Science Quarterly* 97 (Spring 1982): 73–90.

Salamé, Ghassan. "Islam and Politics in Saudi Arabia." *Arab Studies Quarterly* 9 (Summer 1987): 306–25.

Sanjian, Ara. "The Formulation of the Baghdad Pact." *Middle Eastern Studies* 33 (April 1997): 226–66.

Stivers, William. "A Note on the Red Line Agreement." *Diplomatic History* 7 (Winter 1979): 23–34.

Vitalis, Robert. "The Closing of the Arabian Oil Frontier and the Future of Saudi-American Relations." *Middle East Report* 27 (July–September 1997): 15–25.

———. "Crossing Exceptionalism's Frontiers to Discover America's Kingdom." *Arab Studies Journal* 6 (Spring 1998): 10–31.

———. "The 'New Deal' in Egypt: The Rise of Anglo-American Commercial Competition in World War II and the Fall of Neocolonialism." *Diplomatic History* 20 (Spring 1996): 211–39.

Books

Abd al-Wahab, Sayed-Ahmed. *Nasser and American Foreign Policy, 1952–1956.* London: LAAM, 1989.

Abir, Mordechai. *Saudi Arabia: Government, Society and the Gulf Crisis.* London: Routledge, 1993.

———. *Saudi Arabia in the Oil Era: Regime and Elites; Conflict and Collaboration.* Boulder, Colo.: Westview Press, 1988.

Aburīsh, Said K. *The Rise, Corruption and Coming Fall of the House of Saud.* New York: St. Martin's Press, 1995.

Alnasrawi, Abbas. *Arab Nationalism, Oil, and the Political Economy of Dependency.* Westport, Conn.: Greenwood Press, 1991.

Alteras, Isaac. *Eisenhower and Israel: U.S.-Israeli Relations, 1953–1960.* Gainesville: University Press of Florida, 1993.

Ambrose, Stephen E. *Eisenhower.* Vol. 2. *The President.* New York: Simon and Schuster, 1984.

Anderson, Irvine. *Aramco, the United States, and Saudi Arabia: A Study of the Dynamics of Foreign Oil Policy, 1933–1950.* Princeton, N.J.: Princeton University Press, 1981.

———. *The Standard-Vacuum Oil Company and United States East Asian Policy, 1933–1941.* Princeton, N.J.: Princeton University Press, 1975.

Anscombe, Frederick F. *The Ottoman Gulf: The Creation of Kuwait, Saudi Arabia, and Qatar.* New York: Columbia University Press, 1997.

Aronson, Geoffrey. *From Sideshow to Center Stage: U.S. Policy toward Egypt, 1946 1956.* Boulder, Colo.: Lynne Rienner, 1986.

Ashton, Nigel John. *Eisenhower, Macmillan and the Problem of Nasser: Anglo-American Relations and Arab Nationalism, 1955–59.* New York: St. Martin's Press, 1996.

Askari, Hossein. *Saudi Arabia's Economy: Oil and the Search for Economic Development* [Contemporary Studies in Economic and Financial Analysis, vol. 67, ed. Robert J. Thornton and J. Richard Aronson]. Greenwich, Conn.: JAI Press, 1990.

al-Badrī, Ḥasan and Fatīn Aḥmed Farīd. *ḥarb al-tawāṭū' al-thalāthī* [The War of Triple Collusion]. Cairo: al-maktaba al-akādīmīa, 1997.

Batatu, Hanna. *The Old Social Classes and the Revolutionary Movements of Iraq.* Princeton, N.J.: Princeton University Press, 1978.

Beblawi, Hazem and Giacomo Luciani, eds. *The Rentier State.* London: Croom Helm, 1987.

Behbehani, Hashim S.H. *The Soviet Union and Arab Nationalism, 1917–1966.* London: KPI, 1986.

Beiling, Willard A., ed. *King Faisal and the Modernisation of Saudi Arabia.* London: Croom Helm, 1980.

Ben-Zvi, Abraham. *Decade of Transition: Eisenhower, Kennedy, and the Origins of the American-Israeli Alliance.* New York: Columbia University Press, 1998.

Bill, James A. *The Eagle and the Lion: The Tragedy of American-Iranian Relations.* New Haven, Conn.: Yale University Press, 1988.

Bill, James A., and William Roger Louis, eds. *Musaddiq, Iranian Nationalism, and Oil.* London: I. B. Tauris & Co., 1988.

Bird, Kai. *The Chairman: John J. McCloy, the Making of the American Establishment.* New York: Simon and Schuster, 1992.

Black, Jeremy. *Maps and Politics.* Chicago: University of Chicago Press, 1997.

Bligh, Alexander. *From Prince to King: Royal Succession in the House of Saud in the Twentieth Century.* New York: New York University Press, 1984.

Brands, H. W. *Inside the Cold War: Loy Henderson and the Rise of the American Empire, 1918–1961.* New York: Oxford University Press, 1991.

———. *Into the Labyrinth: The United States and the Middle East, 1945–1993.* New York: McGraw Hill, 1994.

———. *The Specter of Neutralism: The United States and the Emergence of the Third World, 1947–1960.* New York: Columbia University Press, 1989.

Bromley, Simon. *American Hegemony and World Oil: The Industry, the State System and the World Economy.* University Park, Pa.: Pennsylvania State University Press, 1991.

———. *Rethinking Middle East Politics.* Austin: University of Texas Press, 1994.

Brown, Anthony Cave. *Oil, God, and Gold: The Story of Aramco and the Saudi Kings.* Boston: Houghton Mifflin, 1999.

Brown, L. Carl, ed. *Imperial Legacy: The Ottoman Imprint on the Balkans and the Middle East.* New York: Columbia University Press, 1996.

———. *International Politics and the Middle East: Old Rules, Dangerous Game.* Princeton, N.J.: Princeton University Press, 1984.

Bulloch, John. *The Gulf: A Portrait of Kuwait, Qatar, Bahrain and the UAE.* London: Century Publishing, 1984.

Bullock, Alan. *Ernest Bevin, Foreign Secretary, 1945–1951.* New York: Norton, 1983.

Carleton, David. *Anthony Eden.* London: Allen Lane, 1981.

Casillas, Rex J. *Oil and Diplomacy: The Evolution of American Foreign Policy in Saudi Arabia, 1933–1945.* New York: Garland, 1987.

Chandler, Alfred D., Jr. *The Visible Hand: The Managerial Revolution in American Business.* Cambridge, Mass.: Belknap Press, 1977.

Chaudhry, Kiren Aziz. *The Price of Wealth: Economies and Institutions in the Middle East.* Ithaca, N.Y.: Cornell University Press, 1997.

Chester, Edward W. *United States Oil Policy and Diplomacy: A Twentieth-Century Overview.* Westport, Conn.: Greenwood Press, 1983.

Clark, John G. *The Political Economy of World Energy: A Twentieth-Century Perspective.* Chapel Hill: University of North Carolina Press, 1991.

Cobbs, Elizabeth A. *The Rich Neighbor Policy: Rockefeller and Kaiser in Brazil.* New Haven, Conn.: Yale University Press, 1992.

Cohen, Michael J. *Palestine and the Great Powers, 1945–1948.* Princeton, N.J.: Princeton University Press, 1982.

Cordesman, Anthony H. *The Gulf and the Search for Strategic Stability: Saudi Arabia, the Military Balance in the Gulf, and Trends in the Arab-Israeli Military Balance.* Boulder, Colo.: Westview Press, 1984.

———. *Saudi Arabia: Guarding the Desert Kingdom.* Boulder, Colo.: Westview Press, 1997.

Costigliola, Frank. *Awkward Dominion: American Political, Economic, and Cultural Relations with Europe, 1919–1933.* Ithaca, N.Y.: Cornell University Press, 1984.

Crystal, Jill. *Oil and Politics in the Gulf: Rulers and Merchants in Kuwait and Qatar.* 2nd ed. Cambridge: Cambridge University Press, 1995.

Dawisha, Adeed, ed. *Islam in Foreign Policy.* New York: Cambridge University Press, 1983.

Dawn, C. Ernest. *From Ottomanism to Arabism: Essays on the Origins of Arab Nationalism.* Urbana: University of Illinois Press, 1973.

DeGaury, Gerald. *Faisal, King of Saudi Arabia.* New York: Praeger, 1966.

Devereux, David R. *The Formulation of British Defence Policy towards the Middle East, 1948–56.* New York: Macmillan, 1990.

Devlin, John F. *The Ba'th Party: A History from Its Origins to 1966.* Stanford, Calif.: Stanford University Press, 1966.

Dorril, Stephen. *MI6: Inside the Covert World of Her Majesty's Secret Intelligence Service.* New York: Free Press, 2000.

Dosal, Paul J. *Doing Business with the Dictators: A Political History of United Fruit in Guatemala, 1899–1944.* Wilmington, Del.: SR Books, 1993.

Dutton, David. *Anthony Eden: A Life and Reputation.* London: Arnold, 1997.

Eickelman, Dale F. *The Middle East: An Anthropological Approach.* 2nd ed. Englewood Cliffs, N.J.: Prentice Hall, 1988.

Evans, Peter. *Ari: the Life and Times of Aristotle Socrates Onassis.* London: Jonathan Cape, 1986.

Farnie, D. A. *East and West of Suez: the Suez Canal in History, 1854–1956.* Oxford: Clarendon Press, 1969.

Fraser, Nicholas, et al. *Aristotle Onassis.* New York: J. B. Lippincott Company, 1977.

Freiberger, Steven Z. *Dawn over Suez: The Rise of American Power in the Middle East, 1953–1957.* Chicago: Ivan R. Dee, 1992.

Gasiorowski, Mark J. *U.S. Foreign Policy and the Shah: Building a Client State in Iran.* Ithaca, N.Y.: Cornell University Press, 1991.

Gause, F. Gregory, III. *Oil Monarchies: Domestic and Security Challenges in the Arab Gulf States.* New York: Council on Foreign Relations Press, 1994.

Gendzier, Irene. *Notes from the Minefield: United States Intervention in Lebanon and the Middle East, 1945–1958.* New York: Columbia University Press, 1997.

Gerges, Fawaz A. *The Superpowers and the Middle East: Regional and International Politics, 1955–1967.* Boulder, Colo.: Westview Press, 1994.

Gershoni, Israel, and James P. Jankowski, *Redefining the Egyptian Nation, 1930–1945.* Cambridge: Cambridge University Press, 1995.

Gibb, H. A. R., and Harold Bowen. *Islamic Society and the West: A Study of the Impact of Western Civilization on Moslem Culture in the Near East.* 2 vols. London: Oxford University Press, 1950, 1957.

Goldberg, Jacob. *The Foreign Policy of Saudi Arabia: The Formative Years, 1902–1918.* Cambridge, Mass.: Harvard University Press, 1986.

Goode, James F. *The United States and Iran: In the Shadow of Musaddiq.* New York: St. Martin's Press, 1997.

Gordon, Joel. *Nasser's Blessed Movement: Egypt's Free Officers and the July Revolution.* New York: Oxford University Press, 1992.

Grayson, Benson Lee. *Saudi-American Relations.* Washington, D.C.: University Press of America, 1982.

Hahn, Peter L. *The United States, Britain, and Egypt, 1945–1956: Strategy and Diplomacy in the Early Cold War.* Chapel Hill: University of North Carolina Press, 1991.

Hawley, Ellis W. *The Great War and the Search for a Modern Order: A History of the American People and Their Institutions, 1917–1933.* New York: St. Martin's Press, 1979.

Heard-Bey, Frauke. *From Trucial States to United Arab Emirates: A Society in Transition.* 2nd ed. London: Longman, 1996.

Heiss, Mary Ann. *Empire and Nationhood: The United States, Great Britain, and Iranian Oil, 1950–1954.* New York: Columbia University Press, 1997.

Helms, Christine Moss. *The Cohesion of Saudi Arabia: Evolution of Political Identity.* London: Croom Helm, 1981.

Hitti, Philip K. *Islam and the West: A Historical Cultural Survey.* Princeton, N.J.: D. Van Nostrand Co., 1962.

Hoff, Joan. *American Business and Foreign Policy, 1920–1933.* Lexington: University Press of Kentucky, 1971.

Hogan, Michael J.. *Informal Entente: The Private Structure of Cooperation in Anglo-American Economic Diplomacy, 1918–1928.* Columbia: University of Missouri Press, 1977.

———. *The Marshall Plan: America, Britain, and the Reconstruction of Western Europe, 1947–1952.* New York: Cambridge University Press, 1987.

Hogan, Michael J., and Thomas G. Paterson, eds. *Explaining the History of American Foreign Relations.* New York: Cambridge University Press, 1991.

Holden, David, and Richard Johns. *The House of Saud.* London: Sidgwick and Johnson, 1981.

Holland, Matthew. *America and Egypt: From Roosevelt to Eisenhower.* New York: Praeger, 1996.

Holt, P. M. *Egypt and the Fertile Crescent, 1516–1922: A Political History.* Ithaca, N.Y.: Cornell University Press, 1966.

Hopwood, Derek. *Egypt: Politics and Society, 1945–1981.* London: Allen and Unwin, 1982.

Hourani, Albert. *Arabic Thought in the Liberal Age, 1798–1939.* London: Oxford University Press, 1962.

Hourani, Albert, Philip Khoury, and Mary C. Wilson, eds. *The Modern Middle East: A Reader.* Berkeley: University of California Press, 1993.

Huntington, Samuel. *Political Order in Changing Societies.* New Haven, Conn.: Yale University Press, 1968.

Ibrahim, Saad Eddin. *The New Arab Social Order: A Study of the Social Impact of Oil Wealth.* Boulder, Colo.: Westview Press, 1982.

Immerman Richard, ed. *John Foster Dulles and the Diplomacy of the Cold War.* Princeton, N.J.: Princeton University Press, 1990.

Inalcik, Halil, and Donald Quataert, eds. *An Economic and Social History of the Ottoman Empire, 1300–1914.* Cambridge: Cambridge University Press, 1994.

Ismael, Jacqueline S. *Kuwait: Dependency and Class in a Rentier State.* Gainesville: University Press of Florida, 1993.

Joyce, Miriam. *Kuwait, 1945–1996: An Anglo-American Perspective.* London: Frank Cass, 1998.

Kaufman, Burton I. *The Arab Middle East and the United States: Inter-Arab Rivalry and Superpower Diplomacy.* New York: Twayne Publishers, 1995.

———. *The Oil Cartel Case: A Documentary History of Antitrust Activity in the Cold War Era.* Westport, Conn.: Greenwood, 1978.

———. *Trade and Aid: Eisenhower's Foreign Economic Policy, 1953–1961.* Baltimore: Johns Hopkins University Press, 1982.

Kelly, John Barrett. *Arabia, the Gulf, and the West.* London: Weidenfeld and Nicolson, 1980.

———. *Eastern Arabian Frontiers.* London: Faber and Faber, 1964.

Kerr, Malcolm. *The Arab Cold War: Gamal 'Abd al-Nasir and His Rivals, 1958–1970.* New York: Oxford University Press, 1971.

Khoury, Philip S. *Syria and the French Mandate: The Politics of Arab Nationalism, 1920–1945.* Princeton, N.J.: Princeton University Press, 1987.

———. *Urban Notables and Arab Nationalism: The Politics of Damascus, 1860–1920.* Cambridge: Cambridge University Press, 1983.

Khoury, Philip S., and Joseph Kostiner, eds. *Tribes and State Formation in the Middle East.* Berkeley: University of California Press, 1990.

Kingston, Paul W. T. *Britain and the Politics of Modernization in the Middle East, 1945–1958.* Cambridge: Cambridge University Press, 1996.

Kolko, Gabriel. *Confronting the Third World: United States Foreign Policy, 1945–1980.* New York: Pantheon Books, 1988.

Korany, Bahgat, and Ali E. Hillal Dessouki, eds. *The Foreign Policies of the Arab States: The Challenge of Change.* 2nd ed. Boulder, Colo.: Westview Press, 1991.

Kostiner, Joseph. *The Making of Saudi Arabia, 1916–1936: From Chieftancy to Monarchical State.* New York: Oxford University Press, 1993.

Kostiner, Joseph, ed. *Middle East Monarchies: The Challenge of Modernity.* Boulder, Colo.: Lynne Rienner Publishers, 2000.

Kunz, Diane B. *Butter and Guns: America's Cold War Economic Diplomacy.* New York: The Free Press, 1997.

———. *The Economic Diplomacy of the Suez Crisis.* Chapel Hill: University of North Carolina Press, 1991.

Kyle, Keith. *Suez.* New York: St. Martin's Press, 1991.

Lacey, Robert. *The Kingdom: Arabia and the House of Saud.* New York: Avon Books, 1981.

Lackner, Helen. *A House Built on Sand: A Political Economy of Saudi Arabia.* London: Ithaca Press, 1978.

Leffler, Melvyn P. *The Elusive Quest: The American Pursuit of European Stability and French Security, 1919–1933.* Chapel Hill: University of North Carolina Press, 1979.

———. *A Preponderance of Power: National Security, the Truman Administration, and the Cold War.* Stanford, Calif.: Stanford University Press, 1992.

Lenczowski, George, ed. *American Presidents and the Middle East.* Durham, N.C.: Duke University Press, 1990.

Lesch, David W. *Syria and the United States: Eisenhower's Cold War in the Middle East.* Boulder, Colo.: Westview Press, 1992.

Lesch, David W., ed. *The Middle East and the United States: A Historical and Political Reassessment.* 2nd ed. Boulder, Colo.: Westview Press, 1999.

Levey, Zach. *Israel and the Western Powers, 1952–1960.* Chapel Hill: University of North Carolina Press, 1997.

Lewis, Bernard. *The Middle East and the West.* Bloomington: Indiana University Press, 1961.

Long, David E. *The United States and Saudi Arabia: Ambivalent Allies.* Boulder, Colo.: Westview Press, 1985.

Louis, William Roger. *The British Empire in the Middle East: Arab Nationalism, the United States, and Postwar Imperialism.* New York: Oxford University Press, 1984.

Louis, William Roger, and William Stookey, eds. *The End of the Palestine Mandate.* Austin: University of Texas Press, 1986.

Louis, William Roger, and Roger Owen, eds. *Suez 1956: The Crisis and Its Consequences.* Oxford: Clarendon Press, 1989.

Love, Kennett. *Suez: The Twice-Fought War.* New York: McGraw-Hill, 1969.

Lucas, W. Scott. *Divided We Stand: Britain, the United States and the Suez Crisis.* London: Hodder and Stoughton, 1991.

Ma'oz, Moshe. *Ottoman Reform in Syria and Palestine, 1840–1861: The Impact of the Tanzimat on Politics and Society.* Oxford: Clarendon Press, 1968.

Marks, Frederick W. *Power and Peace: The Diplomacy of John Foster Dulles.* New York: Praeger, 1993.

al-Sayyid-Marsot, Afaf Lutfi. *Egypt's Liberal Experiment, 1922–1936.* Berkeley: University of California Press, 1977.

McLoughlin, Leslie. *Ibn Saud: Founder of a Kingdom.* New York: St. Martin's Press, 1993.

Melanson, Richard A., and David Mayers, eds. *Reevaluating Eisenhower: American Foreign Policy in the 1950s.* Urbana: University of Illinois Press, 1987.

Meyer, Gail E. *Egypt and the United States: The Formative Years.* Rutherford, N.J.: Fairleigh Dickinson University Press, 1980.

Miller, Aaron David. *Search for Security: Saudi Arabian Oil and American Foreign Policy, 1933–1949.* Chapel Hill: University of North Carolina Press, 1980.

Mosley, Leonard. *Dulles: A Biography of Eleanor, Allen, and John Foster Dulles and Their Family Network.* New York: Dial Press, 1978.

———. *Power Play: Oil in the Middle East.* New York: Random House, 1973.

Neff, Donald. *Warriors at Suez: Eisenhower Takes America into the Middle East.* New York: Linden Press/Simon and Schuster, 1981.

Niblock, Tim, ed. *State, Society and Economy in Saudi Arabia.* London: Croom Helm, 1982.

al-Otaiba, Mana Saed. *OPEC and the Petroleum Industry.* New York: John Wiley and Sons, 1975.

Ovendale, Ritchie. *Britain, the United States and the Transfer of Power in the Middle East, 1945–1962.* New York: Leicester University Press, 1996.

Owen, Roger, and Şevket Pamuk. *A History of Middle East Economies in the Twentieth Century.* Cambridge, Mass.: Harvard University Press, 1999.

———. *The Middle East in the World Economy, 1800–1914*. New York: Methuen, 1981.

Pach, Chester J., Jr. and Elmo Richardson. *The Presidency of Dwight D. Eisenhower.* Lawrence: University Press of Kansas, 1991.

Painter, David S. *Oil and the American Century: The Political Economy of U.S. Foreign Oil Policy, 1941–1954.* Baltimore: Johns Hopkins University Press, 1986.

Palmer, Michael A. *Guardians of the Gulf: A History of America's Expanding Role in the Persian Gulf, 1833–1992.* New York: Free Press, 1992.

Parrini, Carl. *Heir to Empire: United States Economic Diplomacy, 1916–1923.* Pittsburgh: University of Pittsburgh Press, 1969.

Persson, Magnus. *Great Britain, the United States, and the Security of the Middle East: The Formation of the Baghdad Pact.* Lund, Sweden: Lund University Press, 1998.

Petersen, Tore Tingvold. *The Middle East Between the Great Powers: Anglo-American Conflict and Cooperation, 1952–7.* New York: St. Martin's Press, 2000.

Peterson, J. E. *Historical Dictionary of Saudi Arabia.* London: Scarecrow Press, Inc., 1993.

Peters, F. E. *The Hajj: The Muslim Pilgrimage to Mecca and the Holy Places.* Princeton, N.J.: Princeton University Press, 1994.

Philip, George. *The Political Economy of International Oil.* Edinburgh: Edinburgh University Press, 1994.

Polk, W. R., and R. L. Chambers, eds. *The Beginnings of Modernization in the Middle East.* Chicago: University of Chicago Press, 1968.

Porath, Yehoshua. *In Search of Arab Unity, 1930–1945.* London: Frank Cass, 1986.

Pridham, B. R., ed. *The Arab Gulf and the Arab World.* London: Croom Helm, 1988.

———. *The Arab Gulf and the West.* London: Croom Helm, 1985.

al-Qaḥṭānī, Fahd. *ṣirāʿ al-ajnaḥ fī al-ʿāʾila al-Saʿūdiyya: dirāsa fī al-niẓām al-siyāsī wa taʾsus al-dawla* [Factional Conflict within the Saudi Dynasty: A Study of the Political Structure and Foundation of the State]. London: al-ṣafā al-nashr wa al-tawzīʿ, 1988.

Rabe, Stephen G. *The Road to OPEC: United States Relations with Venezuela, 1919–1976.* Austin: University of Texas Press, 1982.

Raffer, Kunibert, and M. A. Mohamed Salih, eds. *The Least Developed and the Oil-Rich Arab Countries: Dependence, Interdependence, or Patronage?* New York: St. Martin's Press, 1992.

Randall, Stephen J. *United States Foreign Oil Policy, 1919–1948: For Profits and Security.* Kingston: McGill-Queen's University Press, 1985.

al-Rashidi, Ibrahim, ed. *The Struggle between Two Princes: The Kingdom of Saudi Arabia in the Final Days of Ibn Saud.* Chapel Hill, N.C.: Documentary Publications, 1985.

Rosenberg, Emily S. *Spreading the American Dream: American Economic and Cultural Expansion, 1890–1945.* New York: Hill and Wang, 1982.

Rustow, Dankwart A. *Oil and Turmoil: America Faces OPEC and the Middle East.* New York: W.W. Norton, 1982.

Safran, Nadav. *Saudi Arabia: The Ceaseless Quest for Security.* Ithaca, N.Y.: Cornell University Press, 1985.

Saʿīd, Amīn. *Taʾrīkh al-dawla al-Saʿūdiyya* [History of the Saudi State]. Vol. 3: *ʿAhd Saʿūd ibn ʿAbd al-ʿAzīz* [The Reign of Saʿūd]. Beirut: dar al-kātib al-ʿArabī, 1970.

Said, Edward. *Covering Islam: How the Media and the Experts Determine How We See the Rest of the World.* New York: Pantheon Books, 1981.

———. *Orientalism.* New York: Vintage Books, 1978.

Salamé, Ghassan. *Al-Siyāsa al-khārjiyya al-Saʿūdiyya mundhu ʿām 19Ɛ0: dirāsa fī al-ʿalāqa al-dawliyya* [Saudi Foreign Policy since 1945: A Study in International Relations]. Beirut: Mahad al-Inmāʾ al-ʿArabī, 1980.

Sampson, Anthony. *The Seven Sisters: The Great Oil Companies and the World They Shaped.* New York: Viking, 1975.

Saunders, Bonnie H. *The United States and Arab Nationalism: The Syrian Case, 1953–60.* New York: Praeger, 1996.

Sayigh, Yusif A. *Arab Oil Policies in the 1970s: Opportunity and Responsibility.* London: Croom Helm, 1983.

Schoenbaum, David. *The United States and the State of Israel.* New York: Oxford University Press, 1993.

Seale, Patrick. *The Struggle for Syria: A Study of Post-War Arab Politics, 1945–1958.* 2nd ed. New Haven, Conn.: Yale University Press, 1986.

Shāmiyya, Jubrān. *Āl Saʿūd: māḍīhim wa mustaqbaluhum* [The Saudi Dynasty: Its Past and Future]. Beirut: dār al-abḥāth wa al-nashr, 1986.

Shārabī, Niẓām. *Amrīkā wa al-ʿArab: al-siyāsa al-Amrīkiyya fī al-waṭan al-ʿArabī fī al-qarn al-ʿashrīn* [America and the Arabs: American Policy in the Arab World in the Twentieth Century]. London: Riad el-Rayyes Books, 1990.

Silverfarb, Daniel. *The Twilight of British Ascendancy in the Middle East: A Case Study of Iraq, 1941–1950.* New York: St. Martin's Press, 1994.

Skeet, Ian. *Opec: Twenty-five Years of Prices and Politics.* Cambridge: Cambridge University Press, 1988.

Sluglett, Peter. *Britain in Iraq, 1914–1932.* London: Ithaca Press, 1976.

Sluglett, Peter, and Marion Farouk-Sluglett. *Iraq since 1958: From Revolution to Dictatorship.* London: KPI, 1987.

Spiegel, Steven. *The Other Arab-Israeli Conflict: Making America's Middle East Policy, from Truman to Reagan.* Chicago: University of Chicago Press, 1985.

Stivers, William. *America's Confrontation with Revolutionary Change in the Middle East, 1948–1983.* New York: St. Martin's Press, 1986.

———. *Supremacy and Oil: Iraq, Turkey, and the Anglo-American World Order, 1918–1930.* Ithaca, N.Y.: Cornell University Press, 1982.

Stoff, Michael B. *Oil, War and American Security: The Search for a National Policy on Foreign Oil, 1941–1947.* New Haven, Conn.: Yale University Press, 1980.

Stookey, Robert. *America and the Arab States: An Uneasy Encounter.* New York: Wiley, 1975.

Takeyh, Ray. *The Origins of the Eisenhower Doctrine: The U.S., Britain, and Nasser's Egypt, 1953–1957.* New York: St. Martin's Press, 2000.

Terzian, Pierre. *OPEC: The Inside Story.* Translated by Michael Pallis. Avon: Bath Press, 1985.

Thompson, Jack H., and Robert D. Reischauer, eds. *The Modernization of the Arab World.* Princeton, N.J.: D. Van Nostrand Co., 1966.

Tripp, Charles. *A History of Iraq.* Cambridge: Cambridge University Press, 2000.

Vassiliev, Alexei. *The History of Saudi Arabia.* London: Saqi Books, 1998.

Weitz, John. *Hitler's Banker: Hjalmar Horace Greeley Schacht.* Boston: Little, Brown, and Co., 1997.

Wiebe, Robert H. *The Search for Order, 1877–1920.* New York: Hill and Wang, 1967.

Wilkinson, John C. *Arabia's Frontiers: The Story of Britain's Boundary Drawing in the Desert.* New York: St. Martin's Press, 1991.

———. *The Imamate Tradition of Oman.* Cambridge: Cambridge University Press, 1987.

Wilson, Mary C. *King Abdullah, Britain and the Making of Jordan.* New York: Cambridge University Press, 1987.

al-Yassini, Ayman. *Religion and State in the Kingdom of Saudi Arabia.* Boulder, Colo.: Westview Press, 1985.

Yergin, Daniel. *The Prize: The Epic Quest for Oil, Money, and Power.* New York: Simon and Schuster, 1992.

Yizraeli, Sarah. *The Remaking of Saudi Arabia: The Struggle between King Saʿūd and Crown Prince Fayṣal, 1953–1962.* Tel Aviv: Moshe Dayan Center for Middle Eastern and African Studies, 1997.

Young, John, ed. *The Foreign Policy of Churchill's Peacetime Administration, 1951–1955.* Worcester, England: Leicester University Press, 1988.

Index

Note: Surnames with the prefixes Abd, Abu, Ben, and Ibn are alphabetized under the prefix. The initial article 'al-' is ignored in alphabetization. Page numbers for photographs are in *italic*.

Photo by Maria Citino

NATHAN J. CITINO
received a Ph.D. in history from Ohio State University. He is an assistant professor of history at Colorado State University and serves as associate editor of *Diplomatic History.*